D1621144

MODERN COMMUNICATION PRINCIPLES

MODERN COMMUNICATION PRINCIPLES

With Application to Digital Signaling

Seymour Stein

Director, Communication Systems Laboratories
Sylvania Electronic Systems
A Division of Sylvania Electric Products, Inc.
Waltham, Massachusetts

J. Jay Jones

Communication Sciences Department
Space and Re-entry Systems Division
Philco-Ford Corporation
Palo Alto, California

McGRAW HILL BOOK COMPANY

New York   San Francisco   Toronto   London   Sydney

200923

MODERN COMMUNICATION PRINCIPLES

Copyright © 1967 by McGraw-Hill, Inc.
All Rights Reserved. Printed in the United States of America.
This book, or parts thereof, may not be reproduced in any form
without permission of the publishers. *Library of Congress
Catalog Card Number* 67-12330

61003

6 7 8 9 0 HDHD 798

QUEEN MARY
COLLEGE
LIBRARY

Preface

In 1964, as part of a program conducted by Sylvania's Applied Research Laboratory, the authors prepared a concise review of the principles of modern communications with special emphasis on digital radio communications. It was required that this review be sufficiently self-contained and tutorial to be useful, without additional references, to practicing engineers many years out of college and at the same time introduce the most advanced theoretical models in radio communication theory. This material, issued as Applied Research Laboratory Research Note No. 509 (October, 1964), was so favorably received by engineers within Sylvania that it was suggested that a similar treatment, with suitable revision, might usefully serve a much larger audience. The result is this book.

A very specific point of view is reflected in the selection and organization of the material here. The authors like to think of it as a "systems engineering" viewpoint of communication theory. Many topics currently covered in related senior-level undergraduate or graduate engineering courses are omitted or only slightly treated. Examples of such omissions are the mechanisms of circuit noise, the detailed concepts of Shannon's information theory, and the formulations of statistical decision theory. (The authors heartily recommend the interested reader to any of the excellent introductory books already available on these topics.) On the other hand, the later chapters highlight material which has until recently been unavailable in book form and which is academically covered (if at all) in specialized second-year graduate courses. The early chapters provide a route whereby the engineer or student, armed with little more than a working recollection of calculus and Fourier series, can reach through to an understanding of these later chapters.

Accordingly, the first eight chapters of the book provide background and review material with emphasis on modern techniques and tools. The next five chapters introduce digital signaling, largely in terms of binary systems with "steady" signals, and include treatments of matched-filtering and correlation detection. Two chapters are then devoted to M-ary and coded transmissions. Finally, in the last two chapters, the results for binary systems are extended to real communication channels with fading signals, including the use of diversity combining techniques for combating such fading.

Greater detail on random processes is available in any of several texts, such as currently used in first-year graduate courses. More detail on the material of the later chapters can be found in the related portions of Communication Systems and Techniques, by M. Schwartz, W. R. Bennett, and S. Stein (McGraw-Hill Book Company, New York, 1966).

The authors wish to thank Sylvania Electronic Systems, a division of the Sylvania Electric Products subsidiary of General Telephone and Electronics, Inc., for encouraging us in this further endeavor. We also express deep appreciation to our many colleagues at the Applied Research Laboratory and elsewhere for the general stimulation, over the years, reflected in our presentation. In addition, we gratefully acknowledge specific contributions by Mr. Alan W. Pierce of the Applied Research Laboratory to the material of Chapters 14 and 15, and thank Dr. John Neil Birch, U. S. Department of Defense, and Capt. Thomas O. Duff, U. S. Air Force, for their helpful comments and criticism in formulating the original Research Note.

SEYMOUR STEIN

J. JAY JONES

Contents

MODERN COMMUNICATION PRINCIPLES

1

Frequency Spectra and Fourier Theory

1-1 Sinusoidal Analysis: The Basis of Fourier Theory

Traditionally, electrical engineering bases the analysis of waveforms and signals in electric systems on the representation of complicated or complex signals as a weighted sum of elementary parts, usually by resolving the signals into a particular set of fundamental components. Many different sets of basic building blocks are possible, some of which are more useful than others. The utility of a particular set of components often depends heavily upon the type of signals to be studied. For example, if the class of signals consists of sequences of positive and negative pulses, a natural choice for the set of basic elements might be the uniform time displacements of a single pulse. By far the most familiar set is that used in conventional Fourier analysis, where the fundamental building blocks are chosen to be a set of harmonically related *sinusoids*. Figure 1-1 illustrates the constituent parts of a sinusoid. The particular representation of waveforms in terms of a discrete set of sinusoids, known as the method of Fourier harmonic series, is an extremely useful analytic tool for the study of periodic waveforms. We shall return to this special topic in Sec. 1-10. As we shall see, the sinusoid is also the fundamental element of Fourier integral theory for the representation of nonperiodic waveforms.

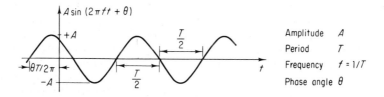

Fig. 1-1 A real sinusoidal time function.

The importance of representing a signal waveform as a weighted sum of elementary parts lies in the *superposition* property of *linear* systems. A linear system is defined by the following properties: Let $X(t)$ be the system response to an input $x(t)$ and independently $Y(t)$ the response to $y(t)$. Then the response to the sum $ax(t) + by(t)$ is $aX(t) + bY(t)$. All passive electrical circuits involving resistance, inductance, and capacitance, with unchanging values of their parameters, are linear. So are a wide variety of active circuits, such as amplifiers and mixers, insofar as they affect the signal components of interest. Note that linear time-invariant systems do not alter or add to the frequencies contained in a signal; however, nonlinear systems can have this ability. The significant nonlinear circuits which we shall discuss later are detectors. Fourier representations cannot then be used for analyzing input-output relations via the simple superposition property. However, they often are very useful in analyzing the operation of nonlinear devices or in analyzing the effects of undesired nonlinearities in nominally linear devices.

Along with the Fourier representation of signal waveforms in terms of components of differing frequency, it is natural also to characterize linear circuits and systems on a frequency basis, in terms of their response to a unit amplitude sinusoidal excitation of an arbitrary frequency. This dependence on sinusoidal testing leads to the well-known impedance concept for one-port electric circuits and to the so-called system transfer function or ratio of output to input as a function of frequency for networks involving more than one port. The modifying effect of a system on a signal can be studied then by examining the individual modifications imposed by the system on the signal's component sinusoids. That is, the effect of a circuit upon a waveform can be described as the net result of individually modifying the amplitude and phase angle of each sinusoid contained in the signal's resolution. These changes of amplitude and/or phase angle of the individual sinusoids are dictated by the impedance function or transfer ratio of the system expressed as a function of frequency. Thus sinusoidal techniques form the cornerstone of both conventional signal analysis and system analysis through the application of Fourier theory.

The familiar Fourier harmonic series can be used only to describe periodic signals. To represent aperiodic (nonperiodic) waveforms such as a single pulse, one resorts to the generalization of Fourier integral theory (Refs. 1-4). This theory also is based on sinusoidal analysis, although it is an *incremental treatment* and is comparable to passing from the study of discrete problems to continuous phenomena. Thus whereas periodic waveforms can be represented in terms of discrete frequencies by means of Fourier series expansions, aperiodic waveforms are representable by Fourier integral transforms involving a continuum of frequencies. In fact the Fourier integral relationships, as given below, can be derived heuristically (Refs. 2-4) by a simple extension of a Fourier series representation composed of discrete, finite-sized sinsuoids to a consideration of a continuum of infinitely many, immeasurably small sinusoidal components. In this text we use Fourier integral transforms to define the frequency spectra of both deterministic and random signals and to characterize linear systems in the frequency domain. In the present chapter we discuss only applications to deterministic (nonrandom) signals and defer until Chap. 4 the extension of Fourier theory to random and noise-like signals. Specifically the discussion here defines and illustrates the frequency spectrum of deterministic signals for both aperiodic and repetitive time functions. We also describe the frequency domain properties of linear time-invariant systems and the way they relate to and interact with signals.

1-2 Fourier Integral Transforms and Frequency Spectra

We have been discussing sinusoidal analysis as the basis of Fourier theory. Let us examine these elementary signal components further. The basic building block is a general sinusoid written in exponential or complex (variable) form as

$$A(f) e^{j2\pi ft} = A(f) \exp(j2\pi ft) \tag{1-1}$$

where $j = \sqrt{-1}$ and f is the sinusoidal frequency in hertz. The amplitude function $A(f)$ of this general sinusoid is generally a complex quantity having both *magnitude* (often termed amplitude) and *phase*. This structure is usually expressed by the form

$$A(f) = |A(f)| e^{j\theta(f)} = \text{Re}\, A(f) + j\text{Im}\, A(f) \tag{1-2}$$

The relationships among the magnitude and phase and the real and imaginary parts of a complex quantity are

$$|A(f)|^2 = [\text{Re}\, A(f)]^2 + [\text{Im}\, A(f)]^2 \tag{1-3a}$$

and

$$\theta(f) = \arctan \frac{\text{Im}\, A(f)}{\text{Re}\, A(f)} \tag{1-3b}$$

Figure 1-2 illustrates the geometrical (cartesian and polar coordinate) interpretation of these relationships. At the same time, (1-1) can be written

$$A(f) e^{j2\pi ft} = |A(f)| \exp j[2\pi ft + \theta(f)]$$

$$= |A(f)| \cos[2\pi ft + \theta(f)] + j|A(f)| \sin[2\pi ft + \theta(f)] \tag{1-4}$$

which perhaps more clearly describes the general complex sinusoid in terms of its magnitude, frequency, and phase angle. Note that the real and imaginary parts of this expression represent components in phase quadrature at frequency f.

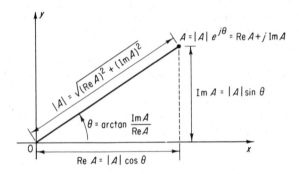

Fig. 1-2 Geometrical relationships among the components of the complex number A.

Arbitrary time functions generally contain a continuum of frequencies. That is, the sinusoids comprising the signal have frequencies lying incrementally close to one another. This implies a very large number of frequency components. Moreover except in limiting situations any individual sinusoid will not contribute heavily to the total. The mathematical formalism for representing such waveforms uses as the basic building block, in place of $A(f) \exp(j2\pi ft)$, the incremental sinusoid $[A(f)\,df] \exp(j2\pi ft)$ where df is an incremental portion of the frequency scale. This latter form may be thought of as representing a general sinusoid lying in the narrow frequency band of width df located at frequency f with an incremental complex amplitude $A(f)\,df$. If a sufficient number of these incremental sinusoids of differing frequency are added together, the resulting sum can be made to approximate closely any member of a rather large, general class of time functions (including all of physical interest). Carried to its natural conclusion, this argument leads to signal representation with the sum of sinusoids replaced by an integration over the entire set of components. Thus it can be shown (Refs. 1–4) that under very general conditions a waveform $a(t)$ can be represented by a relation of the form

$$a(t) \;=\; \int_{-\infty}^{\infty} A(f) e^{j2\pi ft}\,df \qquad\qquad (1\text{-}5)$$

This expression is one of a pair of companion relations known as the Fourier transform integrals. This relates to the fact that to each $a(t)$ there is a unique $A(f)$ and vice versa, as will be described later. Thus it can also be shown (e.g., Ref. 1) that the operation indicated in (1-5) has an unqiue inverse:

$$A(f) = \int_{-\infty}^{\infty} a(t) e^{-j2\pi ft} dt \qquad (1\text{-}6)$$

These Fourier integral relationships are of immeasurable value in the study of signals and systems. For convenience in writing we often will use the symbolism $a(t) \Longleftrightarrow A(f)$ to indicate that $a(t)$ and $A(f)$ are a *Fourier transform pair* as expressed by (1-5) *and* (1-6). It is, incidentally, immaterial which of the pair (1-5) or (1-6) has the exp $(+j2\pi ft)$ factor, so long as the other has exp $(-j2\pi ft)$ and one uses the same definitions throughout any analysis in defining the frequency-time relations.

The frequency function $A(f)$ defined by (1-6) is generally a complex quantity having components as indicated by (1-2). In the terminology of communication engineering, when $a(t)$ is a signal waveform, $A(f)$ is termed the frequency spectrum of $a(t)$. The frequency spectrum $A(f)$ characterizes in the frequency domain (or transform domain) a signal described in the time domain by the time function $a(t)$. The pair of Fourier integrals provides the means of transforming back and forth between the frequency and time descriptions of a signal. Equation (1-6) is often termed an analysis operation because it analyzes or resolves a time function in terms of its frequency content. Similarly relation (1-5) is a synthesis operation since its purpose is to construct a signal from a given frequency spectrum.

When we deal with *real* functions of time (as opposed to *complex* time functions), certain useful properties exist between the components of the signal and those of its frequency spectrum. For example, an arbitrary real function of time can always be resolved into even and odd components of time. That is, given that $a(t)$ is a real time function,

$$a(t) = a_e(t) + a_o(t) \qquad (1\text{-}7)$$

where the even part of $a(t)$,

$$a_e(t) = a_e(-t) = \frac{1}{2}[a(t) + a(-t)], \quad \text{even in } t \qquad (1\text{-}8)$$

is an even function of time and where the odd part of $a(t)$,

$$a_o(t) = -a_o(-t) = \frac{1}{2}[a(t) - a(-t)], \quad \text{odd in } t \qquad (1\text{-}9)$$

is an odd function of time. Figure 1-3 illustrates the even and odd parts of a real time function.

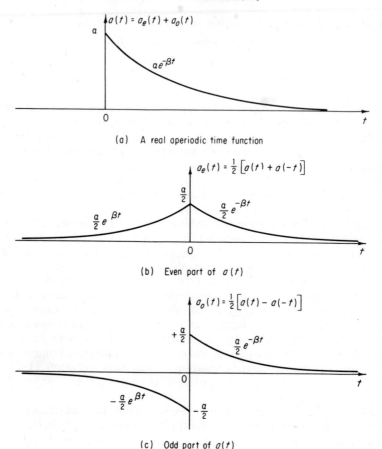

(a)   A real aperiodic time function

(b)   Even part of $a(t)$

(c)   Odd part of $a(t)$

Fig. 1-3 Decomposing a real time function into its even and odd parts.

Given that a real time function has the structure of (1-7) with the properties (1-8) and (1-9), its frequency spectrum can be expressed as

$$A(f) = \int_{-\infty}^{\infty} [a_e(t) + a_o(t)] [\cos 2\pi ft - j \sin 2\pi ft] dt \qquad (1\text{-}10)$$

However, the product of two even functions or of two odd functions results in an even function, whereas the product of an even function and an odd function results in an odd function. Moreover only even functions integrated between limits symmetrical about zero yield nonvanishing results. Hence $A(f)$ reduces to

$$A(f) = \int_{-\infty}^{\infty} a_e(t) \cos 2\pi ft \, dt - j \int_{-\infty}^{\infty} a_o(t) \sin 2\pi ft \, dt \qquad (1\text{-}11)$$

We can now readily identify the parts of (1-11) as the real and imaginary parts of $A(f)$, that is,

$$\text{Re } A(f) = \int_{-\infty}^{\infty} a_e(t) \cos 2\pi ft \, dt, \quad \text{even in } f$$

and

$$\text{Im } A(f) = -\int_{-\infty}^{\infty} a_o(t) \sin 2\pi ft \, dt, \quad \text{odd in } f \qquad (1\text{-}12)$$

These expressions clearly indicate also that the real part of the frequency spectrum of a real time function is an *even* function of frequency, whereas the imaginary part of the spectrum of a real time function is an *odd* function of frequency. Furthermore based on relation (1-3a) these results imply that the magnitude spectrum of a real time function

$$|A(f)| = \sqrt{[\text{Re } A(f)]^2 + [\text{Im } A(f)]^2} \geq 0, \quad \text{even in } f \qquad (1\text{-}13a)$$

is an even function of frequency in addition to being positive everywhere. In a similar manner, when we recognize that the arctangent function is an odd function (actually it is a multivalued odd function), the phase spectrum of a real time function

$$\theta(f) = \arctan \frac{\text{Im } A(f)}{\text{Re } A(f)}, \quad \text{odd in } f \qquad (1\text{-}13b)$$

is an odd function of frequency. A succinct statement of the two results above is that for the frequency spectrum of a real function

$$A(-f) = A^*(f) = \text{Re } A(f) - j \text{Im } A(f) \qquad (1\text{-}13c)$$

where the asterisk denotes a complex conjugate. These properties of a real time function and of its frequency spectrum are quite useful in analytical work.

One further bit of information can be obtained by re-examining (1-12). If we again use the properties of even and odd functions, (1-12) can also be expressed as

$$\text{Re } A(f) \iff a_e(t), \quad j \text{Im } A(f) \iff a_o(t) \qquad (1\text{-}14)$$

These relations state that the real part of the frequency spectrum is the Fourier transform of the even part of the corresponding real time function and that j times the imaginary part of a frequency spectrum is the Fourier transform of the odd part of a real time function. Stated another way, the frequency spectrum of a purely real and even time function is a purely real and even function of frequency. In this special case the frequency spectrum only has a magnitude spectrum since Im $A(f)$ is zero, making the phase spectrum zero, except for possible phase ambiguities to multiples of π because the arctangent function is multivalued (we shall see an example of this condition shortly). Similarly the frequency spectrum of a purely real and odd time function is a purely imaginary and odd function of frequency.

A few examples may help to illustrate these concepts. Consider a decaying exponential, real time function turned on suddenly at $t = 0$ with amplitude V. This signal is described mathematically by

$$a(t) = \begin{cases} Ve^{-t/T}, & t > 0 \\ 0 & , & t < 0 \end{cases} \qquad (1\text{--}15)$$

Its frequency spectrum is computed as

$$A(f) = \int_0^\infty V \exp\left[-\left(\frac{1}{T} + j2\pi f\right)t\right] dt = \frac{V}{(1/T) + j2\pi f} \qquad (1\text{--}16a)$$

After multiplying the numerator and denominator by $(1/T) - j2\pi f$, (1-16a) can be written

$$A(f) = \frac{VT}{1 + (2\pi ft)^2} (1 - j2\pi fT) \qquad (1\text{--}16b)$$

which is in the form of Re $A(f) + j$ Im $A(f)$. Note that indeed the real and imaginary parts of the frequency spectrum are respectively even and odd functions of frequency. We have for the magnitude spectrum of $A(f)$ that

$$|A(f)| = \frac{VT}{\sqrt{1 + (2\pi fT)^2}} \qquad (1\text{--}17a)$$

and for the phase spectrum

$$\theta(f) = \arctan(-2\pi fT) \qquad (1\text{--}17b)$$

Thus in "polar" form $A(f)$ is

$$A(f) = \frac{VT}{\sqrt{1 + (2\pi fT)^2}} \exp\left[j \arctan(-2\pi fT)\right] \qquad (1\text{--}18)$$

Figure 1-4 shows a plot of this time function and plots of its magnitude and phase spectra, which are respectively even and odd frequency functions.

This example has actually provided more information than is at first evident. First, we have derived a basic Fourier transform pair

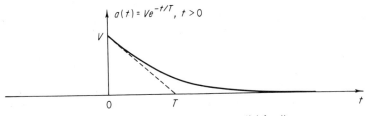

(a) Suddenly occurring, decaying exponential function

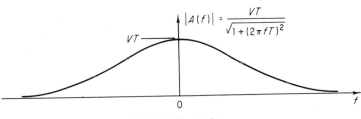

(b) Magnitude spectrum

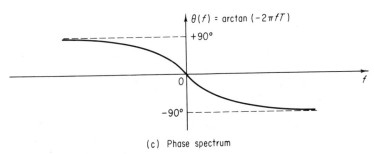

(c) Phase spectrum

Fig. 1-4 Exponential time function and its frequency spectrum.

relation for a suddenly applied, decaying exponential time function, expressed in slightly more general form as

$$\alpha e^{-\beta t}(\beta > 0,\, t > 0) \iff \frac{\alpha}{\beta + j2\pi f} \tag{1-19}$$

Second, since a real time function can always be resolved into its even and odd parts, we have two additional transform pairs, namely,

$$\frac{1}{2}\alpha e^{-\beta |t|}\ (\beta > 0) \iff \frac{\alpha\beta}{\beta^2 + (2\pi f)^2} \tag{1-20a}$$

and

$$\left.\begin{array}{l} \dfrac{1}{2}\alpha e^{-\beta t}\ (\beta > 0,\, t > 0) \\[2ex] -\dfrac{1}{2}\alpha e^{+\beta t}\ (\beta > 0,\, t < 0) \end{array}\right\} \iff \frac{-j2\pi f\alpha}{\beta^2 + (2\pi f)^2} \tag{1-20b}$$

These time functions are shown in Fig. 1-3. Note that the frequency spectra of (1-20) are appropriately real-even and purely imaginary-odd frequency functions.

We see that the even/odd properties discussed above, as well as other properties of the Fourier integrals which we shall develop subsequently, are quite useful in obtaining additional transform-pairs from already known results and in interpreting these results. However, in practice, one often refers to published tables of Fourier transform pairs (e.g., Ref. 5) to facilitate problem solving.

As a second example consider a rectangular pulse of amplitude V and duration T described by

$$p(t) = \begin{cases} V , & |t| \leq T/2 \\ 0 , & |t| > T/2 \end{cases} \tag{1-21}$$

The frequency spectrum of this pulse is

$$P(f) = \int_{-T/2}^{T/2} Ve^{-j2\pi ft}dt = VT \frac{\sin \pi fT}{\pi fT} \tag{1-22}$$

The pulse and its frequency spectrum are shown in Fig. 1-5. Notice that the frequency spectrum $P(f)$ is purely real. This is a direct result of the signal (pulse) being defined as an even function of time. The spectrum of the rectangular pulse has the functional form of a $(\sin x)/x$ function. This function is an important one, occurring frequently in communication engineering, and it is sometimes written sinc x. The sinc (πfT) function has a central peak at $f = 0$ with nulls occuring every $1/T$ hertz on either side of the peak.

Since in this instance Im $P(f) = 0$, the magnitude spectrum is

$$|P(f)| = \sqrt{[\text{Re}\,P(f)]^2} = \sqrt{P^2(f)} = VT \left| \frac{\sin \pi fT}{\pi fT} \right| \tag{1-23}$$

where we must be careful to take the positive sign in calculating $\sqrt{P^2(f)}$. Furthermore since the phase spectrum is

$$\theta_P(f) = \arctan \frac{0}{\text{Re}\,P(f)} \stackrel{?}{=} 0° \tag{1-24}$$

we conclude that no phase spectrum exists. However, because Re $P(f)$ alternates in sign and the arctangent function is multi-valued, we must properly interpret (1-24) as

$$\theta_P(f) = \begin{cases} \arctan \dfrac{0}{+1} = 0 , \ P(f) > 0 \\[3mm] \arctan \dfrac{0}{-1} = \pm\pi \ \text{(to within multiples of } 2\pi) , \ P(f) < 0 \end{cases} \tag{1-25}$$

Note that to properly define a phase spectrum, odd in frequency, it is necessary to alternate the values $\pm\pi$ in the adjacent lobes to which they are appropriate. Figure 1-5 also shows the magnitude spectrum of $P(f)$ and its associated phase spectrum.

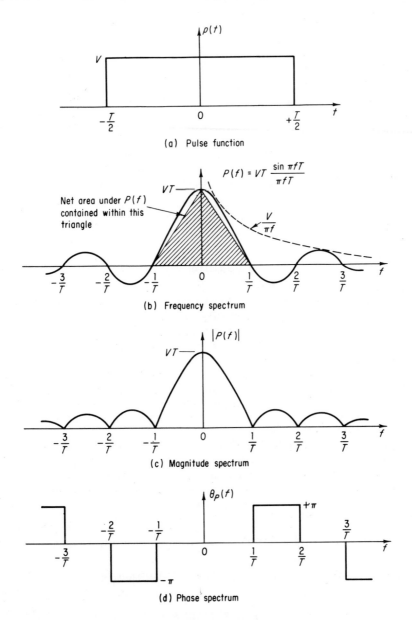

(a) Pulse function

(b) Frequency spectrum

(c) Magnitude spectrum

(d) Phase spectrum

Fig. 1-5 The frequency spectrum of a rectangular pulse function.

Existence of Fourier Transforms

Until now no specific statements have been made regarding the existence of Fourier transforms, i.e., regarding the conditions for convergence of the infinite integral which represents a time function in terms of its frequency spectrum. A few comments are in order on this topic. Although not every time function possesses a Fourier transform, the very large class of useful functions which is Fourier transformable includes essentially all signals and waveforms that can be generated in practice. The Dirichlet conditions (Ref. 2), under which a Fourier integral representation is strictly definable for a given function, state that throughout any infinite range for which the time function is defined, it shall possess the following:

1. A finite number of maxima and minima.
2. A finite number of (finite) discontinuities.
3. A finite number of points where the function becomes infinite.

In short the time function shall be "reasonably well behaved." In addition, the function shall be absolutely integrable; that is, the integral of the magnitude shall be finite,

$$\int_{-\infty}^{\infty} |a(t)|\, dt < \infty \tag{1-26}$$

If the function becomes infinite at some point, this infinity shall be integrable. An example is a logarithmic infinity, the area under which is finite. At a point of discontinuity of the function $a(t)$, the Fourier integral yields the arithmetic average of the two values of the function on opposite sides of this discontinuity. Any function satisfying these strict conditions possesses a *unique* Fourier transform and in turn is reconstructable from its transform. The conditions stated above are sufficient but not necessary. That is, some functions not satisfying these conditions nevertheless have Fourier transforms.

The above conditions form a very strong existence statement for Fourier transformability. A weaker existence statement is available which is often more useful in practical applications. It states that in a limiting sense, if $A(f)$ is the Fourier transform of $a(t)$, then

$$a(t) = \underset{F \to \infty}{\text{l.i.m.}} \int_{-F}^{F} A(f)\, e^{j2\pi ft}\, df \quad \text{(l.i.m. = limit in the mean)} \tag{1-27a}$$

if the integral square of the function exists; that is, if

$$\int_{-\infty}^{\infty} |a(t)|^2\, dt < \infty \tag{1-27b}$$

is finite. Note that the requirement (1-27b) is equivalent to insisting that the function contain finite energy, a condition always met in practice. Thus we can say that if a signal contains finite energy, its spectral representation exists and the signal can be recovered from its spectrum via the Fourier integrals. Furthermore the signal and its spectrum are uniquely related on a one-to-one basis, i.e., the Fourier transform of 0 is uniquely 0.

At times it is convenient for analysis to work with functions which do not satisfy the strict conditions above. The most important such function is $\exp(j2\pi f_0 t)$, defined over all t, for which (1-27b) no longer holds. As we shall see, we can define the spectrum for such a function in a limiting sense, in terms of the delta-function or impulse function, as a single *line spectrum* at frequency f_0.

Multidimensional Fourier Transforms

We shall give no examples here, although we shall later refer to multidimensional Fourier transforms. These are simple extensions of (1-5) and (1-6), applicable under similar existence conditions. Thus if $a(t_1, \ldots, t_N)$ is a function of N variables, we have the following Fourier transform pairs:

$$A(f_1, \ldots f_N) = \int_{-\infty}^{\infty} \cdots \int_{-\infty}^{\infty} a(t_1, \ldots, t_N) e^{-j2\pi(f_1 t_1 + f_2 t_2 + \cdots + f_N t_N)} dt_1 \ldots dt_N$$

$$(1\text{-}28a)$$

$$a(t_1, \ldots t_N) = \int_{-\infty}^{\infty} \cdots \int_{-\infty}^{\infty} A(f_1, \ldots, f_N) e^{j2\pi(f_1 t_1 + \cdots + f_N t_N)} df_1 \ldots df_N$$

$$(1\text{-}28b)$$

1-3 The Impulse Function and System Time/Frequency Representation

One of the most useful functions in signal theory and system analysis is the unit impulse function or delta-function denoted by $\delta(t - t_0)$. This function is often characterized as having zero amplitude everywhere except at the *point* $t = t_0$ where it is infinitely tall, but in such a way that it contains *unit area* under its waveform. For example, it can be pictured as the limit as $T \to 0$ of a rectangle of width T and height $1/T$, centered on $t = t_0$. (A number of equivalent limiting forms can be defined.) As shown in Fig. 1-6, such a rectangular function has unit area under its waveform and in the limit as $T \to 0$ the function becomes infinitesimally narrow and infinitely tall at the point $t = t_0$, yet its area remains finite and fixed at unity.

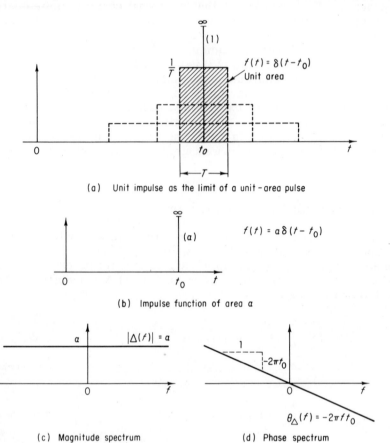

(a)   Unit impulse as the limit of a unit-area pulse

(b)   Impulse function of area a

(c) Magnitude spectrum   (d) Phase spectrum

Fig. 1-6 The impulse function and its frequency spectrum.

Mathematically the impulse function is more properly defined (Ref. 1) in terms of its integral properties. The following integral operation may be taken as defining the impulse function:

$$\int_A^B f(t)\,\delta(t - t_0)\,dt = \begin{cases} f(t_0) & \text{when } A < t_0 < B \\ 0 & \text{when } t_0 < A, \text{ or } t_0 > B \end{cases} \quad (1\text{-}29)$$

Thus the integral over any range that includes the point $t = t_0$ of the product of an arbitrary function $f(t)$ with an impulse function $\delta(t - t_0)$ has the effect of evaluating that function at the time of occurrence of the impulse. The function $a\,\delta(t - t_0)$ is said to be an impulse function with *area* a occurring at $t = t_0$.

The frequency spectrum of the impulse function $\alpha\delta(t - t_0)$ is given by

$$\Delta(f) = \int_{-\infty}^{\infty} \alpha\delta(t - t_0)e^{-j2\pi ft} dt \qquad (1\text{-}30)$$

which according to the definition (1-29) evaluates to

$$\Delta(f) = \alpha e^{-j2\pi ft_0} \Longleftrightarrow \alpha\delta(t - t_0) \qquad (1\text{-}31)$$

The magnitude and phase spectra of the impulse function are

$$|\Delta(f)| = \alpha \qquad (1\text{-}32a)$$

and

$$\theta_\Delta(f) = -2\pi ft_0 \qquad (1\text{-}32b)$$

These spectra are shown in Fig. 1-6 together with the impulse function. It is important to note that the impulse function consists of a uniform frequency content over the entire range from $-\infty$ to $+\infty$; its magnitude spectrum contains all possible frequencies, each with identical amplitude α. Thus the magnitude spectrum is at every point in frequency equal to the area of the impulse. According to (1-32b), the phase of a sinusoidal component of frequency f is linearly proportional to f with the proportionality factor $-2\pi t_0$ where t_0 is the time of occurrence or time delay of the impulse. Hence the slope of the linear phase spectrum of a delayed impulse is -2π times the delay of the impulse, as shown in Fig. 1-6. For the particular case $t_0 = 0$, when the impulse is located at the origin of the time scale, the phase spectrum vanishes since every component has zero phase and only the magnitude spectrum remains; that is, $\alpha\delta(t) \Longleftrightarrow \alpha$ for all f.

Obviously the impulse time function is a very special function, since exciting the input of an electric network or system *by an impulse is equivalent to testing* that system *simultaneously with* sinusoids of *all possible frequencies* and *each with the same amplitude*. Equivalently the time response of a system to unit impulse excitation ($\alpha = 1$) is a time function that characterizes the system; that is, it provides a unique means of describing the system in the time domain. This special response function is termed the *system unit impulse response*. For example, the time response of a simple RC network to a unit impulse voltage is a suddenly occurring, decaying exponential, which is well known to be characteristic of all single time-constant RC networks. This example of an impulse response is illustrated in Fig. 1-7. In general a linear, time-invariant system is characterized uniquely in the time domain by its unit impulse response, which we denote by $h(t)$. Note that, under the assumption that effect can never precede cause, an impulse response $h(t)$ for a *physical* system is *always* identically zero for $t < 0$.

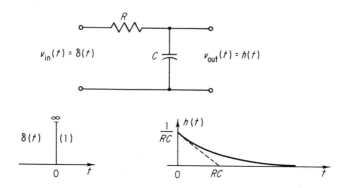

Fig. 1-7 The unit impulse response of an RC circuit.

Just as the unit impulse response characterizes a linear system in the time domain, the system frequency function describes the system's frequency domain properties. The *system frequency function* is defined as the Fourier transform of the unit impulse response $H(f) \Longleftrightarrow h(t)$ and is commonly identified as an impedance function or system transfer ratio. $H(f)$ can be measured for a given system by forming the ratio of the system response to the input excitation, when the system is excited by a single frequency. For each value of f this function describes the system response to a unit amplitude sinusoid of frequency f. For example, consider the RC network of Fig. 1-7, for which (1-19) applies. Setting $\alpha = \beta = 1/RC$, we have

$$ h(t) = \begin{cases} \dfrac{1}{RC}\, e^{-t/RC}, & t > 0 \\[2mm] 0 & , t < 0 \end{cases} \quad \Longleftrightarrow \quad H(f) = \frac{1}{1 + j2\pi f RC} \quad (1\text{-}33) $$

A simple network calculation will verify that the voltage transfer ratio of the RC network of Fig. 1-7 is given by the right-hand side of (1-33).

We now have a representation of a linear system or network in both the time and frequency domains. The system unit impulse response is a unique time description of the system, and the system frequency function is a unique frequency description of the system. In addition, the system unit impulse response and system frequency function are a Fourier transform pair.

1-4 Convolution

A very useful relation between the input and output time functions of a linear system can be written in terms of the unit impulse response that characterizes the system. Figure 1-8 shows a system described by its unit impulse response $h(t)$, an input excitation

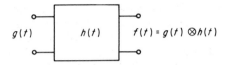

$g(t)$ $h(t)$ $f(t) = g(t) \otimes h(t)$

(a) Time domain relationships of a linea system

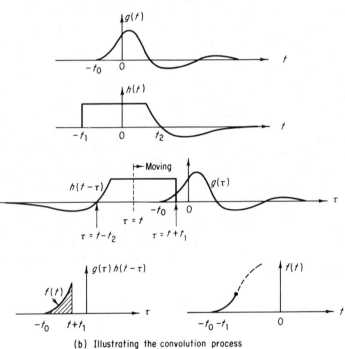

(b) Illustrating the convolution process

Fig. 1-8 Linear system analysis in the time domain.

$g(t)$ to the system, and the resulting output $f(t)$ caused by the input. The output time response is determined by the *convolution integral,* or *superposition integral* as it is also known (Refs. 1, 3, 4, 6), as expressed by either of the equivalent relations.

$$f(t) = \int_{-\infty}^{\infty} g(\tau)\, h(t - \tau)\, d\tau = \int_{-\infty}^{\infty} h(\tau)\, g(t - \tau)\, d\tau \qquad (1\text{-}34)$$

This form of integral is often indicated symbolically by the notation

$$f(t) = h(t) \otimes g(t) \tag{1-35}$$

The validity of the convolution integral is obvious for impulse excitation since, if $g(t) = \delta(t)$ in (1-34), then according to (1-29), $f(t) = h(t)$, which is just the system's unit impulse response. If we regard any more general time function $g(t)$ as composed of a sequence of successive impulses with weights (areas) $g(t)$, the convolution relation is just the statement that, for a linear system, the output is the sum of the responses to the sequence of impulses.

Conceptually in Fig. 1-8, $g(\tau)$ is simply the input function plotted against a new variable τ, while $h(t - \tau)$ is the system unit impulse response function reversed in time on the τ-axis and displaced to the point $\tau = t$. As t takes on all values from $-\infty$ to $+\infty$, the reversed function $h(t - \tau)$ effectively translates or slides along the τ-axis from left to right as time progresses. As $h(t - \tau)$ slips by $g(\tau)$, (1-34) indicates that the product of these functions is formed and then integrated over their common extent, i.e., the area under the product waveform is computed. This calculation is repeated for all values of t. Convolution can be viewed as a process of displacement or scan, multiplication, and computation of the area. Since this sequence of operations depends on the *instantaneous* location of the scanning function, the result of convolving two functions is a new time function. The output time response will have a duration (total time extent) roughly given by the *sum* of the durations of the two functions being convolved. Thus convolution tends to stretch out or lengthen time functions.

As an example of the type of calculation involved in convolution, consider the problem posed in **Fig. 1-9**. The linear system in this instance is a single time constant network (T is termed the time constant), similar to a simple RC network, with a unit impulse response given by

$$h(t) = \begin{cases} h_0 e^{-t/T} , & t > 0 \\ 0 & , & t < 0 \end{cases} \tag{1-36}$$

We are interested in computing the output response of this system to a rectangular pulse excitation

$$g(t) = \begin{cases} V , & |t| \leq T/2 \\ 0 , & |t| > T/2 \end{cases} \tag{1-37}$$

Figure 1-9 illustrates the steps involved in the convolution process. Part b of Fig. 1-9 shows the state of affairs for three selected instants of time. For $t < -T/2$ there is no overlap of the two functions $g(\tau)$ and $h(t - \tau)$; therefore their product is zero and the output response $f(t)$ is zero in this region. However, in the range $-T/2 \leq t \leq T/2$ the two waveforms do overlap and for this interval the response is the integral over the region of overlap of the product waveform as given by

$$|t| < \frac{T}{2}: \; f(t) = \int_{-T/2}^{t} Vh_0 e^{-(t-\tau)/T} d\tau = VTh_0 \left[1 - e^{-(t + T/2)/T} \right] \quad (1\text{--}38a)$$

Note that the output response evaluated at the *point* in time t is given by the shaded area under the product waveform shown in

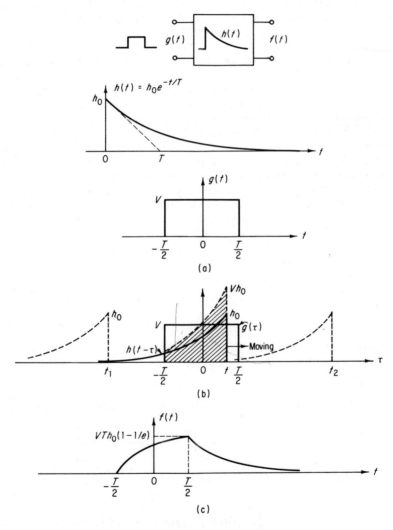

(a)

(b)

(c)

Fig. 1-9 Calculating the response of a linear system by convolution.

Fig. 1-9b. Similarly in the range $+T/2 \leq t$ the response is given by

$$t \geq \frac{T}{2} : f(t) = \int_{-T/2}^{T/2} V h_0 e^{-(t - \tau)/T} d\tau = V T h_0 e^{-t/T} (e^{\frac{1}{2}} - e^{-\frac{1}{2}}) \quad (1\text{-}38b)$$

The combined output response is plotted in part c of Fig. 1-9.

In the time domain the convolution integral is a complete and general description of how linear systems interact with signals transmitted through them. Thus convolution is an important and powerful tool of linear system analysis. In the next section we shall discuss the close relationship of convolution to Fourier theory and describe equivalent frequency domain relationships.

1-5 Linear System Theory in the Frequency Domain

In the previous section we showed by physical reasoning how a convolution integral provides the means of computing the time response of linear systems to various forms of signal waveforms. In the present section we demonstrate linear system analysis in terms of frequency spectra and the system frequency function (Refs. 3, 4, 6). Specifically it is shown that the frequency spectrum of the output response is the product of the system frequency function with the input frequency spectrum, and the output time response is obtained as the Fourier transform of its spectrum.

Consider the convolution integral

$$f(t) = \int_{-\infty}^{\infty} g(\tau) h(t - \tau) d\tau \quad (1\text{-}39)$$

where the input excitation $g(t)$ has a frequency spectrum $G(f)$ related by

$$G(f) \Longleftrightarrow g(t) \quad (1\text{-}40)$$

Similarly the system unit impulse response $h(t)$ is related to the system frequency function $H(f)$ by

$$H(f) \Longleftrightarrow h(t) \quad (1\text{-}41)$$

Expressing $h(t - \tau)$ in terms of $H(f)$, we can write (1-39) as

$$f(t) = \int_{-\infty}^{\infty} g(\tau) \left[\int_{-\infty}^{\infty} H(f) e^{j2\pi f(t - \tau)} df \right] d\tau \quad (1\text{-}42)$$

Inverting the order of integration and rearranging, we find

$$f(t) = \int_{-\infty}^{\infty} H(f) \left[\int_{-\infty}^{\infty} g(\tau) e^{-j2\pi f\tau} d\tau \right] e^{j2\pi ft} df \quad (1\text{-}43)$$

The bracketed integral in (1-43) is recognized as identical to the input frequency spectrum $G(f)$. Making this replacement, we express the output time response as

$$f(t) = \int_{-\infty}^{\infty} H(f)\, G(f)\, e^{j2\pi ft}\, df \qquad (1\text{-}44a)$$

but this relation is in the form of a Fourier integral. Thus the frequency spectrum of the output response is given by

$$F(f) = H(f)G(f) \Longleftrightarrow f(t) \qquad (1\text{-}44b)$$

According to this extremely important result, the frequency spectrum of the output response is obtained by forming the product of the input frequency spectrum with the system frequency function. The output time function is obtained then by computing the inverse Fourier transform of the resulting frequency spectrum. These relationships are illustrated in Fig. 1-10.

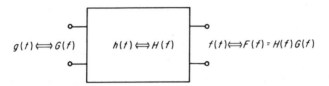

$$g(t) \Longleftrightarrow G(f) \qquad h(t) \Longleftrightarrow H(f) \qquad f(t) \Longleftrightarrow F(f) = H(f)G(f)$$

Fig. 1-10 Frequency domain approach to linear system analysis.

This result should not be surprising, since it is basically the same as derived in conventional sinusoidal circuit analysis. Sinusoidal analysis computes the response of a linear circuit in the following way. Given an input sinusoid $G(f)\exp(j2\pi ft)$, where $G(f)$ contains amplitude and phase information, the output time response is also a sinusoid, namely, $F(f)\exp(j2\pi ft)$. The amplitude and phase factor $F(f)$ of the output is obtained by evaluating the impedance function or system transfer function at the particular input frequency f and by multiplying this quantity with the input factor $G(f)$. Thus $F(f) = H(f)G(f)$ and the output sinusoid is $H(f)G(f)\exp(j2\pi ft)$. Fourier integral theory extends this technique by summing (integrating) the input and output (incremental) sinusoidal components over all frequencies, so as to include more general types of waveforms than purely sinusoidal.

In summary we have demonstrated the important relationship that convolution of time functions is equivalent to multiplication of their frequency spectra. This property can be stated symbolically as follows:

$$h(t) \Longleftrightarrow H(f), \quad g(t) \Longleftrightarrow G(f)$$
$$h(t) \otimes g(t) \Longleftrightarrow H(f)G(f) \qquad (1\text{-}45)$$

1-6 Special Properties of Fourier Transforms

In this section we summarize several basic properties of Fourier transforms which have already been shown or are easily proven.

1 Additive Property (Superposition)

The additive property of Fourier transforms is

$$\alpha f(t) + \beta g(t) \iff \alpha F(f) + \beta G(f) \tag{1-46}$$

For example, the frequency spectrum of a linear sum of signals is the sum of the individual spectra.

2 Area under a Function

Given that $a(t)$ and $A(f)$ are a Fourier transform pair,

$$a(t) = \int_{-\infty}^{\infty} A(f) e^{j2\pi ft} df \tag{1-47}$$

then the zero-time value of $a(t)$ is obtained by setting $t = 0$ in (1-47)

$$a(0) = \int_{-\infty}^{\infty} A(f) df = \text{area under } A(f) \tag{1-48}$$

Thus $a(0)$ is just the total area under the frequency spectrum. Note that, if $a(t)$ is real, the symmetry properties of $A(f)$ guarantee that the computed value will be real also. Similarly

$$A(0) = \int_{-\infty}^{\infty} a(t) dt = \text{area under } a(t) \tag{1-49}$$

These properties of a Fourier transform pair provide useful checks for computations, as well as often aid in the interpretation of functional forms, as will be seen later. The reader might wish to check the examples of Sec. 1-2.

3 Delay or Shift Theorems

a) Time delay

It is useful to know how the frequency spectra of delayed versions of signals are related to the spectra of undelayed signals.

Given a Fourier transform-pair $a(t) \Longleftrightarrow A(f)$, let the time function be delayed an amount t_0. By replacing t with $t - t_0$ in (1-47) and rearranging,

$$a(t - t_0) = \int_{-\infty}^{\infty} A(f) e^{j2\pi f(t - t_0)} df = \int_{-\infty}^{\infty} \left[A(f) e^{-j2\pi f t_0} \right] e^{j2\pi f t} df \qquad (1\text{-}50)$$

The frequency spectrum of the delayed signal can be identified as the bracketed term in (1-50). Thus the (time) delay property of Fourier transforms is

$$a(t - t_0) \Longleftrightarrow A(f) e^{-j2\pi f t_0} \qquad (1\text{-}51)$$

The frequency spectrum of a signal delayed an amount t_0 is the original spectrum of the signal multiplied by the shift or delay factor $\exp(-j2\pi f t_0)$. We have already seen an example of this property, namely, the delayed impulse function $\delta(t - t_0)$ and its frequency spectrum.

$$\delta(t) \Longleftrightarrow 1$$

$$\delta(t - t_0) \Longleftrightarrow (1) e^{-j2\pi f t_0}$$

Hence a signal delayed uniformly without distortion has a linear phase spectrum added to its existing phase spectrum, where every frequency component is given a phase shift proportional to its frequency and to the time delay t_0.

b) Frequency shift

A completely analogous shift property of Fourier transforms exists in the frequency domain. Let every frequency component in a frequency spectrum be shifted an amount f_0,

$$A(f - f_0) = \int_{-\infty}^{\infty} a(t) e^{-j2\pi(f - f_0)t} dt = \int_{-\infty}^{\infty} \left[a(t) e^{+j2\pi f_0 t} \right] e^{-j2\pi f t} dt \qquad (1\text{-}52)$$

The associated time function is the bracketed term in (1-52). Hence the frequency shift property of Fourier transforms is

$$A(f - f_0) \Longleftrightarrow a(t) e^{+j2\pi f_0 t} \qquad (1\text{-}53)$$

Stated inversely, multiplying a signal by the phase shift factor $\exp(+j2\pi f_0 t)$ is equivalent in the frequency domain to shifting every component in its spectrum a uniform amount f_0.

4 Differentiation Property

a) Time domain

Let a time function $a(t)$ be differentiated with respect to the variable t,

$$\frac{da(t)}{dt} = \int_{-\infty}^{\infty} A(f) \frac{d}{dt} e^{j2\pi ft} df = \int_{-\infty}^{\infty} (j2\pi f) A(f) e^{j2\pi ft} dt \qquad (1\text{-}54)$$

and after n such differentiations

$$\frac{d^n a(t)}{dt^n} = \int_{-\infty}^{\infty} (j2\pi f)^n A(f) e^{j2\pi ft} dt \qquad (1\text{-}55)$$

Thus in taking the nth derivative of a signal, we multiply its spectrum by the factor $(j2\pi f)^n$. Symbolically

$$\frac{d^n a(t)}{dt^n} \Longleftrightarrow (j2\pi f)^n A(f) \qquad (1\text{-}56)$$

b) Frequency domain

In a similar manner multiplying a signal by the factor $(-j2\pi t)^n$ is equivalent to taking the nth derivative of the frequency spectrum; that is

$$(-j2\pi t)^n a(t) \Longleftrightarrow \frac{d^n A(f)}{df^n} \qquad (1\text{-}57)$$

5 Time Reversal

For a signal reversed in time,

$$a(-t) \Longleftrightarrow A(-f) \qquad (1\text{-}58)$$

Recall that when $a(t)$ is a *real* function of time

$$A(-f) = A^*(f) \qquad (1\text{-}59)$$

It follows that the frequency spectrum of a real signal reversed in time is the complex conjugate of the original frequency spectrum

$$a(-t) \text{ (real fcn.)} \Longleftrightarrow A(-f) = A^*(f) \qquad (1\text{-}60)$$

6 Duality

The Fourier integrals (1-5) and (1-6) are dual relationships. Given a Fourier transform pair $a(t) \Longleftrightarrow A(f)$, then, after an interchange of t and f,

$$a(\pm f) \Longleftrightarrow A(\mp t) \tag{1-61}$$

Thus if the frequency spectrum of the signal $a(t)$ is $A(f)$, then the spectrum of the signal $A(\mp t)$ is $a(\pm f)$.

7 Multiplication

a) Frequency domain

We have already demonstrated that multiplication of frequency spectra is equivalent to convolution. Thus with

$$h(t) \Longleftrightarrow H(f) \qquad g(t) \Longleftrightarrow G(f)$$
$$h(t) \otimes g(t) \Longleftrightarrow H(f)G(f) \tag{1-62}$$

b) Time domain

Analogous to the above frequency domain multiplication theorem, the product of two time functions transforms to the convolution of their frequency spectra,

$$h(t)g(t) \Longleftrightarrow H(f) \otimes G(f)$$

or

$$h(t)g(t) \Longleftrightarrow \int_{-\infty}^{\infty} G(\lambda)H(f - \lambda)d\lambda \tag{1-63}$$

8 Parseval's Theorem (Ref. 1)

An important result closely related to the multiplication property is the expression

$$\int_{-\infty}^{\infty} g^*(t)h(t)dt = \int_{-\infty}^{\infty} G^*(f)H(f)df \tag{1-64}$$

known as *Parseval's theorem*. For convenience of later discussions we derive the following more general result:

$$\int_{-\infty}^{\infty} g^*(t)\, h(t + \tau)\, dt = \int_{-\infty}^{\infty} g^*(t) \int_{-\infty}^{\infty} H(f)\, e^{j2\pi f(t + \tau)}\, df\, dt$$

$$= \iint_{-\infty}^{\infty} g^*(t)\, e^{j2\pi ft}\, dt\, H(f)\, e^{j2\pi f\tau}\, df \qquad (1\text{-}65)$$

$$= \int_{-\infty}^{\infty} G^*(f)\, H(f)\, e^{j2\pi f\tau}\, df$$

Evaluated for $\tau = 0$, (1-65) reduces to (1-64). For *real* signals Parseval's theorem becomes

$$\int_{-\infty}^{\infty} g(t)\, h(t)\, dt = \int_{-\infty}^{\infty} G^*(f)\, H(f)\, df = \int_{-\infty}^{\infty} G(-f)\, H(f)\, df \qquad (1\text{-}66)$$

If $g(t) = h(t)$, then

$$\int_{-\infty}^{\infty} |g(t)|^2\, dt = \int_{-\infty}^{\infty} |G(f)|^2\, df \qquad (1\text{-}67)$$

for complex signals and

$$\int_{-\infty}^{\infty} g^2(t)\, dt = \int_{-\infty}^{\infty} |G(f)|^2\, df \qquad (1\text{-}68)$$

for real signals. Note that the integral square of a real signal or integral squared magnitude of a complex signal is identified as the energy of the signal. Thus the energy of a signal $g(t)$ is given by the area under the squared magnitude $|G(f)|^2$ of its frequency spectrum. Accordingly $|G(f)|^2$ is termed the *energy density spectrum* of $g(t)$.

1-7 Transform of a Unit Step Function

A function of special interest to linear system analysis is the unit step function defined as a constant equal to unity for all positive t and zero otherwise

$$u(t) = \begin{cases} 1, & t > 0 \\ 0, & t < 0 \end{cases} \qquad (1\text{-}69)$$

Alternately the unit step function can be defined as the integral of the unit impulse function

$$u(t) = \int_{-\infty}^{t} \delta(t)\,dt = \begin{cases} 1, & t > 0 \\ 0, & t < 0 \end{cases} \tag{1-70}$$

That is, the first derivative of the unit step function is the unit impulse function

$$\frac{du(t)}{dt} = \delta(t) \tag{1-71}$$

In a strict sense the step function is like the delta-function in not being Fourier transformable since it violates both of the existence conditions expressed by (1-26) and (1-28), which is to indicate that the step function contains infinite energy. However, we show that in a *limiting* sense a frequency spectrum can be defined for the step function and that it is given by

$$U(f) = \frac{1}{2}\delta(f) + \frac{1}{j2\pi f} \tag{1-72}$$

where $\delta(f)$ is a unit impulse in frequency

A unit step function contains infinite energy, but a unit decaying exponential $\exp(-t/T)$, $t > 0$, contains finite energy equal to $T/2$. Furthermore as the time constant T grows large, the unit decaying exponential closely resembles the unit step function. Figure 1-11a illustrates the approach of the unit decaying exponential to the unit step function. In the limit then as the time constant grows large

$$\lim_{T \to \infty} e^{-t/T} = u(t) \tag{1-73}$$

This is the key to defining a Fourier transform of $u(t)$. First split the unit step function into its even and odd parts

$$u(t) = u_e(t) + u_o(t) = \begin{cases} 1, & t > 0 \\ 0, & t < 0 \end{cases} \tag{1-74a}$$

$$u_e(t) = 1/2 \quad \text{for all } t \tag{1-74b}$$

$$u_o(t) = \begin{cases} 1/2, & t > 0 \\ 0, & t = 0 \\ -1/2, & t < 0 \end{cases} \tag{1-74c}$$

The even part $u_e(t)$ is a true constant for all t and the odd part $u_o(t)$ is a negative constant to the left of the origin and a positive constant to the right of the origin. The unit decaying exponential also can be separated into even and odd parts

$$a(t) = a_e(t) + a_o(t) = e^{-t/T}, \quad t > 0 \tag{1-75a}$$

$$a_e(t) = \frac{1}{2} e^{-|t|/T} \quad \text{for all } t \qquad (1\text{-}75b)$$

$$a_o(t) = \begin{cases} \dfrac{1}{2} e^{-t/T}, & t > 0 \\[2mm] 0, & t = 0 \\[2mm] -\dfrac{1}{2} e^{t/T}, & t < 0 \end{cases} \qquad (1\text{-}75c)$$

As the time constant grows large, the even and odd parts of the unit decaying exponential respectively approach in the limit the even and odd parts of the unit step function. This relationship is illustrated in Fig. 1-11b.

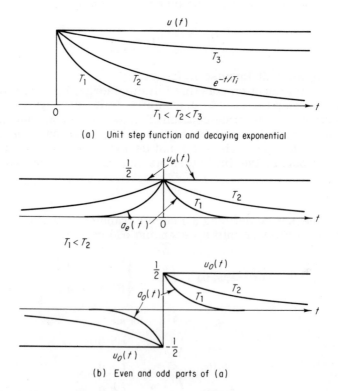

(a)   Unit step function and decaying exponential

(b)   Even and odd parts of (a)

Fig. 1-11 The approach of a decaying exponential to a unit step function.

The frequency spectrum of the decaying exponential was studied earlier in Sec. 1-2 where it was given as

$$A(f) = \frac{1}{(1/T) + j2\pi f} = \frac{1/T}{(1/T)^2 + (2\pi f)^2} - j\frac{2\pi f}{(1/T)^2 + (2\pi f)^2} \qquad (1\text{-}76)$$

Since the decaying exponential is a real function of time, its even part transforms to the real part of $A(f)$ and its odd part transforms to j times the imaginary part of $A(f)$. Figure 1-12 shows the real and imaginary parts of $A(f)$. First consider the real part of $A(f)$ shown in Fig. 1-12a. This function has a *fixed*, finite area under it equal to $a_e(0) = 1/2$ as can be seen by property no. 2 of the previous section

$$a_e(t) = \frac{1}{2} e^{-|t|/T} \iff \text{Re } A(f) = \frac{1/T}{(1/T)^2 + (2\pi f)^2}$$

$$a_e(0) = \frac{1}{2} = \int_{-\infty}^{\infty} \text{Re } A(f)\, df \qquad (1\text{-}77)$$

Figure 1-12a shows that the peak value of $\text{Re } A(f)$ is $\text{Re } A(0) = T$ and that as the time constant T grows large the function grows taller and thinner but maintains a finite area under it equal to $1/2$. Thus *in the limit* $\text{Re } A(f)$ becomes an impulse function of area $1/2$ at the origin of the frequency scale.

$$\lim_{T \to \infty} a_e(t) = \frac{1}{2} \iff \lim_{T \to \infty} \text{Re } A(f) = \frac{1}{2} \delta(f) \qquad (1\text{-}78)$$

Now consider the imaginary part of $A(f)$. As shown in Fig. 1-12b this is an odd function of frequency with a slope at the origin equal to $-2\pi T^2$. Also the highest peaks of $\text{Im } A(f)$ are $T/2$ in magnitude occurring at $\pm 1/2\pi T$. As T grows large, the peaks grow higher but occur closer to the origin where the slope becomes progressively steeper. In the limit then

$$\lim_{T \to \infty} a_o(t) = \begin{cases} \dfrac{1}{2}, & t > 0 \\ -\dfrac{1}{2}, & t < 0 \end{cases} \iff \lim_{T \to \infty} j \text{ Im } A(f) = \frac{1}{j2\pi f} \qquad (1\text{-}79)$$

as can be seen by examining (1-76).

Putting these results together, we can define a frequency spectrum for the unit step function in a limiting sense and it is given by the relation

$$U(f) = \lim_{T \to \infty} A(f) = \frac{1}{2} \delta(f) + \frac{1}{j2\pi f} \qquad (1\text{-}80)$$

Thus we have the transform-pair

$$u(t) = \begin{cases} 1, & t > 0 \\ 0, & t < 0 \end{cases} \iff U(f) = \frac{1}{2} \delta(f) + \frac{1}{j2\pi f} \qquad (1\text{-}81)$$

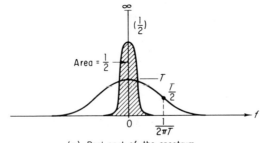

(a) Real part of the spectrum

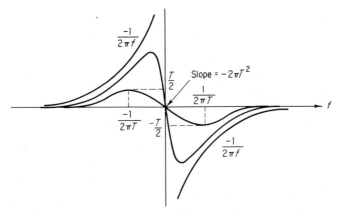

(b) Imaginary part of the spectrum

Fig. 1-12 The frequency spectrum of a unit step function as the limit of the spectrum of a unit decaying exponential.

As a check on the results we should be able to derive the frequency spectrum of a unit impulse function from (1-81), since

$$\delta(t) = \frac{du(t)}{dt}$$

and by property no. 4

$$\Delta(f) = (j2\pi f)\, U(f) = j\pi f\, \delta(f) + 1 = 0 + 1 = 1$$

The check computation is verified.

In addition to determining a frequency spectrum for the step function, we also have obtained an important subsidiary result. Equation (1-78) states that a constant in the time domain transforms to an impulse function in frequency as expressed by

$$1 \iff \delta(f) \tag{1-82}$$

This is completely analogous to the previous result for an impulse in time, namely,

$$\delta(t) \iff 1 \tag{1-83}$$

Thus a constant in either the time or frequency domain transforms to the other domain as an impulse function with area equal to the constant.

Another subsidiary result was obtained from (1-79):

$$\left.\begin{array}{ll} 1/2, & t > 0 \\ 0, & t = 0 \\ -1/2, & t < 0 \end{array}\right\} \Longleftrightarrow \frac{1}{j2\pi f} \qquad (1\text{-}84)$$

These results are summarized in Fig. 1-13.

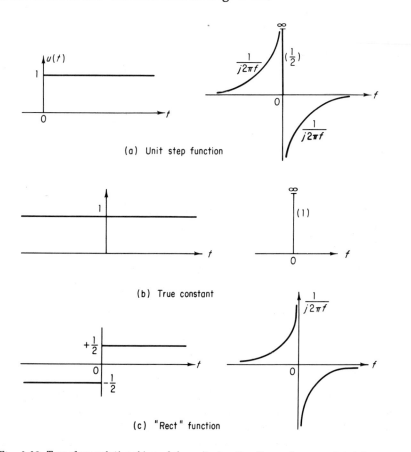

(a) Unit step function

(b) True constant

(c) "Rect" function

Fig. 1-13 Transform relationships of the unit step function and some related functions.

1-8 Example of a System Calculation

To illustrate some of the concepts presented up to this point, we reconsider the example of a system calculation studied earlier to illustrate the convolution process; however, here we treat the problem in terms of frequency functions. Again we consider a linear system specified by the unit impulse response

$$h(t) = \begin{cases} h_0 e^{-t/T}, & t > 0 \\ 0 & , \quad t < 0 \end{cases} \tag{1-85}$$

and driven by a rectangular pulse excitation

$$g(t) = \begin{cases} V, & |t| < T/2 \\ 0, & |t| > T/2 \end{cases} \tag{1-86}$$

The system frequency function

$$H(f) = \frac{h_0}{(1/T) + j2\pi f} \tag{1-87}$$

and the frequency spectrum of the input excitation

$$G(f) = VT \frac{\sin \pi fT}{\pi fT} \tag{1-88}$$

were obtained previously. The problem is to determine the output time response of the system to the given excitation.

The frequency spectrum of the output is the product of the input spectrum with the system function. Thus

$$F(f) = H(f)G(f) = \frac{h_0}{(1/T) + j2\pi f} VT \frac{\sin \pi fT}{\pi fT} \tag{1-89}$$

Accordingly the output time response is given by

$$f(t) = \int_{-\infty}^{\infty} H(f) G(f) e^{j2\pi ft} df \tag{1-90}$$

The direct approach to determining $f(t)$ is to evaluate the integral (1-90). However, direct evaluation of integrals of this type is often difficult. Fortunately another method is available which often provides a simpler means of calculating the output time function. This method is based on separating or expanding the frequency function into a sum of a number of recognizable pieces, each of which can be more readily identified as the transform of a known time function. Of course, this method is premised on finding a suitable expansion and, having done so, on recognizing each of the terms in the expansion. The latter step, that of identifying each term of the expansion with a known time function, is usually implemented by referring to published tables of Fourier transforms (e.g., Ref. 5) or the analyst's own ingenuity.

As an example, applied to (1-89), we first expand the $\sin \pi f T$ function

$$\sin \pi f T = \frac{e^{j2\pi f T/2} - e^{-j2\pi f T/2}}{2j} \tag{1-91}$$

so as to express $F(f)$ in the form

$$F(f) = \left(e^{j2\pi f T/2} - e^{-j2\pi f T/2}\right) \hat{F}(f) \tag{1-92}$$

where the new function $\hat{F}(f)$ is

$$\hat{F}(f) = \frac{Vh_0}{\left(\dfrac{1}{T} + j2\pi f\right) j2\pi f} \tag{1-93}$$

Recalling the time delay property, we recognize the exponential factors in (1-92) to be shift factors arising from time displacements of $\hat{f}(t)$. Given the transform of the function $\hat{F}(f)$,

$$\hat{f}(t) \iff \hat{F}(f) \tag{1-94}$$

we can at once write

$$f(t) = \hat{f}(t + T/2) - \hat{f}(t - T/2) \tag{1-95}$$

Hence for the moment we can neglect the shift factors and concentrate on expanding $\hat{F}(f)$ to obtain $\hat{f}(t)$.

The new frequency function can be expanded by the method of *partial fraction expansion* wherein $\hat{F}(f)$ is expressed as

$$\hat{F}(f) = \frac{A}{\dfrac{1}{T} + j2\pi f} + \frac{B}{j2\pi f} \tag{1-96}$$

The constants A and B can be determined by standard techniques as

$$A = \left(\frac{1}{T} + j2\pi f\right) \hat{F}(f) \Bigg|_{f=-\frac{1}{j2\pi T}} = \frac{Vh_0}{j2\pi f} \Bigg|_{f=-\frac{1}{j2\pi T}} = -VTh_0 \tag{1-97}$$

and

$$B = j2\pi f \hat{F}(f) \Bigg|_{f=0} = \frac{Vh_0}{\dfrac{1}{T} + j2\pi f} \Bigg|_{f=0} = VTh_0 \tag{1-98}$$

Thus $\hat{F}(f)$ is then

$$\hat{F}(f) = \frac{VTh_0}{j2\pi f} - \frac{VTh_0}{\dfrac{1}{T} + j2\pi f} \tag{1-99}$$

each part of which can be identified as the transform of a known time function. Recalling (1-84), we write

$$\left.\begin{array}{ll} VTh_0/2 , & t > 0 \\ -VTh_0/2 , & t < 0 \end{array}\right\} \Longleftrightarrow \frac{VTh_0}{j2\pi f} \tag{1-100}$$

Similarly

$$\left.\begin{array}{ll} -VTh_0 e^{-t/T} , & t > 0 \\ 0 , & t < 0 \end{array}\right\} \Longleftrightarrow - \frac{VTh_0}{\dfrac{1}{T} + j2\pi f} \tag{1-101}$$

Thus

$$\hat{f}(t) = \begin{cases} (VTh_0/2) - VTh_0 e^{-t/T} , & t > 0 \\ -VTh_0/2 & , & t < 0 \end{cases} \tag{1-102}$$

This time function is shown in Fig. 1-14a. The time response of the system $f(t)$ as given by (1-95) is illustrated in Fig. 1-14b. The result is of course identical with that shown earlier in Fig. 1-9.

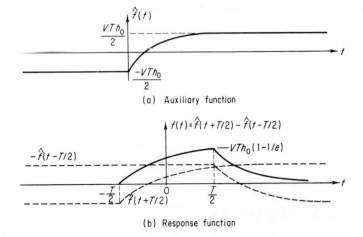

(a) Auxiliary function

(b) Response function

Fig. 1-14 Showing the decomposition of a response function.

1-9 Additional Transforms and Techniques

1 Sinusoidal Functions

We have seen that a constant α in the time domain transforms in a limiting sense to an impulse in frequency

$$\alpha \iff \alpha \, \delta(f) \qquad (1\text{-}103)$$

and the frequency shift theorem states that a signal is multiplied by a shift factor $\exp(j2\pi f_0 t)$ when its spectrum is shifted uniformly by an amount f_0.

$$a(t)\, e^{j2\pi f_0 t} \iff A(f - f_0) \qquad (1\text{-}104)$$

With this in mind a general complex sinusoid defined for all t by

$$A\, e^{j2\pi f_0 t + j\phi} = [A\, e^{j\phi}]\, e^{j2\pi f_0 t} \qquad (1\text{-}105)$$

is recognized as being of the form of a complex constant multiplied by a frequency shift factor. Thus *in a limiting sense* a complex sinusoid has a Fourier transform given by the relation

$$A\, e^{j2\pi f_0 t + j\phi} \iff A\, e^{j\phi}\, \delta(f - f_0) \qquad (1\text{-}106)$$

which is an impulse function in frequency (a *line spectrum*) at $f = f_0$ with complex area $A \exp(j\phi)$.

Consider now a *real* sinusoid defined for all t,

$$A \cos(2\pi f_0 t + \phi) = \frac{A}{2} \left[e^{j2\pi f_0 t + j\phi} + e^{-j2\pi f_0 t - j\phi} \right] \qquad (1\text{-}107)$$

Applying the above result to (1-107), we see that the real sinusoid also has a frequency spectrum defined in a limiting sense as expressed by the transform pair

$$A \cos(2\pi f_0 t + \phi) \iff \frac{A}{2} e^{j\phi} \delta(f - f_0) + \frac{A}{2} e^{-j\phi} \delta(f + f_0) \qquad (1\text{-}108)$$

This spectrum is a pair of impulses in frequency occurring at $f = \pm f_0$ with complex areas $(A/2) \exp(\pm j\phi)$, as shown in Fig. 1-15.

Specializing this result for $\phi = 0$, we see that the frequency spectrum of a real cosine wave is

$$A \cos 2\pi f_0 t \iff \frac{A}{2} \delta(f - f_0) + \frac{A}{2} \delta(f + f_0) \qquad (1\text{-}109)$$

a pair of identical impulses of real area $A/2$ located at $f = \pm f_0$. Similarly, for $\phi = -\pi/2 = -90°$, the spectrum of a real sine wave is seen to be

$$A \sin 2\pi f_0 t \iff \frac{A}{2j} \delta(f - f_0) - \frac{A}{2j} \delta(f + f_0) \qquad (1\text{-}110)$$

a pair of oppositely directed impulses in frequency of purely imaginary area $\pm A/2j$ located at $f = \pm f_0$. These real sinusoids and their frequency spectra are illustrated in Fig. 1-15.

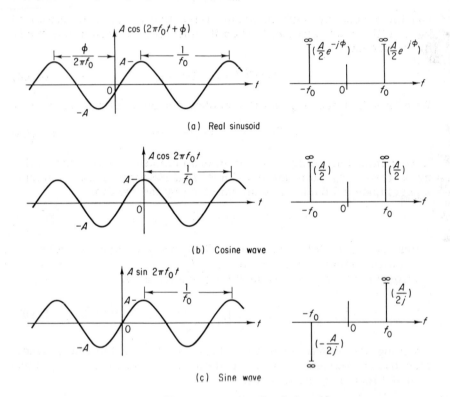

(a) Real sinusoid

(b) Cosine wave

(c) Sine wave

Fig. 1-15 Frequency spectra of real sinusoids.

2 Products of Signals and Sinusoids

Often in communication applications we find sinusoids (*carriers*) multiplied by narrow-band signals (modulation components) in which the largest significant frequency in the signal's spectrum is much smaller than the frequency of the sinusoid. Such product signals are termed *bandpass* signals (Refs. 1, 2) and are discussed in detail in Chap. 3. Here we note some general properties.

Consider a signal of the form

$$f(t) = g(t) \cos (2\pi f_0 t + \phi) \qquad (1\text{-}111)$$

One method for obtaining the frequency spectrum of $f(t)$ is to expand (1-111),

$$f(t) = \frac{1}{2} g(t) \left[e^{j2\pi f_0 t + j\phi} + e^{-j2\pi f_0 t - j\phi} \right] \tag{1-112}$$

and to apply the frequency shift theorem. Given the transform pair $g(t) \Longleftrightarrow G(f)$, the spectrum of $f(t)$ is given directly by

$$f(t) = g(t) \cos(2\pi f_0 t + \phi) \Longleftrightarrow \frac{1}{2} e^{j\phi} G(f - f_0) + \frac{1}{2} e^{-j\phi} G(f + f_0) \tag{1-113}$$

A second method is to apply the multiplication theorem to (1-111). In this case the frequency spectrum of $f(t)$ is given by the convolution of $G(f)$ with the spectrum of the sinusoid

$$F(f) = G(f) \otimes \left[\frac{1}{2} e^{j\phi} \delta(f - f_0) + \frac{1}{2} e^{-j\phi} \delta(f + f_0) \right] \tag{1-114}$$

Since any function convolved with a delayed impulse is identically that function shifted to the location of the impulse, the result is the same by both methods.

A special case of (1-113) for $\phi = 0$,

$$g(t) \cos 2\pi f_0 t \Longleftrightarrow \frac{1}{2} G(f - f_0) + \frac{1}{2} G(f + f_0) \tag{1-115}$$

is a commonly encountered representation of a communication signal. As illustrated in Fig. 1-16, the spectrum of this signal is obtained by shifting the spectrum of the narrow-band function upward in frequency by f_0 hertz and downward by the same amount with a reduction in magnitude by a factor of 1/2. Similarly evaluating (1-113) for the special case $\phi = -90°$, we have the transform pair

$$g(t) \sin 2\pi f_0 t \Longleftrightarrow \frac{1}{2j} G(f - f_0) - \frac{1}{2j} G(f + f_0) \tag{1-116}$$

Consider now a specific narrow-band signal, say, the unit step function

$$u(t) = \begin{cases} 1, & t > 0 \\ 0, & t < 0 \end{cases} \tag{1-117}$$

The frequency spectrum of the unit step function was given earlier as

$$U(f) = \frac{1}{2} \delta(f) + \frac{1}{j2\pi f} \tag{1-118}$$

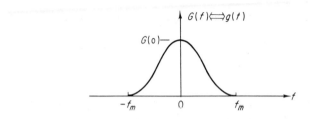

(a) Low-pass signal spectrum

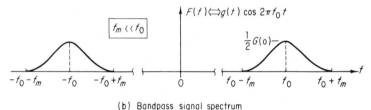

(b) Bandpass signal spectrum

Fig. 1-16 Spectral relations of a bandpass signal.

The bandpass signal $f(t)$ for the case of (1-115) with $g(t) = u(t)$ is

$$f(t) = u(t) \cos 2\pi f_0 t = \begin{cases} \cos 2\pi f_0 t, & t > 0 \\ 0, & t < 0 \end{cases} \tag{1-119}$$

Note that this signal is dead for $t < 0$, and for $t > 0$ it is a cosine wave turned on suddenly at $t = 0$; hence it is *not* equivalent to the continuous cosine wave [see (1-109)]. The frequency spectrum of the suddenly occurring cosine wave as obtained by use of (1-115) and (1-118) is

$$F(f) = \frac{1}{2}\delta(f - f_0) + \frac{1}{2}\delta(f + f_0) + \frac{1/2}{j2\pi(f - f_0)} + \frac{1/2}{j2\pi(f + f_0)}$$

$$= \frac{1}{2}\delta(f - f_0) + \frac{1}{2}\delta(f + f_0) + \frac{jf}{2\pi(f_0^2 - f^2)} \tag{1-120}$$

Comparing this result with (1-109), we see that the frequency spectrum of the suddenly occurring cosine wave has the same impulses as the spectrum of the continuous cosine wave but contains an additional factor. Analogous to this development a suddenly occurring sine wave can be shown to have a frequency spectrum given by

$$\left.\begin{array}{l} \sin 2\pi f_0 t, \quad t > 0 \\ 0, \quad t < 0 \end{array}\right\} \Longleftrightarrow \frac{1}{2j}\delta(f - f_0) - \frac{1}{2j}\delta(f + f_0) + \frac{f_0}{2\pi(f_0^2 - f^2)} \tag{1-121}$$

Compare this result with (1-110) and (1-120).

One further example of a sinusoidal signal deserves mention, namely, a "damped" sinusoid. The narrow-band multiplicative signal in this case is a decaying exponential that causes the sinusoid to damp to zero as t increases; that is,

$$g(t) = \begin{cases} e^{-\beta t}, & t > 0 \\ 0, & t < 0 \end{cases} \iff \frac{1}{\beta + j2\pi f} \qquad (1\text{-}122)$$

and the frequency spectrum of a damped cosine wave is given by the transform relation

$$\begin{cases} e^{-\beta t} \cos 2\pi f_0 t, & \beta > 0, & t > 0 \\ 0, & & t < 0 \end{cases} \iff \frac{1/2}{\beta + j2\pi(f - f_0)} + \frac{1/2}{\beta + j2\pi(f + f_0)}$$

$$= \frac{\beta + j2\pi f}{(j2\pi f)^2 + 2\beta(j2\pi f) + (2\pi f_0)^2 + \beta^2} \qquad (1\text{-}123)$$

For the case of a damped sine wave,

$$\begin{cases} e^{-\beta t} \sin 2\pi f_0 t, & \beta > 0, & t > 0 \\ 0, & & t < 0 \end{cases} \iff \frac{2\pi f_0}{(j2\pi f)^2 + 2\beta(j2\pi f) + (2\pi f_0)^2 + \beta^2}$$

$$(1\text{-}124)$$

3 Impulse Methods

The differentiation properties of the Fourier integrals provide an additional technique for computing transform relationships of functions (Ref. 4). This technique is especially useful when the nth derivative of a function reduces to a sequence of delayed impulse functions. The Fourier transform of a function composed of several impulses can easily be written in terms of exponential shift factors and equated to the Fourier transform of the original function multiplied by a factor $(j2\pi f)^n$. In this way the desired Fourier transform can be found by the solution of an algebraic equation as opposed to solution of an integral. The impulse method is best explained through examples of the technique.

Consider the triangular pulse function

$$a(t) = \begin{cases} V(1 - |t|/T), & |t| < T \\ 0, & |t| > T \end{cases} \qquad (1\text{-}125)$$

shown in Fig. 1-17. The first step is to differentiate the pulse a sufficient number of times to produce impulse functions. Carrying out the first derivative,

$$\frac{da(t)}{dt} = \begin{cases} V/T\,, & -T < t < 0 \\ -V/T\,, & 0 < t < T \\ 0\,, & |t| > T \end{cases} \tag{1-126}$$

and with the second derivative impulses appear

$$\frac{d^2a(t)}{dt^2} = \frac{V}{T}[\delta(t + T) - 2\delta(t) + \delta(t - T)] \tag{1-127}$$

as shown in Fig. 1-17. Using the differentiation and shift properties of Fourier transforms, we can write for (1-127) the transform relation

$$\frac{V}{T}[\delta(t + T) - 2\delta(t) + \delta(t - T)] \Longleftrightarrow (j2\pi f)^2 A(f) = \frac{V}{T}\left[e^{j2\pi fT} - 2 + e^{-j2\pi fT}\right] \tag{1-128}$$

and thus arrive at an algebraic solution for $A(f)$:

$$A(f) = VT\left[\frac{\sin \pi fT}{\pi fT}\right]^2 \tag{1-129}$$

Figure 1-17 illustrates this spectral function.

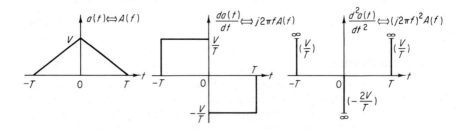

(a) Triangular pulse and its first two derivatives

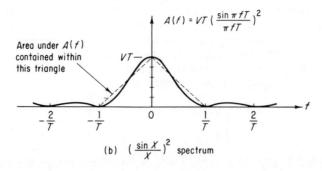

(b) $\left(\frac{\sin X}{X}\right)^2$ spectrum

Fig. 1-17 Computing frequency spectra by impulse methods.

Some functions will never reduce to a sequence composed *entirely* of impulses regardless of the number of derivatives taken. However, in some cases impulse methods are still useful. For example, consider the raised cosine pulse shown in Fig. 1-18:

$$a(t) = \begin{cases} 1 + \cos 2\pi f_0 t, & |t| < T_0/2 \\ 0, & |t| > T_0/2 \end{cases} \qquad (1\text{-}130)$$

where $T_0 = 1/f_0$. Taking the first derivative of $a(t)$, we obtain

$$\frac{da(t)}{dt} = \begin{cases} -(2\pi f_0) \sin 2\pi f_0 t, & |t| < T_0/2 \\ 0, & |t| > T_0/2 \end{cases} \qquad (1\text{-}131)$$

and after the second derivative

$$\frac{d^2 a(t)}{dt^2} = \begin{cases} -(2\pi f_0)^2 \cos 2\pi f_0 t, & |t| < T_0/2 \\ 0, & |t| > T_0/2 \end{cases} \qquad (1\text{-}132)$$

No impulses have appeared. Taking the third derivative, we find

$$\frac{d^3 a(t)}{dt^3} = (2\pi f_0)^2 [\delta(t + T_0/2) - \delta(t - T_0/2)] + (2\pi f_0)^3 \sin 2\pi f_0 t \qquad (1\text{-}133)$$

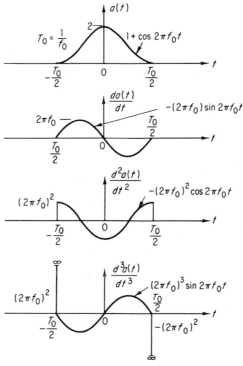

Fig. 1-18 A raised cosine pulse and its first three derivatives.

Impulses now occur but a nonimpulse factor still remains (see Fig. 1-18). However, in this case the additional factor in the third derivative can be related simply to the first derivative

$$\frac{d^3 a(t)}{dt^3} = (2\pi f_0)^2 [\delta(t + T_0/2) - \delta(t - T_0/2)] - (2\pi f_0)^2 \frac{da(t)}{dt} \qquad (1\text{-}134)$$

Thus we write

$$(j2\pi f)^3 A(f) = (2\pi f_0)^2 \left[e^{j\pi f T_0} - e^{-j\pi f T_0} \right] - (2\pi f_0)^2 (j2\pi f) A(f) \qquad (1\text{-}135)$$

or, after rearranging and solving for $A(f)$, we find the frequency spectrum of the raised cosine pulse to be

$$A(f) = \frac{f_0}{f_0^2 - f^2} \frac{\sin \pi f T_0}{\pi f T_0} \qquad (1\text{-}136)$$

The use of impulse methods is not confined to the time domain; analogous procedures are available in the frequency domain to determine time functions from given frequency functions. As an example of this consider the rectangular low-pass filter function shown in Fig. 1-19.

$$H(f) = \begin{cases} 1, & |f| < B/2 \\ 0, & |f| > B/2 \end{cases} \qquad (1\text{-}137)$$

Taking the first derivative of $H(f)$,

$$\frac{dH(f)}{df} = \delta(f + B/2) - \delta(f - B/2) \qquad (1\text{-}138)$$

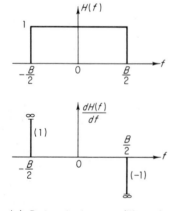

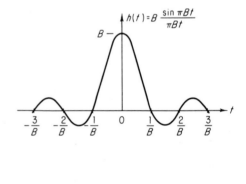

(a) Rectangular low-pass filter and its first derivative

(b) Unit impulse response

Fig. 1-19 Computing a time function by impulse methods.

Impulses in frequency appear immediately. Therefore

$$(-j2\pi t)\,h(t) = e^{-j\pi Bt} - e^{j\pi Bt} \tag{1-139}$$

or solving for $h(t)$, the impulse responses of the rectangular low-pass filter is

$$h(t) = \frac{e^{j\pi Bt} - e^{-j\pi Bt}}{j2\pi t} = B\,\frac{\sin \pi Bt}{\pi Bt} \tag{1-140}$$

4 Higher-Order Functions

Consider now a higher-order function of the form

$$a(t) = \frac{t^{n-1}}{(n-1)!}\,e^{-\beta t}, \quad t > 0, \quad n = 1, 2, 3, \dots \tag{1-141}$$

For $n = 1$ this function reduces to a simple decaying exponential. The frequency spectrum of $a(t)$ is shown below to be given by the transform pair

$$\frac{t^{n-1}}{(n-1)!}\,e^{-\beta t} \left\{ \begin{array}{l} \beta > 0, \quad t > 0 \\[4pt] n = 1, 2, 3, \dots \end{array} \right. \quad \Longleftrightarrow \quad \frac{1}{(\beta + j2\pi f)^n} \tag{1-142}$$

which is recognized as the nth power of the spectrum of a simple decaying exponential.

This transform relation is easily proven by direct evaluation of the defining form of the Fourier integral

$$A(f) = \int_0^\infty \frac{t^{n-1}}{(n-1)!}\,e^{-(\beta + j2\pi f)t}\,dt, \quad n = 1, 2, 3, \dots \tag{1-143}$$

After $n - 1$ integrations by parts the result is

$$A(f) = \frac{1}{(\beta + j2\pi f)^{n-1}}\int_0^\infty e^{-(\beta + j2\pi f)t}\,dt$$

$$= \frac{1}{(\beta + j2\pi f)^n}, \quad n = 1, 2, 3, \dots \tag{1-144}$$

A question now arises how to deal with a frequency function that contains an nth order factor of the form (1-144) so as to obtain its associated time function. The method of partial fraction expansion introduced in Sec. 1-8 applies to this problem with some modification. In general a frequency function of the form

$$F(f) = \frac{P(f)}{(\beta + j2\pi f)^n} \tag{1-145}$$

where $P(f)$ is a polynomial in f can be expanded as

$$F(f) = \frac{A_n}{(\beta + j2\pi f)^n} + \frac{A_{n-1}}{(\beta + j2\pi f)^{n-1}} + \cdots \frac{A_1}{\beta + j2\pi f} \tag{1-146}$$

The constant A_n is evaluated by the relation

$$A_n = (\beta + j2\pi f)^n \left. F(f) \right|_{j2\pi f = -\beta} \tag{1-147}$$

in a manner similar to the example of Sec. 1-8. Next a new function $\hat{F}(f)$ is generated:

$$\hat{F}(f) = F(f) - \frac{A_n}{(\beta + j2\pi f)^n} \tag{1-148}$$

Since the nth order term has been eliminated from $F(f)$, the highest order factor in the new function $\hat{F}(f)$ is of order $n - 1$. $\hat{F}(f)$ is therefore a function of lower order than the original function $F(f)$. The constant A_{n-1} is given by

$$A_{n-1} = (\beta + j2\pi f)^{n-1} \left. \hat{F}(f) \right|_{j2\pi f = -\beta} \tag{1-149}$$

The factor of order $n - 1$ is next removed from $\hat{F}(f)$, resulting in another new function whose highest order factor is of order $n - 2$. This process is repeated successively until all n constants in the expansion (1-146) are determined. The time function associated with $F(f)$ can then be written as a sum of terms of the form

$$f(t) = \begin{cases} \displaystyle\sum_{i=1}^{n} A_i \frac{t^{i-1}}{(i-1)!} e^{-\beta t}, & t > 0 \\ 0 & , \quad t < 0 \end{cases} \tag{1-150}$$

An example may help to illustrate the method described here. Consider the frequency function

$$F(f) = \frac{j2\pi f}{(\beta + j2\pi f)^3} \tag{1-151}$$

or in expanded form

$$F(f) = \frac{A_3}{(\beta + j2\pi f)^3} + \frac{A_2}{(\beta + j2\pi f)^2} + \frac{A_1}{\beta + j2\pi f} \tag{1-152}$$

where, using the above scheme, we find

$$F(f) = \frac{-\beta}{(\beta + j2\pi f)^3} + \frac{1}{(\beta + j2\pi f)^2} \tag{1-153}$$

Thus the inverse transform of $F(f)$ is

$$f(t) = \begin{cases} -\beta \dfrac{t^2}{2} e^{-\beta t} + t e^{-\beta t}, & \beta > 0, \quad t > 0 \\ \\ \\ 0 & , \quad\quad\quad t < 0 \end{cases} \tag{1-154}$$

5 Repetitive Pulse Sequences

Repetititve pulse sequences are another type of communication signal found in practice. Usually these signals consist of an infinite succession of identically shaped pulses commencing at $t = 0$ and repeated regularly thereafter at T second intervals. A repetitive pulse sequence as described here is of the form

$$a(t) = \sum_{n=0}^{\infty} g(t - nT) = g(t) + g(t - T) + g(t - 2T) + \cdots \tag{1-155}$$

where $g(t)$ is the first pulse of the sequence $a(t)$. The pulse sequence is thus an infinite succession of uniformly delayed pulses, as illustrated in **Fig. 1-20.** However, note that the mathematics given below applies even if the pulses overlap one another, so long as the form (1-155) is valid.

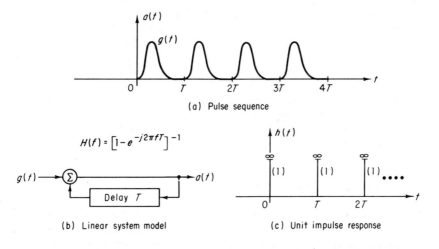

(a) Pulse sequence

(b) Linear system model   (c) Unit impulse response

Fig. 1-20 A repetitive pulse sequence and a linear system model for its generation.

Given that the frequency spectrum of the first pulse $g(t)$ is $G(f)$, we find the spectrum of the $(n+1)$th pulse $g(t - nT)$ to be $G(f) \exp (-j2\pi fnT)$. The frequency spectrum of the entire pulse sequence is therefore

$$A(f) = \sum_{n=0}^{\infty} G(f) e^{-j2\pi fnT} = G(f) \left[1 + e^{-j2\pi fT} + e^{-j4\pi fT} + \cdots \right] \quad (1\text{-}156)$$

Recognizing that the infinite series (1-156) is of the form $(1 - x)^{-1}$, we express the spectrum $A(f)$ as

$$A(f) = \frac{G(f)}{1 - e^{-j2\pi fT}} = G(f)H(f) \quad (1\text{-}157)$$

where the "repetition factor" $H(f)$ is

$$H(f) = \frac{1}{1 - e^{-j2\pi fT}} = 1 + e^{-j2\pi fT} + e^{-j4\pi fT} + \cdots \quad (1\text{-}158)$$

If $H(f)$ is considered to represent the transfer function of a linear system, its unit impulse response is given by

$$h(t) = \delta(t) + \delta(t - T) + \delta(t - 2T) + \cdots$$

$$= \sum_{n=0}^{\infty} \delta(t - nT) \quad (1\text{-}159)$$

This impulse response function and a linear system that implements the system function $H(f)$ are shown in Fig. 1-20. The pulse sequence (1-155) can be considered generated by passing a pulse $g(t)$ through the linear system of Fig. 1-20. Alternately the pulse sequence can be generated by passing the impulse train (1-159) through a linear filter which has unit impulse response $g(t)$.

If an attenuation $\alpha < 1$ is associated with the delay line of Fig. 1-20b, then each pulse of the sequence (1-155) and each impulse of (1-159) is α times smaller than the preceding pulse or impulse. In this way pulse sequences which "die out" with passage of time can be formulated.

1-10 Periodic Functions

Perhaps the most familiar class of waveforms found in engineering practice is the periodic waveform. The method of Fourier harmonic analysis is based on the statement that a periodic function can be represented by an infinite sum of *finite-sized* sinusoids, each with a discrete frequency that is an integral multiple of a fundamental frequency (Refs. 1-4). Note that the building blocks of Fourier harmonic analysis are finite-sized sinusoids as contrasted with Fourier integral theory which constructs functions from infinitesimal-sized sinusoids. The infinite sum of harmonically related sinusoids which represents a periodic function is known as a Fourier harmonic series. The discussion here identifies the Fourier harmonic series as a special case of the Fourier integral representation.

A periodic waveform continuously repeats a basic functional form in successive intervals of time T_0.* Mathematically a periodic function $f(t)$ is defined *for all time* by the relation

$$f(t) = f(t + kT_0) \qquad (1\text{-}160)$$

for $k = 0, \pm 1, \pm 2, \ldots$. The interval of time T_0 is termed the *period* of the waveform and its repetition rate

$$f_0 = 1/T_0 \qquad (1\text{-}161)$$

is termed the *fundamental frequency* or first harmonic frequency of the waveform.

A Fourier harmonic series expresses a periodic function as an infinite sum of sinusoids with harmonic frequencies kf_0 where k is an integer. Several forms of a Fourier series representation are available, one of which is the *exponential series*

$$f(t) = \sum_{k=-\infty}^{\infty} \alpha(k)\, e^{j2\pi k f_0 t} \qquad (1\text{-}162)$$

where $\alpha(k)$ is the kth Fourier *harmonic coefficient*. A complete knowledge of a periodic waveform is contained in its harmonic coefficients $\alpha(k)$ and its period T_0, or fundamental frequency $f_0 = 1/T_0$.

The harmonic coefficients are defined by the relation

$$\alpha(k) = \frac{1}{T_0} \int_{-T_0/2}^{T_0/2} f(t)\, e^{-j2\pi k f_0 t} dt \qquad (1\text{-}163)$$

and are generally complex numbers.

$$\alpha(k) = |\alpha(k)| e^{j\theta_k} \qquad (1\text{-}164)$$

---

*Note the difference between this definition and the form in (1-155) which implies an initial starting point in the process and hence does not satisfy the strict periodicity condition over all t in $(-\infty, \infty)$.

It can be shown that the magnitude function $|\alpha(k)|$ is an even function of the index k and the phase function θ_k is an odd function of k. Additionally the harmonic coefficients possess the conjugate property

$$\alpha(-k) = |\alpha(-k)| e^{j\theta_{-k}} = |\alpha(k)| e^{-j\theta_k} = \alpha^*(k) \qquad (1\text{-}165)$$

that coefficients of similar index except for sign are the complex conjugate of one another. When one uses this property of the $\alpha(k)$, a second useful form is obtained as an infinite sum of real cosine waves.

$$f(t) = \alpha(0) + \sum_{k=1}^{\infty} |\alpha(k)| \left[e^{j2\pi k f_0 t + j\theta_k} + e^{-j2\pi k f_0 t - j\theta_k} \right]$$

$$(1\text{-}166)$$

$$= \alpha(0) + 2 \sum_{k=1}^{\infty} |\alpha(k)| \cos(2\pi k f_0 t + \theta_k)$$

Not all periodic functions can be represented by a Fourier series, but a large class of periodic functions is representable by this means. A very definite set of existence conditions (Ref. 2) is available. Briefly the conditions for a Fourier series representation to be meaningful are essentially identical to the Dirichlet existence conditions discussed earlier in Sec. 1-2 for Fourier integral transformability. The only modification required is that the interval $(-\infty, \infty)$ be replaced by the interval $(-T_0/2, T_0/2)$, particularly in (1-26) and (1-27).

Consider the example of the repeated rectangular pulse waveform of **Fig. 1-21.** Use of the definition (1-163) gives the harmonic coefficients of this periodic waveform as

$$\alpha(k) = \frac{V}{T_0} \int_{-T_0/4}^{T_0/4} e^{-j2\pi kt/T_0} dt = \frac{V}{2} \frac{\sin k\pi/2}{k\pi/2} \qquad (1\text{-}167)$$

For $k = 0$ the right-hand side of (1-167) evaluates to

$$\alpha(0) = \frac{V}{2} \qquad (1\text{-}168)$$

and for $|k| \geq 1$ the harmonic coefficients of this waveform are given by

$$\alpha(k) = \begin{cases} 0 & , \quad k \text{ even} \\ \\ \dfrac{V}{|k|\pi} (-1)^{(|k| - 1)/2} , & k \text{ odd} \end{cases} \qquad (1\text{-}169)$$

Thus the periodic waveform of Fig. 1-21 can be represented by the infinite sum

$$f(t) = \frac{V}{2} \sum_{k=-\infty}^{\infty} \frac{\sin k\pi/2}{k\pi/2} e^{j2\pi k f_0 t} \tag{1-170}$$

or equivalently by the cosine series

$$f(t) = \frac{V}{2} + \sum_{\substack{k=1 \\ k \text{ odd}}}^{\infty} (-1)^{(k-1)/2} \frac{2V}{k\pi} \cos 2\pi k f_0 t \tag{1-171}$$

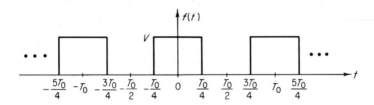

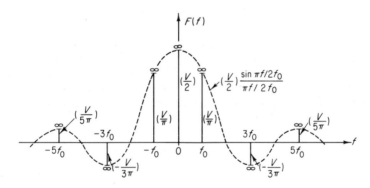

Fig. 1-21 Frequency spectrum of a periodic function.

Frequency Spectra of Periodic Signals

The frequency spectra of periodic functions are obtained from Fourier integral transformation of a Fourier series representation. The Fourier transform of either (1-162) or (1-166) is found to be

$$F(f) = \alpha(0)\,\delta(f) + \sum_{k=1}^{\infty} |\alpha(k)|[e^{j\theta_k}\,\delta(f - kf_0) + e^{-j\theta_k}\,\delta(f + kf_0)] \tag{1-172}$$

$$= \sum_{k=-\infty}^{\infty} \alpha(k)\,\delta(f - kf_0)$$

Thus the frequency spectrum of a periodic signal is an infinite array of weighted impulse functions occurring in frequency at all integral multiples of the fundamental frequency and with areas equal to the corresponding Fourier series harmonic coefficients.

For the example discussed immediately above, the frequency spectrum of the repeated rectangular pulse is

$$F(f) = \frac{V}{2} \sum_{k=-\infty}^{\infty} \frac{\sin k\pi/2}{k\pi/2} \delta(f - kf_0) \qquad (1\text{-}173)$$

This frequency spectrum is shown in **Fig. 1-21**, where for purposes of illustration the heights of the impulses have been adjusted to be indicative of their area.

An important special function, especially in the analysis of sampling theory and pulse modulation as discussed in Chap. 7, is the uniform periodic impulse train. This function can be expressed as the infinite sum

$$s(t) = \sum_{l=-\infty}^{\infty} \delta(t - lT_0) \qquad (1\text{-}174)$$

defined for $-\infty < t < \infty$. As illustrated in **Fig. 1-22**, the uniform periodic impulse train consists of a uniform succession of unit impulses occurring regularly at intervals of T_0 seconds for all time. Since this function is periodic with period T_0, it can be represented by a Fourier harmonic series with coefficients given by

$$\alpha(k) = \frac{1}{T_0} \int_{-T_0/2}^{T_0/2} s(t)\, e^{-j2\pi kt/T_0}\, dt = \frac{1}{T_0} \int_{-T_0/2}^{T_0/2} \delta(t)\, e^{-j2\pi kt/T_0}\, dt = \frac{1}{T_0}$$
$$(1\text{-}175)$$

Equation (1-175) is very simple to evaluate because the range of integration includes only the impulse at $t = 0$. The uniform impulse train can be represented by either a cosine or an exponential series,

$$s(t) = \frac{1}{T_0} + \frac{2}{T_0} \sum_{k=1}^{\infty} \cos 2\pi kf_0 t = \frac{1}{T_0} \sum_{k=-\infty}^{\infty} e^{j2\pi kf_0 t} \qquad (1\text{-}176)$$

According to the definition (1-172), the frequency spectrum of the uniform periodic impulse train is given by

$$S(f) = \frac{1}{T_0} \sum_{k=-\infty}^{\infty} \delta(f - kf_0) \iff s(t) = \sum_{l=-\infty}^{\infty} \delta(t - lT_0) \qquad (1\text{-}177)$$

which is simply another uniform periodic impulse train in frequency as illustrated in Fig. 1-22. Thus *a uniform periodic impulse train in either domain transforms to a similar function in the other domain.* This unique property of a uniform periodic impulse train is useful in calculating the frequency spectra of periodic waveforms *without* first determining the Fourier harmonic coefficients. We demonstrate this method by giving an example.

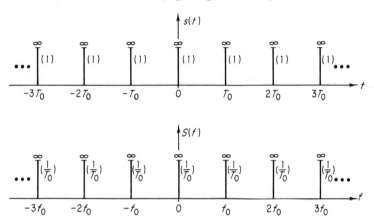

Fig. 1-22 A uniform periodic impulse train and its frequency spectrum.

Reconsider the example of Fig. 1-21 from a different point of view. Consider only the central pulse of the periodic waveform and call this pulse $\hat{f}(t)$; that is,

$$\hat{f}(t) = \begin{cases} V, & |t| \le T_0/4 \\ 0, & |t| > T_0/4 \end{cases} \tag{1-178}$$

The frequency spectrum of this pulse has been shown previously to be a $(\sin x)/x$ function given by

$$\hat{F}(f) = \frac{VT_0}{2} \frac{\sin \pi f T_0/2}{\pi f T_0/2} = \frac{VT_0}{2} \frac{\sin \pi f/2f_0}{\pi f/2f_0} \tag{1-179}$$

If the rectangular pulse $\hat{f}(t)$ is convolved with the uniform periodic impulse train $s(t)$ of Fig. 1-22, the resulting function is identically the periodic waveform $f(t)$ of Fig. 1-21. Thus we may express $f(t)$ as

$$f(t) = s(t) \otimes \hat{f}(t) = \sum_{l=-\infty}^{\infty} \int_{-\infty}^{\infty} \delta(\tau - lT_0)\hat{f}(t - \tau)\,d\tau = \sum_{l=-\infty}^{\infty} \hat{f}(t - lT_0) \tag{1-180}$$

However, since the frequency spectrum of two convolved time functions is the product of their individual spectra, the frequency spectrum of a repeated rectangular pulse is

$$F(f) = S(f)\hat{F}(f) = \sum_{k=-\infty}^{\infty} \frac{V}{2} \frac{\sin \pi f/2f_0}{\pi f/2f_0} \delta(f - kf_0)$$

(1-181)

$$= \frac{V}{2} \sum_{k=-\infty}^{\infty} \frac{\sin k\pi/2}{k\pi/2} \delta(f - kf_0)$$

which is identical with the result (1-173). Notice that because of the impulse train this frequency spectrum exists only at points $f = kf_0$ so that the impulse train effectively "samples" the $(\sin x)/x$ spectrum at these points. Figure 1-21 illustrates this concept.

1-11 The Ideal Low-pass Filter

It is often useful in communication engineering to define the so-called "ideal" low-pass filter described by the frequency function

$$H(f) = \begin{cases} (1) \, e^{-j2\pi f t_0}, & |f| \le B/2 \\ 0 & , |f| > B/2 \end{cases}$$

(1-182)

As indicated in Fig. 1-23, the magnitude function $|H(f)|$ is constant equal to unity and the phase function $\theta(f)$ is linear with slope $-2\pi t_0$ over a band of frequencies B hertz wide about $f = 0$. Outside this band the frequency function vanishes. Thus the ideal low-pass filter passes unmodified, except for a uniform time delay of t_0 seconds, all frequencies within the pass-band of the filter and completely rejects all frequencies outside this band.

A similar low-pass filter but without the linear phase-shift across the band was examined previously. As shown in Fig. 1-19, a rectangular low-pass filter has a unit impulse response in the form of a $(\sin x)/x$ function,

$$B \frac{\sin \pi Bt}{\pi Bt} \Longleftrightarrow \begin{cases} 1, & |f| \le B/2 \\ 0, & |f| > B/2 \end{cases}$$

(1-183)

Since the linear phase function in (1-182) merely introduces a uniform delay of the time function, the unit impulse response of the ideal low-pass filter is given by

$$h(t) = B \frac{\sin \pi B(t - t_0)}{\pi B(t - t_0)}$$

(1-184)

as shown in Fig. 1-23.

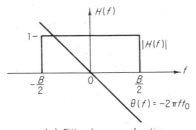

(a) Filter frequency function

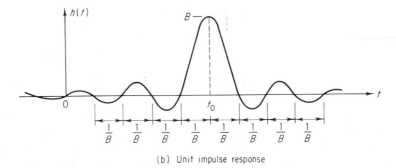

(b) Unit impulse response

Fig. 1-23 The ideal low-pass filter.

Suppose a signal $g(t)$ with a low-pass frequency spectrum $G(f)$ is passed through the ideal low-pass filter. If the signal spectrum is wholly contained within the pass-band of the filter, i.e., $G(f) = 0$ for $|f| > B/2$, then the resulting output signal spectrum is

$$F(f) = H(f)G(f) = G(f)e^{-j2\pi f t_0} \tag{1-185}$$

and the output signal function is

$$f(t) = g(t - t_0) \tag{1-186}$$

In this case the output signal is simply a delayed version of the input signal to the filter. Except for the time delay the signal has passed through the filter without any modification or distortion. Ideal signal transmission requires the filter's magnitude function to be constant independent of frequency and the phase characteristic to be a linear function of frequency. Any departure from these conditions leads to signal distortion. Thus the filter conditions for distortionless transmission of signals are as follows:

    1. $|H(f)| =$ A constant.
    2. $\theta(f) \;\;\; =$ A linear phase.

This holds over the entire band of signal frequencies.

On the other hand suppose the signal's frequency spectrum to be much wider than the pass-band of the filter, so that $G(f) \neq 0$ for $|f| > B/2$. In this case a significant portion of the signal spectrum is lost because the ideal low-pass filter rejects all frequencies outside its pass-band. A considerable amount of signal distortion occurs in this instance.

Another way of looking at (1-185) and (1-186), when the signal spectrum is entirely contained within the filter pass-band, is the following:

$$f(t) = \int_{-\infty}^{\infty} g(\tau)\, h(t - \tau)\, d\tau \qquad (1\text{-}187)$$

where

$$h(t) = B\, \frac{\sin \pi B(t - t_0)}{\pi B(t - t_0)} \qquad (1\text{-}188)$$

The signal function $g(t)$ is scanned by a unit area function $h(t)$ that is essentially of $1/B$ seconds width in time (the area under $h(t)$ can be equivalently contained within a rectangle B units high and $1/B$ units wide). The scanning function $h(t)$ is somewhat akin to a "window" function that looks only at a $1/B$ seconds wide portion of the signal at a time; that is, it can resolve only points on $g(t)$ separated by more than $1/B$ seconds. If significant changes in the signal waveform occur no closer than $1/B$ seconds (one-half the period of a sinusoid of frequency $B/2$), the scanning function can resolve them. In other words, if $g(t)$ contains no significant frequency content above $B/2$ hertz, which is simply the condition assumed for (1-185), the ideal low-pass filter passes the signal with essentially no distortion apart from the uniform time delay.

One often resorts to use of an approximation in dealing with relationships as typified by (1-187) and (1-188). When the signal $g(t)$ contains no significant frequencies above $B/2$ hertz, little harm is done by allowing the pass-band of the filter to grow wider—that is, to let B grow large. In this instance the impulse response $h(t)$ becomes taller and thinner with B but maintains a constant area under it equal to unity. In the limit as $B \to \infty$, the filter becomes infinitely broad and $h(t)$ becomes a unit impulse function

$$h(t) = B\, \frac{\sin \pi B(t - t_0)}{\pi B(t - t_0)} \xrightarrow[B \to \infty]{} \delta(t - t_0) \qquad (1\text{-}189)$$

The integral (1-187) can be approximated then by

$$f(t) \approx \int_{-\infty}^{\infty} g(\tau)\, \delta(t - t_0 - \tau)\, d\tau = g(t - t_0) \qquad (1\text{-}190)$$

leading to a convenient solution. This type of approximation is often employed in analysis of communication problems whenever extension of the filter bandwidth does not substantially change the outcome of a given situation.

REFERENCES

1. A. Papoulis, *The Fourier Integral and Its Applications* (McGraw-Hill Book Co., Inc., New York, 1962).
2. E. A. Guillemin, *The Mathematics of Circuit Analysis* (John Wiley and Sons, Inc., New York, 1949).
3. M. E. Van Valkenburg, *Network Analysis* (Prentice-Hall, Inc., New York, 1957).
4. M. Schwartz, *Information Transmission, Modulation and Noise* (McGraw-Hill Book Company, New York, 1959).
5. G. A. Campbell and R. M. Foster, *Fourier Integrals for Practical Applications* (D. Van Nostrand Co., Princeton, N. J., 1957).
6. E. A. Guillemin, *Theory of Linear, Physical Systems* (John Wiley and Sons, Inc., New York, 1963).

2

Correlation of Deterministic Signals*

One of the most valuable tools of modern analysis is the concept of *correlation*. We introduce it here because of its intimate connection to Fourier theory. The correlation function, as defined below, tells us something about the relationship of two points spaced τ seconds apart at some arbitrary position on the waveform, or about two points on two different waveforms. The correlation function is usually represented as a function of the spacing τ. In addition, when waveforms represent voltages or currents, it will be shown that the Fourier transform of a correlation function describes the spectral distribution of average power for periodic waveforms and the spectral energy density distribution for aperiodic waveforms that contain finite energy, i.e., those that possess a Fourier transform. In this chapter we deal with real, deterministic waveforms in general, and in the following chapter we specialize the theory for bandpass signals. In Chap. 4 a suitably modified correlation function and its Fourier transform arise again in the analysis of random noise waves that contain infinite energy but finite average power. The correlation function for random waves is a fundamental tool of noise analysis. Under certain broad conditions it permits definition of a frequency spectrum in terms of average power for noise waves that otherwise do not possess a spectral representation. Finally correlation theory provides yet another means to describe the interaction of both deterministic signals and random waves with the systems through which they propagate, and it is thereby especially useful in noise analysis.

2-1 Correlation Functions for Periodic Waveforms

Given two *real, periodic* waveforms $v_1(t)$ and $v_2(t)$ of the same fundamental frequency $f_0 = 1/T_0$, the *correlation function* $R_{v_1 v_2}(\tau)$ is

---

*General reference: Y. W. Lee, *Statistical Theory of Communication* (John Wiley and Sons, Inc., New York, 1960).

defined by

$$R_{v_1v_2}(\tau) = \frac{1}{T_0} \int_{-T_0/2}^{T_0/2} v_1(t) v_2(t + \tau) dt \qquad (2\text{-}1)$$

As shown below, the correlation function is also periodic with period T_0 and can be expressed in a Fourier series

$$R_{v_1v_2}(\tau) = \sum_{k=-\infty}^{\infty} \alpha_1^*(k) \alpha_2(k) e^{j2\pi k f_0 \tau} \qquad (2\text{-}2)$$

where $\alpha_1(k)$ and $\alpha_2(k)$ are, respectively, the Fourier harmonic coefficients of $v_1(t)$ and $v_2(t)$. The parameter τ is a continuous time displacement in the range $(-\infty, +\infty)$ between points on the two periodic waveforms.

A most important related quantity is the Fourier transform of the correlation function given by

$$R_{v_1v_2}(\tau) \Longleftrightarrow S_{v_1v_2}(f) = \sum_{k=-\infty}^{\infty} \alpha_1^*(k) \alpha_2(k) \delta(f - kf_0) \qquad (2\text{-}3)$$

where $\delta(\ )$ is the usual delta or impulse function. This frequency function is a weighted impulse train in frequency occurring at all harmonics of the fundamental frequency f_0.

To derive the relationship (2-2), express $v_2(t + \tau)$ in terms of its Fourier exponential series expansion as in Sec. 1-10.

$$R_{v_1v_2}(\tau) = \frac{1}{T_0} \int_{-T_0/2}^{T_0/2} v_1(t) \sum_{k=-\infty}^{\infty} \alpha_2(k) \exp[j2\pi k f_0(t + \tau)] dt \qquad (2\text{-}4)$$

By inverting the order of summation and integration

$$R_{v_1v_2}(\tau) = \sum_{k=-\infty}^{\infty} \alpha_2(k) e^{j2\pi k f_0 \tau} \left[\frac{1}{T_0} \int_{-T_0/2}^{T_0/2} v_1(t) e^{j2\pi k f_0 t} dt \right]$$

$$\qquad (2\text{-}5)$$

$$= \sum_{k=-\infty}^{\infty} \alpha_1^*(k) \alpha_2(k) e^{j2\pi k f_0 \tau}$$

as expressed in (2-2).

Clearly

$$R_{v_1v_2}(\tau) = R_{v_1v_2}(\tau + kT_0) \qquad (2\text{-}6)$$

for $k = 0, \pm 1, \pm 2, \ldots$, which states that $R_{v_1v_2}(\tau)$ is periodic with period T_0. Therefore we have the inverse relation

$$\alpha_1^*(k)\,\alpha_2(k) = \frac{1}{T_0}\int_{-T_0/2}^{T_0/2} R_{v_1v_2}(\tau)\,e^{-j2\pi k f_0 t}\,dt \qquad (2\text{-}7)$$

which defines the Fourier harmonic coefficients of the correlation function. The spectral relationship (2-3) follows directly from the formulas of Sec. 1-10.

In general we can state that the correlation process for periodic waveforms involves the following steps:

1. One of two periodic waveforms $v_2(t)$ is given a time displacement τ relative to the other.
2. The product waveform $v_1(t)v_2(t + \tau)$ of the two periodic functions is formed.
3. The resulting periodic product waveform is time averaged over a complete period.
4. The process is repeated for all displacements τ in the interval $(-\infty, +\infty)$ so that a function of τ is generated. Because of periodicity it suffices to calculate for τ over *any* interval of length T_0.

Thus correlation of periodic waveforms involves the operations of displacement or scan, multiplication, and averaging by integration. This sequence of operations is closely related to the *convolution* process described earlier in Chap. 1, as is apparent from the defining forms.

Autocorrelation

When the two waveforms are identical, the correlation function has a significant physical interpretation. For this special condition, $v_1(t) = v_2(t) = v(t)$, the correlation function (2-1) becomes

$$R_v(\tau) = \frac{1}{T_0}\int_{-T_0/2}^{T_0/2} v(t)v(t + \tau)\,dt = \sum_{k=-\infty}^{\infty} |\alpha(k)|^2 e^{j2\pi k f_0 \tau} \qquad (2\text{-}8)$$

where $f_0 = 1/T_0$ and the complex Fourier harmonic coefficients of $v(t)$ are given by

$$\alpha(k) = \frac{1}{T_0}\int_{-T_0/2}^{T_0/2} v(t)e^{-j2\pi k f_0 t}\,dt = \alpha^*(-k) \qquad (2\text{-}9)$$

The integral expression in (2-8) for $R_v(\tau)$ is termed the *autocorrelation function* for the periodic waveform $v(t)$, and the right-hand side of (2-8) is its Fourier series expansion. An alternate cosine series expansion for the autocorrelation function can be written

$$R_v(\tau) = \alpha^2(0) + 2 \sum_{k=1}^{\infty} |\alpha(k)|^2 \cos 2\pi k f_0 \tau \qquad (2\text{-}10)$$

by recalling that $|\alpha(-k)| = |\alpha(k)|$.

Physically if $v(t)$ represents a voltage or current in a one ohm resistance, then the average power of the kth harmonic of $v(t)$ is $2|\alpha(k)|^2$, $k \neq 0$, and $\alpha^2(0)$ for the zero-frequency term. Therefore the autocorrelation function for periodic waveforms consists of all the harmonic frequencies of the periodic function $v(t)$ with amplitudes equal to the average power of the respective harmonics. In particular note that

$$R_v(0) = \frac{1}{T_0} \int_{-T_0/2}^{T_0/2} v^2(t)\,dt = \alpha^2(0) + 2 \sum_{k=1}^{\infty} |\alpha(k)|^2 \qquad (2\text{-}11)$$

Thus the zero displacement value of the autocorrelation function is the total average power in $v(t)$ and is equal to the sum of all the average powers contained in its individual harmonics. Relationship (2-11) is a special case of *Parseval's theorem* for the periodic function $v(t)$.

This physical interpretation of autocorrelation can be carried over into the frequency domain by taking the Fourier transform of $R_v(\tau)$.

$$R_v(\tau) \Longleftrightarrow S_v(f) = \sum_{k=-\infty}^{\infty} |\alpha(k)|^2 \delta(f - k f_0) \qquad (2\text{-}12)$$

Thus the Fourier transform of the autocorrelation function for periodic waveforms is a line (impulse) spectrum occurring at all the harmonic frequencies of $v(t)$ with weights (areas) equal to the harmonic powers of $v(t)$ at the respective frequencies. This function is a spectral display of the power contained in $v(t)$; hence $S_v(f)$ is termed the *power density spectrum* of $v(t)$ and is measured in units of watts per hertz. To compute the total power, one must sum (integrate) the power (areas) at all frequencies.

$$R_v(0) = \int_{-\infty}^{\infty} S_v(f)\,df = \sum_{k=-\infty}^{\infty} |\alpha(k)|^2 \qquad (2\text{-}13)$$

Hence the total power or the $\tau = 0$ value of the autocorrelation function for the periodic waveform $v(t)$ is the total area under its power density spectrum.

Special properties of the autocorrelation

Clearly the autocorrelation function for periodic waveforms is itself a periodic function of the same period as the waveform $v(t)$:

$$R_v(\tau) = R_v(\tau + T_0) \quad k = \pm1, \pm2, \ldots \tag{2-14}$$

It should also be noted that the autocorrelation function is expressed in terms of only the squared *magnitudes* of the complex harmonic coefficients of $v(t)$ and its harmonic frequencies. That is to say, autocorrelation discards all the phase spectrum information contained in $v(t)$. Therefore autocorrelation is *not* a unique relationship in that many different periodic waveforms of the same fundamental frequency can have the same autocorrelation function. For this to be true, it is necessary only that the waveforms possess the same magnitudes of their complex harmonic coefficients but with different phase angles. Similarly the power density spectrum of a periodic waveform is independent of the harmonic phase angles and can represent the distribution of power for many different periodic waveforms.

Among its other interesting properties the autocorrelation function is a real function, since $v(t)$ is real. Also $R_v(\tau)$ is an even function of the displacement τ. Thus

$$R_v(-\tau) = R_v(\tau) \tag{2-15}$$

The extrema of $R_v(\tau)$ can be obtained by differentiating (2-10) and setting the derivative equal to zero:

$$\frac{dR_v(\tau)}{d\tau} = 2\sum_{k=1}^{\infty} |\alpha(k)|^2 (-2\pi k f_0) \sin 2\pi k f_0 \tau = 0 \tag{2-16}$$

The first, at $\tau = 0$, is clearly a maximum; therefore

$$R_v(\tau) \leq R_v(0) = R_v(kT_0), \quad k = \pm1, \pm2, \ldots \tag{2-17}$$

The largest, positive value of the autocorrelation function occurs for zero displacement and at all integral multiples of a period on either side of $\tau = 0$.

Since the power density spectrum is the Fourier transform of a real, even function, it is itself a real and even function of frequency. Moreover since $|\alpha(k)| \geq 0$, (2-12) indicates that the power density spectrum is also nonnegative, i.e.,

$$S_v(f) \geq 0 \tag{2-18}$$

as it should to be a meaningful power spectrum.

Illustrative examples

Consider an ordinary sinusoid

$$v(t) = A \cos(2\pi f_0 t + \theta) \qquad (2\text{-}19)$$

The autocorrelation function of this waveform is given by

$$R_v(\tau) = \frac{1}{T_0} \int_{-T_0/2}^{T_0/2} v(t) v(t + \tau) dt = \frac{A^2}{2} \cos 2\pi f_0 \tau \qquad (2\text{-}20)$$

Alternately this result could have been obtained directly by use of (2-10), since $v(t)$ in this instance contains only one harmonic frequency and is already in the form of a one-term Fourier series. Thus the autocorrelation function of a sinusoid is itself a cosine wave of the same period, with an amplitude equal to the average power of the waveform. Note that $R_v(\tau)$ is an even function of τ and is completely independent of the phase angle θ of $v(t)$. All sinusoids of the same amplitude and period have this identical autocorrelation function although they have differing initial phase angles.

The power density spectrum of the sinusoid is

$$S_v(f) = \frac{A^2}{4} \delta(f - f_0) + \frac{A^2}{4} \delta(f + f_0) \qquad (2\text{-}21)$$

which is a single pair of impulses at the harmonic frequencies $\pm f_0$ and is a real, even, nonnegative function of frequency. Note also

$$\int_{-\infty}^{\infty} S_v(f) df = R_v(0) = \frac{A^2}{2} = \text{average power in } v(t) \qquad (2\text{-}22)$$

Figure 2-1 illustrates these relationships for the sinusoid.

As a second example consider the periodic pulse train shown in Fig. 2-2a. Recall, from Sec. 1-10, that its Fourier harmonic coefficients are

$$\alpha(k) = \frac{V}{2} \frac{\sin k\pi/2}{k\pi/2} \qquad (2\text{-}23)$$

with magnitudes

$$|\alpha(k)| = \begin{cases} \dfrac{V}{2} & , \quad k = 0 \\[2mm] 0 & , \quad k \text{ even } (k \neq 0) \\[2mm] \dfrac{V}{|k|\pi} & , \quad k \text{ odd} \end{cases} \qquad (2\text{-}24)$$

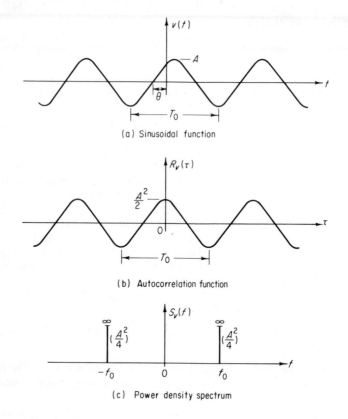

(a) Sinusoidal function

(b) Autocorrelation function

(c) Power density spectrum

Fig. 2-1 Example 1). Autocorrelation of a sinusoidal function.

If one then uses (2-10), the autocorrelation function of this waveform can be written

$$R_v(\tau) = \left[\frac{V}{2}\right]^2 + 2 \sum_{\substack{k=1 \\ k \text{ odd}}}^{\infty} \left[\frac{V}{k\pi}\right]^2 \cos 2\pi k f_0 \tau \qquad (2\text{-}25)$$

With the use of (2-12), the power density spectrum of $v(t)$ is given by

$$S_v(f) = \left[\frac{V}{2}\right]^2 \delta(f) + \sum_{\substack{k=1 \\ k \text{ odd}}}^{\infty} \left[\frac{V}{k\pi}\right]^2 [\delta(f - kf_0) + \delta(f + kf_0)], \qquad (2\text{-}26)$$

As an alternate technique consider the determination of $R_v(\tau)$ by using graphical methods to evaluate the defining form. Because of even symmetry and periodicity it is sufficient to evaluate $R_v(\tau)$ over only one-half period. The remaining portion then can be constructed easily. Part d of Fig. 2-2 shows the details pertaining to this computation. The solid-lined pulse of part d represents $v(t)$ in the time interval $|t| \leq T_0/2$, and the dashed-lined pulse represents $v(t + \tau)$ which is moving to the left as τ increases. For this waveform the product $v(t)v(t + \tau)$ has a nonzero value only between the times $t = -\tau - T_0/4$ and $t = T_0/4$ where its value is V^2. In this time

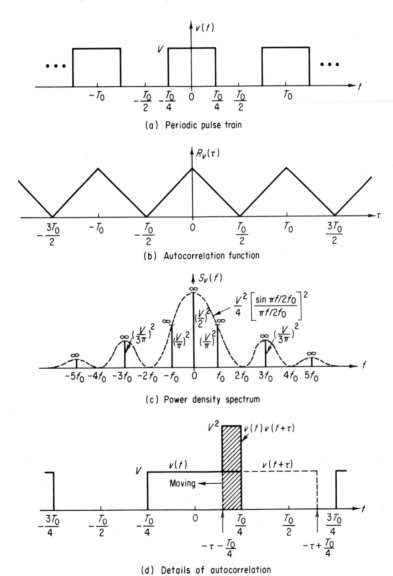

(a) Periodic pulse train

(b) Autocorrelation function

(c) Power density spectrum

(d) Details of autocorrelation

Fig. 2-2 Example 2). Autocorrelation of a periodic pulse train.

interval the product waveform is represented by the shaded pulse in part d of Fig. 2-2. For the particular displacement τ for which this figure is drawn, $R_v(\tau)$ is the area under the shaded pulse divided by T_0. As a function of τ,

$$R_v(\tau) = \frac{1}{T_0} \int_{-\tau-T_0/4}^{T_0/2} V^2 dt = \frac{V^2}{2}\left[1 + \frac{2\tau}{T_0}\right], \quad -T_0/2 \leq \tau \leq 0 \quad (2\text{-}27)$$

and over a whole period

$$R_v(\tau) = \frac{V^2}{2}\left[1 - \frac{2|\tau|}{T_0}\right], \quad |\tau| \leq T_0/2 \quad (2\text{-}28)$$

The complete autocorrelation function is constructed by repeating (2-28) with period T_0, as shown in part b of Fig. 2-2. A Fourier series expansion of this periodic waveform will yield the result given in (2-25).

An alternate technique exists also for determining the power density spectrum of $v(t)$ without first computing the harmonic coefficients of $v(t)$. This involves a direct Fourier transformation of $R_v(\tau)$ once it is obtained as above by graphical methods. Note that $R_v(\tau)$ for this example is equivalent to the triangular pulse (2-28), convolved with a uniform periodic impulse train. (Recall a similar discussion in Sec. 1-10.) Hence the power density spectrum of $v(t)$ is the product of a uniform periodic impulse train in frequency with the spectrum of the triangular pulse which is a $(\sin x)^2/x^2$ frequency function, as part c of Fig. 2-2 illustrates.

Crosscorrelation

If the two real periodic waveforms $v_1(t)$ and $v_2(t)$ are different functions with the same fundamental period, then the correlation function

$$R_{v_1 v_2}(\tau) = \frac{1}{T_0}\int_{-T_0/2}^{T_0/2} v_1(t)v_2(t + \tau)dt \quad (2\text{-}29)$$

is termed a *crosscorrelation function*. As noted previously, $R_{v_1 v_2}(\tau)$ is periodic in τ with the same period T_0 common to $v_1(t)$ and $v_2(t)$. In terms of a Fourier series expansion $R_{v_1 v_2}(\tau)$ is given by either of the forms

$$R_{v_1 v_2}(\tau) = \sum_{k=-\infty}^{\infty} \alpha_1^*(k)\alpha_2(k)e^{j2\pi k f_0 \tau} \quad (2\text{-}30)$$

or

$$R_{v_1 v_2}(\tau) = \alpha_1^*(0)\alpha_2(0) + 2 \sum_{k=1}^{\infty} |\alpha_1^*(k)\alpha_2(k)| \cos(2\pi k f_0 \tau - \theta_1 + \theta_2) \quad (2\text{-}31)$$

One difference between crosscorrelation and autocorrelation is immediately obvious; crosscorrelation does not completely discard phase information about the waveforms being correlated, since phase information is retained in the form of a phase difference, as evidenced by (2-31). However, crosscorrelation is again not a unique property of waveforms, since many different pairs of functions can have the same crosscorrelation function.

In crosscorrelation one must specify which of the two periodic functions is given the displacement τ, since in general $R_{v_1 v_2}(\tau)$ is different from $R_{v_2 v_1}(\tau)$. A change of variable in the defining form yields

$$R_{v_2 v_1}(\tau) = \frac{1}{T_0} \int_{-T_0/2}^{T_0/2} v_2(t) v_1(t + \tau) dt$$

$$(2\text{-}32)$$

$$= \frac{1}{T_0} \int_{-T_0/2 + \tau}^{T_0/2 + \tau} v_1(t') v_2(t' - \tau) dt' = R_{v_1 v_2}(-\tau)$$

Thus the crosscorrelation functions $R_{v_1 v_2}(\tau)$ and $R_{v_2 v_1}(\tau)$ are graphically the mirror images of one another about the value $\tau = 0$. The crosscorrelation function of real periodic waveforms is a real function but in general is not an even function of τ.

The Fourier transform of a periodic crosscorrelation function, given by

$$R_{v_1 v_2}(\tau) \Longleftrightarrow S_{v_1 v_2}(f) = \sum_{k=-\infty}^{\infty} \alpha_1^*(k)\alpha_2(k)\delta(f - k f_0) \quad (2\text{-}33)$$

is a line spectrum in frequency spaced uniformly by the fundamental frequency f_0. For lack of a better name, $S_{v_1 v_2}(f)$ is termed a *cross-power density spectrum*, in analogy to the Fourier transform of a periodic autocorrelation function. However, since in general $v_1(t)$ and $v_2(t)$ are unrelated functions, the cross-power density spectrum is usually not a spectral distribution of real, average power. In fact the impulse areas $\alpha_1^*(k)\alpha_2(k)$ are in general complex numbers, although they do possess the conjugate property

$$\alpha_1^*(-k)\alpha_2(-k) = \alpha_1(k)\alpha_2^*(k) \quad (2\text{-}34)$$

Thus a cross-power density spectrum possesses conjugate symmetry with respect to $f = 0$ but is usually not a real or a nonnegative function of frequency.

A statement analogous to (2-32) can be made in terms of cross-power density spectra. Taking the Fourier transform of (2-32),

$$S_{v_2 v_1}(f) = S_{v_1 v_2}(-f) = S^*_{v_1 v_2}(f) \tag{2-35}$$

Therefore the cross-power density spectrum of real, periodic waveforms is the complex conjugate of the cross-power density spectrum of these waveforms with their order reversed.

Example of crosscorrelation

Consider the crosscorrelation of a cosine wave with a sine wave of the same frequency.

$$v_1(t) = A_1 \cos 2\pi f_0 \tau$$
$$\tag{2-36}$$
$$v_2(t) = A_2 \sin 2\pi f_0 \tau = A_2 \cos [2\pi f_0 \tau - \pi/2]$$

These periodic waveforms are in the form of one-term Fourier series expansions with harmonic coefficients given by

$$\alpha_1(1) = \alpha_1^*(-1) = \frac{A_1}{2} \tag{2-37}$$

and

$$\alpha_2(1) = \alpha_2^*(-1) = \frac{A_2}{2} e^{-j\pi/2}$$

Using (2-31), we write the crosscorrelation function of the cosine and sine waves:

$$R_{v_1 v_2}(\tau) = \frac{A_1 A_2}{2} \cos(2\pi f_0 \tau - \pi/2) = \frac{A_1 A_2}{2} \sin 2\pi f_0 \tau \tag{2-38}$$

In this case $R_{v_1 v_2}(\tau)$ is a real, odd function of τ. Similarly if we use (2-33), the cross-power density spectrum is given by

$$S_{v_1 v_2}(f) = -j \frac{A_1 A_2}{4} \delta(f - f_0) + j \frac{A_1 A_2}{4} \delta(f + f_0) \tag{2-39}$$

Note that, if the roles of $v_1(t)$ and $v_2(t)$ are interchanged in this example, the crosscorrelation function becomes

$$R_{v_2 v_1}(\tau) = \frac{A_1 A_2}{2} \cos(2\pi f_0 \tau + \pi/2) = -\frac{A_1 A_2}{2} \sin 2\pi f_0 \tau = R_{v_1 v_2}(-\tau) \tag{2-40}$$

which is the mirror of $R_{v_1 v_2}(\tau)$, and the cross-power density spectrum becomes

$$S_{v_2 v_1}(f) = j \frac{A_1 A_2}{4} \delta(f - f_0) - j \frac{A_1 A_2}{4} \delta(f + f_0) = S^*_{v_1 v_2}(f) \tag{2-41}$$

2-2 Correlation of Aperiodic Waveforms

For *real, aperiodic* waveforms (i.e., transient-type signals) the correlation function is defined over the range $(-\infty, \infty)$:

$$R_{v_1 v_2}(\tau) = \int_{-\infty}^{\infty} v_1(t) v_2(t + \tau) \, dt \qquad (2\text{-}42)$$

Strictly, (2-42) is defined only for finite energy waveforms $v_1(t)$ and $v_2(t)$ which satisfy the relations

$$\int_{-\infty}^{\infty} v_1^2(t) \, dt < \infty \,, \quad \int_{-\infty}^{\infty} v_2^2(t) \, dt < \infty \qquad (2\text{-}43)$$

Associated with the correlation function (2-42) is the spectral relationship

$$V_1^*(f) V_2(f) \iff R_{v_1 v_2}(\tau) \qquad (2\text{-}44)$$

in which $V_1(f)$ and $V_2(f)$ are the frequency spectra of $v_1(t)$ and $v_2(t)$, respectively.

$$V_1(f) \iff v_2(t) \,, \quad V_2(f) \iff v_2(t) \qquad (2\text{-}45)$$

The spectral relationship (2-44) follows directly from the results given in (1-65) of Sec. 1-6.

The similarity of correlation for aperiodic waveforms to convolution is quite obvious. Both convolution and correlation involve the operations of displacement or scan, multiplication, and integration. One difference, however, concerns the sign in the argument of the displaced function. In convolution the displaced function is reversed (folded over) in time (referring to positive τ) and is displaced to the left with motion or scanning taking place to the right. In correlation the displaced function is *not* reversed in time and is displaced to the right with motion to the left. The Fourier transforms of convolution and correlation functions are quite similar, also, differing only in involving the complex conjugate of one of the frequency functions. This spectral difference is directly attributable to the time reversal, mentioned above, of the displaced function in the convolution process.

Autocorrelation

If the two real, aperiodic functions are identical, $v_1(t) = v_2(t) = v(t)$, the correlation function (2-42) takes the form

$$R_v(\tau) = \int_{-\infty}^{\infty} v(t) v(t + \tau) \, dt \qquad (2\text{-}46)$$

and is termed an *autocorrelation function.* The Fourier transform of an autocorrelation function for the finite energy signal $v(t)$ is from (2-44):

$$W_v(f) = |V(f)|^2 \Longleftrightarrow R_v(\tau) \qquad (2\text{-}47)$$

and is termed the *energy density spectrum* of $v(t)$. The physical significance of this terminology can be seen by use of Parseval's theorem

$$R_v(0) = \int_{-\infty}^{\infty} v^2(t)\,dt = \int_{-\infty}^{\infty} |V(f)|^2\,df = \int_{-\infty}^{\infty} W_v(f)\,df \qquad (2\text{-}48)$$

For an aperiodic function, $R_v(0)$ is the total energy of the signal $v(t)$ and is also the total area under the energy density spectrum $W_v(f)$. Thus $W_v(f)$ is a spectral density distribution of the finite energy of $v(t)$ and is expressed in units of energy per hertz. Recall that the Fourier transform of the autocorrelation function for *periodic* waveforms is a *power density* spectral distribution of the finite average power of the waveforms.

Since the Fourier transform of $R_v(\tau)$ is the squared *magnitude* function $|V(f)|^2$, autocorrelation of an aperiodic function again discards all of the phase spectrum information about the signal $v(t)$. The magnitude frequency spectrum $|V(f)|$ of $v(t)$ can be recovered from the energy density spectrum, but the phase spectrum $\theta_v(f)$ of $v(t)$ is completely lost. Therefore the autocorrelation function of an aperiodic waveform is *not* a unique functional relationship. Many aperiodic signals with identical magnitude spectra but differing phase spectra can have the same autocorrelation function. Recall that this was true also of autocorrelation of periodic functions.

Special properties of autocorrelation

The autocorrelation function of a real, aperiodic waveform is a real, even function which is always less than the value at the origin where $\tau = 0$. These properties can be concisely stated by the relationship

$$R_v(-\tau) = R_v(\tau) < R_v(0) \qquad (2\text{-}49)$$

The evenness of $R_v(\tau)$ can be shown easily by a change of variable in (2-46):

$$R_v(\tau) = \int_{-\infty}^{\infty} v(t)v(t+\tau)\,dt = \int_{-\infty}^{\infty} v(t')v(t'-\tau)\,dt' = R_v(-\tau) \quad (2\text{-}50)$$

Evenness of the autocorrelation function and absence of a phase spectrum go together, since the Fourier transform of a real, even time function has a real, even magnitude frequency function. As a corollary to this property we can state that the energy density spectrum for aperiodic functions is a real, even function

$$W_v(f) = |V(f)|^2 = |V(-f)|^2 \geq 0 \qquad (2\text{-}51)$$

From its form it is clearly also nonnegative.

To show that the autocorrelation function for aperiodic functions has its maximum value at the origin, consider the expression

$$\int_{-\infty}^{\infty} [v(t) \pm v(t+\tau)]^2 dt > 0 \quad \text{for } \tau \neq 0 \qquad (2\text{-}52)$$

This integral is always a positive, nonzero quantity for $\tau \neq 0$. It is positive because the integrand is squared. The integral is also nonzero unless $v(t)$ is a constant. By expansion of (2-52) this expression becomes

$$\int_{-\infty}^{\infty} v^2(t) dt \pm 2 \int_{-\infty}^{\infty} v(t)v(t+\tau) dt + \int_{-\infty}^{\infty} v^2(t+\tau) dt > 0$$
$$(2\text{-}53)$$

$$\text{for } \tau \neq 0$$

in which we recognize the first and last terms as $R_v(0)$ and the middle term as $2R_v(\tau)$. Therefore

$$R_v(0) \pm R_v(\tau) > 0 \quad \text{for } \tau \neq 0 \qquad (2\text{-}54\text{a})$$

or equivalently

$$R_v(0) > |R_v(\tau)| \qquad (2\text{-}54\text{b})$$

which indicates that for aperiodic waveforms the maximum value of the autocorrelation function is at the origin. No other value of the function can exceed or even equal in absolute magnitude $R_v(0)$ which is the total energy of the signal.

Example of autocorrelation

Consider the aperiodic function

$$v(t) = \begin{cases} e^{-t}, & t > 0 \\ 0, & t < 0 \end{cases} \qquad (2\text{-}55)$$

Figure 2-3 shows the details of computing $R_v(\tau)$ for two selected values of the displacement τ. For $\tau < 0$, $R_v(\tau)$ is given by

$$R_v(\tau) = \int_{-\tau}^{\infty} e^{-t} e^{-(t+\tau)} dt = \frac{1}{2} e^{\tau}, \quad \tau < 0 \qquad (2\text{-}56a)$$

and for $\tau > 0$,

$$R_v(\tau) = e^{-\tau} \int_{0}^{\infty} e^{-2t} dt = \frac{1}{2} e^{-\tau}, \quad \tau > 0 \qquad (2\text{-}56b)$$

Therefore the entire autocorrelation function is

$$R_v(\tau) = \frac{1}{2} e^{-|\tau|} \qquad (2\text{-}57)$$

as shown in Fig. 2-3.

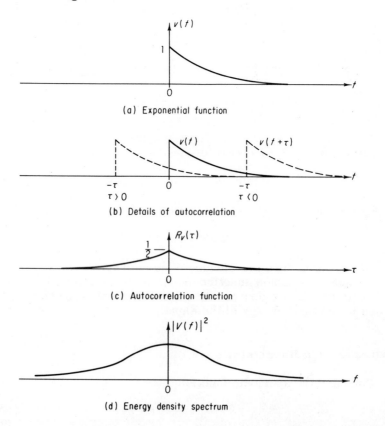

(a) Exponential function

(b) Details of autocorrelation

(c) Autocorrelation function

(d) Energy density spectrum

Fig. 2-3 Autocorrelation of an aperiodic function.

Taking the Fourier transform of (2-57), the energy density spectrum of this function is given by

$$W_v(f) = \int_{-\infty}^{\infty} R_v(\tau)e^{-j2\pi f\tau}d\tau = \frac{1}{1 + (2\pi f)^2} \qquad (2\text{-}58)$$

Alternately the same $W_v(f)$ can be obtained by forming the squared magnitude of the frequency spectrum $V(f)$. This energy density spectrum is illustrated in Fig. 2-3.

Crosscorrelation

When the two real aperiodic waveforms $v_1(t)$ and $v_2(t)$ are different functions, the correlation function

$$R_{v_1 v_2}(\tau) = \int_{-\infty}^{\infty} v_1(t)v_2(t + \tau)dt \qquad (2\text{-}59)$$

is termed a *crosscorrelation function.* By analogy to autocorrelation the Fourier transform of a crosscorrelation function for aperiodic waveforms

$$W_{v_1 v_2}(f) = V_1^*(f)V_2(f) \iff R_{v_1 v_2}(\tau) \qquad (2\text{-}60)$$

is termed a *cross-energy density spectrum.* However, this terminology for $W_{v_1 v_2}(f)$ is weak since discussion of only the energy of a single waveform is meaningful. In no sense is the area under the cross-energy density spectrum

$$\int_{-\infty}^{\infty} W_{v_1 v_2}(f)df = \int_{-\infty}^{\infty} V_1^*(f)V_2(f)df = \int_{-\infty}^{\infty} v_1(t)v_2(t)dt = R_{v_1 v_2}(0) \quad (2\text{-}61)$$

a physical energy although $W_{v_1 v_2}(f)$ is measured in units of energy per hertz.

As with crosscorrelation of periodic functions, it is important to specify the ordering of the functions $v_1(t)$ and $v_2(t)$, since $R_{v_1 v_2}(\tau)$ is generally different from $R_{v_2 v_1}(\tau)$. To show the relationship between these two crosscorrelation functions, make a change of variable $t' = t + \tau$ in (2-59):

$$R_{v_1 v_2}(\tau) = \int_{-\infty}^{\infty} v_2(t')v_1(t' - \tau)dt' = R_{v_2 v_1}(-\tau) \qquad (2\text{-}62)$$

The crosscorrelation functions $R_{v_1 v_2}(\tau)$ and $R_{v_2 v_1}(\tau)$ are the mirror images of one another about the value $\tau = 0$. A comparable spectral relationship is that the cross-energy density spectra are the complex conjugates on one another.

$$W_{v_1 v_2}(f) \;=\; V_1^*(f) V_2(f) \;=\; [V_2^*(f) V_1(f)]^* \;=\; W_{v_2 v_1}^*(f) \qquad (2\text{-}63)$$

These properties of crosscorrelation are a direct consequence of the fact that crosscorrelation, unlike autocorrelation, does not completely discard the phase spectrum information about the functions $v_1(t)$ and $v_2(t)$. The phase spectrum of the cross-energy density spectrum $W_{v_1 v_2}(f)$ is in fact the phase spectrum of $v_2(t)$ minus the phase spectrum of $v_1(t)$. However, as with autocorrelation, crosscorrelation is *not* a unique functional relationship, since many aperiodic functions can have the same crosscorrelation function.

Since the cross-energy density spectrum is in general a complex function of frequency, a crosscorrelation function is in general *not* an even function as is an autocorrelation function.

2-3 Relationship between Linear Systems and Correlation

In Chap. 1 we studied the interaction of signals with the linear systems through which they propagate, characterized by convolution in the time domain and by spectral multiplication in the frequency domain. To summarize briefly, the output time response $v_o(t)$ of a linear system with system unit impulse response $h(t)$ to an input $v_i(t)$ is given by the convolution

$$v_o(t) \;=\; v_i(t) \otimes h(t) \qquad (2\text{-}64)$$

Given the Fourier transform pairs

$$v_i(t) \iff V_i(f) \quad v_o(t) \iff V_o(f) \qquad (2\text{-}65a)$$

and

$$h(t) \iff H(f) \qquad (2\text{-}65b)$$

then

$$V_o(f) \;=\; H(f) V_i(f) \qquad (2\text{-}66)$$

We now inquire into the effect of linear systems upon waveform correlation functions and their spectra. Here this question is considered in terms of finite energy signals, but as pointed out the results apply as well to periodic functions.

Autocorrelation

It follows directly from (2-47) and (2-66) that

$$W_{v_o}(f) \;=\; |V_{v_o}(f)|^2 \;=\; |H(f)|^2 |V_{v_i}(f)|^2 \;=\; |H(f)|^2 W_{v_i}(f) \qquad (2\text{-}67)$$

That is, the energy density spectrum of the output is equal to that of the input, multiplied by the squared magnitude of the system transfer function. The quantity $|H(f)|^2$ may be interpreted in terms of the autocorrelation function of the system unit impulse response

$$R_h(\tau) = \int_{-\infty}^{\infty} h(t)h(t + \tau)\,dt \qquad (2\text{-}68)$$

whence it is readily shown that

$$R_h(\tau) \iff |H(f)|^2 \qquad (2\text{-}69)$$

The time domain relationship corresponding to (2-67) is then the simple convolutional statement

$$R_{v_o}(\tau) = R_h(\tau) \otimes R_{v_i}(\tau) = \int_{-\infty}^{\infty} R_{v_i}(t)R_h(\tau - t)\,dt \qquad (2\text{-}70)$$

This result is valid for finite energy signals as well as periodic signals. As an alternate point of view, $R_{v_o}(\tau)$ may be considered the output time response of a *new* linear system described by a system unit impulse response $R_h(\tau)$ which is driven by an input time function $R_{v_i}(\tau)$. Figure 2-4 illustrates this concept.

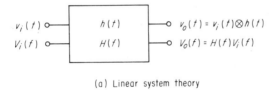

(a) Linear system theory

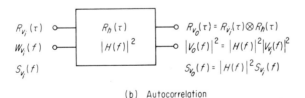

(b) Autocorrelation

Fig. 2-4 Illustrating the relationship between autocorrelation and linear systems.

If we are dealing with periodic functions, the analogous relation is that the output power density spectrum is given by the expression

$$S_{v_o}(f) = |H(f)|^2 S_{v_i}(f) \qquad (2\text{-}71)$$

where $S_{v_i}(f)$ is the power density spectrum of the input.

Crosscorrelation

Another set of useful relations exist for the crosscorrelation of the input and output of a linear system. The first of these is the crosscorrelation function

$$R_{v_o v_i}(\tau) = \int_{-\infty}^{\infty} v_o(t) v_i(t + \tau) dt \qquad (2\text{-}72)$$

Directly then

$$R_{v_o v_i}(\tau) \iff W_{v_o v_i}(f) = V_o^*(f) V_i(f) = H^*(f) |V_i(f)|^2 = H^*(f) W_{v_i}(f) \quad (2\text{-}73)$$

Hence in the time domain we have the equivalent correlation statement

$$R_{v_o v_i}(\tau) = \int_{-\infty}^{\infty} h(t) R_{v_i}(t + \tau) dt \qquad (2\text{-}74)$$

Therefore the crosscorrelation function $R_{v_o v_i}(\tau)$ is equivalent to crosscorrelating the system unit impulse response $h(t)$ with the input autocorrelation function $R_{v_i}(\tau)$. It is important to preserve the order of these functions. If the order is reversed, we have the crosscorrelation function

$$R_{v_i v_o}(\tau) \iff W_{v_i v_o}(f) = V_i^*(f) V_o(f) = H(f) |V_i(f)|^2 = H(f) W_{v_i}(f) \quad (2\text{-}75)$$

or hence

$$R_{v_i v_o}(\tau) = R_{v_o v_i}(-\tau) = \int_{-\infty}^{\infty} R_{v_i}(t) h(t + \tau) dt \qquad (2\text{-}76)$$

When dealing with periodic functions, the spectrum of $R_{v_o v_i}(\tau)$ is the cross-power density spectrum

$$S_{v_o v_i}(f) = H^*(f) S_{v_i}(f) \qquad (2\text{-}77)$$

and the spectrum of $R_{v_i v_o}(\tau)$ is the cross-power density spectrum

$$S_{v_i v_o}(f) = H(f) S_{v_i}(f) \qquad (2\text{-}78)$$

3

Narrow-Band, Bandpass Signals and Systems

3-1 Bandpass Signal Representation

A general bandpass signal $a(t)$ may be described by an expression of the form

$$a(t) = \rho(t) \cos[2\pi f_c t + \theta(t)] \qquad (3\text{-}1)$$

This waveform is said to be a *bandpass* signal when its frequency spectrum is concentrated in the vicinity of the frequencies $f = \pm f_c$ where f_c is termed the *carrier frequency* or simply the *carrier*. The amplitude $\rho(t)$ and phase $\theta(t)$ of this bandpass signal are, in general, time-varying functions that, for example, convey some form of intelligence or information. However, the information-bearing aspects of $\rho(t)$ and $\theta(t)$ are not pertinent to the present discussion, whose purpose rather is to present some mathematical tools for dealing with bandpass signals and the bandpass systems that process these signals. The presentation here is restricted to bandpass signals in which the spectral bandwidth B, measured about the carrier in some reasonable sense, is much smaller than the carrier frequency. Bandpass signals which satisfy the condition

$$B \ll f_c \qquad (3\text{-}2)$$

are termed *narrow-band*, bandpass signals. Since the majority of communication signals are of this type, it is useful to develop special techniques for dealing with their essential properties. The amplitude $\rho(t)$ and phase $\theta(t)$ characterize the *modulation components* of the bandpass signal. When the modulation components are "slowly varying" time functions with respect to the period $1/f_c$ of the carrier, the narrow-band condition (3-2) is usually fulfilled. We assume this narrow-band restriction to apply to all the bandpass signals involved in this discussion.

Expansion of the representation (3-1) yields the alternate form

$$a(t) = u_r(t) \cos 2\pi f_c t - u_i(t) \sin 2\pi f_c t \qquad (3\text{-}3)$$

where the quantities $u_r(t)$ and $u_i(t)$ are given by

$$u_r(t) = \rho(t) \cos \theta(t) \qquad (3\text{-}4)$$

and

$$u_i(t) = \rho(t) \sin \theta(t) \qquad (3\text{-}5)$$

These are termed the *quadrature components* of the signal. Since $u_r(t)$ and $u_i(t)$ are functions of only the modulation components, these quadrature components are also slowly varying relative to the period of the carrier. The quadrature components, or the amplitude and phase, are the distinguishing features of the modulation components of a bandpass signal. A useful bandpass signal representation that emphasizes these features is embodied in the concept of complex signals. We associate the *complex* bandpass signal

$$u(t)\, e^{j2\pi f_c t} \qquad (3\text{-}6)$$

with the *real* bandpass signal

$$a(t) = \mathrm{Re}\left\{ u(t)\, e^{j2\pi f_c t} \right\} \qquad (3\text{-}7)$$

A real bandpass signal $a(t)$ is the real part of its complex equivalent. The complex sinusoid $\exp(j2\pi f_c t)$ serves as a complex carrier whereas the function $u(t)$ is a complex modulation component related to $u_r(t)$ and $u_i(t)$ by the expression

$$u(t) = u_r(t) + j u_i(t) \qquad (3\text{-}8)$$

Alternately the complex modulation function $u(t)$, which is often termed the *complex envelope* of $a(t)$, may be expressed as

$$u(t) = |u(t)| \exp[j \arg u(t)] = \rho(t)\, e^{j\theta(t)} \qquad (3\text{-}9)$$

where

$$\rho(t) = |u(t)| = \text{envelope of } a(t) = \sqrt{u_r^2(t) + u_i^2(t)} \qquad (3\text{-}10)$$

and

$$\theta(t) = \arg u(t) = \text{phase of } a(t) = \arctan \frac{u_i(t)}{u_r(t)} \qquad (3\text{-}11)$$

The magnitude of the complex envelope, $|u(t)| = \rho(t)$, is commonly termed the *envelope* of the bandpass signal and is the low-frequency response of the ordinary envelope detector used extensively in communication systems (see also Chap. 5). Similarly the phase of the complex envelope is identical to the phase angle of $a(t)$ and is the low-frequency response of a phase detector operating at the frequency f_c.

Thus a bandpass signal is completely described by a knowledge of its carrier frequency f_c and its low-frequency complex envelope $u(t)$. Equivalently the frequency spectrum of a bandpass signal is completely determined by its carrier frequency and the frequency spectrum of its complex envelope. Specifically we now show that the frequency spectrum $A(f)$ of the bandpass signal $a(t)$ is given by the expression

$$A(f) = \frac{1}{2} U(f - f_c) + \frac{1}{2} U^*(-f - f_c) \qquad (3\text{-}12)$$

where the frequency spectrum of the complex envelope is

$$U(f) = \int_{-\infty}^{\infty} u(t) e^{-j2\pi f t} dt \qquad (3\text{-}13)$$

Taking the Fourier transform of (3-7), we have

$$A(f) = \int_{-\infty}^{\infty} a(t) e^{-j2\pi f t} dt = \int_{-\infty}^{\infty} \text{Re}\left\{ u(t) \, e^{j2\pi f_c t} \right\} e^{-j2\pi f t} dt \qquad (3\text{-}14)$$

Recall that the real part of a complex quantity z is equal to one-half the sum of itself and its complex conjugate, i.e.,

$$\text{Re}\, z = \frac{1}{2}(z + z^*) \qquad (3\text{-}15)$$

Using this relation to re-express $a(t)$, (3-14) becomes

$$A(f) = \frac{1}{2} \int_{-\infty}^{\infty} [u(t) \, e^{j2\pi f_c t} + u^*(t) \, e^{-j2\pi f_c t}] e^{-j2\pi f t} dt$$

$$= \frac{1}{2} \int_{-\infty}^{\infty} u(t) \exp[-j2\pi(f - f_c) t] dt + \frac{1}{2} \int_{-\infty}^{\infty} u^*(t) \exp[j2\pi(-f - f_c) t] dt \qquad (3\text{-}16)$$

The result (3-12) immediately follows then by comparison with (3-13).

Note that, by definition, $U(f)$ is a low-pass frequency function concentrated in the vicinity of the origin $f = 0$, while the bandpass spectrum $A(f)$ is concentrated about the carrier frequencies $f = \pm f_c$.

In fact $A(f)$ can be split into two parts, a positive frequency part and a negative frequency part. The positive frequency part of $A(f)$ is the spectrum of the complex envelope shifted up in frequency and centered on $f = f_c$,

$$A(f)\Big|_{f>0} = U(f - f_c) \tag{3-17}$$

whereas the negative frequency part of $A(f)$ is the complex conjugate of $U(f)$ folded over in frequency and shifted down to $f = -f_c$.

$$A(f)\Big|_{f<0} = U^*(-f - f_c) \tag{3-18}$$

The implication of the narrow-band restriction is that these positive and negative portions of the bandpass spectrum do not extend beyond the origin on the "wrong" side, so as to interfere with the interpretation given here.*

3-2 Linear Bandpass System Representation

A *bandpass system* is defined as a system whose transfer function or frequency function is nonvanishing only in a band of frequencies concentrated about the *band-center* frequencies $f = \pm f_c$. As in the case of bandpass signals the unit impulse response and transfer function can be usefully represented in terms of complex low-frequency equivalents.

A *linear* bandpass system is uniquely described by its system frequency function $G(f)$ and its system unit impulse response $g(t)$, related by

$$g(t) = \int_{-\infty}^{\infty} G(f) e^{j2\pi ft} df \tag{3-19}$$

We can rewrite (3-19) by splitting the range of integration; then we have

$$g(t) = \int_{0}^{\infty} G(f) e^{j2\pi ft} df + \int_{-\infty}^{0} G(f) e^{j2\pi ft} df \tag{3-20}$$

---

*However, a rigorous statement can be based upon identifying $U(f)$ with the positive frequency part of the spectrum $A(f)$, referred to f_c as the center frequency, i.e.,

$$U(f) = \begin{cases} 0 & , \quad f < -f_c \\ A(f + f_c), & f > -f_c \end{cases}$$

The mathematics below are then correct for arbitrary spectra.

If in the second integral of this latter equation a change of variable is made such that $f = -\lambda$, then

$$g(t) = \int_0^\infty G(f) \, e^{j2\pi ft} \, df + \int_0^\infty G(-\lambda) \, e^{-j2\pi\lambda t} \, d\lambda \qquad (3\text{-}21)$$

However, since $g(t)$ is the unit impulse response of a physical system, it is a *real* time function, and hence $G(-f) = G^*(f)$. Using this fact and the relation (3-15), it becomes clear that the unit impulse response of the bandpass system can be rewritten as

$$g(t) = 2\,\mathrm{Re}\left\{\int_0^\infty G(f) \, e^{j2\pi ft} \, df\right\} \qquad (3\text{-}22)$$

If we now restrict the discussion to narrow-band systems, the positive frequency part of $G(f)$ can be expressed as

$$G(f)\bigg|_{f>0} = H(f - f_c) \qquad (3\text{-}23)$$

where $H(f)$ is a low-pass frequency function nonvanishing only in the vicinity of the origin (when its total argument is around zero). Using this representation in terms of a low-pass function, (3-22) becomes

$$g(t) = 2\,\mathrm{Re}\left\{\int_0^\infty H(f - f_c) \, e^{j2\pi ft} \, df\right\} \qquad (3\text{-}24)$$

Since by the narrow-band restriction, now

$$H(f - f_c) = 0 \quad \text{when } f < 0 \qquad (3\text{-}25)$$

the lower limit on the integral (3-24) can be replaced by $-\infty$ and

$$g(t) = 2\,\mathrm{Re}\left\{\int_{-\infty}^\infty H(f - f_c) \, e^{j2\pi ft} \, df\right\} \qquad (3\text{-}26)$$

Finally with the change of variable $\lambda = f - f_c$ we obtain the form

$$g(t) = 2\,\mathrm{Re}\left\{e^{j2\pi f_c t} \int_{-\infty}^\infty H(\lambda) \, e^{j2\pi\lambda t} \, d\lambda\right\} = 2\,\mathrm{Re}\left\{h(t) \, e^{j2\pi f_c t}\right\} \qquad (3\text{-}27)$$

where

$$h(t) \Longleftrightarrow H(f) \qquad (3\text{-}28)$$

Since $H(f)$ is an equivalent low-pass system transfer function, $h(t)$ is an equivalent low-pass impulse response.

To summarize, with the results (3-27) and (3-28) we are able to express a linear narrow-band, bandpass system in terms of the band-center frequency f_c and an *equivalent low-pass system* described by $H(f)$ and $h(t)$. The unit impulse response $g(t)$ of the bandpass system is given by

$$g(t) = 2\,\text{Re}\left\{h(t)\,e^{j2\pi f_c t}\right\} \tag{3-29}$$

where $h(t)$ is the unit impulse response of the equivalent low-pass system. This latter expression, apart from a factor of 2, is of the same form as the complex signal representation of a bandpass signal. The equivalent low-pass system function $H(f)$ is defined by (3-23) as the positive frequency lobe of the bandpass system function $G(f)$. Drawing on the result (3-12) for the spectrum of a bandpass signal and taking into account the factor of 2, $G(f)$ and $H(f)$ are also related by the expression

$$G(f) = H(f - f_c) + H^*(-f - f_c) \tag{3-30}$$

Just as the bandpass system function $G(f)$ and bandpass unit impulse response $g(t)$ are a Fourier transform pair, so are the system function $H(f)$ and unit impulse response $h(t)$ of the equivalent low-pass system. It is important to note, however, that for a physical system $g(t)$ is a *real* function, whereas for the equivalent low-pass system the unit impulse response $h(t)$ may be a *complex* function. Therefore, while the equivalent low-pass system exists mathematically, $h(t)$ and $H(f)$ may generally not correspond in a physical sense to any actual low-pass system.* However, the representation of a narrow-band bandpass system in terms of an equivalent low-pass system is mathematically valid and an extremely useful analysis tool.

Example

Consider the bandpass RLC network of Fig. 3-1. The open-circuit voltage transfer function for this circuit can be shown to be

$$G(f) = \frac{Q(f)}{A(f)} = \frac{R}{R + j2\pi fL + \dfrac{1}{j2\pi fC}} = \frac{j2\pi f\,\dfrac{R}{L}}{(j2\pi f)^2 + j2\pi f\,\dfrac{R}{L} + \dfrac{1}{LC}} \tag{3-31}$$

---

*The requirement for $h(t)$ real is that $H(f) = H^*(-f)$ This corresponds to the assumption of a filter response symmetric about center frequency (even in amplitude, odd in phase). As in the example below, this is often a reasonable assumption for narrow-band filters.

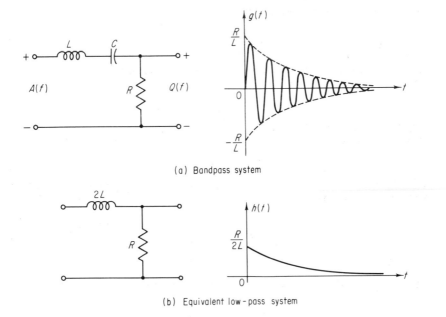

(a) Bandpass system

(b) Equivalent low-pass system

Fig. 3-1 Example of a bandpass system and its equivalent low-pass system, showing the unit impulse response of each.

By factoring the denominator of (3-31), $G(f)$ can be expressed in the form of a partial-fraction expansion

$$G(f) = \frac{A}{j2\pi f + \dfrac{R}{2L} - j\sqrt{\dfrac{1}{LC} - \left(\dfrac{R}{2L}\right)^2}} + \frac{B}{j2\pi f + \dfrac{R}{2L} + j\sqrt{\dfrac{1}{LC} - \left(\dfrac{R}{2L}\right)^2}}$$

(3-32)

The constants are given by

$$A = \frac{\dfrac{R}{L}\left[-\dfrac{R}{2L} + j\sqrt{\dfrac{1}{LC} - \left(\dfrac{R}{2L}\right)^2}\right]}{j2\sqrt{\dfrac{1}{LC} - \left(\dfrac{R}{2L}\right)^2}}$$

(3-33)

$$B = A^*$$

The band-center frequency f_c of this bandpass filter is given exactly by the relation

$$f_c = \frac{1}{2\pi}\sqrt{\frac{1}{LC} - \left(\frac{R}{2L}\right)^2}$$

(3-34)

For the narrow-band condition

$$\frac{1}{\sqrt{LC}} \gg \frac{R}{2L} \tag{3-35}$$

(i.e., for a high "Q" circuit) f_c is closely given by

$$f_c \approx \frac{1}{2\pi\sqrt{LC}} \tag{3-36}$$

Applying the narrow-band condition to (3-33), the constant A is approximately

$$A \approx R/2L \tag{3-37}$$

Therefore, using the definition (3-23) for the positive frequency lobe of $G(f)$, we have

$$H(f - f_c) = G(f)\bigg|_{f>0} \approx \frac{R/2L}{\frac{R}{2L} + j2\pi(f - f_c)} \tag{3-38}$$

and the transfer function of the equivalent low-pass system is given by

$$H(f) = \frac{R/2L}{\frac{R}{2L} + j2\pi f} = \frac{R}{R + j2\pi f(2L)} \tag{3-39}$$

The equivalent low-pass system function $H(f)$ can be recognized easily in this case as an RL network composed of a resistor R and an inductance $2L$, as shown in Fig. 3-1. The unit impulse response $h(t)$ of the equivalent low-pass system is therefore

$$h(t) = \begin{cases} \dfrac{R}{2L} e^{-Rt/2L}, & t > 0 \\ 0, & t < 0 \end{cases} \tag{3-40}$$

In this particular example the equivalent low-pass system corresponds to a physical circuit and $h(t)$ is a real function. For the bandpass system of Fig. 3-1, the unit impulse response $g(t)$ under the narrow-band condition (3-35) is

$$g(t) = 2\,\mathrm{Re}\left\{\frac{R}{2L} e^{-Rt/2L} \exp(jt/\sqrt{LC})\right\}$$

$$= \begin{cases} \dfrac{R}{L} e^{-Rt/2L} \cos(t/\sqrt{LC}), & t > 0 \\ 0, & t < 0 \end{cases} \tag{3-41}$$

Figure 3-1 also shows the bandpass and low-pass equivalent impulses responses $g(t)$ and $h(t)$ for this system.

3-3 Response of a Bandpass System

We have expressed both a narrow-band bandpass signal and the unit impulse response of a linear narrow-band, bandpass system in compact forms in terms of complex equivalents. The objective now is to express in a similar form the response or output of such a system when driven by a bandpass signal with a carrier frequency at the band-center frequency of the system. Incidentally we need never consider a situation in which the carrier is not aligned with the band-center frequency, since we have considerable freedom in designating the carrier and band-center frequency. A change in choice of carrier or the band-center frequency merely requires a modification of that which we term the complex envelope or the equivalent low-pass impulse response, as the case may be. Changing f_c by an amount Δf_c corresponds to merely absorbing (or removing) a factor of $\exp(\pm j2\pi \Delta f_c t)$ in the complex envelope of the signal or the unit impulse response of the equivalent low-pass system.

The response or output $q(t)$ of a bandpass system is also a bandpass signal and therefore can be expressed in the form

$$q(t) = \mathrm{Re}\left\{v(t)\, e^{j2\pi f_c t}\right\} \tag{3-42}$$

where $v(t)$ is the complex envelope of $q(t)$. According to our previous results, the bandpass frequency spectrum $Q(f)$ is related to the spectrum $V(f)$ of the complex envelope by the expression

$$Q(f) = \frac{1}{2}V(f - f_c) + \frac{1}{2}V^*(-f - f_c) \tag{3-43}$$

If $q(t)$ is the response of a bandpass system with impulse response $g(t)$ driven by a bandpass signal $a(t)$, then $q(t)$ is given by the convolution

$$q(t) = \int_{-\infty}^{\infty} a(\tau)g(t - \tau)\,dt \tag{3-44}$$

The equivalent spectral relationship among these functions is

$$Q(f) = G(f)A(f) \tag{3-45}$$

However, both $A(f)$ and $G(f)$ are expressible in terms of their associated low-pass spectra $U(f)$ and $H(f)$, respectively. Using the results (3-12) and (3-30), the bandpass output spectrum $Q(f)$ is given by

$$Q(f) = \frac{1}{2}\left[H(f - f_c) + H^*(-f - f_c)\right]\left[U(f - f_c) + U^*(-f - f_c)\right] \quad (3\text{-}46)$$

Since two of the indicated products terms in (3-46) are formed from nonoverlapping functions (the narrow-band condition),

$$H(f - f_c)U^*(-f - f_c) = H^*(-f - f_c)U(f - f_c) = 0 \quad (3\text{-}47)$$

the expression for $Q(f)$ reduces to

$$Q(f) = \frac{1}{2}H(f - f_c)U(f - f_c) + \frac{1}{2}H^*(-f - f_c)U^*(-f - f_c) \quad (3\text{-}48)$$

By comparison of (3-43) and (3-48) it is clear that the low-pass output spectrum is thus

$$V(f) = H(f)U(f) \quad (3\text{-}49)$$

Therefore we have the important result that the complex envelope $v(t)$ of the bandpass output signal is the convolution of the input complex envelope $u(t)$ with the impulse response $h(t)$ of the equivalent low-pass system, i.e.,

$$v(t) = \int_{-\infty}^{\infty} u(\tau)h(t - \tau)\,d\tau \quad (3\text{-}50)$$

The bandpass output signal is expressible then by the relation

$$q(t) = \text{Re}\left\{e^{j2\pi f_c t}\int_{-\infty}^{\infty} u(\tau)h(t - \tau)\,d\tau\right\} \quad (3\text{-}51)$$

These relationships suffice to completely describe how the bandpass system operates on any bandpass inputs. In dealing with bandpass signals and systems we need only deal with the equivalent low-pass functions. The significance of this result is that a computation, complicated by sinusoidal carrier terms, is reduced to an equivalent but *simpler* low-pass problem, which contains the essence of all signal-shaping effects. For deterministic waveforms this is all the information we need to describe processing of bandpass signals in bandpass systems. Figure 3-2 illustrates the complex signal representation of bandpass signals and systems and their relationship to the associated low-pass signals and systems.

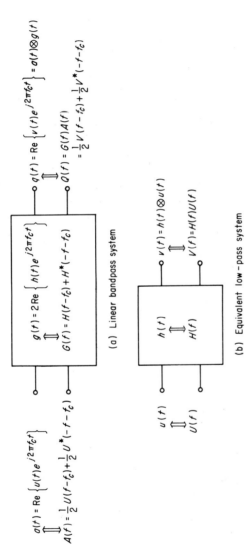

$$a(t) = \text{Re}\left\{u(t)e^{j2\pi f_c t}\right\}$$
$$\Longleftrightarrow$$
$$A(f) = \frac{1}{2}U(f-f_c) + \frac{1}{2}U^*(-f-f_c)$$

$$g(t) = 2\text{Re}\left\{h(t)e^{j2\pi f_c t}\right\}$$
$$\Longleftrightarrow$$
$$G(f) = H(f-f_c) + H^*(-f-f_c)$$

$$q(t) = \text{Re}\left\{v(t)e^{j2\pi f_c t}\right\} = a(t)\otimes g(t)$$
$$\Longleftrightarrow$$
$$Q(f) = G(f)A(f)$$
$$= \frac{1}{2}V(f-f_c) + \frac{1}{2}V^*(-f-f_c)$$

(a) Linear bandpass system

$$u(t)$$
$$\Longleftrightarrow$$
$$U(f)$$

$$h(t)$$
$$\Longleftrightarrow$$
$$H(f)$$

$$v(t) = h(t)\otimes u(t)$$
$$\Longleftrightarrow$$
$$V(f) = H(f)U(f)$$

(b) Equivalent low-pass system

Fig. 3-2 Complex signal representation of narrow-band, bandpass signals and systems.

Example of a Bandpass System Calculation

Reconsider the bandpass system of Fig. 3-1 when the input driving function is a rectangular pulse of r.f. carrier with a pulse duration of T seconds. The input signal $a(t)$ is then of the form

$$a(t) = \text{Re}\left\{A_0 e^{j2\pi f_c t}\right\}, \quad |t| \leq T/2 \tag{3-52}$$

and its complex envelope $u(t)$ is a rectangular function

$$u(t) = \begin{cases} A_0, & |t| \leq T/2 \\ 0, & |t| > T/2 \end{cases} \tag{3-53}$$

which in this case happens to be a real function. The unit impulse response of the bandpass system is, as given earlier,

$$g(t) = \begin{cases} 2\,\text{Re}\left\{\dfrac{R}{2L} e^{-Rt/2L} e^{j2\pi f_c t}\right\}, & t > 0 \\ 0, & t < 0 \end{cases} \tag{3-54}$$

where the band—center frequency is

$$f_c = \frac{1}{2\pi \sqrt{LC}} \tag{3-55}$$

and the equivalent low-pass system is described by the unit impulse response $h(t)$ given by

$$h(t) = \begin{cases} \dfrac{R}{2L} e^{-Rt/2L}, & t > 0 \\ 0, & t < 0 \end{cases} \tag{3-56}$$

To determine the bandpass output signal, we deal entirely with low-pass functions. Straightforwardly the complex envelope $v(t)$ of the output response is given by

$$v(t) = \int_{-\infty}^{\infty} u(\tau) h(t-\tau)\,d\tau = A_0 \int_{-T/2}^{T/2} h(t-\tau)\,d\tau$$

$$= \begin{cases} 0, & t < -T/2 \\ A_0 - A_0 \exp\left[-\dfrac{R}{2L}(t+T/2)\right], & |t| < T/2 \\ A_0\left[1 - \exp\left(-\dfrac{RT}{2L}\right)\right]\exp\left[-\dfrac{R}{2L}(t-T/2)\right], & t > T/2 \end{cases} \tag{3-57}$$

If the input pulse duration T is long relative to the time constant of the system (i.e., $T > 2L/R$), the output pulse $v(t)$ is a reasonably good reproduction of the input. In any case the bandpass output signal is

$$q(t) = \text{Re}\left\{v(t)e^{j2\pi f_c t}\right\} \tag{3-58}$$

where the complex envelope $v(t)$ is described by (3-57). Figure 3-3 shows the input and output bandpass signals for this example.

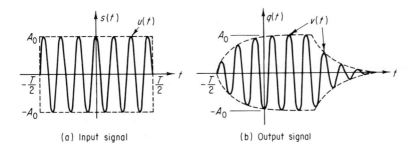

(a) Input signal   (b) Output signal

Fig. 3-3 Input and output signals of the circuit of Fig. 3-1.

3-4 Operations with Bandpass Signals

Sum of Signals

Given two bandpass signals $a_1(t)$ and $a_2(t)$ of the same carrier frequency f_c and having complex envelopes $u_1(t)$ and $u_2(t)$, the sum of these signals is a new bandpass signal $a(t)$ of the same carrier frequency and with a complex envelope $u(t)$ which is the sum $u_1(t) + u_2(t)$. That is,

$$a(t) = a_1(t) + a_2(t) = \text{Re}\left\{u_1(t)e^{j2\pi f_c t}\right\} + \text{Re}\left\{u_2(t)e^{j2\pi f_c t}\right\}$$

$$= \text{Re}\left\{u(t)e^{j2\pi f_c t}\right\} \tag{3-59}$$

where the complex envelope of the sum signal is

$$u(t) = u_1(t) + u_2(t) \tag{3-60}$$

However, the *envelope* $|u(t)|$ of the sum signal is generally not the sum of the envelopes $|u_1(t)|$ and $|u_2(t)|$, but is

$$|u(t)| = |u_1(t) + u_2(t)|$$

$$= \sqrt{\rho_1^2(t) + \rho_2^2(t) + 2\rho_1(t)\rho_2(t)\cos[\theta_1(t) - \theta_2(t)]} \tag{3-61}$$

where ρ_1, ρ_2, and θ_1, θ_2 are the envelopes and phases of $u_1(t)$ and $u_2(t)$, respectively.

Product of Signals

Let two bandpass signals $a_1(t)$ and $a_2(t)$ with complex envelopes $u_1(t)$ and $u_2(t)$ have different carrier frequencies f_1 and f_2, respectively. Taking the product of two such signals, given by

$$a_1(t)a_2(t) = \operatorname{Re}\left\{u_1(t)e^{j2\pi f_1 t}\right\}\operatorname{Re}\left\{u_2(t)e^{j2\pi f_2 t}\right\} \qquad (3\text{-}62)$$

is a common operation in communication systems. Using the easily proven relation

$$(\operatorname{Re} z_1)(\operatorname{Re} z_2) = \frac{1}{2}\operatorname{Re} z_1 z_2 + \frac{1}{2}\operatorname{Re} z_1^* z_2 \qquad (3\text{-}63)$$

for the complex numbers z_1 and z_2, the product signal is expressible as the combination of two new bandpass signals.

$$\begin{aligned} a_1(t)a_2(t) &= \operatorname{Re}\left\{\frac{1}{2}u_1(t)u_2(t)\exp[j2\pi(f_1 + f_2)t]\right\} \\ &+ \operatorname{Re}\left\{\frac{1}{2}u_1^*(t)u_2(t)\exp[j2\pi(f_2 - f_1)t]\right\} \end{aligned} \qquad (3\text{-}64)$$

One of these new signals has a carrier at the sum frequency $f_1 + f_2$ and the other has a carrier at the difference frequency $f_2 - f_1$. Since the spectra of these bandpass signals are concentrated in the vicinity of their carrier frequencies, bandpass filters centered on the sum and difference frequencies can separate the product signal into two individual signals given by

$$a_1(t)a_2(t)\bigg|_{\text{sum freq.}} = \operatorname{Re}\left\{\frac{1}{2}u_1(t)u_2(t)\exp[j2\pi(f_1 + f_2)t]\right\} \qquad (3\text{-}65)$$

and

$$a_1(t)a_2(t)\bigg|_{\text{dif. freq.}} = \operatorname{Re}\left\{\frac{1}{2}u_1^*(t)u_2(t)\exp[j2\pi(f_2 - f_1)t]\right\} \qquad (3\text{-}66)$$

The complex envelopes and low-pass spectra of these sum and difference frequency signals are given by

$$u_{SF}(t) = \frac{1}{2}u_1(t)u_2(t) \iff U_{SF}(f) = \frac{1}{2}\int_{-\infty}^{\infty} U_1(\lambda)U_2(f - \lambda)\,d\lambda \qquad (3\text{-}67)$$

and

$$u_{DF}(t) = \frac{1}{2}u_1^*(t)u_2(t) \iff U_{DF}(f) = \frac{1}{2}\int_{-\infty}^{\infty} U_1^*(\lambda)U_2(\lambda + f)\,d\lambda \qquad (3\text{-}68)$$

respectively. In communication practice, devices known as muli-pliers and frequency converters perform operations such as de-scribed above.

3-5 Correlation of Bandpass Signals

Crosscorrelation

Consider two real bandpass signals at the same carrier fre-quency f_c,

$$a(t) = \mathrm{Re}\left\{u(t)e^{j2\pi f_c t}\right\} \qquad (3\text{-}69)$$

and

$$q(t) = \mathrm{Re}\left\{v(t)e^{j2\pi f_c t}\right\} \qquad (3\text{-}70)$$

Their crosscorrelation is defined by the familiar expression

$$R_{aq}(\tau) = \int_{-\infty}^{\infty} a(t)q(t + \tau)\,dt \qquad (3\text{-}71)$$

Using the relationship (3-64), the crosscorrelation function (3-71) becomes

$$R_{aq}(\tau) = \mathrm{Re}\left\{e^{j2\pi f_c \tau}\int_{-\infty}^{\infty} \frac{1}{2}u(t)v(t + \tau)e^{j4\pi f_c t}\,dt\right\}$$

$$\qquad (3\text{-}72)$$

$$+ \mathrm{Re}\left\{e^{j2\pi f_c \tau}\int_{-\infty}^{\infty} \frac{1}{2}u^*(t)v(t + \tau)\,dt\right\}$$

The first of the integrals in (3-72) involves two terms multiplied by $\exp(j4\pi f_c t)$. The result is zero, cycle by cycle, in the integration over t since the multiplicative terms $u(t)$ and $v(t + \tau)$ are low-pass functions which vary much slower than a period $1/2f_c$. Therefore because of the narrow-band condition the crosscorrelation function $R_{aq}(\tau)$ reduces to

$$R_{aq}(\tau) = \mathrm{Re}\left\{e^{j2\pi f_c \tau}\int_{-\infty}^{\infty} \frac{1}{2}u^*(t)v(t + \tau)\,dt\right\} = \mathrm{Re}\left\{R_{uv}(\tau)e^{j2\pi f_c \tau}\right\} \qquad (3\text{-}73)$$

which is of the form of a bandpass function. Hence, the cross-correlation function of two real, narrow-band, bandpass signals is itself a bandpass function at the carrier frequency of the signals and with a complex envelope given by

$$R_{uv}(\tau) = \int_{-\infty}^{\infty} \frac{1}{2} u^*(t) v(t + \tau) dt \qquad (3\text{-}74)$$

We define $R_{uv}(\tau)$ as the *complex crosscorrelation function* of the complex envelopes $u(t)$ and $v(t)$. It is in general a complex quantity, since $u(t)$ and $v(t)$ are generally complex. In addition $R_{uv}(\tau)$ is a low-pass function that varies slowly relative to a period $1/f_c$ of the carrier. Note that the crosscorrelation function $R_{aq}(\tau)$ is real and bandpass in nature, and that $R_{aq}(\tau)$ and $R_{uv}(\tau)$ are related to one another in exactly the same way as are a real, bandpass signal and its low-pass complex envelope.

By analogy to correlation involving real, aperiodic functions, we term the Fourier transform of the complex crosscorrelation function $R_{uv}(\tau)$,

$$R_{uv}(\tau) \Longleftrightarrow W_{uv}(f) = \frac{1}{2} U^*(f) V(f) \qquad (3\text{-}75)$$

the cross-energy density spectrum of the complex envelopes $u(t)$ and $v(t)$. Setting $\tau = 0$, we have

$$R_{uv}(0) = \int_{-\infty}^{\infty} W_{uv}(f) df \qquad (3\text{-}76)$$

or in a more familiar form, Parseval's theorem for complex envelopes given by

$$\int_{-\infty}^{\infty} \frac{1}{2} u^*(t) v(t) dt = \int_{-\infty}^{\infty} \frac{1}{2} U^*(f) V(f) df \qquad (3\text{-}77)$$

If the two complex functions $u(t)$ and $v(t)$ are identical, Parseval's theorem for complex envelopes becomes

$$\int_{-\infty}^{\infty} \frac{1}{2} |u(t)|^2 dt = \int_{-\infty}^{\infty} \frac{1}{2} |U(f)|^2 df = \text{energy of } u(t) \qquad (3\text{-}78)$$

Note the definition of energy for *complex* waveforms involves the squared magnitude of the function. Additionally the factor of 1/2 appearing in (3-78) is required because the function in this case is a complex envelope.

Autocorrelation

Drawing on the above results, the autocorrelation function of the real bandpass signal $a(t)$ is given by

$$R_a(\tau) = \int_{-\infty}^{\infty} a(t) a(t + \tau) dt = \mathrm{Re}\left\{R_u(\tau) e^{j2\pi f_c \tau}\right\} \qquad (3\text{-}79)$$

This autocorrelation function has all the properties of an ordinary real autocorrelation function and in addition has all the properties of a bandpass function. The carrier frequency of $R_a(\tau)$ is the same as that of $a(t)$ and its complex envelope is $R_u(\tau)$. We term $R_u(\tau)$, given by the expression

$$R_u(\tau) = \int_{-\infty}^{\infty} \frac{1}{2} u^*(t) u(t + \tau) dt \qquad (3\text{-}80)$$

the *complex autocorrelation function* of the complex envelope $u(t)$. The energy of the bandpass signal $a(t)$ is, therefore, given by

$$R_a(0) = \int_{-\infty}^{\infty} a^2(t) dt = \mathrm{Re}\{R_u(0)\} = \int_{-\infty}^{\infty} \frac{1}{2} |u(t)|^2 dt \qquad (3\text{-}81)$$

which is consistent with Parseval's theorem noted above and previous definitions of energy.

Based on the result (3-75), the *energy density spectrum* $W_u(f)$ of the complex envelope $u(t)$ is defined by

$$R_u(\tau) \Longleftrightarrow W_u(f) = \frac{1}{2} |U(f)|^2 \qquad (3\text{-}82)$$

This low-pass spectrum is not quite the same as an ordinary energy density spectrum. It is true that $W_u(f)$ is a real, nonnegative function, but $W_u(f)$ in general is not an even function of frequency. The nonnegativeness of $W_u(f)$ is obvious, but in a more subtle way the noneven symmetry of $W_u(f)$ is due to the complex nature of $u(t)$ and therefore of $R_u(\tau)$. The complex envelope $u(t)$ possesses both real and imaginary parts, the quadrature components $u_r(t)$ and $u_i(t)$, both of which may be composed of even and odd parts; e.g.,

$$u(t) = u_r(t) + ju_i(t) = u_{re}(t) + u_{ro}(t) + ju_{ie}(t) + ju_{io}(t) \qquad (3\text{-}83)$$

Consequently $U(f)$, the Fourier transform of $u(t)$, can be expressed as

$$U(f) = U_{re}(f) + jU_{ro}(f) + jU_{ie}(f) - U_{io}(f) \qquad (3\text{-}84)$$

and its squared magnitude as

$$|U(f)|^2 = [U_{re}(f) - U_{io}(f)]^2 + [U_{ro}(f) + U_{ie}(f)]^2$$

$$= U_{re}^2(f) - 2U_{re}(f)U_{io}(f) + U_{io}^2(f) + U_{ro}^2(f) \qquad (3\text{-}85)$$

$$+ 2U_{ro}(f)U_{ie}(f) + U_{ie}^2(f)$$

Examination of (3-85) shows that $|U(f)|^2$ is a real function but generally is not an even function, since it contains even as well as odd components. Therefore the low-pass energy density spectrum $W_u(f)$ is real, nonnegative, generally not even in f, and can never be purely an odd function. This latter restriction is based on an examination of the cross-product terms in (3-85). Under certain circumstances $W_u(f)$ may be purely even in f. The conditions for evenness of $W_u(f)$ are as follows:

1. The complex envelope $u(t)$ is either purely real or purely imaginary.
2. The quadrature components $u_r(t)$ and $u_i(t)$ are both simultaneously purely even or purely odd functions.

In the usual sense we can define an energy density spectrum for the bandpass signal $a(t)$ as

$$W_a(f) \Longleftrightarrow R_a(\tau) = \text{Re}\left\{R_u(\tau)e^{j2\pi f_c \tau}\right\} \qquad (3\text{-}86)$$

However, since the autocorrelation function $R_a(\tau)$ has the properties of a bandpass function, the bandpass energy density spectrum $W_a(f)$ can be expressed in terms of the low-pass spectrum $W_u(f)$ by the relationship

$$W_a(f) = \frac{1}{2}W_u(f - f_c) + \frac{1}{2}W_u^*(-f - f_c) \qquad (3\text{-}87)$$

Since the low-pass energy density spectrum $W_u(f)$ is always a real function, (3-87) becomes

$$W_a(f) = \frac{1}{2}W_u(f - f_c) + \frac{1}{2}W_u(-f - f_c) \qquad (3\text{-}88)$$

This bandpass spectrum may be interpreted as $W_u(f)/2$ shifted up in frequency by f_c hertz and $W_u(f)/2$ folded over in frequency and shifted down to $-f_c$ hertz. Therefore, the bandpass spectrum $W_a(f)$ is a real, nonnegative, *even* function of frequency, as a proper energy density spectrum should be, despite the possible nonevenness of the low-pass spectrum $W_u(f)$.

Bandpass Filtering

Let the bandpass signal $a(t)$ with complex envelope $u(t)$ pass through a linear bandpass system described by its equivalent low-pass system with unit impulse response $h(t)$ and system function $H(f)$. The output response of the bandpass system to the input $a(t)$ is a bandpass signal $q(t)$ with complex envelope $v(t)$. The energy density spectrum $W_u(f)$ of the input complex envelope $u(t)$ is

$$W_u(f) = \frac{1}{2}|U(f)|^2 \qquad (3\text{-}89)$$

where $U(f)$ is the Fourier transform of $u(t)$. In a similar manner the energy density spectrum $W_v(f)$ of the output complex envelope $v(t)$ is

$$W_v(f) = \frac{1}{2}|V(f)|^2 \qquad (3\text{-}90)$$

where $V(f)$ is the Fourier transform of $v(t)$. However, from linear bandpass system theory we know that $u(t)$ and $v(t)$ are related by the convolution

$$v(t) = \int_{-\infty}^{\infty} u(\tau)h(t - \tau)\,d\tau \qquad (3\text{-}91)$$

and hence

$$V(f) = H(f)U(f) \qquad (3\text{-}92)$$

Substituting (3-92) in (3-90), we have the result

$$W_v(f) = \frac{1}{2}|H(f)U(f)|^2 = \frac{1}{2}|H(f)|^2\,|U(f)|^2 = |H(f)|^2 W_u(f) \qquad (3\text{-}93)$$

relating the input and output low-pass energy density spectra of the complex envelopes. Using this result, the output bandpass energy density spectrum $W_q(f)$, given by

$$W_q(f) = \frac{1}{2}W_v(f - f_c) + \frac{1}{2}W(-f - f_c) \qquad (3\text{-}94)$$

may be expressed in terms of low-pass input and system functions as

$$W_q(f) = \frac{1}{2}|H(f - f_c)|^2 W_u(f - f_c) + \frac{1}{2}|H(-f - f_c)|^2 W_u(-f - f_c) \qquad (3\text{-}95)$$

4

Random Processes and Noise
Analysis

By electrical noise one means undesired voltages, often of natural origin. All electrical components generate noise, owing to microscopic fluctuation phenomena associated with their macroscopic properties. A familiar example is the resistor, whose macroscopic property depends upon the average velocity with which electrons move through the body. However, in their motion, these electrons interact through collisions with the heavier particles of the resistor, causing some of their kinetic energy to be converted to heat energy. The fluctuations in the velocity of the electrons, about their average drift through the resistor, imply additional currents in the resistor, the so-called thermal noise. Similarly antennas of all communication systems are subject to and detect electromagnetic fields arising from sources such as lightning strokes (atmospheric noise) or distant sources of intense radiation, such as the sun or radio stars (cosmic noise).

As these examples imply, much electrical noise is of a random nature. That is, it is not possible to determine or estimate a sufficient number of describing parameters so that the noise wave can be predicted as a specific waveform. Nevertheless certain *average properties* of the noise waveform can be described, such as the average power in the waveform, or the way in which this power is spectrally distributed on the average. Such averages represent *statistical* properties or *statistics* of the noise processes. The body of mathematics through which these statistics are employed to provide representations of the noise is known as the theory of random processes. In this chapter we review some highlights of this theory and its applications, again referring the reader to other literature for more detail (Refs. 1, 2, 3). We do not attempt mathematical rigor with respect to the axiomatic foundations of the theory of random processes, preferring an intuitive presentation of these foundations sufficiently rigorous for our communication theory applications.

4-1 Probability Distribution and Density Functions

A real *random variable* or *random variate* is a quantity whose value is specified only by the statement that it is one of a *collection* or *ensemble* of possible real values, with a further statement as to the relative frequency of occurrence of each of these values.* The latter statement describes the *probability distribution* of the random variable. For example, consider a rectangular wave whose amplitudes are either one or zero, with sharp transitions which occur at random. Suppose further that, over a long interval, the wave is in the "1" state for a fraction p of the time, and in the "0" state the remaining $1-p$ fraction of the time. If one samples the wave at some arbitrary instant, he will find either a "0" or a "1" value. Furthermore if the experiment is repeated at wide intervals (so that a random number of transitions will have occurred in the intervening times), the accumulation of samples will tend toward having a fraction p which are 1's and a fraction $1-p$ of 0's.

A *discrete* random variable is one whose possible values are discrete, such as in the 1 or 0 example cited above. The set of discrete values may be countably infinite, e.g., the set of all integers. A *continuous* random variable is one whose values are infinitely dense in some range, e.g., all the real numbers in the interval $(-1, 1)$.

For a *discrete random variable* X, whose possible values are the set $\{x_n\}$, one specifies the *probability* $P(x_n)$ that X takes on the value x_n, i.e., the relative frequency of occurrence of x_n in a long set of repeated, independent samples of X. By definition, summing over all n,

$$\sum_n P(x_n) = 1 \tag{4-1}$$

One can also define a *probability distribution function.* If the set of numbers x_n are ordered so that

$$\cdots < x_{-2} < x_{-1} < x_0 < x_1 < x_2 < \cdots \tag{4-2}$$

then the distribution function is the probability that a value of X selected at random will equal or be smaller than some value x_m,

$$\text{prob}\,(X \leq x_m) = \sum_{n=-\infty}^{m} P(x_n) \tag{4-3}$$

---

*Often, relative frequency of occurrence of a value x is formally identified as $\lim\limits_{N \to \infty} \dfrac{M(x,N)}{N}$ where $M(x,N)$ is the number of occurrences of the value x in a total of N samples.

Alternatively one often works with the complementary function,

$$\text{prob }(X \geq x_m) = \sum_{n=m}^{\infty} P(x_n) \tag{4-4}$$

or some statement such as

$$\text{prob }(x_k < X \leq x_m) = \sum_{n=k}^{m} P(x_n) \tag{4-5}$$

If X is a *continuous random variable*, it is also basically described by its cumulative distribution, termed its *distribution function*,

$$\text{prob }(X \leq x) = P(x) \tag{4-6}$$

Thus the probability that X lies in the interval (x_1, x_2) is given by

$$\text{prob }(x_1 < X \leq x_2) = P(x_2) - P(x_1) \tag{4-7}$$

and

$$\text{prob }(X > x) = 1 - P(x) \tag{4-8}$$

It is often notationally convenient, when it causes no confusion, to use a letter such as x to refer both generically (and loosely) to the random variable and to a specific value (rather than using X and x, respectively, as above).

If $P(x)$ is a continuously differentiable function, its derivative

$$p(x) = \frac{d}{dx} P(x) \tag{4-9}$$

is a density, termed the *probability density function* (p.d.f.) of the random variable. Clearly then we have the relation

$$P(x) = \int_{-\infty}^{x} p(x)\,dx \tag{4-10}$$

and

$$\text{prob }(x_1 < x \leq x_2) = P(x_2) - P(x_1) = \int_{x_1}^{x_2} p(x)\,dx \tag{4-11}$$

and so forth. The alternative definition often stated is that

$$p(x)\,dx = \begin{array}{l}\text{probability that the random variable}\\\text{takes on values in the range } (x, x + dx)\end{array} \tag{4-12}$$

If $P(x)$ is not continuously differentiable, e.g., if it has discontinuities, then a p.d.f. often can still be defined provided one allows use of the mathematics of δ-functions or impulses. Thus if x actually occupies only the discrete set of values $\{x_n\}$, the p.d.f. will have the form

$$p(x) = \sum_n a_n \delta(x - x_n) \qquad (4\text{-}13)$$

Here a_n is the area associated with the impulse in probability density at x_n and is in fact the probability of the value x_n (among the set of discrete values); thus a_n is identical to the quantity $P(x_n)$ utilized earlier in (4-1) through (4-5). That (4-13) along with (4-10) reproduces these earlier equations is readily verified.

Note that by the definition of (4-6) the distribution function $P(x)$ is a monotonically increasing function, such that

$$P(-\infty) = 0 \qquad (4\text{-}14a)$$

and

$$P(\infty) = 1 \qquad (4\text{-}14b)$$

Thus $p(x)$, the p.d.f., is always nonnegative,

$$p(x) \geq 0 \qquad (4\text{-}15a)$$

and has unit area

$$\int_{-\infty}^{\infty} p(x)\,dx = 1 \qquad (4\text{-}15b)$$

Any real function satisfying both conditions of (4-15) is a possible p.d.f.; one may include δ-function terms if the random variable has discrete values. Figure 4-1 shows the probability distribution function and its associated probability density function for such a random variable.

An important set of *statistics* which characterize a p.d.f., $p(x)$, are its *moments*. The simplest of these is the mean value, the average of the set of values of x which would be obtained in a long sequence of independent trials. Recalling the interpretation of (4-12), this so-called *ensemble-mean* value is given by

$$\bar{x} = \int_{-\infty}^{\infty} x\, p(x)\,dx \qquad (4\text{-}16)$$

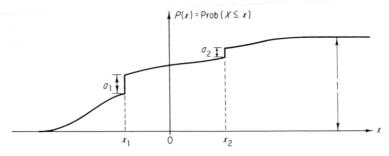

(a) Probability distribution function

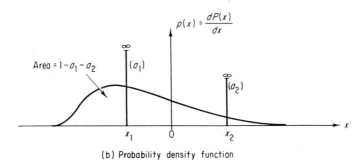

(b) Probability density function

Fig. 4-1 Probability distribution and density functions of a random variable.

Similarly the nth moment is the average value of x^n, defined by*

$$\overline{x^n} = \int_{-\infty}^{\infty} x^n p(x)\, dx$$

More generally, if $f(x)$ is some function defined on the set of values of x, the average value of $f(x)$ is given by

$$\overline{f(x)} = \int_{-\infty}^{\infty} f(x) p(x)\, dx \qquad (4\text{-}17)$$

For example, if x represents a voltage, $f(x)$ might represent a logarithmic version (such as a measurement on a dB scale), and one might be interested in the average value of the logarithm, i.e., $\overline{\ln x}$. Note that in general $\overline{\ln x} \neq \ln \overline{x}$, and more generally

$$\overline{f(x^n)} \neq f(\overline{x^n}) \qquad (4\text{-}18)$$

---

*In mathematical statistics the term "expectation" is often used instead of average and the notation $E[x^n]$ rather than the overbar as in $\overline{x^n}$.

However, taking the average of an average does not change its value. That is, since $\overline{f(x)}$ is a constant (i.e., a number),

$$\overline{\left[\overline{f(x)}\right]} = \int_{-\infty}^{\infty} \overline{f(x)}\, p(x)\, dx = \overline{f(x)} \int_{-\infty}^{\infty} p(x)\, dx = \overline{f(x)} \qquad (4\text{-}19)$$

Note also that the average of a sum of terms is the sum of the averages of the individual terms.

Many probability density functions are of primary interest only with respect to fluctuations which they describe about their mean value. Thus one often defines *central moments* $\overline{(x - \bar{x})^n}$. The most important of these is the second central moment, termed the *variance*,

$$\sigma^2 = \overline{(x - \bar{x})^2} = \overline{(x^2 - 2x\bar{x} + \bar{x}^2)} = \overline{x^2} - 2\bar{x}^2 + \bar{x}^2 = \overline{x^2} - \bar{x}^2 \quad (4\text{-}20)$$

The quantity σ, the square-root of the variance, is termed the *standard deviation* of the distribution. It is a measure of the width of the functional form $p(x)$. Electrically, when x is a voltage, σ is the r.m.s. value of the fluctuation of x about its mean value (i.e., of the "a.c. component," since the mean represents the "d.c. component"). Sometimes higher-order central moments are utilized to further characterize shape characteristics of the functional form of $p(x)$.

Unlike the usual mathematical representations the term $p(\ )$ is often used to generically indicate the p.d.f. of the random variable, without denoting per se a functional form. Thus if x and y are random variables, one may denote $p(x)$ and $p(y)$ as their respective p.d.f.'s, without meaning that the functional forms are the same. It is usually evident from the context that this generic use of $p(\ )$ is intended, with special notation introduced when functional relationships are involved.

Suppose now that $p(x)$ is the p.d.f. of a random variable X, and there is another variable Y which is one-to-one related to X through the functional form

$$Y = f(X) \qquad (4\text{-}21a)$$

or its inverse

$$X = g(Y) \qquad (4\text{-}21b)$$

That is, to every value x there corresponds a value

$$y = f(x) \qquad (4\text{-}22a)$$

or inversely

$$x = g(y) \qquad (4\text{-}22b)$$

Although the functional relationship is one-to-one, the different weights assigned by the functional relationship to the various values of x may result in a distribution of the ensemble of values y which is substantially different from the distribution of the values x. Let $q(y)$ be the p.d.f. of Y. To determine its relation to $p(x)$, note that when X lies in the range

$$x < X < x + dx \qquad (4\text{-}23)$$

Y lies in the corresponding range

$$y < Y < y + dy \qquad (4\text{-}24)$$

where y is related to x by (4-22a), and

$$y + dy = f(x + dx) = f(x) + f'(x)\,dx$$

That is,

$$dy = f'(x)\,dx \qquad (4\text{-}25)$$

But $p(x)\,dx$ is the probability that values of X fall in the range $(x, x + dx)$, and since Y is one-to-one related to X, the value $p(x)\,dx$ must also be the probability that Y falls in the equivalent range given by (4-24). Thus

$$q(y)\,dy = p(x)\,dx \qquad (4\text{-}26)$$

with x and y related by (4-22) and (4-25). Thus

$$p(x) = q[f(x)]f'(x) \qquad (4\text{-}27)$$

or, in the inverse direction,

$$q(y) = p[g(y)]g'(y) \qquad (4\text{-}28)$$

The latter states, for example, that the functional form for $q(y)$ is obtained by replacing x in $p(x)$ by its representation in terms of y and weighing the result by the derivative of the transformation.

As an example consider the p.d.f. (later identified as the Rayleigh distribution),

$$p(x) = \frac{x}{\alpha} e^{-x^2/2\alpha}, \qquad 0 < x < \infty \qquad (4\text{-}29)$$

This p.d.f. peaks at the value $x = \sqrt{\alpha}$, with the value

$$p(\sqrt{\alpha}) = \frac{1}{\sqrt{\alpha}} e^{-\frac{1}{2}} \qquad (4\text{-}30)$$

Now consider the transformation

$$y = x^2$$

$$\tag{4-31}$$

$$x = \sqrt{y}$$

According to (4-28), the p.d.f. of y is given by

$$q(y) = \left[\frac{\sqrt{y}}{\alpha} e^{-y/2\alpha} \right] \frac{1}{2\sqrt{y}} = \frac{1}{2\alpha} e^{-y/2\alpha}, \quad 0 < y < \infty \tag{4-32}$$

Note this exponential p.d.f. peaks at the value $y = 0$, with the value $q(0) = 1/2\alpha$, and in no particular relation to the peaking of $p(x)$. This is a reflection of the redistribution of the "probability mass" under the change of variables. Figure 4-2 illustrates the probability density functions involved in this transformation.

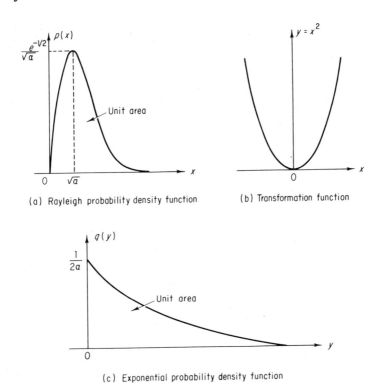

(a) Rayleigh probability density function

(b) Transformation function

(c) Exponential probability density function

Fig. 4-2 Illustrating a transformation of probability variables.

Finally in this section, note that $p(x)$ as a function of x may be represented in many ways by integral transformations. Consider

Fourier transformation* (the most commonly used in this context) as an example. Thus let

$$F(\xi) = \int_{-\infty}^{\infty} p(x) e^{-j\xi x} dx \tag{4-33}$$

Then

$$p(x) = \frac{1}{2\pi} \int_{-\infty}^{\infty} F(\xi) e^{j\xi x} d\xi \tag{4-34}$$

But, with (4-17), the transformation of (4-33) has the useful interpretation of being a statistical average

$$F(\xi) = \overline{e^{-j\xi x}} \tag{4-35}$$

where the average is over the probability space of the variable X.

One interesting property of the Fourier transform of $p(x)$ follows by using the power series expansion for the exponential

$$e^{-j\xi x} = \sum_{n=0}^{\infty} \frac{(-j\xi)^n}{n!} x^n \tag{4-36}$$

From this and the property that the average of a sum is the sum of the averages, it follows that

$$F(\xi) = \overline{e^{-j\xi x}} = \sum_{n=0}^{\infty} \frac{(-j\xi)^n}{n!} \overline{x^n} \tag{4-37}$$

That is, the coefficients in the power series expansion of $F(\xi)$ around $\xi = 0$ give the moments $\overline{x^n}$. Thus, for example, if one can easily calculate $F(\xi)$, a convenient method for calculating the moments of the p.d.f. is to use the expression

$$\overline{x^n} = (j)^n \left[\left(\frac{\partial}{\partial \xi} \right)^n F(\xi) \right]_{\xi = 0} \tag{4-38}$$

For this reason the Fourier transform of the p.d.f. is termed in statistics the *moment-generating function* or, more often, the *characteristic function* (ch.f.). The property (4-38) is perhaps made even more readily apparent by using it with the form in (4-33) and

---

*In this context it is common to write the Fourier transform in terms of a radian measure variable ξ. This corresponds in our earlier discussion to use of the variable $\omega = 2\pi f$ in place of f.

interchanging the orders of the integration and differentiation operations.

The characteristic function has another useful property in transformation of variables. Consider again the case where one introduces a new variable $Y = f(X)$, with a p.d.f. of $q(y)$. The ch.f. of y can be written as

$$F_y(\xi) = \overline{e^{-j\xi y}} = \int_{-\infty}^{\infty} q(y) e^{-j\xi y} dy \qquad (4\text{-}39)$$

Now, while the average (4-39) refers to the probability ensemble of the Y, it can be *equally well interpreted* as a statistical average over any equivalent probability space, equivalent in the sense of (4-26). Thus with $y = f(x)$, one can write

$$F_y(\xi) = \overline{e^{-j\xi y}} = \int_{-\infty}^{\infty} p(x) e^{-j\xi f(x)} dx \qquad (4\text{-}40)$$

while still writing

$$q(y) = \frac{1}{2\pi} \int_{-\infty}^{\infty} F_y(\xi) e^{j\xi y} d\xi \qquad (4\text{-}41)$$

It is readily ascertained that (4-40) and (4-38) lead directly again to the result expressed in (4-28). Although the example cited earlier was treated simply by the relation (4-28), there are many cases in which the *characteristic function method* described above proves extremely useful. This is especially true in connection with multivariate distributions, described later.

4-2 Examples of Probability Distributions

The Rectangular Distribution

As shown in Fig. 4-3a, the random variable in this case is uniformly distributed between two limits, with a p.d.f. given by

$$p(x) = \begin{cases} \dfrac{1}{\beta}, & \alpha < x < \alpha + \beta \\ 0, & \text{elsewhere} \end{cases} \qquad (4\text{-}42)$$

Note the constant value $1/\beta$ satisfies the requirement that the area under the p.d.f. be unity; i.e.,

$$1 = \int_{-\infty}^{\infty} p(x) dx = \int_{\alpha}^{\alpha+\beta} \frac{1}{\beta} dx \qquad (4\text{-}43)$$

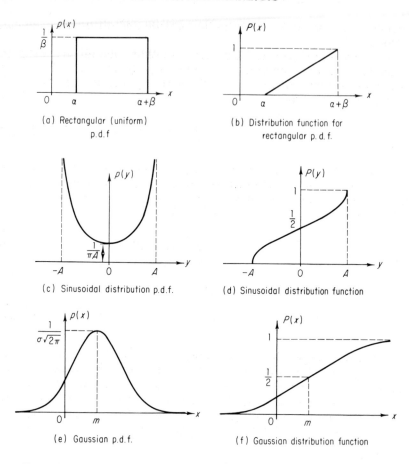

(a) Rectangular (uniform)
p.d.f

(b) Distribution function for
rectangular p. d. f.

(c) Sinusoidal distribution p.d.f.

(d) Sinusoidal distribution function

(e) Gaussian p.d.f.

(f) Gaussian distribution function

Fig. 4-3 Examples of probability density functions and distribution functions.

The mean value of the distribution is

$$\bar{x} = \int_{\alpha}^{\alpha+\beta} x \, \frac{1}{\beta} \, dx = \alpha + \frac{\beta}{2} \tag{4-44}$$

and the mean-square is

$$\overline{x^2} = \int_{\alpha}^{\alpha+\beta} x^2 \, \frac{1}{\beta} \, dx = \alpha^2 + \alpha\beta + \frac{\beta^2}{3} \tag{4-45}$$

The variance is then

$$\sigma^2 = \overline{x^2} - \bar{x}^2 = \beta^2/12 \tag{4-46a}$$

and the standard deviation is

$$\sigma = \frac{\beta}{2\sqrt{3}} \tag{4-46b}$$

The cumulative distribution for the rectangular distribution, illustrated in Fig. 4-3, is

$$P(x) = \int_{-\infty}^{x} p(y)\,dy = \begin{cases} 0 & , \quad x \le \alpha \\ \dfrac{x-\alpha}{\beta} & \alpha < x \le \alpha + \beta \\ 1 & \alpha + \beta < x \end{cases} \tag{4-47}$$

The ch.f. is

$$F(\xi) = \int_{\alpha}^{\alpha+\beta} \frac{1}{\beta} e^{-j\xi x}\,dx = \exp\left[-j\xi\left(\alpha + \frac{\beta}{2}\right)\right] \frac{\sin(\xi\beta/2)}{(\xi\beta/2)} \tag{4-48}$$

The Sinusoidal Distribution

Consider the sinusoidal waveform

$$y(t) = A\sin(2\pi ft + \theta) \tag{4-49}$$

Consider taking a large set of samples of $y(t)$ at completely random instants (i.e., irregularly related to the period $1/f$). The values of the argument $(2\pi ft + \theta)$ will then be completely random, and, when considered modulo 2π, the resulting ensemble of values may be regarded as arising from the transformation

$$y = A\sin\phi \tag{4-50}$$

where ϕ is a random variable, uniformly distributed. The range of ϕ might be taken as $(-\pi, \pi)$, although we can recognize that the values of $\sin\phi$ are the same in the second quadrant as in the first, and similarly the same in the third as in the fourth. Hence, most simply, we take ϕ to be uniformly distributed over the range $\left(-\dfrac{\pi}{2}, \dfrac{\pi}{2}\right)$

$$p(\phi) = \begin{cases} \dfrac{1}{\pi}, & -\dfrac{\pi}{2} \le \phi < \dfrac{\pi}{2} \\ 0, & \text{elsewhere} \end{cases} \tag{4-51}$$

We also recognize from (4-50) that the values of y are limited to the range $(-A, A)$.

Applying the transformation rule to (4-49), we find the values y to be distributed according to the p.d.f.

$$p(y) = p[\phi(y)] \frac{d\phi}{dy} = \frac{1}{\pi} \frac{d}{dy} \arcsin\left(\frac{y}{A}\right) = \frac{1}{\pi} \frac{1}{\sqrt{A^2 - y^2}}, \qquad |y| < A \quad (4\text{-}52)$$

This p.d.f. is sketched in Fig. 4-3c.

Note that if we had assumed ϕ to be distributed uniformly over a 2π-range, say

$$p(\phi) = \begin{cases} \dfrac{1}{2\pi}, & -\pi \le \phi < \pi \\[2mm] 0, & \text{elsewhere} \end{cases} \qquad (4\text{-}53)$$

we would have had to recognize a "doubling-up" in the values of y which result from the transformation, and supply this factor of 2 to the result of applying the transformation rule (4-27) to the p.d.f. (4-53). One of the advantages of the characteristic function method is that it obviates the need for such auxiliary recognition. It also obviates the need for recognizing by inspection the resulting range for y. (While these recognitions can be achieved by inspection in simple cases, more complex situations can create real difficulties.) As an example consider ϕ to be defined by the p.d.f. of (4-53) and y defined by the relation of (4-50). Then the ch.f. for y is

$$F_y(\xi) = \overline{e^{-j\xi y}} = \overline{e^{-j\xi A \sin\phi}} = \frac{1}{2\pi} \int_{-\pi}^{\pi} \exp(-j\xi A \sin\phi)\, d\phi = J_0(\xi A)$$

$$(4\text{-}54)$$

where J_0 is the Bessel function of the first kind and the integral is a familiar representation for J_0. Note exactly the same ch.f. would be obtained if the p.d.f. (4-51) had been used instead. In either case the p.d.f. $p(y)$ is now the inverse Fourier transform

$$p(y) = \frac{1}{2\pi} \int_{-\infty}^{\infty} F_y(\xi) e^{j\xi y}\, d\xi = \frac{1}{2\pi} \int_{-\infty}^{\infty} J_0(\xi A) e^{j\xi y}\, d\xi$$

and this is recognized as another standard integral whose value is

$$p(y) = \begin{cases} \dfrac{1}{\pi\sqrt{A^2 - y^2}}, & |y| \le A \\[2mm] 0, & |y| > A \end{cases} \qquad (4\text{-}55)$$

Note the resulting range of y appears automatically in the result, and there is no question about whether or not ϕ is "folded over" into the y-set.

For the p.d.f. of (4-55), we obtain the mean value

$$\bar{y} = \int_{-A}^{A} \frac{y}{\pi\sqrt{A^2 - y^2}}\, dy = 0 \qquad (4\text{-}56)$$

and the mean-square value

$$\overline{y^2} = \int_{-A}^{A} \frac{y^2}{\pi\sqrt{A^2 - y^2}}\, dy = \frac{A^2}{2} \qquad (4\text{-}57)$$

Since $\bar{y} = 0$, $\overline{y^2}$ is also the variance. The standard deviation, or r.m.s. value, is

$$\sigma = \frac{A}{\sqrt{2}} \qquad (4\text{-}58)$$

Note that the p.d.f. (4-55) tends to become infinite near the limits of the range, as $|y| \to A$. However, the function is still integrable. Indeed the distribution function is simply

$$P(y) = \int_{-A}^{y} p(x)\, dx = \frac{1}{2} + \frac{1}{\pi} \arcsin\left(\frac{y}{A}\right) \qquad (4\text{-}59)$$

This function is shown in Fig. 4-3d.

The Gaussian Distribution

The most important probability distribution in problems of random noise is the *Gaussian* or *normal* distribution. This has the general p.d.f.

$$p(x) = \frac{1}{\sigma\sqrt{2\pi}} \exp\left[-\frac{(x-m)^2}{2\sigma^2}\right], \qquad -\infty < x < \infty \qquad (4\text{-}60)$$

The distribution function is

$$P(x) = \int_{-\infty}^{x} p(y)\, dy = \frac{1}{2} + \frac{1}{2}\operatorname{erf}\left(\frac{x-m}{\sigma\sqrt{2}}\right) = 1 - \frac{1}{2}\operatorname{erfc}\left(\frac{x-m}{\sigma\sqrt{2}}\right) \qquad (4\text{-}61)$$

where we have introduced the tabulated *error function* and the *complementary error function*, defined respectively by

$$\operatorname{erf} x = \frac{2}{\sqrt{\pi}} \int_{0}^{x} e^{-t^2}\, dt \qquad (4\text{-}62)$$

and

$$\text{erfc } x = 1 - \text{erf } x = \frac{2}{\sqrt{\pi}} \int_x^\infty e^{-t^2} dt \qquad (4\text{-}63)$$

These functions have the properties

$$\text{erf}(-x) = -\text{erf } x \qquad (4\text{-}64a)$$

$$\text{erfc}(-x) = 2 - \text{erfc } x \qquad (4\text{-}64b)$$

and the special values

$$\text{erf } 0 = 0 \qquad (4\text{-}64c)$$

$$\text{erf } \infty = \text{erfc } 0 = 1 \qquad (4\text{-}64d)$$

$$\text{erfc } \infty = 0 \qquad (4\text{-}64e)$$

$$\text{erfc}(-\infty) = 2 \qquad (4\text{-}64f)$$

The p.d.f. and distribution function are illustrated in Figs. 4-3e and f.

Note that the p.d.f. (4-60) is symmetric about $x = m$. Hence the mean value is just

$$\bar{x} = m \qquad (4\text{-}65)$$

The Gaussian distribution is more familiarly written, for the case of zero mean, as

$$p(x) = \frac{1}{\sigma\sqrt{2\pi}} e^{-x^2/2\sigma^2} \qquad (4\text{-}66)$$

The ch.f. for the p.d.f. (4-60) is

$$F_x(\xi) = \overline{e^{-j\xi x}} = \int_{-\infty}^\infty \frac{1}{\sigma\sqrt{2\pi}} \exp\left[-j\xi x - \frac{(x-m)^2}{2\sigma^2}\right] dx$$

$$= e^{-j\xi m} e^{-\xi^2 \sigma^2/2} \qquad (4\text{-}67)$$

Thus the magnitude of the characteristic function is also "Gaussian-shaped."

As is readily shown now, the variance is

$$\overline{(x-\bar{x})^2} = \sigma^2 \qquad (4\text{-}68)$$

and hence the parameter σ which characterizes the major properties of the distribution is just the standard deviation. A detailed plot of the Gaussian p.d.f. is given in Fig. 4-4, illustrated for the case of zero mean.

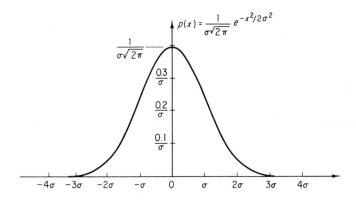

Fig. 4-4 The Gaussian p.d.f.

The major importance of the Gaussian distribution arises from the fact, discussed later, that this distribution law represents the limiting situation when a large number of independent fluctuation phenomena add together (such as thermal motions of individual electrons adding to comprise a noise current).

4-3 Multivariate Distributions

Often we are simultaneously interested in two or more random processes, whose values may be independent or may somehow be interrelated. To describe such *multivariate* processes, we extend the definitions of Sec. 4-1.

Thus, consider N random variables $\{X_1, \cdots, X_N\}$. Their *joint probability density function* is defined as a multivariable function $p(x_1, \cdots, x_N)$, by the relation

$$p(x_1, \cdots, x_N)\, dx_1 \cdots dx_N = \text{prob}\,(x_1 \leq X_1 < x_1 + dx_1,\ and$$

$$x_2 \leq X_2 \leq x_2 + dx_2, \cdots,\ and$$

$$x_N \leq X_N < x_N + dx_N) \qquad (4\text{-}69)$$

That is, $p(x_1, \cdots, x_N)$ defines the ensemble density function of sets of values $(x_1, \cdots, x_N)$ as the simultaneous values of the N different (but not necessarily unrelated) processes. Thus also,

$$\text{prob}\,(a_1 \leq X_1 < b_1,\, a_2 \leq X_2 < b_2,\, \cdots,\, a_N \leq X_N < b_N)$$

$$= \int_{a_1}^{b_1} \int_{a_2}^{b_2} \cdots \int_{a_N}^{b_N} p(x_1,\, \cdots,\, x_N)\, dx_1 \cdots dx_N \qquad (4\text{-}70)$$

and the *joint distribution function* is

$$P(x_1,\, \cdots,\, x_N) = \int_{-\infty}^{x_1} \cdots \int_{-\infty}^{x_N} p(t_1,\, \cdots,\, t_N)\, dt_1 \cdots dt_N \qquad (4\text{-}71)$$

One can also define *marginal* p.d.f.'s and distribution functions, which describe the probabilities of subsets of the variables. Thus, from the basic definition it follows, for example, that the joint p.d.f. of just X_1 and X_3 (i.e., the p.d.f. for X_1 and X_3 regardless of the values of the other variables, or, equivalently, averaged over all values of these variables) is expressed as

$$p(x_1, x_3) = \int_{a_2}^{b_2} \int_{a_4}^{b_4} \cdots \int_{a_N}^{b_N} p(x_1, x_2, x_3, x_4, \cdots, x_N)\, dx_2\, dx_4\, dx_5 \cdots dx_N$$

$$(4\text{-}72)$$

For a two-dimensional distribution, where we term the variables x and y, we have

$$p(x) = \int p(x, y)\, dy, \qquad p(y) = \int p(x, y)\, dx \qquad (4\text{-}73)$$

where $p(x)$ and $p(y)$ are simple one-dimensional p.d.f.'s.

We can also define *conditional* distributions. For example, in the two-dimensional case we may ask: For the random variables X, Y, with the probability of joint occurrence of values (x, y) defined by $p(x, y)$, what are the ensemble of values of X connected with the occurrence of a particular *single* value of Y? Let the latter be some value y. Then the ensemble of values of X associated in occurrence with this particular value, $Y = y$, defines the *conditional p.d.f.* $p_y(x)$,

$$p_y(x)\, dx = \text{prob}\,(x \leq X < x + dx \text{ when } Y = y) \qquad (4\text{-}74)$$

Another common notation for the conditional p.d.f. is

$$p_y(x) \equiv p(x|y) \qquad (4\text{-}75)$$

For a more general multivariate distribution one would have as a typical conditional p.d.f.,

$$p_{x_a, x_b, x_c, \ldots}(x_\alpha, x_\beta, \cdots)$$

or

$$p(x_\alpha, x_\beta, x_\gamma, \cdots | x_a, x_b, \cdots)$$

for the p.d.f. of the variables X_α, X_β, ... (with values x_α, x_β, ...) conditional on the values x_a, x_b, ... for the variables X_a, X_b, ...

From basic considerations of the various ways to partition the total ensemble in the two-variable case, it becomes apparent that

$$p_y(x)\, p(y)\, dxdy \;=\; \text{prob}[y \le Y \le y + dy \;\; and \;\; x \le X \le x + dx] \quad (4\text{-}76)$$

or therefore,

$$p_y(x)\, p(y) \;=\; p(x, y) \qquad (4\text{-}77)$$

Hence we have a method for constructing the conditional p.d.f. from the joint p.d.f. and a marginal p.d.f.,

$$p_y(x) \;=\; \frac{p(x, y)}{p(y)} \qquad (4\text{-}78)$$

More generally, of course,

$$p_{x_a, x_b, \cdots}(x_\alpha, x_\beta, \cdots) \;=\; \frac{p(x_a, x_b, \cdots, x_\alpha, x_\beta, \cdots)}{p(x_a, x_b, \cdots)} \qquad (4\text{-}79)$$

Instead of (4-78), one might also have the relation involving the values of Y conditioned on a value of X, $p_x(y)$, for which

$$p_x(y) \;=\; \frac{p(x, y)}{p(x)} \qquad (4\text{-}80)$$

By comparing (4-78) and (4-80), one obtains *Bayes' rule*:

$$p_x(y) \;=\; \frac{p_y(x)\, p(y)}{p(x)} \qquad (4\text{-}81)$$

The generalization for many variables should be obvious.

Cumulative distributions (distribution functions) can be defined for conditional p.d.f.'s, in the usual manner. Note that, as should be expected,

$$\int_{-\infty}^{\infty} p_x(y)\, dy \;=\; \int_{-\infty}^{\infty} \frac{p(x, y)}{p(x)}\, dy \;=\; \frac{p(x)}{p(x)} \;=\; 1 \qquad (4\text{-}82a)$$

and likewise

$$\int_{-\infty}^{\infty} p_y(x)\, dx \;=\; 1 \qquad (4\text{-}82b)$$

Averages, or moments, are defined in the same general manner for multivariate distributions as for a single-variable p.d.f., except that the integrations are now over a multivariable probability space. Thus

$$\overline{f(x_1,\cdots,x_N)} = \int_{-\infty}^{\infty} \cdots \int_{-\infty}^{\infty} f(x_1,\cdots,x_N)\,p(x_1,\cdots,x_N)\,dx_1\cdots dx_N \qquad (4\text{-}83)$$

For example, the nth moment of x_k is

$$\overline{x_k^n} = \int_{-\infty}^{\infty} \cdots \int_{-\infty}^{\infty} x_k^n\,p(x_1,\cdots,x_N)\,dx_1\cdots dx_N = \int_{-\infty}^{\infty} x_k^n\,p(x_k)\,dx_k \qquad (4\text{-}84)$$

Since several variables are involved, higher-order moments can be defined which involve several variables. Generally these are of the form $x_1^{k_1} x_2^{k_2} \cdots x_N^{k_N}$; the order of the moment is defined by $(k_1 + k_2 + \cdots + k_N)$. Of these the most commonly used moments, in addition to the mean and mean-square values of each of the variables, are the *second cross-moments* or *crosscorrelations*,

$$\overline{x_j x_k} = \int_{-\infty}^{\infty} \cdots \int_{-\infty}^{\infty} x_j x_k\,p(x_1,\cdots,x_N)\,dx_1\cdots dx_N$$

$$= \int_{-\infty}^{\infty} \int_{-\infty}^{\infty} x_j x_k\,p(x_j,x_k)\,dx_j dx_k \qquad (4\text{-}85)$$

Central moments can also be defined as earlier, with respect to the means of individual variables. Thus for the second-order moments we have the variances

$$\sigma_k^2 = \overline{(x_k - \bar{x}_k)^2} = \overline{x_k^2} - \bar{x}_k^2 \qquad (4\text{-}86)$$

and, corresponding to the crosscorrelation, we have the *covariance*

$$\mu_{jk} = \overline{(x_j - \bar{x}_j)(x_k - \bar{x}_k)} = \overline{x_j x_k} - \bar{x}_j \bar{x}_k \qquad (4\text{-}87)$$

When $j = k$, $\mu_{jk} \equiv \sigma_k^2$. Often one refers to μ_{kk} as an *autocovariance* and μ_{jk}, $j \neq k$ as a *crosscovariance*. As will be seen later, cross-covariances describe the probabilistic interrelationships between the pairs of variables. Their actual values are often significant in this sense only with respect to the r.m.s. values of the variables themselves. Hence one defines the *normalized covariance* or *correlation coefficient*,

$$\rho_{jk} = \frac{\mu_{jk}}{\sigma_j \sigma_k} = \frac{\overline{x_j x_k} - \bar{x}_j \bar{x}_k}{\sqrt{\left(\overline{x_j^2} - \bar{x}_j^2\right)\left(\overline{x_k^2} - \bar{x}_k^2\right)}} \qquad (4\text{-}88)$$

The correlation coefficient ρ_{jk} can also be regarded as the cross-correlation of normalized or *standardized* variables, defined by

$$y_k = \frac{x_k - \bar{x}_k}{\sigma_k} \qquad (4\text{-}89)$$

These standardized variables have zero mean and unit variance. The relations

$$(y_j \pm y_k)^2 \geq 0 \qquad (4\text{-}90)$$

then can be used to show that ρ_{jk} is always smaller than unity in magnitude,

$$|\rho_{jk}| \leq 1 \qquad (4\text{-}91)$$

and furthermore, that $\rho_{jk} = 1$ only if y_j is identically equal to y_k for all occurrences (i.e., the two variables are "perfectly correlated"). Likewise $\rho_{jk} = -1$ implies $y_j = -y_k$, often termed perfect negative correlation.

For a multivariate distribution the characteristic function can also be generalized as a multidimensional Fourier transform,

$$F(\xi_1, \cdots, \xi_N) = \int_{-\infty}^{\infty} \cdots \int_{-\infty}^{\infty} \exp\left[-j \sum_{k=1}^{N} \xi_k x_k\right] p(x_1, \cdots, x_N) \, dx_1 \cdots dx_N$$

$$= \overline{\exp\left[-j \sum_{k=1}^{N} \xi_k x_k\right]} \qquad (4\text{-}92)$$

Again it is observed that the moments can be derived by differentiations on the ch.f.,

$$\overline{x_k^{k_1} x_2^{k_2} \cdots x_N^{k_N}} =$$

$$(-j)^{k_1 + k_2 + \cdots k_N} \left[\frac{\partial^{k_1}}{\partial \xi_1^{k_1}} \frac{\partial^{k_2}}{\partial \xi_2^{k_2}} \cdots \frac{\partial^{k_N}}{\partial \xi_N^{k_N}} F(\xi_1, \cdots, \xi_N)\right]_{\xi_1 = \xi_2 = \cdots \xi_N = 0}$$

$$(4\text{-}93)$$

Again the ch.f. often provides a useful intermediary for calculating the joint p.d.f. of a new set of variables defined by some functional transformation on the given set.

When there is a transformation of variables which involves a *one-to-one* mapping from one N-fold set of variates to another

N-fold set, such as

$$y_1 = g_1(x_1, \cdots, x_N)$$

$$\vdots \qquad (4\text{-}94)$$

$$y_N = g_N(x_1, \cdots, x_N)$$

(with corresponding inverse transformation relations), then one can write an equation which is a generalization of (4-27). This now involves the *Jacobian* of the transformation, defined by the magnitude of the determinant

$$\frac{\partial(y_1, \cdots, y_N)}{\partial(x_1, \cdots, x_N)} = \begin{vmatrix} \dfrac{\partial g_1}{\partial x_1} & \dfrac{\partial g_1}{\partial x_2} & \cdots & \dfrac{\partial g_1}{\partial x_N} \\[2ex] \dfrac{\partial g_2}{\partial x_1} & \dfrac{\partial g_2}{\partial x_2} & \cdots & \vdots \\[2ex] \dfrac{\partial g_N}{\partial x_1} & & \cdots & \dfrac{\partial g_N}{\partial x_N} \end{vmatrix} \qquad (4\text{-}95)$$

Note

$$\frac{\partial(x_1, \cdots, x_N)}{\partial(y_1, \cdots, y_N)} = \left[\frac{\partial(y_1, \cdots, y_N)}{\partial(x_1, \cdots, x_N)}\right]^{-1} \qquad (4\text{-}96)$$

With $q(y_1, \cdots, y_N)$ representing the new p.d.f., the result is

$$p(x_1, \cdots, x_N) = q[g_1(x_1, \cdots, x_N), g_2(x_1, \cdots, x_N), \cdots, g_N(x_1, \cdots, x_N)]$$

$$\cdot \left| \frac{\partial(y_1, \cdots, y_N)}{\partial(x_1, \cdots, x_N)} \right| \qquad (4\text{-}97)$$

As an example, in the two-space, consider replacing the variables x, y (regarded for intuitive purposes as Cartesian coordinates of a point in the two-space) by the one-to-one mapping (into polar coordinates)

$$\begin{aligned} x &= R\cos\theta \\ y &= R\sin\theta \end{aligned} \quad \begin{cases} 0 \le R < \infty \\ 0 \le \theta < 2\pi \end{cases} \qquad (4\text{-}98)$$

Then

$$\frac{\partial(x, y)}{\partial(R, \theta)} = \begin{vmatrix} \cos\theta & -R\sin\theta \\ \sin\theta & R\cos\theta \end{vmatrix} = R \qquad (4\text{-}99)$$

Hence if $p(x, y)$ was the p.d.f. for x, y, the p.d.f for the corresponding variables R, θ is given by

$$q(R, \theta) = Rp(R \cos\theta, R \sin\theta) \qquad (4\text{-}100)$$

We shall give examples of this transformation, for the Gaussian distribution, in Sec. 4-6.

Quite often, however, one is interested in transformations which reduce the number of variables, so that results such as (4-97) are not directly applicable and the ch.f method becomes quite useful. For example, one may be interested only in the p.d.f. for the sum of the given variables $x_1, \cdots, x_N$,

$$y = \sum_{k=1}^{N} x_k \qquad (4\text{-}101)$$

Then for the p.d.f. $q(y)$ one may introduce the ch.f.

$$G_y(\xi) = \int_{-\infty}^{\infty} q(y) e^{-j\xi y} dy = \overline{e^{-j\xi y}} \qquad (4\text{-}102)$$

and quite properly interpret the latter as an average over the total probability space,

$$G_y(\xi) = \int_{-\infty}^{\infty} \cdots \int_{-\infty}^{\infty} e^{-j\xi y} p(x_1, \cdots, x_N) dx_1 \cdots dx_N \qquad (4\text{-}103)$$

With the relation (4-101), this becomes

$$G_y(\xi) = \int_{-\infty}^{\infty} \cdots \int_{-\infty}^{\infty} \exp\left[-j\xi \sum_{k=1}^{N} x_k\right] p(x_1, \cdots, x_N) dx_1 \cdots dx_N$$

$$= F(\xi, \xi, \xi, \cdots) \qquad (4\text{-}104)$$

where $F(\xi_1, \xi_2, \cdots, \xi_N)$ was the ch.f. defined in (4-92). That is, $G_y(\xi)$ is obtained by setting all the ch.f. variables $(\xi_1, \cdots, \xi_N)$ simultaneously equal to ξ. To obtain $q(y)$ then requires the Fourier transform inversion of $G_y(\xi)$. Examples of such a transformation are given later.

Finally in this section we introduce the notion of *statistical independence*. Consider two variables, with joint p.d.f. $p(x, y)$. Then y is said to be statistically independent of x if, and only if,

$$p_x(y) = p(y) \qquad (4\text{-}105)$$

That is, the conditional distribution of the values of y is the same for all values of x (or, equivalently, is independent of the value of x). From (4-77), another equivalent statement of statistical independence is

$$p(x, y) = p(x)p(y) \tag{4-106}$$

For N variables, mutual statistical independence implies

$$p(x_1, \cdots, x_N) = p(x_1)p(x_2) \cdots p(x_N) = \prod_{k=1}^{N} p(x_k) \tag{4-107}$$

Note that use here of the notation $p(x_k)$ is a generic use of the notation $p(\ )$ and does *not* imply that the individual variables have identical p.d.f.'s.

With (4-107), higher cross-moments become separable. That is, for statistically independent variables,

$$\overline{x_1^{k_1} x_2^{k_2} \cdots x_N^{k_N}} = \overline{x_1^{k_1}} \, \overline{x_2^{k_2}} \cdots \overline{x_N^{k_N}} \tag{4-108}$$

Particularly, for the covariances,

$$\mu_{jk} = \overline{(x_j - \bar{x}_j)(x_k - \bar{x}_k)} = \overline{x_j x_k} - \overline{x_j}\,\overline{x_k} = 0 \quad \text{when } j \neq k \tag{4-109}$$

That is, the crosscovariance of statistically independent random variables is *zero*. Note the converse statement is *not* generally true. That is, zero covariance does not imply statistical independence between variables, and higher-order cross-moments may still be generally nonseparable. It is one of the unusual characteristics of the Gaussian distribution (see Sec. 4-4) that zero covariance does imply statistical independence, as well as vice versa.

Note that the mean value of a sum of variables is always the sum of their means, and that *when* the variables have zero covariances with each other, the mean square of the sum is the sum of the component mean-squares. For statistically independent variables, the ch.f. also has a simple form. Thus with (4-107) the general form of (4-92) becomes

$$
\begin{aligned}
F(\xi_1, \cdots, \xi_N) &= \overline{\exp\left(-j \sum_k \xi_k x_k\right)} \\
&= \int_{-\infty}^{\infty} p(x_1) e^{-j\xi_1 x_1} \, dx_1 \int_{-\infty}^{\infty} p(x_2) e^{-j\xi_2 x_2} \, dx \quad \cdots \\
&= F_1(\xi_1) F_2(\xi_2) \cdots F_N(\xi_N) \tag{4-110}
\end{aligned}
$$

where $F_k(\xi)$ is the ch.f. corresponding to the p.d.f. of the kth variable. Thus

$$F(\xi_1,\cdots,\xi_N) = \prod_{k=1}^{N} F_k(\xi_k) \qquad (4\text{-}111)$$

In particular if all the N variables have the *same* p.d.f., with ch.f. of $F_k(\xi)$, the ch.f. for their joint p.d.f. reduces to the simple form

$$F(\xi_1,\cdots,\xi_N) = \prod_{k=1}^{N} F(\xi_k) \qquad (4\text{-}112)$$

Recalling also (4-104), the ch.f. for the *sum* of N *independent* variables is then given by

$$G(\xi) = \prod_{k=1}^{N} F_k(\xi) \qquad (4\text{-}113)$$

and, if all the variables are identically distributed,

$$G(\xi) = [F(\xi)]^N \qquad (4\text{-}114)$$

Note that (4-113) is in the form of a product. As is well known (Chap. 1), the resulting inverse transform has the form of a convolution integral. For example, if $p_1(x_1)$ and $p_2(x_2)$ are the respective p.d.f.'s for a pair of statistically independent variables, the p.d.f. for their sum y is thus given by the form

$$p(y) = \int_{-\infty}^{\infty} p_1(y-x)p_2(x)\,dx = \int_{-\infty}^{\infty} p_1(x)p_2(y-x)\,dx \quad (4\text{-}115)$$

Although this could be deduced by other arguments, it has indeed been simply shown via the ch.f. approach.

4-4 The Multivariate Gaussian Distribution

The multivariate Gaussian distribution is defined most simply in terms of its characteristic function. With $p(x_1,\cdots,x_N)$ the p.d.f. of N jointly Gaussian variables, the ch.f. defined by

$$F(\xi_1,\cdots,\xi_N) = \overline{\exp\left(-j\sum_{k=1}^{N}\xi_k x_k\right)}$$

has for the multivariate Gaussian distribution the form

$$F(\xi_1, \cdots, \xi_N) = \exp\left[-j \sum_{k=1}^{N} \xi_k m_k\right] \exp\left[-\frac{1}{2} \sum_{k,m=1}^{N} \mu_{km} \xi_k \xi_m\right] \quad (4\text{-}116)$$

Recalling the moment-generating properties of the ch.f., the m_k are clearly identifiable as the means of the corresponding x_k, and the μ_{kn} as the covariances between x_k and x_n. Note that since $\overline{x_k x_n} = \overline{x_n x_k}$, one has the symmetry property

$$\mu_{kn} = \mu_{nk} \quad (4\text{-}117)$$

The characteristic function in (4-116) is the most general that can be defined in the form of an exponential whose exponent consists of all possible linear and second-degree terms, with the requirement of (4-117). Clearly, also (e.g., by considering the moments implied by the p.d.f.) the individual variables are Gaussianly distributed via a distribution of the type described earlier in Sec. 4-2.

To define the inverse Fourier transform, it is convenient to consider the μ_{kn} to comprise the components of a symmetric $N \times N$ matrix, μ (termed the *covariance matrix*), whose inverse* is the symmetric $N \times N$ matrix $\Lambda = \mu^{-1}$. The elements of Λ, λ_{kn}, are given by the transposed matrix of the cofactors of μ, divided by det μ (the determinant of μ). For example, for two variables x_1 and x_2, with variances σ_1^2 and σ_2^2 and normalized covariance ρ, the covariance matrix μ would have the form

$$\mu = \begin{pmatrix} \sigma_1^2 & \sigma_1\sigma_2\rho \\ \sigma_1\sigma_2\rho & \sigma_2^2 \end{pmatrix} \quad (4\text{-}118)$$

and its inverse will be

$$\Lambda = \mu^{-1} = \frac{1}{\sigma_1^2\sigma_2^2(1-\rho^2)} \begin{pmatrix} \sigma_2^2 & -\sigma_1\sigma_2\rho \\ -\sigma_1\sigma_2\rho & \sigma_1^2 \end{pmatrix} \quad (4\text{-}119)$$

In general in terms of Λ, the inverse transform of the ch.f. in (4-116) can be shown to have the form

$$p(x_1, \cdots, x_N) = \frac{1}{(2\pi)^{N/2}(\det\mu)^{1/2}} \exp\left[-\frac{1}{2} \sum_{k,n=1}^{N} \lambda_{kn}(x_k - m_k)(x_n - m_n)\right] \quad (4\text{-}120)$$

---

*It can be shown that this inverse exists (the matrix is nonsingular) provided the set $x_1, \cdots, x_N$ does not have any complete linear dependence, i.e., there is no *deterministic* relation by which the values for one of the variables is always precisely some *fixed* linear combination of the values of a set of the other variables.

For example, in the two-dimensional case,

$$p(x_1, x_2) = \frac{1}{2\pi \sigma_1 \sigma_2 \sqrt{1 - \rho^2}}$$

$$\exp\left\{ -\frac{1}{2(1 - \rho^2)} \left[\frac{(x_1 - m_1)^2}{\sigma_1^2} + \frac{(x_2 - m_2)^2}{\sigma_2^2} - 2\rho \frac{(x_1 - m_1)(x_2 - m_2)}{\sigma_1 \sigma_2} \right] \right\}$$

$$(4\text{-}121)$$

Note the general form for the p.d.f. again involves simply an exponential in linear and second-order terms and that in the case of zero mean ($m_1 = m_2 = \ldots = m_N = 0$), the exponential contains only second-order terms. Note also that the joint distribution is *completely characterized by the means and covariances.* Hence, for the multivariate Gaussian p.d.f., all higher-order moments are given in terms of the means and second moments (formulas being readily obtained, for example, by differentiation of the ch.f.).

Now consider the situation when all the crosscovariances are zero. Defining the autocovariances as $\{\sigma_k^2\}$, the covariance matrix μ has the diagonal form

$$\mu = \begin{pmatrix} \sigma_1^2 & & & 0 \\ & \sigma_2^2 & & \\ & & \ddots & \\ 0 & & & \sigma_N^2 \end{pmatrix} \qquad (4\text{-}122)$$

and its inverse is simply another diagonal form

$$\Lambda = \mu^{-1} = \begin{pmatrix} \frac{1}{\sigma_1^2} & & & 0 \\ & \frac{1}{\sigma_2^2} & & \\ & & \ddots & \\ 0 & & & \frac{1}{\sigma_N^2} \end{pmatrix} \qquad (4\text{-}123)$$

Then the p.d.f. of (4-120) is simply

$$p(x_1, x_2, \ldots, x_N) = \frac{1}{(2\pi)^{N/2} \sigma_1 \sigma_2 \cdots \sigma_N} \exp\left[-\frac{1}{2} \sum_{k=1}^{N} \frac{(x_k - m_k)^2}{\sigma_k^2} \right] \qquad (4\text{-}124)$$

$$= \prod_{k=1}^{N} \left\{ \frac{1}{\sigma_k \sqrt{2\pi}} e^{-(x_k - m_k)^2 / 2\sigma_k^2} \right\} \qquad (4\text{-}125)$$

As an example, the two-dimensional p.d.f. for independent Gaussian variates with equal variances is pictured in Fig. 4-5. From (4-125), when the crosscovariances vanish, the joint p.d.f. is the product of the p.d.f.'s of the individual variables, and hence they are statistically independent. Thus *for the Gaussian distribution, statistical independence and vanishing of the crosscovariances* are equivalent statements!

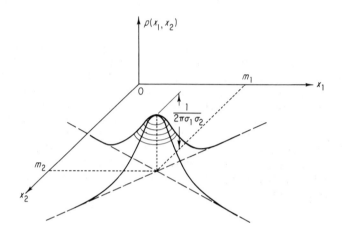

Fig. 4-5 Two-dimensional Gaussian p.d.f.

If a set of N variables are jointly Gaussian, so is any subset (again this can be seen, for example, by examining the totality of moments implied by the ch.f.). Thus any conditional p.d.f. will be Gaussian in form, since by (4-79) it will involve just the ratio of a pair of exponential forms, hence, differencing of the exponents. For the two-dimensional zero-mean case, as an example again,

$$p_{x_1}(x_2) = \frac{p(x_1, x_2)}{p(x_1)}$$

$$= \frac{1}{\sigma_2 \sqrt{2\pi(1 - \rho^2)}} \exp\left\{ -\frac{1}{2(1 - \rho^2)} \left[\frac{x_1^2}{\sigma_1^2} + \frac{x_2^2}{\sigma_2^2} - \frac{2\rho_1 x_1 x_2}{\sigma_1 \sigma_2} \right] + \frac{x_1^2}{2\sigma_1^2} \right\}$$

This can be reduced to the form

$$p_{x_1}(x_2) = \frac{1}{[\sigma_2\sqrt{1 - \rho^2}]\sqrt{2\pi}} \exp\left[-\frac{\left(x_2 - \frac{\rho\sigma_2}{\sigma_1} x_1 \right)^2}{2\sigma_2^2(1 - \rho^2)} \right] \qquad (4\text{-}126)$$

Thus, although x_2 is a zero-mean variable, the fact that it is non-vanishingly correlated with x_1 implies that when x_1 is given, the range of associated values of x_2 is more constrained. Indeed the conditional mean for x_2 is just $\rho x_1 \sigma_2/\sigma_1$ (i.e., the value of x_1 is multiplied by the normalized covariance ρ and by a factor σ_2/σ_1 which reflects the difference in r.m.s. values between x_1 and x_2), and the conditional variance is only $\sigma_2^2(1 - \rho^2)$. Thus knowledge of x_1 not only biases the likely value of x_2 (the conditional mean) but narrows the uncertainty below that which holds in the absence of knowledge of the value of the related variate x_1.

Another fact which is evident from the general form of the Gaussian ch.f. is that any *linear sum of jointly Gaussian variates is also Gaussian*. This follows by observing that the characteristic function of the sum, as given by (4-104), is described by an exponential with only linear or second-order terms. Such self-reproduction in form is not a general property of other distributions. For example (recalling the convolution property), the sum of two identically, uniformly distributed variables has a triangular-shaped distribution. It is extremely fortunate that the property does hold for the Gaussian *and* that the Gaussian describes a large number of processes of physical interest. Regarding any integral as the limit of a sum, this property leads to the important observation that a *linear system operating on a Gaussian noise input* has a *Gaussian noise output*. The ability to predict the output p.d.f. from the system input enables analysis of a large class of linear systems and thereby allows most of the major results of communication theory.

The conclusion that a linear sum of Gaussian variables results in another Gaussian variable and the fact that only first and second moments are needed to completely characterize Gaussian variables lead to extremely simple procedures for defining the resulting p.d.f.'s. Thus, suppose $x_1, \cdots, x_N$ are jointly Gaussian with covariances μ_{mn}, and one defines a new set of M variables by the sums

$$y_k = \sum_{n=1}^{N} \alpha_{kn} x_n \qquad k = 1, \cdots, M \qquad (4\text{-}127)$$

Then it follows immediately that the y_k are also jointly Gaussian. Their means are

$$\bar{y}_k = \sum_{n=1}^{N} \alpha_{kn} \bar{x}_n \qquad (4\text{-}128)$$

and their covariances are

$$\overline{(y_j - \overline{y}_j)(y_k - \overline{y}_k)} = \sum_{n=1}^{N} \sum_{m=1}^{N} \alpha_{jn}\alpha_{km}\overline{(x_n - \overline{x}_n)(x_m - \overline{x}_m)}$$

$$(4\text{-}129)$$

$$= \sum_{n,m=1}^{N} \alpha_{jn}\alpha_{km}\mu_{nm}$$

With these parameters one can then immediately write the joint Gaussian p.d.f. for the new variables, without need for examining any other detailed properties of the transformations defined by (4-127).

Finally we cite (without proof) the important *central limit theorem*. This theorem states that, under very general assumptions, the joint p.d.f. of a set of variates which are in turn weighted sums formed from a large number of other independently distributed quantities, approaches a joint Gaussian p.d.f. as the number of terms in the sums increase, no matter what the individual distributions of the latter quantities are within a wide class (but not all). This follows from the observation that the peak value for any ch.f. $F(\xi)$ is unity, at $\xi = 0$, and that it tends to decrease away from $\xi = 0$. Hence the product of a very large number of characteristic functions tends to drop to 0 rapidly away from $\xi = 0$. However, when one defines the mean and variance of the sum to be finite (meaning that the corresponding values for the component processes become infinitesimal as the number of variates being added becomes infinite), the product of the characteristic functions approaches a Gaussian ch.f. to within factors which are asymptotically unity (i.e., are unity to within terms which vanish as the number of variates being added in each sum becomes infinite).

Random electrical noise which results, for example, from thermal fluctuations of the electrons which comprise a current is the addition of just such a large number of independent random quantities and hence is Gaussian. It is this and similar origins which lead to the major role of Gaussian distributions in communication theory and applications. At the same time it is because the unusual mathematical features of the Gaussian distribution enable great mathematical tractability that the theory and its applications have been so extensively developed.

4-5 Continuous Processes: Autocorrelation Functions and Power Spectra

In communication theory applications we are generally interested in random processes (usually Gaussian or derived from a Gaussian) which are continuous in time and with operations upon such processes. Here we shall discuss the basic statistical characterization of such processes.

First is the concept of stationarity. We have referred hitherto to statistical ensembles. For a continuous process the ensemble consists of a set of waveforms (*realizations or sample functions*), whose values (over the set) at any instant of time t conform to the one-dimensional p.d.f. defining the ensemble of process values. Moreover one can define joint ensemble statistics for the values at spaced instants of time. If these joint statistics (the joint p.d.f. and all derived moments) remain the same for any shift in the time base (the spacings between the selected instants remaining fixed), the process is said to be *statistically stationary*, in a strict sense. In reality, of course, one deals simply with physical waveforms, and it is the concept that time averages or distributions derived from one long section of such a waveform will be the same as for any other long section, which underlies the use of ensemble statistics. Mathematically the statement that time and ensemble averages will be equivalent for a stationary process is the assumption of an *ergodic* process. This definition has meaning where one has physically an ensemble of processes, as, for example, when one is considering the motions of all (statistically equivalent) molecules in a gas. In most communication applications ergodicity generally enters only as an assumption that one could construct a number of statistically equivalent systems where, because of stationarity in the time processes, ergodicity would also hold.

Next we proceed to the particular statistics of most interest to us in this section. We consider a random process $X(t)$. That is, we consider an ensemble of waveforms, of which a typical realization is $x(t)$. We can designate its values at instants $t_1, \cdots, t_N$ (N arbitrary for the moment) by the values

$$x_k \equiv x(t_k) \qquad k = 1, \cdots, N \tag{4-130}$$

Then over the ensemble one can define the joint p.d.f. for the values $x_1, \cdots, x_N$. Such a p.d.f., and the moments derived from it, comprise the *joint process statistics* for $X(t)$. In principle all possible dimensionalities of the p.d.f. have to be defined. Usually it suffices to characterize up to that dimensionality involved in the problem at hand. For the Gaussian process, the process for which all joint p.d.f.'s are multivariate Gaussian, the important feature is that *all* higher-order p.d.f.'s, for arbitrary dimensionality, are described completely by the means and the matrix of covariances. That is, the basic parameters are only those involved in defining pair-wise (two-dimensional) joint p.d.f.'s.

For a continuous stationary process the second moments are defined by an autocovariance or autocorrelation *function*. Thus let

$$x_1 = x(t_1)$$
$$x_2 = x(t_1 + \tau) \tag{4-131}$$

Because of stationarity their mean values are equal and can be written notationally as

$$\bar{x}_1 = \bar{x}_2 = \bar{x} = \overline{x(t)} \qquad (4\text{-}132)$$

Likewise, because of stationarity, their covariance $\overline{(x_1 - \bar{x}_1)(x_2 - \bar{x}_2)}$ is a function *only* of the time spacing τ. If one considers the value of this covariance for arbitrary τ, one thereby indeed defines a function of τ, the *autocovariance function* of the process, written in the general form

$$\mu_x(\tau) = \overline{[x(t) - \bar{x}][x(t + \tau) - \bar{x}]} \qquad (4\text{-}133)$$

The variable τ defining an autocovariance function is often denoted the *time-lag*. In a similar way the *autocorrelation function* is

$$R_x(\tau) = \overline{x(t)x(t + \tau)} \qquad (4\text{-}134)$$

Note

$$\mu_x(\tau) = R_x(\tau) - [\overline{x(t)}]^2 \qquad (4\text{-}135)$$

The variances of x_1 and x_2 are obviously equal, because of stationarity, with the value given by the autocovariance at zero time-lag,

$$\sigma_x^2 = \mu_x(0) = \overline{[x_1 - \bar{x}]^2} = \overline{[x_2 - \bar{x}]^2} = \overline{[x(t) - \overline{x(t)}]^2} \qquad (4\text{-}136)$$

This is the mean-square value, or *mean power* of the fluctuation component of the process (when x is visualized as a voltage across a 1Ω resistor). The *normalized autocovariance function* is then

$$\rho_x(\tau) = \frac{\mu_x(\tau)}{\sigma_x^2} = \frac{\overline{[x(t) - \bar{x}][x(t + \tau) - \bar{x}]}}{\sigma^2} \qquad (4\text{-}137)$$

Note that if $x(t)$ is real, $\mu(\tau)$ is an even function in τ, i.e.,

$$\mu(-\tau) = \mu(\tau) \qquad (4\text{-}138)$$

Likewise, if $x(t)$ and $y(t)$ represent two different continuous random processes, each has its own mean and autocovariance functions, and the most general second-moment statistical relation between the two is defined by their *normalized crosscovariance function*,

$$\rho_{xy}(\tau) = \frac{\overline{[x(t) - \bar{x}][y(t + \tau) - \bar{y}]}}{\sqrt{\overline{[x(t) - \bar{x}]^2}\,\overline{[y(t) - \bar{y}]^2}}} \qquad (4\text{-}139)$$

The correlation or covariance functions are important for two reasons. One, mentioned above, is that they provide complete description of the Gaussian process. The other, described immediately below, is their intimate relation with a definable process spectrum, which in turn allows simple calculations of the effect of linear systems (filters) upon the correlation or covariance functions or the equivalent spectra.

In introducing spectra, note first that a stationary random process $x(t)$ has infinite energy and therefore it does not have a definable Fourier transform in any ordinary sense; its behavior as $t \to \infty$ is no different than in any finite part of the plane, and this precludes meaningful convergence to a limit value for integrals such as

$$\lim_{T \to \infty} \int_{-T}^{T} x(t) \, e^{-j2\pi ft} \, dt$$

On the other hand, one expects *time averages* on $x(t)$ to have reasonable convergence (to approach meaningful limits) as the time domain over which averaging is taken increases without limit.* Particularly, for a stationary ergodic process, such as we are assuming, these time averages must be equal to the defined ensemble averages. Thus one can write

$$\overline{x(t)} = \lim_{T \to \infty} \frac{1}{2T} \int_{-T}^{T} x(t) \, dt \tag{4-140}$$

$$\sigma_x^2 = \overline{[x(t) - \bar{x}]^2} = \lim_{T \to \infty} \frac{1}{2T} \int_{-T}^{T} [x(t) - \overline{x(t)}]^2 \, dt \tag{4-141}$$

Particularly also, the autocorrelation function is

$$R_x(\tau) = \overline{x(t)x(t + \tau)} = \lim_{T \to \infty} \frac{1}{2T} \int_{-T}^{T} x(t)x(t + \tau) \, dt \tag{4-142}$$

Considered as a function of τ, $R_x(\tau)$ has a Fourier transform, which we denote by $S_x(f)$,

$$S_x(f) = \int_{-\infty}^{\infty} R_x(\tau) e^{-j2\pi f\tau} \, d\tau \tag{4-143}$$

---

*These characteristics are similar to those described earlier, in Chap. 2, for periodic (harmonic) deterministic functions. As shown below, one is again led to defining power density spectra rather than the kind of energy density spectra which can be used to characterize aperiodic, deterministic, finite-energy waveforms.

The inverse relation is

$$R_x(\tau) = \int_{-\infty}^{\infty} S_x(f) e^{j2\pi f\tau} df \qquad (4\text{-}144)$$

In particular

$$R_x(0) = \int_{-\infty}^{\infty} S_x(f) df = \overline{x^2} = \sigma_x^2 + \bar{x}^2 \qquad (4\text{-}145)$$

It can be shown (below) that $S_x(f)$ is nonnegative real. Hence it is tempting (and has physical interpretation indicated below) to regard $S_x(f) df$ as the mean power contained in those spectral components of the process which lie in the frequency range $(f, f + df)$. Thus $S_x(f)$ is denoted the *power spectral density* or *power density spectrum* of $x(t)$. Its dimensions are watts per hertz.

A power density spectrum corresponding to the autocovariance function can also be defined, in analogy to (4-143). However, recalling (4-135), the autocorrelation function differs from the autocovariance function by a constant (the square of the mean value of the process), so that the power density spectrum for the covariance will differ only by the subtraction of a term of the form $\bar{x}^2 \delta(f)$, corresponding to the transform of the constant term. A power density spectrum for the normalized autocorrelation can also be defined; it will be equal to simply $S_x(f)/\sigma_x^2$.

Note the definition of the power density spectrum includes negative as well as positive frequencies. However, from the even symmetry of $R_x(\tau)$ it is readily shown that (4-143) can be written in the form

$$S_x(f) = \int_{-\infty}^{\infty} R_x(\tau) \cos 2\pi f\tau \, d\tau = 2 \int_{0}^{\infty} R_x(\tau) \cos 2\pi f\tau \, d\tau \qquad (4\text{-}146)$$

Hence $S_x(f)$ is also an even function,

$$S_x(-f) = S_x(f) \qquad (4\text{-}147)$$

Furthermore, one can then rewrite (4-144) as

$$R_x(\tau) = 2 \int_{0}^{\infty} S_x(f) \cos 2\pi f\tau \, d\tau \qquad (4\text{-}148)$$

This relation shows that $R_x(\tau)$ can be represented in terms of a one-sided power density spectrum, of value $2S_x(f)$, representing the equivalence of positive and negative frequencies. It also demonstrates a kind of Fourier cosine transform relationship between $R_x(\tau)$ and $S_x(f)$; this form is little used in the more recent literature.

Thus far we have defined $S_x(f)$ only as a mathematical quantity, a Fourier transform on the autocorrelation function. We have not, however, related it directly to the spectral properties of the time process depicted by $x(t)$. Such a relationship is important in that, for example, the response of a filter to an input voltage can be readily written in terms of the filter transfer function and the spectrum of the input. We pointed out earlier that one cannot strictly define a spectrum for a sample function of a stationary random process. However, if $x(t)$ is such a sample function, one *can* write a spectrum (transform) for the process defined by

$$x_T(t) = \begin{cases} x(t), & |t| \le T \\ 0, & |t| > T \end{cases} \qquad (4\text{-}149)$$

Let this function have the voltage spectrum (Fourier transform)

$$X_T(f) = \int_{-\infty}^{\infty} x_T(t) e^{-j2\pi ft} dt = \int_{-T}^{T} x(t) e^{-j2\pi ft} dt \qquad (4\text{-}150)$$

Since $x(t)$ and $x_T(t)$ are real functions, $X_T(f)$ will have the property

$$X_T(-f) = X_T^*(f) \qquad (4\text{-}151)$$

The inverse is

$$x_T(t) = \int_{-\infty}^{\infty} X_T(f) e^{j2\pi ft} df \qquad (4\text{-}152)$$

Now consider the autocorrelation function defined in (4-142). (Note the autocorrelation function rather than autocovariance is chosen here for simplicity in the presentation; the reader can readily verify similar results for the autocovariance and its power density spectrum.) We alter the definition slightly (negligibly) and write

$$R_x(\tau) = \lim_{T \to \infty} \frac{1}{2T} \int_{-\infty}^{\infty} x_T(t) x_T(t + \tau) d\tau \qquad (4\text{-}153)$$

Then, with (4-152), it is readily shown that

$$R_x(\tau) = \lim_{T \to \infty} \frac{1}{2T} \int_{-\infty}^{\infty} |X_T(f)|^2 e^{j2\pi f\tau} df \qquad (4\text{-}154)$$

Denoting the power density spectrum of $R_x(\tau)$ as $S_x(f)$, it is tempting to interchange the order of integration and limiting processes in (4-154), to write

$$S_x(f) = \lim_{T \to \infty} \frac{1}{2T} |X_T(f)|^2 \qquad (4\text{-}155)$$

However, it can be shown that this is not strictly correct, since in fact $X_T(f)$ is itself a random process. What can be stated in a correct manner is that if one takes the ensemble average of (4-153) over the class of all sample functions, recognizing that $R_x(\tau)$ is unchanged by such averaging, then one obtains a deterministic relation which can be written as

$$R_x(\tau) = \int_{-\infty}^{\infty} S_x(f) e^{j2\pi f \tau} df \qquad (4\text{-}156a)$$

where

$$S_x(f) = \lim_{T \to \infty} \frac{\overline{|X_T(f)|^2}}{2T} \qquad (4\text{-}156b)$$

This relationship is known as the *Wiener-Khinchine* theorem.

Note that (4-156) immediately demonstrates that $S_x(f)$ is non-negative. The same immediately holds also for the power density spectrum corresponding to the autocovariance function, since the two can differ only by the possible presence of a $\delta(f)$ term in $S_x(f)$.

Furthermore, if any sample function $x_T(t)$ is passed through a filter (or any linear system) with transfer function $H(f)$, the filter output which we denote by $y_T(t)$ will have a spectrum

$$Y_T(f) = H(f) X_T(f) \qquad (4\text{-}157)$$

Hence

$$\overline{|Y_T(f)|^2} = |H(f)|^2 \overline{|X_T(f)|^2} \qquad (4\text{-}158)$$

and we can immediately deduce that the power density spectrum for the autocorrelation of the filter output (random) process will be related to that of the random input process by

$$S_y(f) = |H(f)|^2 S_x(f) \qquad (4\text{-}159)$$

The quantity $|H(f)|^2$ is the *power transfer function* of the filter (recall Chap. 2). Thus, if the autocorrelation or autocovariance of the input process is known, (4-159) provides a recipe, analogous to the usual filter response calculation typified by (4-157), for calculating the autocorrelation or autocovariance of the output process. As in Chap. 2, one can in fact define a direct convolutional statement equivalent to (4-159). If the filter impulse response is

$$h(t) \Longleftrightarrow H(f) \qquad (4\text{-}160)$$

then one can define the filter autocorrelation function

$$R_h(\tau)^{\cdot} = \int_{-\infty}^{\infty} h(t) h(t + \tau) dt \Longleftrightarrow |H(f)|^2 \qquad (4\text{-}161)$$

Hence (4-159) corresponds to the equivalent statements

$$R_y(\tau) = \int_{-\infty}^{\infty} R_h(\tau - \tau_1) R_x(\tau_1) d\tau_1 = \int_{-\infty}^{\infty} R_h(\tau_1) R_x(\tau - \tau_1) d\tau_1 \quad (4\text{-}162)$$

and similar statements apply for the autocovariance function.

As the simplest example of a calculation using these results, note that the mean power in the output process is given by

$$R_y(0) = \int_{-\infty}^{\infty} S_y(f) df = \int_{-\infty}^{\infty} |H(f)|^2 S_x(f) df \quad (4\text{-}163)$$

Again the major importance of these results is that, for the Gaussian process, where the means and covariances completely describe all joint p.d.f.'s, the knowledge of the input process and the transfer characteristics of a linear system operating upon the process serve to *completely* describe the output process. Equivalent results are not generally available for non-Gaussian processes.

Examples of power density spectra and corresponding autocorrelation functions can be interpreted from the Fourier transform pairs in Chaps. 1 and 2. From a practical point of view the most important process is that idealization known as *white noise*. This is the zero-mean process whose power density spectrum is flat over *all* frequencies. If this constant density is $n_0/2$ watts per hertz,*

$$S(f) = n_0/2 \quad (4\text{-}164)$$

the corresponding autocorrelation function is

$$R(\tau) = \int_{-\infty}^{\infty} \frac{n_0}{2} e^{j2\pi f \tau} df = \frac{n_0}{2} \delta(\tau) \quad (4\text{-}165)$$

This process, strictly speaking, has infinite mean power, but nevertheless convenient mathematical properties. Thus, in (4-159), if a filter input process has a power density spectrum flat (constant) over just the band of the filter response, its value outside that band is irrelevant to determining the parameters of the output process and, if convenient, the input noise power density spectrum may be regarded to have the same constant value over all frequencies. Thus one has the common statement that if a Gaussian noise process has a spectrum much wider than a system bandwidth

---

*The white noise spectral density $n_0/2$ is defined for both positive and negative frequencies (i.e., a double-sided spectrum); n_0 is then the spectral density for a one-sided definition of the spectrum.

and has a constant power density spectrum over that band, it may as well be regarded as white Gaussian noise with that constant value for its power density spectrum.

One also sometimes defines ''band-limited'' white noise. In this case the power spectrum is spread uniformly over a specified range of frequencies and vanishes outside. In theory it is obtained by passing white noise through an ideal rectangular filter. (Since neither white noise nor ideal filters exist, it is only an approximation to reality.) We shall continue for computational simplicity the model containing both positive and negative frequencies and write for this case

$$S(f) = \begin{cases} n_0/2, & f_1 < |f| < f_2 \\ 0, & |f| < f_1 \text{ and } |f| > f_2 \end{cases} \qquad (4\text{-}166)$$

The plot of this spectrum is shown in Fig. 4-6a. The mean total power is equal to the area of the two rectangles, giving

$$P = n_0(f_2 - f_1) \qquad (4\text{-}167)$$

The autocorrelation function $R(\tau)$ is found to be

$$R(\tau) = \left[\int_{-f_2}^{-f_1} + \int_{f_1}^{f_2} \right] \frac{n_0}{2} e^{j2\pi f\tau} df = P \frac{\sin \pi (f_2 - f_1)\tau}{\pi (f_2 - f_1)\tau} \cos \pi (f_1 + f_2)\tau \qquad (4\text{-}169)$$

Special cases of band-limited white noise of considerable importance are given below.

The Low-pass Case (Fig. 4-6b):

$$f_1 = 0, f_2 = F, \qquad R(\tau) = P \frac{\sin 2\pi F\tau}{2\pi F\tau} \qquad (4\text{-}169)$$

The Narrow-band Case (Figs. 4-6c and d):

$$f_1 \gg f_2 - f_1$$

Here we write for convenience

$$f_1 + f_2 = 2f_c, \qquad f_2 - f_1 = B$$

$$R(\tau) = P \frac{\sin \pi B\tau}{\pi B\tau} \cos 2\pi f_c \tau \qquad (4\text{-}170)$$

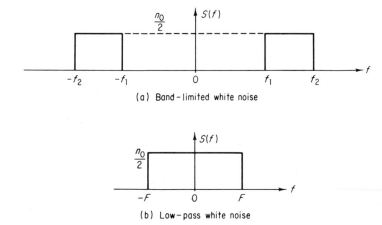

(a) Band-limited white noise

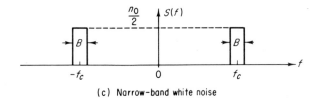

(b) Low-pass white noise

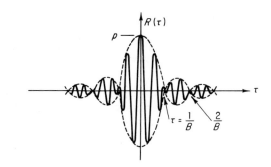

(c) Narrow-band white noise

(d) Autocorrelation function of narrow-band white noise

Fig. 4-6 Power density spectra of band-limited white noise.

4-6 Narrow-band Signal Plus Noise

A wide class of communication problems involve detecting some property of a signal in the presence of electrical noise. In radio, the application area which we emphasize, this usually involves some relatively narrow band of frequencies which contain the signal and the noise of interest.

Narrow-band Noise

If $n(t)$ is a representative wave of a narrow-band process with spectrum roughly centered on some frequency f_c, it is convenient to seek a resolution of the form discussed in Chap. 3,

$$n(t) = x(t) \cos 2\pi f_c t - y(t) \sin 2\pi f_c t \qquad (4\text{-}171)$$

where $x(t)$ and $y(t)$ are slowly varying functions of time relative to oscillations of frequency f_c. It can be shown that $x(t)$ and $y(t)$ are obtainable by linear operations upon $n(t)$, these operations involving coherent detection, as defined in later chapters. Since $x(t)$ and $y(t)$ are linearly related to $n(t)$, it follows that if $n(t)$ is Gaussian, so are $x(t)$ and $y(t)$.

The representation (4-171) can be written in terms of a complex equivalent,

$$n(t) = \text{Re}\left[z(t)e^{j2\pi f_c t}\right] \qquad (4\text{-}172)$$

where we have introduced the *complex envelope* (recall Chap. 3),

$$z(t) = x(t) + jy(t) = \rho(t)e^{j\phi(t)} \qquad (4\text{-}173)$$

Thus

$$\rho(t) = |z(t)| = \text{envelope of } z(t) = \sqrt{x^2(t) + y^2(t)} \qquad (4\text{-}174)$$

$$\phi(t) = \arg z(t) = \text{phase of } z(t) = \arctan \frac{y(t)}{x(t)} \qquad (4\text{-}175)$$

For stationary zero-mean Gaussian noise, the low-pass quadrature components $x(t)$ and $y(t)$ are themselves zero-mean Gaussian. They comprise a bivariate Gaussian process described by the following ensemble moments:

$$\overline{x(t)} = \overline{y(t)} = 0 \qquad (4\text{-}176)$$

$$\overline{x(t)x(t + \tau)} = \overline{y(t)y(t + \tau)} = R_c(\tau) \qquad (4\text{-}177)$$

$$\overline{x(t)y(t + \tau)} = -\overline{x(t + \tau)y(\tau)} = R_s(\tau) \qquad (4\text{-}178)$$

The left-hand equalities in (4-177) and (4-178) are consequences of the assumption of stationarity. Furthermore, then, $R_c(\tau)$ is an even function of τ and $R_s(\tau)$ is odd:

$$R_c(-\tau) = R_c(\tau) \qquad (4\text{-}179)$$

$$R_s(-\tau) = -R_s(\tau) \qquad (4\text{-}180)$$

The complex envelope process $z(t)$ in (4-173) is a *complex Gaussian process,* i.e., its real and imaginary parts are Gaussian. Its moments are defined by

$$\overline{z(t)} = 0 \tag{4-181}$$

$$\frac{1}{2}\overline{z^*(t)z(t + \tau)} = R_z(\tau) = R_c(\tau) + jR_s(\tau) \tag{4-182}$$

$$\frac{1}{2}\overline{z(t)z(t + \tau)} = 0 \tag{4-183}$$

The last of these is an explicit statement of stationarity. The factor $1/2$ is used above so as to simply relate the properties of $z(t)$ to those of $x(t)$ and $y(t)$. From (4-172) the autocorrelation of the real zero-mean bandpass process can now be written as

$$R_n(\tau) = \overline{n(t)n(t + \tau)}$$

$$= \overline{\frac{1}{2}\left[z(t)e^{j2\pi f_c t} + z^*(t)e^{-j2\pi f_c t}\right]\frac{1}{2}\left[z(t + \tau)e^{j2\pi f_c(t + \tau)} + z^*(t+\tau)e^{-j2\pi f_c(t+\tau)}\right]}$$

$$= \mathrm{Re}\left[R_z(\tau)e^{j2\pi f_c \tau}\right] \tag{4-184}$$

Thus, $R_z(\tau)$, the complex autocorrelation function of the complex envelope $z(t)$, completely describes all the covariance properties of $n(t)$ aside from the nominal center frequency.

If one defines corresponding power density spectra,

$$S_n(f) \iff R_n(\tau) \tag{4-185}$$

for the bandpass noise and

$$S_z(f) \iff R_z(\tau) \tag{4-186}$$

for the complex envelope, it is apparent that since $R_z(\tau)$ is a correlation involving only "modulation frequency terms," $S_z(f)$ is therefore a low-pass power spectrum. From the symmetry properties (4-179) and (4-180) for the components of $R_z(\tau)$, it is incidentally readily shown that $S_z(f)$ is real, as a meaningful power density spectrum should be. Finally, since we can write (4-184) as

$$R_n(\tau) = \frac{1}{2}\left[R_z(\tau)e^{j2\pi f_c \tau} + R_z^*(\tau)e^{-j2\pi f_c \tau}\right] \tag{4-187}$$

it is apparent that the power spectra are related by

$$S_n(f) = \frac{1}{2} S_z(f - f_c) + \frac{1}{2} S_z(-f - f_c) \tag{4-188}$$

As depicted in Fig. 4-7, $S_n(f)$ has its two-sided spectrum centered about $+f_c$ and $-f_c$, the two parts being mirror-symmetric in shape. Indeed, then, if one were rather to define a *one-sided* spectrum for $R_n(\tau)$, regarding all power to be concentrated in positive frequency components only, this would be identical in magnitude and shape with $S_z(f)$, except with the latter translated upwards in frequency to be centered at f_c. Thus, in dealing with bandpass noise, we can concentrate on the *equivalent low-pass process* describing the "modulation" components only. In this we further recognize that their complex autocorrelation function $R_z(\tau)$ as defined by (4-176)-(4-183) has a *two-sided low-pass* spectrum identical in form with the one-sided bandpass spectrum (concentrated about the nominal center frequency) of the real bandpass process.

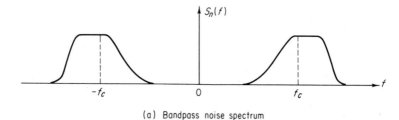

(a) Bandpass noise spectrum

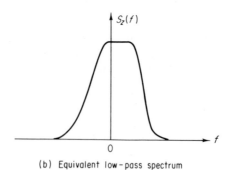

(b) Equivalent low-pass spectrum

Fig. 4-7 Power density spectrum of bandpass noise.

Note that $S_z(f)$ is *not* generally an even function of frequency. It is easily shown that such symmetry occurs only when $x(t)$ and $y(t)$ have a zero crosscovariance function (or, if Gaussian, are independent processes). In the latter event, $R_s(\tau) = 0$ and $R_z(\tau) = R_c(\tau)$, and $S_z(f)$ will be a real, even nonnegative function.

Finally, now, referring to the action of a bandpass filter as described in Chap. 3, we see that the input and output noise processes are related in terms of the equivalent low-pass response of the filter $h(t)$ by

$$z_{out}(t) = \int_{-\infty}^{\infty} h(t - \tau) z_{in}(\tau) d\tau \tag{4-189}$$

or

$$x_{out}(t) + jy_{out}(t) = \int_{-\infty}^{\infty} h(t - \tau)[x_{in}(\tau) + jy_{in}(\tau)] d\tau \tag{4-190}$$

Thus the output quadrature processes are linear transformations of the input Gaussian processes and hence are also zero-mean Gaussian processes. Further, in view of the earlier result (4-159), we see immediately that the equivalent low-pass power density spectra are related by

$$S_{out}(f) = |H(f)|^2 S_{in}(f) \tag{4-191}$$

and this is sufficient to complete the statistical description of the output process.

The mathematical model for stationary narrow-band Gaussian noise can now be completed by writing the appropriate probability density functions. Recall that the crosscorrelation function $R_s(\tau)$ of the quadrature components $x(t)$ and $y(t)$ is an odd function of τ and hence

$$R_s(0) = \overline{x(t)y(t)} = 0 \tag{4-192}$$

Since the ensemble is jointly Gaussian, this implies that at any time t, $x(t)$ and $y(t)$ are statistically independent.* Therefore the joint probability density function of x and y evaluated *at the same instant of time* is the product of single-variable Gaussian functions in x and y. That is,

$$p(x,y) = \frac{1}{2\pi \sigma^2} e^{-(x^2 + y^2)/2\sigma^2} \tag{4-193}$$

where

$$\sigma^2 = R_c(0) = R_z(0) = R_n(0) = \overline{n^2(t)} = \overline{x^2(t)} = \overline{y^2(t)} = \frac{1}{2}\overline{\rho^2(t)} \tag{4-194}$$

is the total average power in $n(t)$. The p.d.f. of (4-193) is the same as pictured earlier in Fig. 4-5.

---

*Note that $x(t)$ and $y(t + \tau)$ for $\tau \neq 0$ are *not* generally statistically independent. In general, quadrature components $x(t)$ and $y(t)$ of zero-mean noise are statistically independent for all time lags τ if and only if $R_s(\tau) = 0$ for all τ.

For the zero-mean noise, the quadrature components are related to the envelope and phase defined in (4-173)–(4-175) by

$$x(t) = \rho(t) \cos\phi(t)$$

$$y(t) = \rho(t) \sin\phi(t)$$

(4-195)

Hence transforming from noise quadrature components to envelope and phase of the noise is like transforming from rectangular to polar coordinates. Hence (recall Sec. 4-3), if $q(\rho,\phi)$ is the probability density of the envelope and phase of the noise wave,

$$p(x,y)\,dx\,dy = p(\rho\cos\phi, \rho\sin\phi)\,\rho\,d\rho\,d\phi = q(\rho,\phi)\,d\rho\,d\phi \quad (4\text{-}196)$$

and hence

$$q(\rho,\phi) = \frac{\rho}{2\pi\sigma^2} e^{-\rho^2/2\sigma^2} \quad (4\text{-}197)$$

The probability density function of just the noise envelope of Gaussian noise is obtained by averaging over all phases and is therefore

$$q_1(\rho) = \int_0^{2\pi} q(\rho,\phi)\,d\phi = \frac{\rho}{\sigma^2} e^{-\rho^2/2\sigma^2} \quad (4\text{-}198)$$

This is known as the *Rayleigh distribution* (see Fig. 4-8). The probability density function of phase ϕ is

$$q_2(\phi) = \int_0^{\infty} q(\rho,\phi)\,d\rho = \frac{1}{2\pi} \quad (4\text{-}199)$$

The values of $\phi(t)$ thus have a rectangular distribution. Thus also

$$q(\rho,\phi) = q_1(\rho)\,q_2(\phi) \quad (4\text{-}200)$$

and envelope and phase *at any instant* are statistically independent. (This is a statement of the circular symmetry evident in Fig. 4-5.)

Signal Plus Noise

Now let us turn to the case where a signal is also present in the narrow band. Let this signal be a cosine wave at frequency f_c,

$$s(t) = A \cos 2\pi f_c t \quad (4\text{-}201)$$

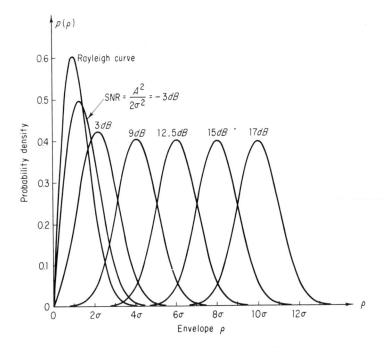

Fig. 4-8 Probability density function of envelope for sine wave plus Gaussian noise.

It is convenient to use the same frequency f_c as the nominal center frequency for the noise. The signal-plus-noise ensemble of interest is then represented by

$$e(t) = n(t) + s(t) = [x(t) + A] \cos 2\pi f_c t - y(t) \sin 2\pi f_c t \qquad (4\text{-}202)$$

Correspondingly this can be written in terms of envelope and phase functions (recall Chap. 3), as

$$e(t) = \rho(t) \cos[2\pi f_c t + \phi(t)] \qquad (4\text{-}203)$$

where

$$\rho(t) = \sqrt{[x(t) + A]^2 + y^2(t)}, \quad \rho \geq 0 \qquad (4\text{-}204)$$

and

$$\tan \phi(t) = \frac{y(t)}{x(t) + A} \qquad (4\text{-}205)$$

We can obtain the probability density function for the combination of the cosine signal and noise by substituting $\xi(t) = x(t) + A$ in (4-193). The resulting joint probability density function for ξ and y, the quadrature components of the total waveform, is

$$p(\xi, y) = \frac{1}{2\pi\sigma^2} e^{-[(\xi - A)^2 + y^2]/2\sigma^2} \tag{4-206}$$

Now transform to polar coordinates by

$$\xi = \rho \cos\phi, \quad y = \rho \sin\phi \tag{4-207}$$

where per (4-203)-(4-205), ρ now represents the envelope and ϕ the phase of the *signal plus noise.* Then the joint probability density function $q(\rho, \phi)$ is

$$q(\rho, \phi) = \frac{\rho}{2\pi\sigma^2} e^{-(\rho^2 + A^2 - 2A\rho\cos\phi)/2\sigma^2} \tag{2-208}$$

Note that now we cannot write $q(\rho, \phi)$ as a product $q_1(\rho)q_2(\phi)$, since a term in the equation appears with both variables multiplied together as $\rho \cos\phi$. This indicates that ρ and ϕ are *dependent* variables when $A \neq 0$.

We can find $q_1(\rho)$ again by integrating over all values of ϕ. This gives

$$q_1(\rho) = \frac{\rho}{2\pi\sigma^2} e^{-(\rho^2 + A^2)/2\sigma^2} \int_0^{2\pi} e^{\rho A \cos\phi/\sigma^2} d\phi \tag{4-209}$$

The integral in (4-209) can be identified in terms of the defining integral for the modified Bessel function of the first kind and zero order,

$$I_0(z) = \frac{1}{2\pi} \int_0^{2\pi} e^{z \cos\theta} d\theta \tag{4-210}$$

Accordingly

$$q_1(\rho) = \frac{\rho}{\sigma^2} I_0\left[\frac{A\rho}{\sigma^2}\right] e^{-(\rho^2 + A^2)/2\sigma^2} \tag{4-211}$$

This is often referred to as the *Rice* (Rician) or sometimes the *Nakagami-Rice* distribution and is shown in Fig. 4-8 for various values of the ratio $A^2/2\sigma^2$.

The modified Bessel function can be written as an infinite series,

$$I_0(z) = \sum_{n=0}^{\infty} \frac{z^{2n}}{2^{2n}(n!)^2} \tag{4-212}$$

For $z \ll 1$,

$$I_0(z) = 1 + \frac{z^2}{4} + \cdots \approx e^{z^2/4} \tag{4-213}$$

Thus, letting $A \to 0$ in (4-211), one finds the Rayleigh distribution again, as in the previous result for the zero-signal case.

Equation (4-211) contains the term $A^2/2\sigma^2$. Since σ^2 is the mean noise power and $A^2/2$ the mean signal power (in a 1 Ω resistor), $A^2/2\sigma^2$ is just the signal-to-noise power ratio (SNR). Calling this γ, we may write the probability distribution of the envelope of signal plus noise as

$$q_1(\rho) = \frac{\rho}{\sigma^2} I_0 \left[\frac{\rho\sqrt{2\gamma}}{\sigma} \right] e^{-\gamma - \rho^2/2\sigma^2} \quad , \quad \gamma = \frac{A^2}{2\sigma^2} \qquad (4\text{-}214)$$

We have indicated that for $\gamma \to 0$ this reduces to the Rayleigh distribution. For large γ, $(A \gg \sigma)$, one can use another known property of the modified Bessel function; for large values of the argument it approaches asymptotically an exponential function. Thus for $z \gg 1$,

$$I_0(z) \approx \frac{e^z}{\sqrt{2\pi z}} \qquad (4\text{-}215)$$

Letting $\rho\sqrt{2\gamma}/\sigma \gg 1$ (or $\rho A \gg \sigma^2$), we can make use of this property to put $q_1(\rho)$ in the form

$$q_1(\rho) = \sqrt{\frac{\rho}{2\pi A \sigma^2}} \; e^{-(\rho - A)^2/2\sigma^2} \qquad (4\text{-}216)$$

This function peaks sharply about the point $\rho = A$, dropping off rapidly as we move away from this point (see Fig. 4-8). Most of the contribution to the area under the $q_1(\rho)$ curve (or the largest values of the probability density of ρ) comes from points in the vicinity of $\rho = A$. In this range of ρ, then, we can let $\rho = A$ in the nonexponential (and slowly varying) portions of $q_1(\rho)$ and obtain the approximation

$$q_1(\rho) = \frac{1}{\sqrt{2\pi\sigma^2}} \; e^{-(\rho - A)^2/2\sigma^2} \quad , \quad \gamma \gg 1 \qquad (4\text{-}217)$$

Thus in the vicinity of the point $\rho = A$, which becomes essentially the mean value of the envelope ρ, the distribution approximates a Gaussian distribution. This is of course valid only for $A^2 \gg \sigma^2$ or $\gamma \gg 1$. Note that this Gaussian distribution has an average amplitude A and variance σ^2.

So far as the signal-plus-noise at the output is concerned, then, the nonlinear operation of an envelope detector has little effect on the form of the distribution, for large SNR. A similar result is found to hold true for other nonlinear demodulators.

Returning now to complete our statistical description, one can show the probability density function of the phase of the signal plus Gaussian noise to be

$$q_2(\phi) = \int_0^\infty q(\rho, \phi)\, d\rho$$

$$= \frac{1}{2\pi} e^{-A^2/2\sigma^2} + \frac{A \cos\phi}{2\sigma\sqrt{2\pi}} \left\{ 1 + \mathrm{erf}\left[\frac{A \cos\phi}{\sigma\sqrt{2}} \right] \right\} e^{-A^2 \sin^2\phi/2\sigma^2} \tag{4-218}$$

or, again using $\gamma = A^2/2\sigma^2$,

$$q_2(\phi) = \frac{1}{2\pi} e^{-\gamma} \left\{ 1 + \sqrt{\pi\gamma} \cos\phi [1 + \mathrm{erf}(\sqrt{\gamma} \cos\phi)] e^{\gamma \cos^2\phi} \right\} \tag{4-219}$$

Notice that for $\gamma = A = 0$, $q_2(\phi)$ reduces to $1/2\pi$, as the phase takes on the uniform distribution of random noise in the absence of signal. On the other hand, for large SNR and using the standard approximation

$$\mathrm{erf}(x) \approx 1 - \frac{e^{-x^2}}{x\sqrt{\pi}}, \quad x \gg 1 \tag{4-220}$$

the p.d.f. for the phase of signal plus Gaussian noise becomes

$$q_2(\phi) \approx \sqrt{\frac{\gamma}{\pi}} \cos\phi\, e^{-\gamma \sin^2\phi}, \quad \gamma \gg 1 \tag{4-221}$$

Because of the exponential factor in (4-221), this function drops away rapidly with ϕ, but for $\phi = 0$ it takes on the large value $\sqrt{\gamma/\pi}$.

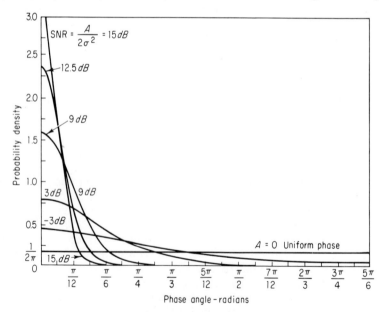

Fig. 4-9 Probability density function of phase for sine wave plus Gaussian noise.

Thus for large SNR the phase of signal plus noise concentrates in the vicinity of the signal's phase (zero in this case). This behavior is illustrated by the curves of Fig. 4-9.

REFERENCES

1. A. Papoulis, *Probability, Random Variables, and Stochastic Processes* (McGraw-Hill Book Company, New York, 1965).
2. W. B. Davenport, Jr. and W. L. Root, *Random Signals and Noise* (McGraw-Hill Book Company, New York, 1958).
3. J. M. Wozencraft and I. M. Jacobs, *Principles of Communication Engineering* (John Wiley and Sons, Inc., New York, 1965).

5

Amplitude (Linear) Modulation

The object of any communication system is to convey intelligence of some type from an information source to an intended distant user. When converted to simplest electrical form, the intelligence usually has a low-pass (audio or video) spectrum. However, to make efficient use of the available transmission media a narrow-band (bandpass) transmission at much higher frequencies is usually required. The process of transforming the intelligence into this form is termed *modulation*. Following the modulation process, the communication system transmitter provides the necessary power amplification and coupling to the medium. At the distant receiving terminal, after passing through the medium and possibly being corrupted by interference, the bandpass waveform is recovered from the medium. Implicit in all types of modulation is the subsequent ability to reverse or undo the modulation process (*demodulation*), to retrieve after demodulation a reasonable facsimile of the original information.

In addition to making possible utilization of favorable radio frequencies, modulation techniques can often be selected so as to minimize the effects of interference or other disturbances owing to changes in the medium. Even if all the above were not considered, one problem, selectivity, would still necessitate modulation. If information signals were transmitted directly, they would in general overlap one another in frequency, causing disturbances and creating confusion. There would be no means to separate the messages belonging to one information source from those of another whereas, through modulation, each source can be assigned to an individual frequency band and conveniently filtered out at the receiver.

All modulation techniques involve at least two quantities. One of these is the *modulating waveform* containing the message to be transmitted. The second quantity is the high-frequency *carrier* wave, which is *modulated* by an appropriate variation of one or more of its parameters. Most commonly, the carrier is a single frequency sinusoid. It can also be some other continuously generated function, even a noise waveform or a discrete time function composed of a sequence of pulses. In any case the modulating wave varies some characteristic of the carrier in a prescribed manner. For example, the modulating wave can vary the amplitude, frequency, or phase of a sinusoid, or the pulse amplitude, width, or position (timing) of a pulsed carrier. The first of these, amplitude modulation (AM) of a sinusoidal carrier, is the subject of the present chapter. Frequency and phase modulation (FM and PM) are discussed jointly in Chap. 6, and pulse modulation is considered in Chap. 7. As will become evident, amplitude modulation is characterized as a linear process which involves a simple frequency translation of the message spectrum to higher frequencies in the vicinity of the carrier. On the other hand, angle modulation (both frequency and phase) and pulse modulation are nonlinear techniques which, in addition to frequency translation, involve the generation of new frequencies.

5-1 Double-sideband (DSB) Modulation

Double-sideband (*DSB*) modulation is a straightforward multiplicative operation in which the modulating time function and carrier signal can be regarded as multiplied together. For a bandpass carrier this is usually accomplished in a device known as a *balanced modulator* (Refs. 1, 2, 3). This is a nonlinear device that provides multiplication of the message and carrier signals as one term resulting from the nonlinearity. It usually takes advantage of a symmetry condition of the device to balance or cancel out from the output a carrier frequency term that would otherwise appear in the same band as the product term. This operation is indicated in Fig. 5-1, where the carrier signal $c(t)$ is simply a sinusoid of frequency f_c. In principle the carrier signal could be any high-frequency wave, for example, a pulsed carrier or a bandpass noise process.

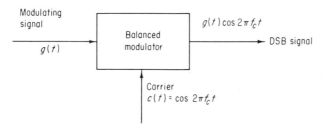

Fig. 5-1 Double-sideband modulation.

The message or modulating time function $g(t)$ is considered to be a band-limited signal whose spectrum is confined to some region $|f| \leq f_m$. Band-limited low-pass signals are sometimes termed *baseband* signals and the interval $0 \leq f \leq f_m$ is the baseband width, with f_m termed the highest modulation frequency. In analog modulation systems (for example, undigitized voice communications), $g(t)$ intentionally contains no zero-frequency component; that is, the average value of $g(t)$ is zero. Because of this fact and the cancellation property of the balanced modulator, a DSB signal contains no carrier frequency component in its spectrum. For this reason the DSB modulation process is more properly termed double-sideband suppressed-carrier (DSB-SC) modulation. However, for brevity and convenience we shall use throughout the notation DSB in place of DSB-SC to imply a double-sideband signal with no carrier component present.

For a given modulating function and sinusoidal carrier, the product

$$e_{\text{DSB}}(t) = g(t)c(t) = g(t)\cos 2\pi f_c t, \quad f_c \gg f_m \qquad (5\text{-}1)$$

represents a DSB signal. Thus, whereas $g(t)$ is a baseband signal, the DSB signal $e_{\text{DSB}}(t)$ is a bandpass waveform. (Recall earlier discussions of such signals.) Figure 5-2 illustrates a typical modulating waveform and the associated DSB signal. Note that the *envelope* of the DSB signal is not a true reproduction of the modulation $g(t)$, but instead follows $|g(t)|$. Thus envelope detection (to be discussed presently) of a DSB signal is not suitable for recovery of $g(t)$.

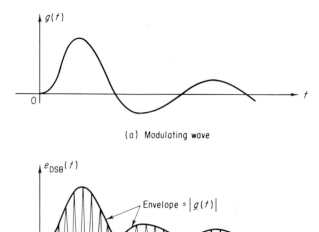

(a) Modulating wave

(b) Modulated carrier

Fig. 5-2 Baseband signal and double-sideband waveforms.

Since the spectrum of the product of any two time functions is the convolution of their spectra, the relationship

$$e_{\text{DSB}}(t) \Longleftrightarrow E_{\text{DSB}}(f) = G(f) \otimes C(f) \tag{5-2}$$

expresses the DSB spectrum in terms of the spectra

$$G(f) \Longleftrightarrow g(t), \quad C(f) \Longleftrightarrow c(t) \tag{5-3}$$

of the baseband and carrier signals. For a general, nonzero width carrier spectrum, the relation (5-2) indicates a spreading or smearing of the signal spectrum in addition to frequency translation. However, for the sinusoidal carrier case examined here, the carrier spectrum is just a pair of impulses at $\pm f_c$ and the DSB signal spectrum is therefore

$$E_{\text{DSB}}(f) = \frac{1}{2} G(f - f_c) + \frac{1}{2} G(f + f_c) \tag{5-4}$$

a simple frequency translation to the vicinity of the carrier. Figure 5-3 shows the magnitude spectrum of a baseband signal band-limited to $\pm f_m$ and the associated DSB spectrum. Note the presence

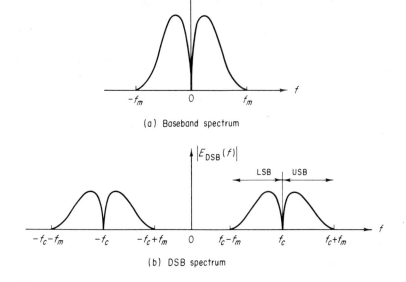

(a) Baseband spectrum

(b) DSB spectrum

Fig. 5-3 Spectra of double-sideband signals.

of both upper and lower *sideband* components around both $+f_c$ and $-f_c$. In fact these sidebands are complex conjugate mirror images of one another. Thus, the message is doubly contained in the spectrum of a DSB signal, since either sideband component contains the full description of the message. Figure 5-3 also shows clearly that a DSB signal requires a transmission bandwidth of $2f_m$ or twice the baseband width.

Demodulation or detection of a DSB signal involves essentially reinsertion of the missing carrier by a process known as *synchronous* or *coherent detection.* This involves multiplying the received signal $e_r(t)$ by a locally generated carrier signal $c_o(t)$, accurately controlled in frequency and phase, followed by low-pass filtering. As shown in **Fig. 5-4**, the multiplication operation is accomplished by a product detector, a nonlinear device similar to

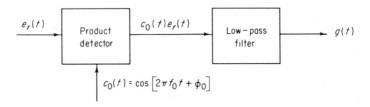

Fig. 5-4 Coherent detection.

a balanced modulator. The DSB signal arrives at the receiver with an unknown phase ϕ_c:

$$e_r(t) = g(t) \cos[2\pi f_c t + \phi_c] \qquad (5\text{-}5)$$

Assuming for the moment that both the frequency and phase of the local carrier may be different from those of the received carrier,

$$c_o(t) = \cos[2\pi f_o t + \phi_o] \qquad (5\text{-}6)$$

the output of the product detector will be given by

$$c_o(t)e_r(t) = g(t) \cos[2\pi f_o t + \phi_o] \cos[2\pi f_c t + \phi_c]$$

$$= \frac{1}{2} g(t) \left\{ \cos[2\pi (f_c - f_o)t + \phi_c - \phi_o] \right. \qquad (5\text{-}7)$$

$$\left. + \cos[2\pi (f_c + f_o)t + \phi_c + \phi_o] \right\}$$

When no frequency or phase error exists between the two carriers ($f_c = f_o$ and $\phi_c = \phi_o$), the output is

$$c_o(t)e_r(t) = \frac{1}{2} g(t) + \frac{1}{2} g(t) \cos[4\pi f_c t + 2\phi_c] \qquad (5\text{-}8)$$

In this case, low-pass filtering (of frequencies out to f_m or beyond but cutting off well below f_c) then recovers the baseband signal and rejects the spurious term generated at twice the carrier frequency.

In terms of spectral analysis, (5-8) is equivalent to the relationship

$$c_0(t)e_r(t) \iff \frac{1}{2}\left[e^{j\phi_c}G(f - f_c) + e^{j\phi_c}G(f + f_c)\right]$$

$$\otimes \frac{1}{2}\left[e^{j\phi_c}\delta(f - f_c) + e^{-j\phi_c}\delta(f + f_c)\right]$$

$$= \frac{1}{2}G(f) + \frac{1}{4}\left[e^{j2\phi_c}G(f - 2f_c) + e^{-j2\phi_c}G(f + 2f_c)\right] \qquad (5\text{-}9)$$

The first term here is the desired result, obtainable by low-pass filtering. For this term it is seen that multiplying the received DSB signal by a frequency- and phase-synchronzied local carrier has the effect of translating the signal spectrum back down to its original location on the frequency axis, where the upper and lower sidebands coherently combine.

If only a phase error exists between the two carriers ($f_c = f_o$, $\phi_c \neq \phi_o$), the final output of a coherent detector is given by

$$\frac{1}{2}g(t)\cos(\phi_c - \phi_o) \qquad (5\text{-}10)$$

In this case the message is recovered undistorted but reduced in magnitude by the cosine of the phase error (difference). Maximum signal amplitude occurs for zero phase error and complete loss of the message results from a phase error of $\pi/2$. Of course for optimum performance *both* the local carrier frequency and phase must be identical to the received (missing) carrier frequency and phase. Thus in DSB detection there exists a stringent requirement for accurate frequency and phase synchronization of a local oscillator to hold frequency and phase errors to tolerable levels. In practice this is often accomplished either by use of various forms of automatic frequency/phase controlled loops (AF/PC) that automatically lock the local oscillator in frequency and phase to a received vestige of the carrier, or else by use of a nonlinear circuit to regenerate the carrier term from the received DSB signal. Some DSB systems transmit a greatly reduced (vestigial) pilot carrier or pilot tone for this purpose. In any case DSB receivers tend to be somewhat sophisticated, and in some instances coherent detection is not feasible because of insufficiently stable carrier frequency and phase information owing to, perhaps, an unstable medium.

5-2 Conventional Amplitude Modulation (AM)

In conventional amplitude modulation the instantaneous carrier envelope varies about a mean value in a manner linearly related to the modulating wave. The distinguishing feature of AM is that the modulated *carrier envelope* is a true reproduction of the modulating wave. Conceptually, AM waves can be generated by adding a constant or average value to the modulating wave and multiplying the sum with a sinusoidal carrier. The resulting AM wave is

$$e_{AM}(t) = [1 + g(t)] \cos 2\pi f_c t \qquad (5\text{-}11)$$

This has the form of the linear sum of a DSB signal and a phase-coherent unmodulated carrier.

Usually an AM wave is written as

$$e_{AM}(t) = [1 + m_a g(t)] \cos 2\pi f_c t \qquad (5\text{-}12)$$

where m_a is termed the *modulation index* and both m_a and the modulating function $g(t)$ are constrained such that*

$$|g(t_{max})| \le 1, \quad 0 < m_a < 1 \qquad (5\text{-}13)$$

As previously, $g(t)$ is spectrally confined to the region $|f| \le f_m$ with $f_m \ll f_c$ and $g(t)$ contains no average value of its own. The modulation index m_a measures the *degree* of modulation and is often stated as $100 m_a$ %, the percentage modulation. Figure 5-5 illustrates how the modulated carrier envelope follows the modulation. Note that to transmit the same information (with the same power in the information carrying sidebands), the envelope of an AM signal is larger than that of a corresponding DSB signal; therefore AM requires larger peak powers than DSB.

The frequency spectrum of the AM signal is the Fourier transform of (5-12). For a given baseband spectrum, $G(f) \Longleftrightarrow g(t)$, the AM signal spectrum $E_{AM}(f)$ is obtained from the relationship

$$e_{AM}(t) \Longleftrightarrow E_{AM}(f) = [\delta(f) + m_a G(f)] \otimes \frac{1}{2}[\delta(f - f_c) + \delta(f + f_c)]$$

$$= \underbrace{\frac{1}{2}[\delta(f - f_c) + \delta(f + f_c)]}_{\text{carrier}} + \underbrace{\frac{m_a}{2}[G(f - f_c) + G(f + f_c)]}_{\text{sidebands}}$$

$$(5\text{-}14)$$

This is shown in Fig. 5-6. The AM signal spectrum contains a carrier component in addition to frequency translation of the baseband spectrum to the vicinity of the carrier. The latter appears in

*If the conditions of (5-13) are violated, one has *overmodulation*, in which distortion occurs since the carrier *envelope* cannot take on a negative value.

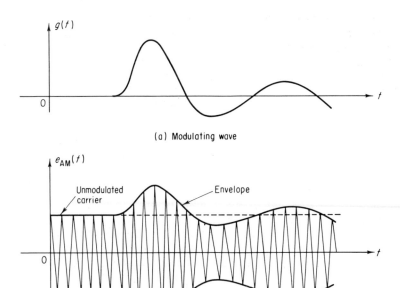

(a) Modulating wave

(b) Modulated carrier

Fig. 5-5 Baseband and amplitude modulated waveforms.

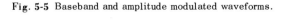

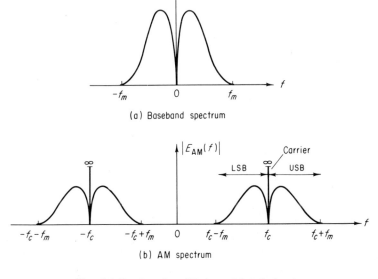

(a) Baseband spectrum

(b) AM spectrum

Fig. 5-6 Spectra of amplitude modulated signals.

the form of upper and lower sideband components that are complex conjugate mirror images of one another. The AM signal requires a transmission bandwidth of $2f_m$, the same as a DSB signal modulated by the same $g(t)$.

For the case of sinusoidal modulation, $g(t) = \cos 2\pi f_m t$, the AM signal is

$$e_{AM}(t) = A_c(1 + m_a \cos 2\pi f_m t) \cos 2\pi f_c t$$

$$= A_c \cos 2\pi f_c t + \frac{m_a A_c}{2}[\cos 2\pi(f_c + f_m)t + \cos 2\pi(f_c - f_m)t]$$

$$(5\text{-}15)$$

Thus it can be expressed as a sum of sinusoids where A_c is the unmodulated carrier amplitude. Equation (5-15) illustrates decomposition of the AM wave into a carrier term and upper and lower sideband terms at the frequencies $f_c \pm f_m$. The extension to a modulating wave composed of several sinusoids is obvious. The frequency spectrum

$$E_{AM}(f) = \frac{A_c}{2}[\delta(f - f_c) + \delta(f + f_c)]$$

$$+ \frac{m_a A_c}{4}[\delta(f - f_c - f_m) + \delta(f + f_c + f_m) + \delta(f - f_c + f_m) + \delta(f + f_c - f_m)]$$

$$(5\text{-}16)$$

of the sinusoidally modulated AM wave is shown in Fig. 5-7. Again, the modulation process involves a simple frequency translation plus the inclusion of a carrier component.

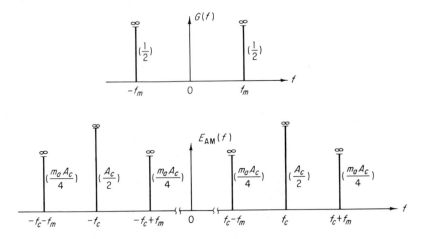

Fig. 5-7 Spectrum of sinusoidally modulated AM wave.

A study of the power relationships implied by (5-15) is of importance in evaluating the modulation technique. Assuming each component of the modulated wave is the voltage across a 1 Ω resistor, we have an average power in the carrier of

$$P_C = A_c^2/2 \qquad (5\text{-}17)$$

and in each sideband an average power of

$$P_{USB} = P_{LSB} = \frac{m_a^2 A_c^2}{8} \qquad (5\text{-}18)$$

Thus the total average sideband power is

$$P_{SB} = P_{USB} + P_{LSB} = \frac{m_a^2 A_c^2}{4} \qquad (5\text{-}19)$$

In order to maximize the power in the information bearing portion of the signal, namely, the sidebands, set m_a to unity, its highest permissible value. In this case

$$P_{SB} = \frac{A_c^2}{4} = \frac{1}{2} P_C \qquad (5\text{-}20)$$

so that the maximum possible total sideband power is one-half the carrier power. Thus, at best, only one-third of the total available power is utilized in the information-carrying sideband, the remainder representing carrier power. Recall that in DSB there is no transmitted unmodulated carrier component, so that power utilization can be regarded as three times as efficient as in AM. However, as we shall see, the presence of a carrier in AM does simplify the receiver implementation.

In principle, AM signals can be demodulated by coherent detection; however, this technique does not take advantage of the carrier component present in AM. The most common method of AM demodulation, known as envelope detection, is illustrated in Fig. 5-8. The received AM wave is passed through a diode, which eliminates the negative portions of the wave, converting it to a positive function with a nonzero average value. Since the message is contained in the low-frequency variations (i.e., the envelope) of this average about some nominal value, low-pass filtering recovers the modulation by separating out the envelope from the high-frequency components. Note that if the envelope of the received wave is not a true reproduction of the modulation, envelope detection produces a distorted message. For this reason, as noted earlier, the largest tolerable modulation index m_a in AM is unity or 100% modulation, sometimes termed *full modulation*. In *overmodulation* the modulation index exceeds unity $(m_a > 1)$, and the envelope of the AM wave is a distorted version of the modulation.

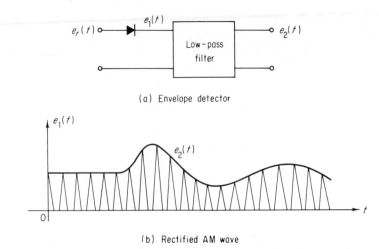

(a) Envelope detector

(b) Rectified AM wave

Fig. 5-8 Envelope detection of AM waves.

Obviously envelope detection of AM signals leads to much simpler receiver configurations than does coherent detection of DSB signals. This is due solely to the inclusion of the carrier component in AM. However, the price of the receiver simplification is a loss of two-thirds or more of the total available power to supply the carrier. AM also requires larger peak powers than does DSB.

5-3 Single-sideband (SSB) Modulation

Although DSB modulation reduces the required transmitter power, it still requires the same transmission bandwidth as ordinary AM and transmits both sidebands, either one of which fully describes the information. If the required transmission bandwidth can be compressed further, more information channels can be placed in a given frequency band. This capability exists in a modified AM technique that halves the transmission bandwidth by eliminating the carrier and one sideband. This modulation process is known as *single-sideband suppressed-carrier (SSB-SC)* transmission or simply *single-sideband (SSB)*. In SSB systems all the available power is allotted to the information and this is transmitted in the minimum bandwidth possible. Thus SSB systems provide good economy of both transmitted power and utilization of frequency space. SSB is theoretically feasible because the message is separately contained in the upper and lower sidebands of AM and DSB waves and hence only one sideband is necessary to convey the information.

Several methods are available for the generation of SSB signals, but probably the most commonly used technique is to first form a

DSB signal with a balanced modulator and then to reject one sideband by filtering. This technique is illustrated in Fig. 5-9. The "tight" requirements of such sideband filters dictate that specially designed filters be used. In fact because of this rather difficult filter requirement other techniques have been developed (Refs. 1, 2, 3) for the generation of SSB signals. These alternate SSB techniques all involve generation of two DSB signals using carriers in 90°-phase quadrature and use of phasing arrangements such that upon recombination of the two DSB signals the unwanted sideband is balanced out. However, the degree to which the undesired sideband may be suppressed depends upon very careful control of amplitudes and phases and requires accurate balancing. All these SSB phasing methods of generation involve more sophistication than that required of either AM or DSB systems. We will not further discuss these alternate generating techniques here.

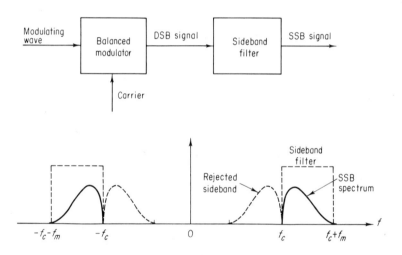

Fig. 5-9 Generation of single-sideband wave.

Except for trivial cases, such as sinusoidal modulation, time representations of SSB signals are not simple. Perhaps the most useful method for representing SSB involves the concept of the *analytic signal* and the use of *Hilbert transforms* (Refs. 1, 3). This involves a form of representation applicable to any signals and closely related to the complex envelope notation introduced in Chap. 3. However, since our later purposes are well served by the complex envelope notation and lucid discussions of the analytic signal method are readily available in the literature, we will not dwell further on this subject.

Reception of SSB signals usually involves filtering and product detection. A predetector bandpass filter is employed whose bandwidth equals the modulation bandwidth. Otherwise, SSB demodulation is quite similar to DSB detection in that the received signal is multiplied in a product detector by a *locally generated carrier*, which provides frequency translation down to baseband. Low-pass filtering then removes the undesired double-frequency term. However, in SSB systems the local oscillator frequency and phase may not have to be so accurately controlled as in DSB transmission. It has been subjectively judged in voice SSB systems that up to 20 or 30 Hz variation between local and received carrier frequencies does not cause too objectionable an amount of distortion. However, if the modulating waveform must be preserved, then true coherent detection is required with accurate control of local oscillator frequency *and* phase necessary. In this case, some SSB systems transmit an appreciably reduced vestigial carrier or pilot tone to facilitate proper frequency and phase control at the receiver. Carrier information is obtained then by placing a very sharply tuned filter at the carrier frequency to recover the almost missing carrier wave. The recovered carrier is then greatly amplified and used either directly as the local carrier or indirectly to synchronize the local oscillator.

Since SSB combines the two advantages of lower transmitted power and less bandwidth, one may ask why it is not used more extensively. The reasons are equipment complexity and cost of both the transmitter and receiver, and problems of equipment changeover (compatibility) that prevent its widespread introduction into existing services. Particularly, because generation of SSB signals necessarily occurs at low power levels, the SSB transmitter requires a *linear* power amplifier (which is inherently inefficient) to prevent distortion of the transmission. In contrast convenient methods exist for generating AM and DSB signals *directly* at high power levels and therefore these systems may employ more efficient nonlinear power amplifiers. Also it can be shown that for complex modulating signals, SSB tends to involve a much higher ratio of peak-to-average power than either DSB or AM. Then too, the availability of a carrier in conventional AM greatly simplifies receiver requirements with consequential good realiability. However, SSB is widely employed in frequency division multiplexing systems. It has also found other recent usage in the crowded h.f. and v.h.f. bands because of its property of spectrum conservation.

5-4 Signal-to-noise Ratios in AM Systems

There exist many criteria by which one can judge the performance of communication systems. Of particular interest is performance in additive Gaussian noise. The most commonly used criterion is the ratio of average signal power to average noise power, both measured at the same point in the system. This is called the *signal-to-noise power ratio (SNR)*. In this section we compute the SNR's prior to and following detection for the various systems described above and show the relationship between these ratios. For simplicity we assume single-frequency sinusoidal modulation in each case.

DSB Transmission

Following initial frequency selection and amplification in the receiver, one has a waveform

$$e_r(t) = A_c \cos 2\pi f_m t \cos 2\pi f_c t + n(t) \qquad (5\text{-}21)$$

which consists of a DSB signal of carrier amplitude A_c and an additive narrow-band Gaussian noise process $n(t)$. The latter originates either externally or in the initial stages of the receiver. The appropriate SNR for $e_r(t)$ is obtained by forming the mean-square value, av $e_r^2(t)$. This average is interpreted as involving a combination of statistical averaging and a time averaging of the form $(1/T) \int_0^T dt$. The deterministic (nonrandom) components of $e_r^2(t)$ are not affected by statistical averaging and similarly, since the noise is statistically stationary, time averaging has no effect on averages of random components. Therefore, since also both the DSB signal and noise are zero-mean,

$$\text{av} e_r^2(t) = \frac{1}{T} \int_0^T A_c^2 \cos^2 2\pi f_m t \cos^2 2\pi f_c t \, dt + \overline{n^2(t)} = \frac{A_c^2}{4} + N \qquad (5\text{-}22)$$

where N is the average noise power. The noise is assumed to be band-limited to the bandwidth $2f_m$ of the DSB signal. For white noise with double-sided spectral density $n_0/2$, $N = 2n_0 f_m$. Thus the predetection SNR of the DSB system is given by

$$\left(\frac{S}{N}\right)_{i(\text{DSB})} = \frac{A_c^2}{4N} \qquad (5\text{-}23)$$

Since the coherent detection process involves multiplying the received signal by a frequency and phase synchronized local carrier, it is instructive to express the noise process $n(t)$ in terms of quadrature "modulated" components (Chap. 4).

$$n(t) = x(t) \cos 2\pi f_c t - y(t) \sin 2\pi f_c t \qquad (5\text{-}24)$$

The Gaussian variables $x(t)$ and $y(t)$ are slowly varying random functions relative to f_c and are confined to the baseband $|f| \leq f_m$.

Furthermore, recall

$$\overline{x^2(t)} = \overline{y^2(t)} = \overline{n^2(t)} = N \tag{5-25}$$

As in Fig. 5-4, the output of the product detector is then

$$c_o(t)e_r(t) = A_c \cos 2\pi f_m t \cos^2 2\pi f_c t + x(t) \cos^2 2\pi f_c t$$
$$- y(t) \sin 2\pi f_c t \cos 2\pi f_c t \tag{5-26}$$

The final output following low-pass filtering is then (to within an unimportant factor of 1/2 which equally applies to signal and noise)

$$e_o(t) = A_c \cos 2\pi f_m t + x(t) \tag{5-27}$$

Note that the modulation has been recovered and the *out-of-phase noise component rejected by coherent detection.* Forming the mean-square of (5-27),

$$\text{av } e_o^2(t) = \frac{A_c^2}{2} + N \tag{5-28}$$

the postdetection SNR is then

$$\left(\frac{S}{N}\right)_{o(\text{DSB})} = \frac{A_c^2}{2N} \tag{5-29}$$

or in terms of $(S/N)_i$ the output SNR is

$$\left(\frac{S}{N}\right)_{o(\text{DSB})} = 2\left(\frac{S}{N}\right)_{i(\text{DSB})} \tag{5-30}$$

Thus coherent detection provides a 3-dB *detection gain* in DSB demodulation. This effect may be explained either by rejection of one of the noise components or by coherent addition in voltage of the DSB signal sidebands, whereas the sidebands of the noise combine noncoherently (add in power). That is, a factor of 4 times the power of one set of signal sidebands results for the recovered signal while a factor of 2 results for power addition of the noise sidebands.

Another important effect may be observed from these results. The output SNR is *always* proportional to the input SNR even under poor receiving conditions (low-input SNR's). That is, there is no threshold effect below which system performance degrades rapidly with reduction in received SNR. This property of DSB systems is due primarily to the *linear* processing of coherent detection. As we shall see presently, other detection techniques that employ nonlinear processing do experience such a threshold effect.

Conventional AM Transmission

In an AM system operating under the same conditions as above, the received signal is

$$e_r(t) = A_c[1 + m_a \cos 2\pi f_m t] \cos 2\pi f_c t + n(t) \tag{5-31}$$

where, for the analysis, $n(t)$ is more conveniently written in terms of its envelope and phase,

$$n(t) = \rho(t) \cos[2\pi f_c t + \theta(t)] \tag{5-32}$$

The predetection SNR is obtained from the mean-square value

$$\text{av } e_r^2(t) = \frac{1}{T}\int_0^T A_c^2[1 + m_a \cos 2\pi f_m t]^2 \cos^2 2\pi f_c t\, dt + \overline{n^2(t)} \tag{5-33}$$

$$= \frac{A_c^2}{2}\left(1 + m_a^2/2\right) + N$$

However, since the carrier power is *not* considered part of the signal (sideband) power,* we have

$$\left(\frac{S}{N}\right)_{i(\text{AM})} = \frac{m_a^2 A_c^2}{4N} \tag{5-34}$$

The output of an envelope detector operating on $e_r(t)$ generates the envelope

$$e_o(t) = \sqrt{A_c^2[1 + m_a \cos 2\pi f_m t]^2 + \rho^2(t) + 2A_c[1 + m_a \cos 2\pi f_m t]\rho(t)\cos\theta(t)} \tag{5-35}$$

In general, analysis of this function so as to separate it into appropriate signal and noise fluctuation components and thereby compute a corresponding SNR is a somewhat difficult chore. However, in the case of large carrier-to-noise ratios, $A_c^2/2N \gg 1$, $e_o(t)$ can be approximated by

$$e_o(t) \approx A_c[1 + m_a \cos 2\pi f_m t] + \rho(t)\cos\theta(t) \tag{5-36}$$

with mean-square value

$$\text{av } e_o^2(t) = A_c^2\left(1 + m_a^2/2\right) + N \tag{5-37}$$

where

$$N = \frac{1}{2}\overline{\rho^2(t)} = \overline{n^2(t)} \tag{5-38}$$

---

*Note that the carrier-to-noise power ratio is $(C/N)_i = A_c^2/2N$.

Dropping the constant term in (5-37) owing to the carrier, the postdetection SNR is

$$\left(\frac{S}{N}\right)_{o(AM)} = \frac{m_a^2 A_c^2}{2N} = 2\left(\frac{S}{N}\right)_i \qquad (5\text{-}39)$$

Thus, for large carrier-to-noise ratios an AM system experiences a factor of 2 improvement in detection gain, the same as a DSB system. That is, under good reception conditions an envelope detector performs as well as a coherent detector. Note that this result neglects the power wasted by the carrier. In terms of the carrier-to-noise power ratio, $(S/N)_{o(AM)}$ may be expressed in the often stated form

$$\left(\frac{S}{N}\right)_{o(AM)} = m_a^2 \left(\frac{C}{N}\right)_i \qquad (5\text{-}40)$$

Under adverse reception conditions resulting in small $(C/N)_i$, the envelope $e_o(t)$ may be approximated by

$$e_o(t) \approx \rho(t) + A_c[1 + m_a \cos 2\pi f_m t] \cos\theta(t) \qquad (5\text{-}41)$$

In this case the modulation function is multiplied by the random function $\cos\theta(t)$ as well as immersed in the Rayleigh variable $\rho(t)$. Consequently the desired signal may be lost in the noise below some critical value of $(C/N)_i$ and performance degrades rapidly below this point. This property of envelope detection is an example of the threshold effect mentioned earlier, a condition not experienced in DSB systems but common to all systems which employ nonlinear detection techniques. When coherent detection of AM is employed, this threshold condition is avoided.

As noted above, AM and DSB system performance is identical under good reception conditions for the AM system and equal sideband powers for both systems. However, taking into account the carrier and equating the total average transmitted powers, the postdetection SNR's differ at least by a factor of 3; that is,

$$\frac{(S/N)_{o(DSB)}}{(S/N)_{o(AM)}} \geq 3 \qquad (5\text{-}41)$$

with equality applying for 100% AM modulation. The factor of 3 arises from the property of AM that at most only one-third the total available power is alloted to the sidebands, the remainder appearing as carrier power. In this respect, DSB transmission has about a 5 dB advantage over AM transmission.

SSB Transmission

Since the process of SSB detection is a straightforward frequency translation from r.f. to baseband, all of the signal and noise components are transferred unmodified to low frequencies. Therefore the relationship between signal and noise remains unchanged by SSB detection and the pre- and postdetector SNR's are equal, i.e.,

$$\left(\frac{S}{N}\right)_{o(\text{SSB})} = \left(\frac{S}{N}\right)_{i(\text{SSB})} \tag{5-42}$$

Thus there is no detection gain in SSB such as we observed in DSB and AM operating under good conditions, where $(S/N)_o = 2(S/N)_i$. However, since the bandwidth of SSB signals is one-half that of DSB and AM signals, the noise power admitted by the SSB predetector filter is one-half that of DSB and AM systems. Consequently, for the same total average transmitted signal power the ratio $(S/N)_i$ in SSB systems is a factor of 2 larger than in these other systems, and therefore

$$\left(\frac{S}{N}\right)_{o(\text{SSB})} = \left(\frac{S}{N}\right)_{o(\text{DSB or AM})} \tag{5-43}$$

REFERENCES

1. P. F. Panter, *Modulation, Noise, and Spectral Analysis* (McGraw-Hill Book Company, New York, 1965).
2. M. Schwartz, *Information Transmission, Modulation, and Noise* (McGraw-Hill Book Company, New York, 1959).
3. M. Schwartz, W. R. Bennett, and S. Stein, *Communication Systems and Techniques* (McGraw-Hill Book Company, New York, 1966).

6

Angle (Nonlinear) Modulation

Angle modulation is a general term applied to both frequency modulation (FM) and phase modulation (PM), which are closely related techniques. FM conveys the information as variations of the carrier frequency, whereas for PM the modulating wave directly varies the carrier's phase. In Chap. 5 amplitude modulation was characterized as essentially a *linear* process in which no new frequencies are created aside from frequency translation of the modulation spectrum to the vicinity of the carrier. Angle modulation also involves frequency translation, but in contrast to AM, this modulation technique transforms the message spectrum into an entirely new set of related frequency components. Generally the transmitted FM or PM spectrum is broader than the original baseband spectrum. This property of angle modulation of generating new frequency components, is characteristic of all forms of *nonlinear* processing.

Angle modulation often finds application where high fidelity or accuracy of message waveform reproduction is required, because these systems more successfully overcome noise disturbances and other forms of interference than do AM systems. It is well known, for example, that an FM system has noise-suppression properties such that large improvements in SNR are realized in detection. However, a price is paid for this advantage, part of which lies in increased bandwidth requirements. FM is probably the most common example of communication systems that exchange bandwidth or spectral occupancy for improved SNR performance. But, as with the other *bandwidth-exchange* systems, the SNR improvement is realized only for received SNR's above a certain critical threshold range. Below the threshold region, the FM output SNR decreases rapidly with received SNR until eventually FM is at a disadvantage compared to linear systems such as SSB-AM. Extending the FM improvement by using wider bandwidths usually involves a higher threshold. However, several methods have been suggested for extending the range of FM improvement without changing the threshold region. These topics are mentioned briefly following a discussion of conventional FM and PM systems.

6-1 Frequency and Phase Modulated Waves
(Refs. 1, 2, 3)

Consider an unmodulated carrier wave of unit amplitude expressed conveniently in the form

$$c(t) = \cos \psi(t) \qquad (6\text{-}1)$$

In the absence of any angle modulation, the carrier "angle" $\psi(t)$ has the linear form

$$\psi(t) = 2\pi f_c t + \psi_c \qquad (6\text{-}2)$$

where f_c and ψ_c are, respectively, the carrier frequency and a phase constant. By angle modulation is meant a form for the angle function,

$$\psi(t) = 2\pi f_c t + g(t) + \psi_c \qquad (6\text{-}3)$$

where the time-variable phase function $g(t)$ conveys the message. Thus a general angle modulated wave, with the convenient choice of time reference such that $\psi_c = 0$, may be expressed as

$$e(t) = \cos[2\pi f_c t + g(t)] \qquad (6\text{-}4)$$

As mentioned previously, for PM the modulation directly varies the carrier phase. That is, to form a PM wave, $g(t)$ is made proportional to the modulating wave $m(t)$,

$$g(t) = k_p m(t), \quad \text{for PM} \qquad (6\text{-}5)$$

A PM wave is then of the form

$$e_{\text{PM}}(t) = \cos[2\pi f_c t + k_p m(t)] \qquad (6\text{-}6)$$

with k_p a constant of the system.

A very useful tool for the study of angle modulation and FM in particular is the concept of *instantaneous frequency* $f_i(t)$, defined as

$$f_i(t) = \frac{1}{2\pi} \frac{d\psi(t)}{dt}, \quad \psi(t) = 2\pi \int_{-\infty}^{t} f_i(t)\, dt \qquad (6\text{-}7)$$

This relation is consistent with the usual definition of frequency, since for time invariant frequency and phase as in (6-2), $f_i(t) = f_c$. For FM the modulation is made to cause proportional variations of the instantaneous frequency about the carrier frequency. With $m(t)$ the modulation $f_i(t)$ has the form

$$f_i(t) = f_c + \frac{k_f}{2\pi} m(t), \quad \text{for FM} \qquad (6\text{-}8)$$

In the FM case, the time-varying phase function $g(t)$ is then the integral of the modulating wave

$$g(t) = k_f \int_{-\infty}^{t} m(t)\,dt \,, \quad \text{for FM} \tag{6-9}$$

with k_f a system constant. Thus the form

$$e_{\text{FM}}(t) = \cos\left[2\pi f_c t + k_f \int_{-\infty}^{t} m(t)\,dt\right] \tag{6-10}$$

expresses an FM wave directly in terms of the modulation.

Comparing conventional AM and FM modulation waveshapes, as in Fig. 6-1, points up immediately the significant qualitative differences between the two techniques.

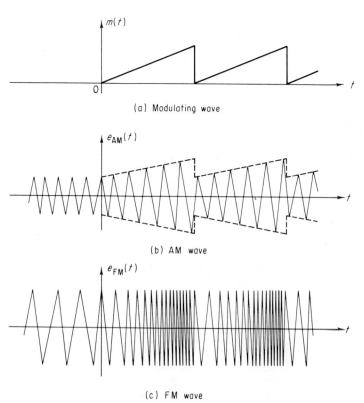

(a) Modulating wave

(b) AM wave

(c) FM wave

Fig. 6-1 Comparison of AM and FM waveforms.

At this point a few quantities are defined which will be useful in the discussions to follow. An angle modulated wave of carrier amplitude A_c is generally written as

$$e(t) = A_c \cos[2\pi f_c t + \beta g_n(t)] \tag{6-11}$$

where $g_n(t)$ represents a time-varying phase function normalized to unit peak amplitude; that is,

$$g_n(t) = \frac{g(t)}{|g(t_{max})|}, \quad |g_n(t)| \leq 1 \tag{6-12}$$

The constant β in (6-11), often termed the *modulation index*, corresponds to the maximum phase deviation of the carrier.

$$\beta = |g(t_{max})| \tag{6-13}$$

For a PM wave,

$$\beta = k_p |m(t_{max})|, \quad \text{for PM} \tag{6-14}$$

where $m(t_{max})$ is the peak value of the modulating wave. Another interpretation of β is given subsequently for an FM wave.

Often we are interested in the instantaneous frequency deviation from the carrier frequency, i.e., the difference

$$f_i(t) - f_c = \frac{\beta}{2\pi} g_n'(t) = \Delta F \, h_n(t) \tag{6-15}$$

where $g_n'(t) = dg_n/dt$. For a general angle modulated wave the quantities ΔF and $h_n(t)$ in (6-15) are given by*

$$\Delta F = \frac{1}{2\pi} |g'(t_{max})| \tag{6-16}$$

and

$$h_n(t) = \frac{g'(t)}{|g'(t_{max})|}, \quad |h_n(t)| \leq 1 \tag{6-17}$$

Here $h_n(t)$ represents the normalized *instantaneous* frequency deviation from f_c and ΔF is termed the *peak frequency deviation* of the carrier. For an FM wave as in (6-10)

$$\Delta F = \frac{k_f}{2\pi} |m(t_{max})|, \quad \text{for FM} \tag{6-18}$$

and

$$h_n(t) = \frac{m(t)}{|m(t_{max})|}, \quad \text{for FM} \tag{6-19}$$

---

*Note that the value t_{max} that maximizes $g'(t)$ is not the same value that maximizes $g(t)$.

Since the parameter ΔF is indicative of the maximum instantaneous excursion of frequency from the original carrier frequency, it is reasonable to expect that the required transmission bandwidth will depend on ΔF; such is the case. The transmission bandwidth is a function of the modulation index β as well.

Consider now a special example of an FM wave in which the modulation is a single-frequency tone:

$$m(t) = A_m \cos 2\pi f_m t \qquad (6\text{-}20)$$

Using (6-18) and (6-19), we find the peak and normalized instantaneous frequency deviations from f_c to be given by

$$\Delta F = \frac{k_f A_m}{2\pi} \qquad (6\text{-}21)$$

and

$$h_n(t) = \cos 2\pi f_m t \qquad (6\text{-}22)$$

or, combining these,

$$f_i(t) - f_c = \Delta F \cos 2\pi f_m t \qquad (6\text{-}23)$$

The FM wave modulated with this particular $m(t)$ appears as

$$e_{FM}(t) = A_c \cos\left[2\pi f_c t + k_f A_m \int_{-\infty}^{t} \cos 2\pi f_m t\, dt\right]$$

$$= A_c \cos[2\pi f_c t + \beta \sin 2\pi f_m t] \qquad (6\text{-}24)$$

where the modulation index β is given by

$$\beta = \frac{k_f A_m}{2\pi f_m} = \frac{\Delta F}{f_m} \qquad (6\text{-}25)$$

Thus we have arrived at an alternate definition for the modulation index in FM: For sinusoidal modulation, β is the ratio of the maximum frequency deviation from the carrier to the modulating frequency. In this context, β is then often also termed the *peak frequency deviation ratio* or simply the *deviation ratio*.

Aside from these definitions, note that the average signal power in an angle modulated wave is independent of the modulating signal, as contrasted with amplitude modulation. In fact for both PM and FM the average power depends solely on the carrier amplitude and therefore is fixed, since this amplitude is not varied in the modulation process. Obviously the average signal power is then the constant value $A_c^2/2$. Likewise the peak-to-average power ratio is also fixed. This aspect of angle modulation has important practical implications, since it permits very efficient operation of PM and FM transmitters with power amplifiers having nonlinear input-output characteristics and without fear of distortion owing to overloads.

6-2 Narrow-band FM

At this point we examine a narrow-band FM signal as a prelude to discussion of the more important wide-band FM application. To this end, consider the FM wave

$$e_{\mathrm{FM}}(t) = \cos[2\pi f_c t + \beta g_n(t)] \qquad (6\text{-}26)$$

which after a simple expansion can be written as

$$e_{\mathrm{FM}}(t) = \cos 2\pi f_c t \, \cos[\beta g_n(t)] - \sin 2\pi f_c t \, \sin[\beta g_n(t)] \qquad (6\text{-}27)$$

The narrow-band assumption is equivalent to constraining the modulation index β to small values or $\beta \ll 1$. For this case, using the small angle approximations for trigonometric functions, we can then write

$$\cos[\beta g_n(t)] \approx 1 \qquad (6\text{-}28a)$$

and

$$\sin[\beta g_n(t)] \approx \beta g_n(t) \qquad (6\text{-}28b)$$

Thus for a very small modulation index the narrow-band FM wave can be written approximately as

$$e_{\mathrm{FM}}(t) \approx \cos 2\pi f_c t - \beta g_n(t) \sin 2\pi f_c t \qquad (6\text{-}29)$$

The frequency spectrum of this wave is given by

$$E_{\mathrm{FM}}(f) = \frac{1}{2}[\delta(f - f_c) + \delta(f + f_c)] + \frac{j\beta}{2}[G_n(f - f_c) - G_n(f + f_c)] \qquad (6\text{-}30)$$

where $G_n(f) \Longleftrightarrow g_n(t)$. Note that (6-30) includes both carrier and sideband terms.

Notice the similarity of form of narrow-band FM and conventional AM signals. For a modulating wave $m(t) \Longleftrightarrow M(f)$ and modulation index m_a, the AM wave is

$$e_{\mathrm{AM}}(t) = \cos 2\pi f_c t + m_a m(t) \cos 2\pi f_c t \qquad (6\text{-}31)$$

with the spectrum

$$E_{\mathrm{AM}}(f) = \frac{1}{2}[\delta(f - f_c) + \delta(f + f_c)] + \frac{m_a}{2}[M(f - f_c) + M(f + f_c)] \qquad (6\text{-}32)$$

For comparison the spectrum of the narrow-band FM wave (6-29) modulated by the same $m(t)$ is

$$E_{FM}(f) = \frac{1}{2}[\delta(f - f_c) + \delta(f + f_c)] + \frac{k_f}{4\pi}\left[\frac{M(f - f_c)}{f - f_c} - \frac{M(f + f_c)}{f + f_c}\right] \quad (6\text{-}33)$$

where

$$\beta g_n'(t) = k_f m(t) \quad (6\text{-}34)$$

Study of these two spectra reveals that, aside from a distortion factor, the major difference is a 180°-phase shift of the lower sideband of the FM wave.

Perhaps this effect may be pointed up more clearly by examination with a particular modulating wave. For example, consider the cosine wave of (6-20) leading to the FM wave (6-24). Again for $\beta \ll 1$ and for convenience setting $A_c = A_m = 1$, we write

$$e_{FM}(t) \approx \cos 2\pi f_c t - \beta \sin 2\pi f_m t \sin 2\pi f_c t \quad (6\text{-}35)$$

corresponding to (6-29) or after further expansion

$$e_{FM}(t) = \cos 2\pi f_c t - \frac{\beta}{2}[\cos 2\pi(f_c - f_m)t - \cos 2\pi(f_c + f_m)t] \quad (6\text{-}36)$$

Similarly, corresponding to (6-31) the AM wave for the same $m(t)$ is

$$e_{AM}(t) = \cos 2\pi f_c t + m_a \cos 2\pi f_m t \cos 2\pi f_c t$$

$$\quad (6\text{-}37)$$

$$= \cos 2\pi f_c t + \frac{m_a}{2}[\cos 2\pi(f_c - f_m)t + \cos 2\pi(f_c + f_m)t]$$

Here again the 180°-phase inversion of the lower sideband is evident. The spectrum of the narrow-band FM wave is entirely analogous to the spectrum of the AM wave except for this lower sideband phase inversion. This relationship is illustrated in Fig. 6-2. Note that the bandwidth required for transmission of narrow-band FM is identical to that required for the corresponding AM signal, namely, $2f_m$ where f_m is the highest modulating frequency.

6-3 Wide-band FM

Narrow-band FM, as we shall see in Chap. 11, represents an important operational mode for digital communications, in a form known as frequency-shift keying. In that application SNR's need only be large enough to preclude frequent decision errors. However, in analog communication, such as high-quality voice communications, one is usually more interested in operation at

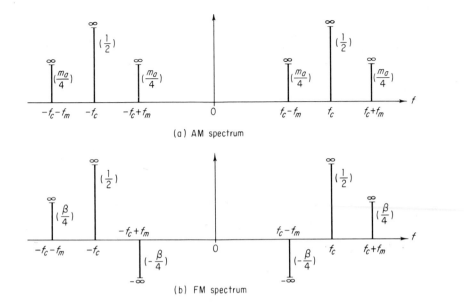

(a) AM spectrum

(b) FM spectrum

Fig. 6-2 AM and narrow-band FM spectra.

relatively high SNR's after demodulation and the performance improvements offered by wide-band FM become significant. Wide-band FM implies greater spectral bandwidth, through a larger modulation index β and peak frequency deviation ΔF. This invalidates the approximations made above in analyzing narrow-band FM. Note, however, that altering β or ΔF does not affect the carrier amplitude and therefore the total average transmitted signal power remains unchanged.

As an approach to analyzing wide-band FM, one may consider successively increasing the modulation index and consequently requiring the inclusion of more and more terms for the series expansions of the functions (6-28a and b). For example, consider a modulation index larger than previously but small enough ($\beta^2 \ll 6$) to validate the following power series approximations

$$cos\left[\beta g_n(t)\right] \approx 1 - \frac{\beta^2}{2} g_n^2(t) \qquad (6\text{-}38a)$$

$$sin\left[\beta g_n(t)\right] \approx \beta g_n(t) \qquad (6\text{-}38b)$$

This allows writing the FM wave (6-26) as

$$e_{\mathrm{FM}}(t) \approx \left[1 - \frac{\beta^2}{2} g_n^2(t)\right] cos\, 2\pi f_c t - \beta g_n(t)\, sin\, 2\beta f_c t \qquad (6\text{-}39)$$

Since the spectrum of the square of a function is the convolution of its spectrum with itself, the larger modulation index FM wave

(6-39) has a broader bandwidth (by a factor of 2) than the narrow-band FM wave (6-29). Furthermore, study of (6-39) reveals that the strength of the carrier term has decreased and the average power has been redistributed within the signal spectrum. Thus, as observed earlier, a change of modulation level does not disturb the total average power of the modulated wave but affects only the bandwidth and distribution of power among the components of the wave.

We could proceed indefinitely in the manner described above, each time increasing β and allowing more terms in the power series expansions. However, for the special case of sinusoidal modulation a more direct method is available. We concern ourselves then with the particular FM wave

$$e_{FM}(t) = A_c \cos(2\pi f_c t + \beta \sin 2\pi f_m t) \tag{6-40}$$

as in (6-24), or after an initial expansion

$$e_{FM}(t) = A_c \cos 2\pi f_c t \cos(\beta \sin 2\pi f_m t) - A_c \sin 2\pi f_c t \sin(\beta \sin 2\pi f_m t) \tag{6-41}$$

Expressions of the form $\cos(\beta \sin x)$ and $\sin(\beta \sin x)$ are expandable into well-known series forms:

$$\cos(\beta \sin x) = J_0(\beta) + 2 \sum_{n=1}^{\infty} J_{2n}(\beta) \cos 2nx \tag{6-42a}$$

and

$$\sin(\beta \sin x) = 2 \sum_{n=0}^{\infty} J_{2n+1}(\beta) \sin(2n + 1)x \tag{6-42b}$$

where

$$J_n(\beta) = \sum_{m=0}^{\infty} \frac{(-1)^m (\beta/2)^{2m+n}}{m!(m + n)!} \tag{6-43}$$

is the well-tabulated nth-order Bessel function of the first kind and of argument β (Ref. 4). Using these series expressions, we can write the FM wave (6-40) in the expanded form

$$e_{FM}(t) = A_c \left[J_0(\beta) + 2 \sum_{n=1}^{\infty} J_{2n}(\beta) \cos 4\pi n f_m t \right] \cos 2\pi f_c t$$

$$- 2A_c \sum_{n=0}^{\infty} J_{2n+1}(\beta) \sin[2\pi(2n + 1)f_m t] \sin 2\pi f_c t \tag{6-44}$$

and finally, after trigonometric reduction, as

$$e_{FM}(t) = A_c J_0(\beta) \cos 2\pi f_c t$$

$$- A_c \sum_{n=0}^{\infty} J_{2n+1}(\beta) \{\cos 2\pi [f_c - (2n+1)f_m]t - \cos 2\pi [f_c + (2n+1)f_m]t\}$$

$$+ A_c \sum_{n=1}^{\infty} J_{2n}(\beta) [\cos 2\pi (f_c - 2nf_m)t + \cos 2\pi (f_c + 2nf_m)t] \tag{6-45}$$

The amplitude of each term depends on the modulation index $\beta = \Delta F/f_m$ and an appropriate Bessel function. Several of these amplitude factors are plotted in Fig. 6-3 as a function of β (see Refs. 2, 5). Note that the number of significant terms increases with modulation index or peak frequency deviation.

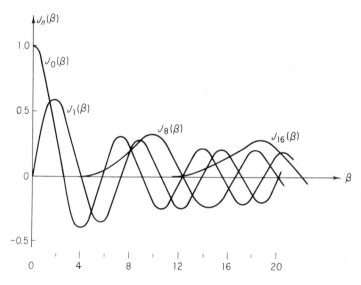

Fig. 6-3 Bessel functions of the first kind.

Thus, this FM wave with sinusoidal modulation of frequency f_m consists of a term at the carrier frequency f_c and an *infinite* number of sideband components spaced symmetrically $\pm f_m$ Hz from the carrier and from each other; i.e., at the frequencies $f_c \pm nf_m$, $n = 0, 1, 2, \ldots$. This is in contrast to amplitude modulation in which only a single set of sidebands exist. Frequency modulation has caused the information to be spread out over a band of frequencies much wider than the original baseband spectrum. Note that while sideband components of similar order are symmetrically spaced with respect to the carrier term and have amplitudes equal in magnitude, only the even-order sideband components are in phase with each other and with the carrier,* the odd-order lower sideband terms are 180° out of phase with their upper sideband equivalents. This phase relationship of the odd-order sideband components is the wide-band FM extension of the lower sideband inversion effect, noted earlier in the narrow-band FM case where only the first-order sidebands are present. Representative spectra of sinusoidally modulated FM signals are shown in **Fig. 6-4.**

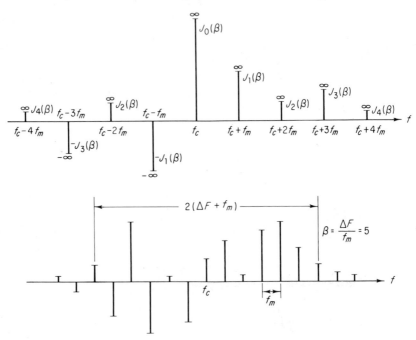

Fig. 6-4 FM spectra for sinusoidal modulation (positive frequencies only shown).

Although the total number of sidebands surrounding the carrier term of an FM signal is infinite, the number of sideband components with significant magnitudes is limited to a finite number. A question naturally arises now of just how many terms are important, for example, in determining the necessary transmission bandwidth. We have noted that the number of significant sideband amplitude factors increases with the modulation index β. As a function of β, a typical high-order ($n \gg 1$) Bessel function $J_n(\beta)$ is essentially zero except in the vicinity of $\beta \approx n$ and the next higher-order

---

*By which we specifically mean that the even-order sideband components and the carrier are in the same relation to each other as for a conventional AM signal.

factor $J_{n+1}(\beta)$ is small enough often to be neglected. Hence truncation with $J_n(\beta)$ as the highest-order significant factor or after approximately $n + 1 \approx \beta + 1$ terms (including the carrier) encompasses most of the important sideband components. Since a term of order n represents a contribution to the spectrum at the frequencies $f_c \pm nf_m$, the sinusoidally modulated FM wave has a bandwidth given approximately by

$$B \approx 2nf_m \approx 2\beta f_m = 2\Delta F \qquad (6\text{-}46)$$

or twice the peak frequency deviation. However, we recall that for narrow-band FM the required bandwidth is only $2f_m$. Hence an often-used excellent "rule of thumb," which quite well includes the narrow- and wide-band extremes and intermediate cases as well, is that the necessary FM transmission bandwidth is approximately twice the sum of the peak frequency deviation and the highest modulating frequency

$$B = 2(\Delta F + f_m) \qquad (6\text{-}47)$$

or alternately in terms of the modulation index

$$B = 2(\beta + 1)f_m \qquad (6\text{-}48)$$

The above comparatively lengthy discussion on FM sideband components and bandwidth requirements is based on the simple case of a single-frequency sinusoidal modulating signal. Extension of this analysis to include more complex, nonsinusoidal modulating signals is a more difficult problem and is not easily carried out. The inherent nonlinearity of the FM process precludes the use of superposition so that even the sideband analysis of an FM signal modulated by only two sinusoids becomes a tedious task. A general approach to this problem would be to decompose a nonsinusoidal modulating signal into a number of sinusoidal frequency components and assign each frequency its individual modulation index. The FM process then produces sideband components arrayed about the carrier frequency at all possible sum and difference combinations of these modulating frequencies and their harmonics. The amplitude factors for these sideband components consist of a product of Bessel functions of appropriate orders, one for each of the modulating frequencies, with arguments given by the associated modulation indices. Needless to say, such a computation is a complicated process. Only when the individual modulation indices are very small is the superposition principle applicable and then only approximately. Under this condition the significant sideband components are essentially those we would expect from a single-frequency analysis performed for each of the modulating frequencies, but this holds only to a first approximation.

In general the spectrum of an FM wave does not even have symmetrical sidebands about the carrier. It turns out that the significant sideband components tend to cluster around the frequencies that the instantaneous frequency concept would indicate. If the instantaneous frequency of the FM wave has a particular value during a large portion of a cycle of the modulating signal, then the sideband power tends to concentrate in components in the vicinity of that frequency. Although we shall not delve further into it here, the instantaneous frequency concept does provide insight into the spectrum of FM waves and additionally is very useful for studying the response of linear networks to FM waves. In any case, however, for wideband FM the spectral lines still tend to fall within the band of frequencies $\pm\Delta F$ about the carrier, ΔF usually being a constant of the system. Thus the bandwidths determined by the single-frequency analysis are still applicable to more general modulating signals and so provide useful engineering information. The rule of thumb for bandwidth in FM systems is still $2(\Delta F + f_m)$, where f_m now represents the largest significant frequency component in the modulating wave.

6-4 Generation and Detection of FM Waves

Of the several methods available for the generation of FM signals (see also Refs. 2, 3), probably the most commonly employed technique is that depicted in Fig. 6-5. The transmitter of the FM system contains a carrier frequency oscillator involving a resonant circuit in which the major frequency-determining elements are fixed inductance L and capacitance C. A small change in any of the reactive elements (either L or C) of this circuit

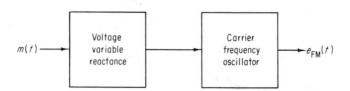

Fig. 6-5 Variable reactance method of FM generation.

causes small variations about the carrier frequency. Frequency modulation of the carrier is accomplished then by varying a reactive device in the resonant circuit in accordance with the modulation. That is, a voltage proportional to the modulating signal controls the reactance of the variable device. Such devices, known generically as voltage-variable reactances, have common implementations as so-called reactance tubes or transistors. Semiconductor devices such as varactors (voltage-variable capacitors) are used extensively also, and some current-controlled inductances are available.

A phase-modulated wave can be generated with this same technique by first processing the information wave through a differentiating circuit (i.e., a circuit whose magnitude response is proportional to frequency over the bandwidth of the signal). In this case the modulating wave, and hence instantaneous carrier frequency deviations, are proportional to the derivative of the information; therefore the instantaneous carrier phase deviations vary directly with the information wave.

It is also common to generate wide-band FM by first using the modulating wave to produce a narrow-band FM signal at some convenient low-carrier frequency. Processing the narrow-band FM signal through an appropriate frequency multiplier chain (i.e., nonlinear devices whose responses are rich in harmonics, followed by bandpass circuits centered at one such harmonic) then translates and broadens the frequency deviation. Frequency multiplication, as implemented in practice, multiplies the deviation *without* changing the modulating waveform and hence acts to multiply the modulation index and deviation ratio by the same factor as applies to the carrier.

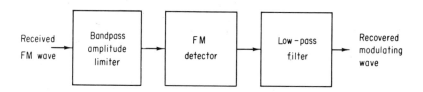

Fig. 6-6 Conventional FM receiver.

A simplified block diagram of an FM receiver is shown in Fig. 6-6. The essential component of this receiver is the FM demodulator or detector, usually termed a frequency discriminator. This is a device whose output voltage follows instantaneous frequency variations of carrier wave; that is, it responds to the instantaneous frequency deviation

$$f_i(t) - f_c = \frac{1}{2\pi} \frac{d\psi(t)}{dt} - f_c \qquad (6\text{-}49)$$

where $\psi(t)$ is the angle function of the received wave. Thus the output voltage of the FM detector is proportional to the modulation carried by the FM signal. FM detection compresses or converts the large frequency excursions of the carrier wave into the low frequencies of the slowly varying modulating wave. Figure 6-7 illustrates the transfer characteristic of both ideal and practical

FM detectors. The distance in frequency between the peaks of the practical FM detector's characteristics (i.e., roughly the linear response region) must be the same as the bandwidth of the received FM signal or approximately $2(\Delta F + f_m)$. A low-pass filter with upper cutoff frequency f_m follows the FM detector. This filter eliminates a large portion of the postdetection noise in FM systems.

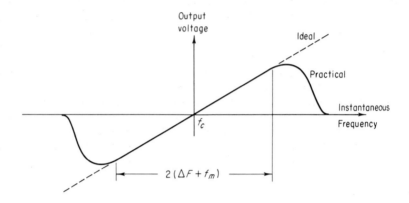

Fig. 6-7 FM detector characteristic.

Other forms of FM demodulators are available, although the type described above is the most popular. One example is the counter-type discriminator. This device counts zero-crossings of the modulated wave by producing a narrow voltage pulse of single polarity at each zero-crossing. The cumulative area under these pulses, integrated over a fixed time period, produces a voltage proportional to the instantaneous frequency deviations and hence to the modulation. Generally speaking this discriminator involves greater circuit complexity than the more conventional type.

One reason why FM systems are relatively unaffected by some forms of noise and disturbances is because the detectors are amplitude insensitive. Since the amplitude of an FM wave remains fixed regardless of the modulation, one can remove amplitude variations by use of a bandpass amplitude limiter in the receiver. The bandpass limiter is a nonlinear device that strips off or removes any amplitude variations that may be present on the signals falling within its passband. Thus the limiter provides a constant amplitude signal to the FM detector, essentially eliminating any amplitude sensitivity. However, bandpass amplitude limiting does not alter the angle variations (neither frequency nor phase) of the received signal. In this manner the effects of a variety of amplitude disturbances can be minimized. However, it should be emphasized that amplitude limiting serves as an adjunct to the FM detection process and not as an essential operation.

6-5 SNR Improvement in Wide-band FM Systems

As noted previously, wide-band FM systems possess the advantageous property of exchanging increased bandwidth requirements for improved SNR performance after demodulation. For suitable conditions the output SNR of a wide-band FM system can exceed the predetection carrier-to-noise power ratio (CNR) by a large factor. This desirable property of wide-band FM is due mainly to the inherent noise-reducing abilities of the nonlinear FM detection process. Known as the *capture effect,* this weak signal-suppression phenomenon of FM is not possessed by any linear demodulation technique. However, FM demodulation also exhibits a threshold effect common to envelope detection and other nonlinear demodulation methods. This threshold must be exceeded by the FM signal in order to achieve the full performance improvement. These concepts of FM strong signal capture and threshold are discussed briefly here, together with a calculation of the FM improvement in output SNR.

For purposes of discussion, we assume a conventional FM receiver consisting of a limiter/discriminator combination followed by low-pass filtering. Since the transmitted FM signal

$$e_{FM}(t) = A_c \cos[2\pi f_c t + \beta g_n(t)] \qquad (6\text{-}50)$$

requires a passband at least $2(\beta + 1)f_m = 2(\Delta F + f_m)$ Hz wide, all r.f. and i.f. receiver circuits including the limiter and discriminator must have this wide bandwidth. Only the final low-pass filter at the detector output with cutoff at f_m Hz has a narrow bandwidth; i.e., it passes the frequency band $|f| \leq f_m$ where f_m is the highest modulating frequency.

The signal $e_r(t)$ arriving at the receiver front-end

$$e_r(t) = e_{FM}(t) + n(t) \qquad (6\text{-}51)$$

consists of the FM signal (6-50) immersed in bandpass Gaussian noise $n(t)$ of the same bandwidth. As in Chaps. 4 and 5, we represent this type of noise by the convenient forms

$$n(t) = x(t) \cos 2\pi f_c t - y(t) \sin 2\pi f_c t = \rho(t) \cos[2\pi f_c t + \theta(t)] \quad (6\text{-}52)$$

with average noise power N given by

$$N = \overline{n^2(t)} = \overline{x^2(t)} = \overline{y^2(t)} = \frac{1}{2}\overline{\rho^2(t)} \qquad (6\text{-}53)$$

Thus the composite of signal plus noise appearing in the receiver i.f. circuits prior to limiting is

$$e_r(t) = A_c \cos[2\pi f_c t + \beta g_n(t)] + \rho(t) \cos[2\pi f_c t + \theta(t)]$$

$$= v(t) \cos[2\pi f_c t + \phi(t)] = v(t) \cos\psi(t) \tag{6-54}$$

At this point in the receiver the carrier-to-noise power ratio (CNR) is clearly

$$\left(\frac{C}{N}\right)_{(\text{FM})} = \frac{A_c^2}{2N} \tag{6-55}$$

Note that this is measured in the i.f. bandwidth. The amplitude limiting operation in the receiver then strips off the envelope $v(t)$ from the i.f. signal but leaves the angle variation $\psi(t)$ unchanged. Therefore the post–limiter signal ready for FM demodulation has the constant amplitude form

$$\hat{e}_r(t) = \cos[2\pi f_c t + \phi(t)] = \cos\psi(t) \tag{6-56}$$

Using the instantaneous phase angle $\beta g_n(t)$ of the FM signal as a reference, the instantaneous phase angle $\phi(t)$ of the i.f. signal (6-54) or (6-56) is given by the expression

$$\phi(t) = \beta g_n(t) + \arctan \frac{\rho(t) \sin[\theta(t) - \beta g_n(t)]}{A_c + \rho(t) \cos[\theta(t) - \beta g_n(t)]} \tag{6-57}$$

whereas, if the instantaneous phase angle $\theta(t)$ of the noise is taken as the reference, then

$$\phi(t) = \theta(t) + \arctan \frac{A_c \sin[\beta g_n(t) - \theta(t)]}{\rho(t) + A_c \cos[\beta g_n(t) - \theta(t)]} \tag{6-58}$$

For the usual situation of interest (above threshold), the CNR is large enough that the noise represents only a minor disturbance. In this case, most of the time $A_c \gg \rho(t)$ and (6-57) simplifies to

$$\phi(t) \approx \beta g_n(t) + \frac{\rho(t)}{A_c} \sin[\theta(t) - \beta g_n(t)] \tag{6-59}$$

Thus, when the FM signal is much stronger than the noise, the signal strongly suppresses the small random phase variation introduced by the noise; that is, the signal is said to *capture* the detector. On the other hand, when the noise is much stronger than the signal (small CNR), usually $A_c \ll \rho(t)$ and (6-58) reduces to

$$\phi(t) \approx \theta(t) + \frac{A_c}{\rho(t)} \sin[\beta g_n(t) - \theta(t)] \tag{6-60}$$

Thus in the weak signal case the random phase variation $\theta(t)$ of the noise controls (or captures) the instantaneous phase angle of the

composite i.f. signal. The desired phase information of the FM
signal is then lost in the much stronger random phase variation of
the noise, and subsequent FM detection can no longer successfully
recover the intended message.

Following amplitude limiting in the FM receiver, the FM detector performs the operation

$$\frac{1}{2\pi} \frac{d\psi(t)}{dt} - f_c = \frac{1}{2\pi} \frac{d\phi(t)}{dt} \qquad (6\text{-}61)$$

It will be useful in the discussion below to think of the operation
indicated in the RHS of (6-61) in terms of a linear system described
by the impulse response $h(t)$ and transfer function $H(f)$ given by

$$h(t) = \frac{1}{2\pi} \frac{d}{dt} \Longleftrightarrow H(f) = jf \qquad (6\text{-}62)$$

with $\phi(t)$ as the input (recall Sec. 1-6). Finally as the last step
in the FM demodulation process, the resultant of the above operation is low-pass filtered to discard any spurious components.

To determine the postdetection improvement in SNR possible
with FM systems, we examine the strong signal situation in which
this improvement is realized. In this case the FM detector operates
on the i.f. signal's instantaneous phase angle $\phi(t)$ as given approximately by

$$\phi(t) \approx \beta g_n(t) + \frac{\rho(t)}{A_c} \sin[\theta(t) - \beta g_n(t)] \qquad (6\text{-}63)$$

and valid only for large CNR; i.e., $A_c^2/2N \gg 1$. Note that the disturbance component in (6-63), with peak value $\rho(t)/A_c$, depends on
the instantaneous phase difference $\theta(t) - \beta g_n(t)$. Since $\theta(t)$ is uniformly distributed in the range $(-\pi, \pi)$, the quantity $\theta(t) - \beta g_n(t)$ is
also uniformly distributed in a 2π range about the instantaneous
value $\beta g_n(t)$. Therefore it follows that in computing the mean-
square perturbations of the noise output of an FM detector for high
CNR, the noise output is independent of the modulation and depends
only on the carrier level and the noise characteristics. The analysis
can be simplified somewhat, then, by ignoring the modulation term
in the disturbance component of (6-63). Thus we have

$$\phi(t) \approx \beta g_n(t) + \frac{\rho(t)}{A_c} \sin\theta(t) = \beta g_n(t) + \frac{y(t)}{A_c} \qquad (6\text{-}64)$$

where $y(t)$ is the so-called "out-of-phase" low-pass quadrature
component of the noise as in (6-52). For high CNR, the output of
the FM detector is then

$$\frac{1}{2\pi} \phi'(t) = \frac{\beta}{2\pi} g_n'(t) + \frac{y'(t)}{2\pi A_c} \qquad (6\text{-}65)$$

where the prime symbol implies differentiation.

The demodulated output signal component is clearly the term $\beta g'_n(t)/2\pi$ in (6-65); however, to be explicit we assume single-tone sinusoidal modulation, as in the example of Sec. 6-1 in which

$$\beta g_n(t) = \frac{\Delta F}{f_m} \sin 2\pi f_m t \tag{6-66}$$

In this case the recovered modulation is given by

$$m(t) = \frac{\beta g'_n(t)}{2\pi} = \Delta F \cos 2\pi f_m t \tag{6-67}$$

with average signal power

$$S_o = \frac{(\Delta F)^2}{2} \tag{6-68}$$

Prior to FM detection, the disturbance component introduced into the instantaneous phase angle by the noise is a function of the low-pass noise component $y(t)$. This Gaussian distributed random quantity varies slowly relative to a cycle of the carrier, but contains frequency components spread over the i.f. bandwidth $B = 2(\Delta F + f_m)$. For example, for white noise and a rectangular i.f. passband, the predetection power density spectrum of $y(t)$ is given by

$$S_y(f) = \begin{cases} \dfrac{N}{B}, & |f| \le \dfrac{B}{2} \\[2mm] 0, & |f| > \dfrac{B}{2} \end{cases} \tag{6-69}$$

After FM detection the output noise component in (6-65) is the quantity

$$\eta(t) = \frac{y'(t)}{2\pi A_c} \tag{6-70}$$

As mentioned previously, it is useful to think of the detector as performing a *linear* operation (namely, differentiation) on, in this case, $y(t)$. It follows, therefore, from the results of Chap. 4 that the output noise power density spectrum is given by

$$S_\eta(f) = |H(f)|^2 S_y(f) \tag{6-71}$$

where the linear system transfer function is

$$H(f) = \frac{j2\pi f}{2\pi A_c} = \frac{jf}{A_c} \tag{6-72}$$

Thus $S_\eta(f)$ is then

$$S_\eta(f) = \frac{f^2 S_y(f)}{A_c^2} \qquad (6\text{-}73)$$

which is valid for any low-pass power density spectrum $S_y(f)$. However, in the special case of interest (6-69), the output noise power density spectrum reduces to simply

$$S_\eta(f) = \frac{f^2 N}{B A_c^2} = \frac{f^2/2B}{(C/N)_{(\text{FM})}} , \quad |f| \le \frac{B}{2} \qquad (6\text{-}74)$$

This well-known result states that, for white bandpass noise, the FM detected output noise power density spectrum varies parabolically with frequency, as indicated in Fig. 6-8. This also includes the familiar statement that the FM detected *r.m.s. noise voltage* varies linearly with frequency (see also Fig. 6-8). Note, however, that the output noise power density spectrum is distributed over the wide-frequency band $|f| \le \Delta F + f_m$ with the higher

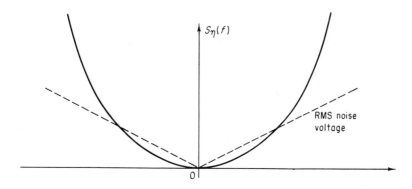

Fig. 6-8 FM detector output noise power density spectrum (large CNR).

frequencies accentuated. This result is of great practical value because the subsequent low-pass filtering recovers the modulation, which is limited to the frequency range $(-f_m, f_m)$, and discards the large portion of output noise lying outside this range. Assuming a filter cutoff at f_m, we write the total average noise power of the final filtered output as

$$\int_{-f_m}^{f_m} S_\eta(f)\, df = \frac{f_m^3/3B}{(C/N)_{(\text{FM})}} \qquad (6\text{-}75)$$

We can now make use of the results obtained above to determine the improvement in the FM signal-to-noise power ratio for high

CNR and white noise in a rectangular i.f. passband. Defined as the ratio of average output signal power to average output noise power, the FM postdetection SNR is given from (6-68) and (6-75) as

$$\left(\frac{S}{N}\right)_{o(\text{FM})} = \frac{3B(\Delta F)^2}{2f_m^3}\left(\frac{C}{N}\right)_{\text{FM}} = 3\beta^2(\beta + 1)\left(\frac{C}{N}\right)_{(\text{FM})} , \quad \left(\frac{C}{N}\right)_{(\text{FM})} \gg 1 \tag{6-76}$$

where the modulation index $\beta = \Delta F/f_m$ and the FM bandwidth is $B = 2(\Delta F + f_m)$. Thus the detection gain possible in wide-band FM systems is $3\beta^2(\beta + 1)$ or asymptotically $3\beta^3$ for very broad-band systems (i.e., large modulation index). For a common value of 5 for β, FM realizes a detection gain of 450 over the CNR.

Often the above result is stated in terms of a comparison with a conventional AM system with the same carrier power and operating in the same noise environment. In this case

$$\left(\frac{S}{N}\right)_{o(\text{FM})} = 3\beta^2\left(\frac{C}{N}\right)_{(\text{AM})} , \quad \left(\frac{C}{N}\right)_{(\text{AM})} \gg 1 \tag{6-77}$$

where the average noise power in the narrower AM bandwidth $2f_m$ is $2f_m(N/B)$. Since the quantity $(C/N)_{(\text{AM})}$ also represents the maximum achievable output SNR in the AM system (recall Sec. 5-4), the wide-band FM system is a factor of $3\beta^2$ better in output SNR than the equivalent AM system, but requires a factor of $\beta + 1$ more bandwidth than AM. For example, again using $\beta = 5$, the FM system trades a factor of 6 in bandwidth expansion for a factor of 75 improvement in SNR over the AM system.

We have seen above that the output noise power density spectrum of the FM detector grows parabolically with frequency (i.e., as f^2). Furthermore it is generally true of the modulating signals that the amplitudes of their frequency components decrease with increasing frequency. Thus after FM detection these weak high-frequency signal components are buried in strong output noise, resulting in poor SNR for the higher frequencies of the modulating signal. In FM systems this difficulty is often overcome by a compensating technique known as pre-emphasis/de-emphasis. Using this technique, before being modulated on the carrier, the modulating signal is passed through a pre-emphasis filter which boosts up (i.e., strengthens) the higher frequencies tending to equalize the distribution of energy within signal's spectrum. At the receiver, immediately after demodulation, the recovered signal and the detected noise pass through a de-emphasis filter which reduces or weakens the higher-frequency components in exactly the opposite manner in which they were strengthened by pre-emphasis. This inverse operation then restores the frequency components of the modulating signal to their proper relationship, but most importantly de-emphasis sharply diminishes the strengths of the higher frequency detected noise components. In effect, pre-emphase/de-emphasis leaves the modulating signal unchanged but tends to flatten out or equalize the output noise spectrum resulting in improved SNR. How much SNR improvement can be achieved with this technique depends on the cutoff frequency f_m of the low-pass filter at the detector output. For example, it can be shown (Refs. 1, 2) that for f_m = 3 kHz the SNR improvement is 3 dB, for f_m = 10 kHz the improvement is 10 dB, for f_m = 15 kHz the improvement is 13 dB, etc. For practical systems, the application of pre-emphasis/de-emphasis techniques can provide a significant improvement factor in system performance.

It should be strongly emphasized that the validity of all the above results on FM improvements holds only for large CNR and for large modulation indices. As pointed out earlier, when the noise voltage at the input to the FM detector is momentarily larger than the desired signal, then the noise suppresses the signal, just as a strong signal will suppress a weaker noise (stronger signal capture). Accordingly, when continuous noise has an amplitude great enough to cause noise peaks to instantaneously exceed the amplitude of the desired signal an appreciable fraction of the time, then the desired signal will be intermittently replaced by noise. This causes the zero-crossings of the modulated wave to change in number as well as in position, resulting in a lowering (actually a less-than-expected improvement) in postdetection SNR. This effect is found to depend very sharply upon FM carrier-to-noise ratio and is called a *threshold effect*. It is found in practice that, for large β, threshold phenomena begin to be noticeable in the range of about 10 to 13 dB carrier-to-noise ratio. Threshold effects are common to all wide-band noise improvement systems that exchange bandwidth for SNR as, for example, also in PCM systems, as discussed in the next chapter. For CNR's above the threshold region, FM improvement accrues; but below threshold the performance of FM rapidly deteriorates until eventually it becomes inferior to ordinary AM.

In conventional demodulation, SNR performance cannot be improved indefinitely by increasing the peak frequency deviation and hence the bandwidth. This comes about for several reasons. First, all communication systems are power limited so we may consider the available carrier power fixed. Furthermore, even though the noise power density spectrum (noise power per unit bandwidth) remains constant, as β and the FM bandwidth increase, more noise power must be accepted by the detector. Consequently, with fixed carrier power, the CNR in the wider bandwidth is reduced. Hence, as the FM transmission bandwidth increases with β, larger signal powers are needed to remain above threshold at the detector input and thereby to attain higher FM improvement factors. Figure 6-9 illustrates the (idealized) SNR performance characteristics of wide-band FM. So in the final analysis the FM improvement in output SNR must be paid for by *both* wider bandwidths and larger carrier power inputs.

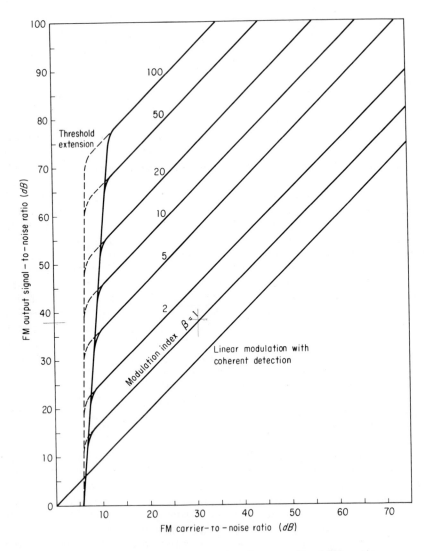

Fig. 6-9 Signal-to-noise characteristics of a conventional FM system.

Several special receiver techniques exist for partially over-coming the threshold effect limitation of FM systems (Ref. 5). These techniques, known as *FM feedback* (FMFB) or *frequency-compressive feedback* (FCF), leave unchanged the FM performance above threshold, but offer the possibility of extending the range of

FM improvement by narrowing the required predetector bandwidth to a value independent of the deviation ratio. Figure 6-9 illustrates the type of threshold extension possible with FMFB. These systems are based on the concept that a wide-band FM signal does not instantaneously fill the entire FM transmission bandwidth. Instead the wide-band FM signal occupies a much smaller instantaneous bandwidth that sweeps back and forth within the wide FM bandwidth at approximately the rate of change of the modulation. Thus the r.f. circuits of an FMFB system require the full FM bandwidth but the i.f. circuits need only a substantially smaller bandwidth and thereby reject a large portion of the noise power. The narrower i.f. bandwidth is achieved by introducing in the FM receiver a mixer (multiplier) driven by the incoming FM signal and by a voltage-controlled oscillator in a feedback loop from the FM detector. In effect this technique compresses the instantaneous frequency deviations of the wide-band signal and at the same time rejects a portion of the noise. The resulting receiver concept is much like a *tracking filter* that follows the slowly varying frequency deviations of the carrier within the wide bandwidth. A closely related approach is the phase-lock system which involves locking a local oscillator to the incoming FM signal by means of a feedback loop and recovering a voltage proportional to the instantaneous phase difference between the local oscillator and the received signal.

REFERENCES

1. H. S. Black, *Modulation Theory* (D. Van Nostrand Co., Inc., Princeton, New Jersey, 1953).
2. P. F. Panter, *Modulation, Noise, and Spectral Analysis* (McGraw-Hill Book Company, New York, 1965).
3. M. Schwartz, *Information Transmission, Modulation, and Noise* (McGraw-Hill Book Company, New York, 1959).
4. E. Jahnke and F. Emde, *Tables of Functions with Formulae and Curves* (Dover Publications, New York, 1945).
5. A. Hund, *Frequency Modulation* (McGraw-Hill Book Company, New York, 1942).

7

Pulse Modulation

As stated earlier, all modulation schemes involve both a modulating signal and a carrier function. In the two preceding chapters we have described use of a sinusoidal waveform as the carrier function. Another useful form is pulse modulation, in which the carrier function is a uniform pulse sequence or pulse train, some parameter of which is modified in accordance with the modulating signal. For example, in *pulse amplitude modulation* (PAM) systems, the modulation is carried in variations of the individual pulse amplitudes. In *pulse width modulation* (PWM) and *pulse position modulation* (PPM) systems, the modulating signal changes, respectively, the pulse width and relative time of occurrence of the individual carrier pulses. Carrier pulse waveshapes range the gamut from impulse-like waveforms to rectangular pulses with steep wavefronts and trailing edges to "smooth" waveforms with only faintly discernible beginning and ending points. Pulse modulation finds application where the data to be transmitted occurs naturally on an intermittent basis or where some benefit such as noise immunity is provided by transmission on a sampled data basis.

Sampling of the information source at a rate exceeding twice the highest frequency contained in the message waveform is a fundamental operation to all forms of pulse modulation for conveying analog waveforms. For this reason an understanding of the principles of sampling is essential to the study of pulse modulation. We preface this chapter with a discussion of these principles.

Since pulse modulation involves information in sampled form, it also provides the opportunity for messages from several information sources to share common communications equipment and a single transmission channel by utilizing those "vacant" time intervals between samples of any one message. This technique of combining several sampled message functions, known as *time division multiplexing* (TDM), is described more fully in Chap. 8.

Perhaps the most important aspect of pulse modulation and of all forms of digital data transmission is an inherent immunity to noise and disturbances similar to, and in some ways even better than, FM systems. The degree to which this noise immunity is effective is dependent upon the individual pulse modulation techniques. Quantized and coded systems, such as *pulse code modulation* (PCM), excel in this respect. As will be evident, pulse modulation is from this view another means of spreading the information spectrum over a wider bandwidth to achieve some useful improvement in system performance.

7-1 Sampling Principles

A basic tool in analyzing waveform sampling is a so-called *sampling function* in the form of a uniform impulse train, periodic in time with period T. This type of function was discussed previously in Sec. 1-10 where it was represented as

$$s(t) = \sum_{l=-\infty}^{\infty} \delta(t - lT) \tag{7-1}$$

The frequency spectrum of this sampling function was shown in (1-177) also to be a uniform impulse train in frequency, namely,

$$s(t) \iff S(f) = \frac{1}{T} \sum_{k=-\infty}^{\infty} \delta(f - k/T) \tag{7-2}$$

Figure 7-1 shows the impulse sampling function and its frequency spectrum.

This particular sampling function derives its usefulness from the property of impulses that multiplication of an arbitrary function $g(t)$ by a unit impulse simply changes the impulse weight (area) to the value of $g(t)$ at the time of occurrence of the impulse; i.e.,

$$g(t)\delta(t - T) = g(T)\delta(t - T) \tag{7-3}$$

Thus, taking the product of a function with an impulse *samples* the amplitude of the function at the time of occurrence of the impulse. An information wave $g(t)$ can therefore be sampled *periodically* by multiplication with the above sampling function $s(t)$, leading to the expression

$$v(t) = g(t)s(t) = \sum_{l=-\infty}^{\infty} g(lT)\delta(t - lT) \tag{7-4}$$

The sampled data function $v(t)$ corresponds to sampling the information wave periodically at intervals of T seconds, as Fig. 7-2 illustrates.

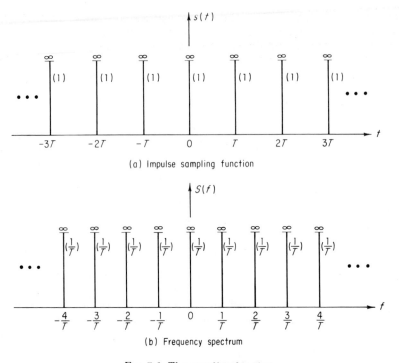

(a) Impulse sampling function

(b) Frequency spectrum

Fig. 7-1 The sampling function.

illustrates. In sampled form the information wave is then a periodic impulse whose weights are the values of the original function at the respective sampling instants, namely, the samples $g(lT)$.

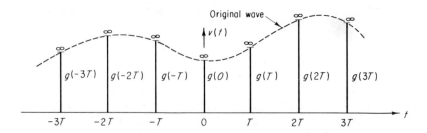

Fig. 7-2 Impulse sampled wave (impulse heights drawn to indicate sample size).

Further useful insight into the sampling process can be gained through frequency analysis. In this connection recall from Chap. 1 that multiplication and convolution of functions are dual operations in the time and frequency domains. Accordingly, since a sampled data function is the product of the information wave and the sampling function, its spectrum is given by convolution of the information spectrum with the periodic impulse spectrum (7-2). Using (7-2), the sampled data spectrum $V(f) \iff v(t)$ is given by

$$V(f) = G(f) \otimes S(f) = \frac{1}{T} \sum_{k=-\infty}^{\infty} G(f - k/T) \qquad (7\text{-}5)$$

where $G(f) \iff g(t)$ is the information spectrum. Apart from a scaling factor of $1/T$, this sampled data spectrum is simply the information spectrum repeated periodically in frequency, as illustrated in Fig. 7-3. Note that the sampling frequency $f_c = 1/T$, or the rate of taking samples, is very analogous to a carrier frequency, and that each lobe of the sampled data spectrum resembles a DSB-SC spectrum. Furthermore Fig. 7-3 has been drawn with the implication that the sampling frequency is slightly greater than twice the highest frequency contained in the original signal spectrum. For this relationship note that no overlap occurs between adjacent spectral lobes and that the original waveform can be recovered by passing the sampled representation through a filter which passes, say, the central lobe without distortion, but stops all others. (If any other lobe is used, recovery will have to include a form of DSB-SC demodulation.)

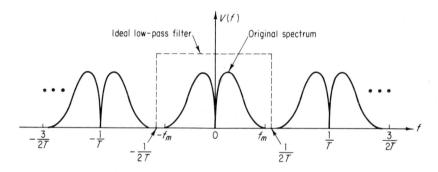

Fig. 7-3 Frequency spectrum of an impulse sampled wave.

A fundamental principle of sampling describes the least number of samples of a function necessary to completely and unambiguously define or represent that function. Waveform sampling always deals with band-limited functions. For example, it can be shown that a *real, low-pass* function band-limited to a maximum frequency f_m

$$G(f) = 0, \quad |f| > f_m \qquad (7\text{-}6)$$

is completely described by (i.e., can be reconstructed from) its sample values taken every $1/2f_m$ seconds throughout its entire time extent. The sampling frequency f_c, or rate of taking samples, must be then

$$f_c \geq 2f_m \qquad (7\text{-}7)$$

That is, f_c must exceed twice the highest signal frequency contained in the band-limited function. This conclusion is also apparent from an examination of **Fig. 7-3.** As pointed out above, this rate provides a complete representation of the original function, while any smaller sampling rate would allow adjacent spectral lobes of the sampled function to overlap each other, causing distortion in the recovery process.*

The minimum sampling rate for a band-limited function $2f_m$ is known as the *Nyquist* sampling rate. It can be shown that similar relationships apply to bandpass functions of bandwidth B in which the band-center frequency is much larger than the bandwidth. Samples (of amplitude and phase) of such a bandpass function taken at the Nyquist rate $2B$ per second completely describe the function. Thus there is no need to transmit an entire continuous function of time. It suffices to send only the instantaneous samples values obtained by sampling the signal amplitude at a regular rate of $2f_m$ or $2B$ samples per second.

Alternately stating the sampling principle, a signal which contains no frequencies greater than f_m Hz can assume *at most* $2f_m$ *independent* values per second. One often then speaks of a signal as being completely specified by $2f_m$ numbers per second, or conveying a maximum of $2f_m$ independent pieces of information per second. It follows then that a filter or a communications channel of bandwidth B Hz can be used to transmit a maximum of $2B$ independent samples per second.

We now describe a conventional proof of the sampling principle and show that an ideal low-pass filter limited to $|f| \leq f_m$ can be used to completely recover the original function from its sampled form.

The original band-limited information function is

$$g(t) \Longleftrightarrow G(f)$$

where

$$G(f) = 0, \quad |f| > f_m \qquad (7\text{-}8)$$

Since the information spectrum is confined to the finite region $(-f_m, f_m)$, $G(f)$ can be treated as though it were *periodic in frequency* with period $2f_m$ and expanded in a Fourier series. The Fourier

---

*That is, when overlap occurs, there is ambiguity as to the original spectrum of the signal which was sampled.

series expansion will be a valid representation of $g(t)$, of course, only within the primary region $(-f_m, f_m)$. Thus

$$
G(f) = \begin{cases} 0, & |f| > f_m \\ \sum_{k=-\infty}^{\infty} \alpha(k) e^{-j2\pi kf/2f_m} = \sum_{k=-\infty}^{\infty} \alpha(k) e^{-j\pi kf/f_m}, & |f| \le f_m \end{cases} \tag{7-9}
$$

where the Fourier harmonic coefficients are given by

$$
\alpha(k) = \frac{1}{2f_m} \int_{-f_m}^{f_m} G(f) e^{j\pi kf/f_m} df \tag{7-10}
$$

From the relationships of (7-8) it is recognized that

$$
g(t) = \int_{-f_m}^{f_m} G(f) e^{j2\pi ft} df \tag{7-11}
$$

and therefore that

$$
\alpha(k) = \frac{1}{2f_m} g\left(\frac{k}{2f_m}\right) \tag{7-12}
$$

Thus the Fourier harmonic coefficients are proportional to sample values of the original function taken at the Nyquist sampling rate. The Fourier series expansion of $G(f)$ is then also determined by these Nyquist samples

$$
G(f) = \frac{1}{2f_m} \sum_{k=-\infty}^{\infty} g\left(\frac{k}{2f_m}\right) e^{-j\pi kf/f_m} \tag{7-13}
$$

Using (7-11) and (7-13), we note it now follows that the original function is given by

$$
g(t) = \frac{1}{2f_m} \sum_{k=-\infty}^{\infty} g\left(\frac{k}{2f_m}\right) \int_{-f_m}^{f_m} e^{j2\pi f(t - k/2f_m)} df
$$
$$
= \sum_{k=-\infty}^{\infty} g\left(\frac{k}{2f_m}\right) \frac{\sin[2\pi f_m(t - k/2f_m)]}{2\pi f_m(t - k/2f_m)} \tag{7-14}
$$

This latter expression establishes the sampling principle, namely, that a real, band-limited function is completely determined by its sample values $g(k/2f_m)$ taken every $1/2f_m$ seconds. Each term of

(7-14) is an appropriately delayed $(\sin x)/x$ function whose amplitude at the associated sampling instant is exactly the sample value and at every other sampling instant is exactly zero. Furthermore, (7-14) indicates that at all intermediate points in time the entire collection of terms combines to yield exactly $g(t)$ everywhere. This is illustrated in Fig. 7-4.

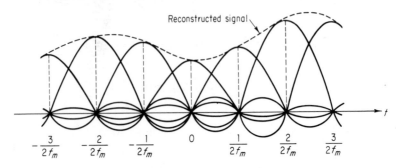

Fig. 7-4 Reconstruction of a signal from its Nyquist samples by low-pass filtering.

Based on the above discussion of the sampling principle, it becomes clear that a sampled data function of the form

$$v(t) = \sum_{l=-\infty}^{\infty} g(lT)\,\delta(t - lT)\,, \qquad T \leq \frac{1}{2f_m} \qquad (7\text{-}15)$$

where the samples are taken at a rate slightly greater than $2f_m$ per second, contains all of the information in the original function. It also seems evident from an examination of Fig. 7-3, which illustrates the spectrum of $v(t)$, that $g(t)$ can be recovered from its sampled form by lowpass filtering. That this is true is easily shown. Consider an ideal low-pass filter with cutoff frequency $1/2T \geq f_m$:

$$H(f) = \begin{cases} 1, & |f| < \dfrac{1}{2T} \\[2mm] 0, & |f| > \dfrac{1}{2T} \end{cases} \quad\Longleftrightarrow\quad h(t) = T\,\frac{\sin 2\pi t/2T}{2\pi t/2T} \qquad (7\text{-}16)$$

such as described earlier in Sec. 1-11. Passing the sampled data function $v(t)$ through the low-pass filter $H(f)$ equivalently convolves $v(t)$ with the filter unit impulse response $h(t)$; hence

$$V(f)H(f) \quad\Longleftrightarrow\quad v(t) \otimes h(t) \qquad (7\text{-}17)$$

where

$$v(t) \otimes h(t) = \sum_{l=-\infty}^{\infty} g(lT)\,\delta(t - lT) \otimes h(t) = \sum_{l=-\infty}^{\infty} g(lT)\,h(t - lT) \qquad (7\text{-}18)$$

Substituting from (7-16), we write the result of low-pass filtering the sampled data function as

$$v(t) \otimes h(t) = T \sum_{l=-\infty}^{\infty} g(lT) \, \frac{\sin[2\pi(t - lT)/2T]}{2\pi(t - lT)/2T} \qquad (7\text{-}19)$$

Comparing this expression with (7-14) and recalling that the interval between samples is

$$T \leq 1/2f_m \qquad (7\text{-}20)$$

it becomes clear that (7-19) reduces to

$$v(t) \otimes h(t) = T \, g(t) \qquad (7\text{-}21)$$

Thus, ideal low-pass filtering will *exactly* recover the original function (to within a constant multiplier) from its sampled form when the sampling rate exceeds the Nyquist rate.*

7-2 Sampling with Narrow Pulses: Pulse Amplitude Modulation

In practice impulse functions are impossible to realize, but they can be closely approached by narrow pulses of finite height, having little adverse effect on the above results. A more practical sampling function is the rectangular pulse sampling wave $s_p(t)$, shown in Fig. 7-5a. The sampled data function $v_{PAM}(t)$ resulting from ideal multiplication of an information wave with $s_p(t)$ is shown in Fig. 7-6. This sampled function is an example of a *pulse amplitude modulated* (PAM) wave.

To study the effect of using a finite width sampling pulse, we again employ frequency analysis. First, the rectangular pulse train $s_p(t)$ can be mathematically generated by convolving a *single* pulse $p(t)$ located at the origin of the time scale with the impulse train $s(t)$ of (7-1). Thus,

$$s_p(t) = p(t) \otimes s(t) = \sum_{l=-\infty}^{\infty} p(t - lT) \qquad (7\text{-}22)$$

where

$$p(t) = \begin{cases} 1, & |t| \leq T_p/2 \\ 0, & |t| > T_p/2 \end{cases} \Longleftrightarrow P(f) \qquad (7\text{-}23)$$

---

*Indeed (7-21) is apparent from (7-5) and Fig. 7-3. Hence (7-16) to (7-19) can be regarded as an alternative proof of the sampling principle.

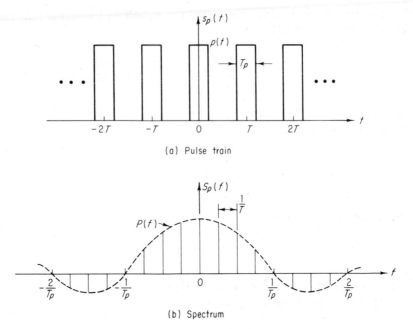

(a) Pulse train

(b) Spectrum

Fig. 7-5 Rectangular pulse sampling function and its spectrum (impulse heights drawn to show variation in weight).

The spectrum of the single pulse $p(t)$ is a $(\sin x)/x$ function with its first zero at $f = 1/T_p$,

$$P(f) = T_p \frac{\sin \pi f T_p}{\pi f T_p} \qquad (7\text{-}24)$$

The spectrum of $s_p(t)$ is then the product of the pulse spectrum $P(f)$ with the uniform periodic impulse spectrum $S(f)$ as given by

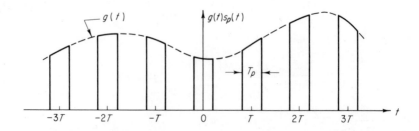

Fig. 7-6 A PAM wave with shaped-top pulses.

$$S_p(f) = P(f)S(f) = \frac{T_p}{T} \frac{\sin \pi f T_p}{\pi f T_p} \sum_{k=-\infty}^{\infty} \delta(f - k/T)$$

$$= \frac{T_p}{T} \sum_{k=-\infty}^{\infty} \frac{\sin(\pi k T_p/T)}{\pi k T_p/T} \delta(f - k/T)$$

(7-25)

This line spectrum is shown in **Fig. 7-5b.**

The pulse amplitude modulated wave $v_{\mathrm{PAM}}(t)$ formed by multiplying the information wave $g(t)$ with the pulse train $s_p(t)$ is

$$v_{\mathrm{PAM}}(t) = g(t) s_p(t) = g(t)[p(t) \otimes s(t)] \qquad (7\text{-}26)$$

This wave is shown in **Fig. 7-6.** The spectrum of $v_{\mathrm{PAM}}(t)$ is easily determined by convolution of the information spectrum with the weighted impulse train (7-25).

$$V_{\mathrm{PAM}}(f) = G(f) \otimes S_p(f) = G(f) \otimes [P(f)S(f)] \qquad (7\text{-}27)$$

As illustrated in **Fig. 7-7,** the PAM spectrum is periodic in frequency with spectral lobes *identical* in *form* and *shape* to the original information spectrum. The only essential difference between the spectra of impulse sampled and finite-width pulse sampled waveforms is that in the latter, the individual spectral lobes vary in amplitude by a *scaling factor* that is determined by both the spectrum of the sampling pulse and by the pulse width. Note, however, the individual spectral lobes of $v_{\mathrm{PAM}}(t)$ are undistorted since each individual lobe is reduced *uniformly* in amplitude by a constant factor. Figure 7-7 illustrates the effect of sampling with finite width pulses as compared with Fig. 7-3.

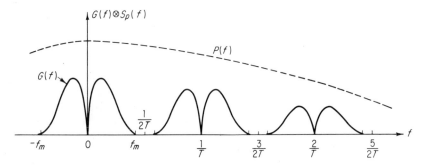

Fig. 7-7 Effect of sampling with finite width pulses.

Recovery of the information wave is again by low-pass filtering, which results in an *exact* reproduction of the original wave. This distortion-free recovery is directly attributable to permitting the sampling pulses to follow the exact shape of the information wave during the brief existence of the pulses; that is, the tops of the pulses are shaped by the information waveform. PAM waves of this type can be generated by a sampling *"gate"* as indicated in Fig. 7-8a.

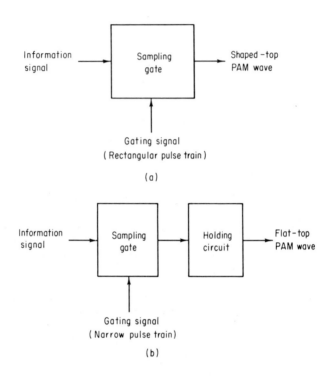

Fig. 7-8 Generation of PAM waves.

In practice, *"shaped-top"* PAM pulses are not usually employed because of the difficulties involved with maintaining the pulse shapes in an environment of noise and communication channel distortions. Instead *"flat-topped"* pulses are normally used where the pulse height is determined by the sample value of the information wave at some point within the duration of the pulse, usually the middle or beginning of the pulse. Eliminating the shaped pulse tops allows more flexibility in circuit implementations for these systems and reduces the sensitivity to noise and distortion. (Other pulse modulation techniques, such as pulse code modulation described later, go even further in noise sensitivity reduction by transmitting pulses of fixed heights.) A flat-topped PAM wave can be generated by sampling the information wave with a very narrow pulse (ideally an impulse) and then stretching this pulse in time with a *"holding circuit."* Figure 7-8b illustrates this latter PAM method.

The analysis of this latter type of PAM is performed by simply reversing the application of some of the operations used in the preceding analysis. First the information wave is sampled by the impulse train $s(t)$, resulting in the sampled data function

$$v(t) = g(t)s(t) = \sum_{l=-\infty}^{\infty} g(lT)\,\delta(t - lT) \qquad (7\text{-}28)$$

Then this function is convolved with the rectangular pulse $p(t)$ in (7-23), producing a PAM wave with flat-topped pulses as expressed by

$$v_{PAM}(t) = v(t) \otimes p(t) = [g(t)s(t)] \otimes p(t) \qquad (7\text{-}29)$$

The spectrum of this PAM wave is just the product of the pulse spectrum $P(f)$ with the spectrum of Fig. 7-3, i.e.,

$$V_{PAM}(f) = V(f)P(f) = [G(f) \otimes S(f)]P(f) \qquad (7\text{-}30)$$

This flat-topped pulse PAM wave and its spectrum are shown in Fig. 7-9. The effect of using flat-topped pulses instead of shaped

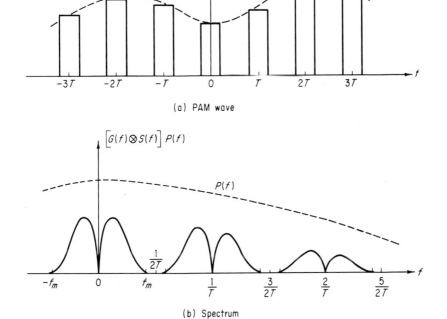

(a) PAM wave

(b) Spectrum

Fig. 7-9 Waveform and spectrum of a flat-topped pulse PAM wave.

ones is seen to be a slight nonuniform or asymmetrical distortion of the spectral lobes as well as a reduction of amplitude, again determined by the sampling pulse spectrum and pulse width. Processing by low-pass filtering recovers the original information wave but with a small amount of distortion. However, for narrow sampling pulse widths this distortion can be negligible. It can also be completely removed if one can construct an "equalizing filter," with response proportional to $1/P(f)$ over the signal bandwidth.

7-3 Pulse Code Modulation (PCM)

Quantization

In the descriptions of pulse modulation given above, instantaneous samples of the information signal directly modulate the amplitude of a uniform carrier pulse train. This simple form of PAM transmits all possible signal amplitudes without further modification. In any physical system it is, of course, impossible to recover the *exact* amplitude of a sample because of noise and other disturbances introduced during transmission that mask the fine variations of amplitude. In addition to this ultimate limitation, the final recipient of the information, both human and electronic, is also limited in its abilities to distinguish fine detail of the signal. Therefore it is pointless to attempt to retain a degree of signal "quality" far in excess of that which can be efficiently utilized. With this recognition it becomes unnecessary then to transmit all possible signal amplitudes. Moreover it is possible to use this to advantage by designing a system in which only certain *discrete* levels of amplitude are allowed. Then, when the signal is sampled, the amplitude level nearest to the true signal value is sent. A PAM system then transmits only a set of specified (fixed) pulse heights corresponding to the discrete allowed amplitude levels. Since the set of fixed amplitude levels is known also to the receiver, a detector circuit can more easily recognize these levels in the presence of noise. If the noise and distortion are not too great, the detector can correctly decide which of the amplitude levels was sent. The discrete samples of the signal can then be completely reformed at the receiver, free of transmission noise and distortion.

Representing a signal by only certain allowed discrete amplitude levels is known as *quantizing*. The "rounding-off" of the last few digits of a numeral in numerical processing represents an entirely analogous procedure. Figure 7-10 shows a signal in sampled and quantized form, in which instantaneous samples of varying amplitude are replaced by the nearest to the true value of a set of fixed levels. Quantization transforms a signal in *analog* (continuous) form into a *digital* (discrete) form. After conversion to quantized or digitized form, the original analog signal can never be *exactly* recovered even in a noiseless environment. The quantizing process introduces an initial irreducible amount of signal distortion, termed *quantization noise*. However, as we shall see, this signal distortion can be negligible with a small enough spacing between amplitude levels or equivalently a sufficiently large number or quantization levels. We shall return to discuss this quantization noise later.

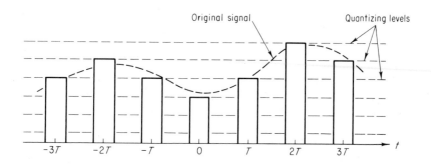

Fig. 7-10 Sampled and quantized signal.

The example of Fig. 7-10 shows a uniform spacing between amplitude levels; however, systems with variable level separation are used also. A variable spacing between amplitude levels favors small amplitude signals, which need more protection against noise, at the expense of large amplitude signals. This effect is somewhat analogous to the previously discussed pre-emphasis/de-emphasis technique used in FM. In this discussion, however, we will consider only the uniform spacing.

Keep in mind the outstanding feature of quantization. Once a signal is in a quantized state, it can be transmitted and relayed any distance without further loss in quality, provided only that the noise and distortion are not too great to prevent correct decisions as to which amplitude level a particular pulse represents. Given error-free decisions, the quantized signal can be reformed *exactly* and the original analog signal recovered to within the quantization distortion, which can be made small.

Coding

So-called quantized PAM could be used to transmit each quantized signal amplitude as a discrete pulse height. However, if too large a number of amplitude levels are allowed, it becomes difficult to make error-free decisions and the advantage of quantization is then lost. On the other hand it is relatively easy to distinguish between just two pulses, or between the presence or absence of a pulse. Suppose then that each discrete amplitude level is represented by a particular group of several pulses which individually have only a small number of possible pulse heights. This is an example of waveform *coding*. In this case coding transforms the information conveyed by a *single* pulse height into the arrangement (pattern) of a group of several pulses known as a *code group*. To each quantization level is associated a unique code group. The individual pulses of the code group also have fixed pulse heights assigned from a small set of values (usually just two levels). Coding achieves a greater immunity to noise mainly for two reasons:

1. Only a portion of the total information is affected by loss or corruption of one or more of the pulses of a code group.
2. Large amounts of noise and distortion can be tolerated in the detection of an individual pulse because the selection is from among a small number of possibilities.

A commonly used coding scheme converts the sampled and quantized signal pulses into code groups of two-level (*binary*) pulses using fixed amplitudes. Binary pulses are commonly used in two forms, the first *on-off* (or unipolar) pulses in which the pulse can be on (1) or off (0), the other *plus-minus* (or *bipolar*) pulses (+1, −1). The most common binary code, in fact, represents the quantized amplitude levels written in binary notation (base 2). The binary code table shown below illustrates this coding technique for code groups composed of three pulses. In addition an example of binary coded pulse groups using the relations of this table is shown in **Fig. 7-11.**

Binary Code

Amplitude Level	On-off Pulses	Bipolar Pulses
0	000	−1 −1 −1
1	001	−1 −1 1
2	010	−1 1 −1
3	011	−1 1 1
4	100	1 −1 −1
5	101	1 −1 1
6	110	1 1 −1
7	111	1 1 1

In binary notation the place-values are 1, 2, 4, 8, ... ; that is, a unit in the right-hand column represents 1, a unit in the second column represents 2, a unit in the third column represents 4, etc. We see that with binary pulses a code group of n pulses can represent 2^n amplitude levels. For example, 32 levels require five binary pulses, 128 levels require seven pulses.

The binary code described above is just one of many possible different ways of coding with binary pulses. It is also possible to

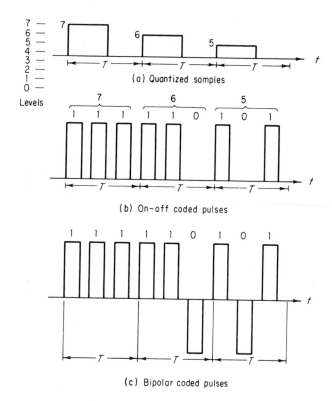

(a) Quantized samples

(b) On-off coded pulses

(c) Bipolar coded pulses

Fig. 7-11 Binary pulse coding.

code the amplitude in terms of pulses of more than just two levels. For example, we can use pulses with three allowed levels (base 3 or ternary code), or four levels (base 4 or quaternary code), etc. Further discussion of the detection of pulses in binary and m-ary coded signaling is deferred to later chapters. It suffices to point out here that a code composed of code groups of n pulses, each pulse having m allowed levels (base m), can represent m^n quantization levels; that is, n pulses, each with m possible heights, may be combined in m^n different ways. One possible practical reason for employing pulses of more than two allowed levels would be to conserve transmission bandwidth; however, as the number of levels increase, multilevel coded systems (large m) eventually fall prey to the same ailments as uncoded systems. In this chapter we concentrate on binary coding only.

A PCM System

Pulse code modulation (PCM) is a practical pulse modulation scheme that incorporates in an effective manner all the above described techniques of sampling, quantizing, and coding. In PCM systems, analog information is transmitted in a quantized and coded digital form that efficiently exchanges transmission bandwidth for improvements in postdetection SNR, bettering even the performance of wide-band FM. Here we describe briefly the basic functional operations involved in a PCM system. Refer to Fig. 7-12.

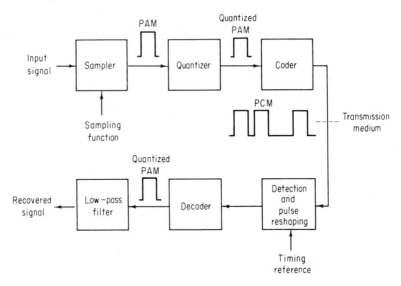

Fig. 7-12 Basic operations of a PCM system.

An information signal band-limited to f_m Hz is first sampled periodically with narrow pulses at a rate slightly exceeding $2f_m$ samples per second. This produces an ordinary PAM wave in which the pulse heights correspond to the instantaneous signal amplitudes at the sampling instants. The PAM pulse heights are then quantized to the nearest of a set of discrete levels that span the entire amplitude range of the original signal. The quantized PAM waveform closely resembles the *un*quantized PAM waveform with the exception of a slight modification of the pulse heights. At this point the quantized samples are encoded into PCM code groups, each code group containing n pulses.

Since the encoding process converts one pulse into a group of n pulses, these n pulses must be squeezed into the time interval previously allotted to a single pulse. Hence the pulse width must be decreased by a factor of n and the bandwidth increased accordingly. Conserving the peak pulse amplitude rather than pulse shape is of primary interest here, so that the bandwidth is determined solely by the pulse width. Now, to transmit a signal of bandwidth f_m by PCM requires $2f_m$ code groups per second (each code group represents an independent piece of information), and therefore the individual pulses flow at a rate of $2nf_m$ pulses per second. This requires a minimum transmission bandwidth $B = nf_m$ (recall that a transmission channel of bandwidth B Hz can convey $2B$ independent pieces of information per second). Thus the transmission bandwidth for PCM is n times as great as that required for direct transmission of the signal, where n is the number of pulses per code group. The code groups can be transmitted either as a time sequence of pulses over the same transmission channel, or in parallel over n separate channels. In either case the total bandwidth occupied will be the same. Of course, if any form of double-sideband transmission is used, the total bandwidth will be $2nf_m$ (i.e., doubled). A PCM system is, therefore, a *coded wide-band* system in which the transmission bandwidth is purposely widened a factor of n by the coding process to achieve improved immunity to noise.

At the receiver the PCM pulses are individually detected and regenerated (reshaped and cleaned-up). These "clean" pulses are then regrouped (*framed*) into code groups and decoded (converted back) to a quantized PAM form. The decoding process (which we shall not go into here) involves generating a pulse which is the linear sum of all the pulses in the code group, each pulse weighted by its place-value (1, 2, 4, 8 ...) in the code. The final step in the recovery of the message is to low-pass filter (with cutoff frequency f_m) the reconstructed PAM wave. If the detection process is (almost) error-free, then the recovered signal *includes no noise* with the exception of the initial distortion introduced by the quantization process.

Over long transmission distances communication systems often employ a chain of repeater stations to strengthen and rebroadcast the signals. In ordinary analog modulation systems the transmission noise introduced in the individual links is amplified at the repeaters and sent along to the next repeater. Consequently, the noise and distortion in these systems rapidly cumulates and degrades the system performance. In these systems the longer the overall transmission distance, the more severe are the requirements on each link. On the other hand, this need not be the case in PCM systems. In PCM systems the transmission noise introduced during the previous link can be completely eliminated (except for errors) at each repeater station by pulse regeneration. This involves detecting the individual pulses and reshaping them, but does not include decoding. These cleaned-up pulses are then amplified and retransmitted to the next repeater to be regenerated again, etc. In this way the noise is not carried along from one repeater to the next. If the transmission noise introduced in each single link does not cause an undue rate of detection errors, the pulses can be regenerated as often as necessary. Thus the transmission requirements for a PCM system are almost independent of the total physical length of the system.

Detection of Binary Pulses

We have been describing a PCM system transmitting binary pulses of, say, the on-off variety. To detect the presence or absence of a pulse, the receiver first filters the pulse stream to remove out-of-band noise and then the detector samples the output of this filter at an instant when the peak amplitude of a pulse is expected. (The timing reference necessary to accomplish this sampling must be supplied external to the detection process but is not of concern to us here.) The sampled filter output is then compared with a decision threshold level to decide whether or not a pulse is present. If the threshold level is exceeded at the sampling instant, a pulse is said to be present; if not exceeded, no pulse is present. Obviously, if the peak pulse amplitude is too low relative to the noise, the detector will make errors and occasionally indicate a pulse when in fact there is none, and vice versa. Reliable pulse detection, therefore, requires a sufficiently large signal-to-noise ratio. We examine this relationship here, assuming low-pass pulse streams. (A more general discussion of binary pulse signaling and detection in radio communications is given in Chaps. 10 to 14).

Suppose the peak pulse amplitude at the filter output is A volts and this pulse is corrupted by additive noise $n(t)$. Having been filtered, the noise is of the same bandwidth as the pulse. Let the filter output $u(t)$ be sampled at the instant $t = T$, the time of occurrence of the peak pulse amplitude. Then, when a pulse is present, the sampled filter output $u(T)$ is a sample from a noise process $n(T)$ plus the peak pulse amplitude A; and when a pulse is not present, $u(T)$ is a sample of noise only,

$$u(T) = \begin{cases} n(T) + A , & \text{pulse present} \\ n(T) , & \text{pulse not present} \end{cases} \tag{7-31}$$

The decision threshold level is set at one-half the peak pulse amplitude $A/2$, and if $u(T)$ exceeds this level, the detector decides a pulse is present, and vice versa. The pulse/no pulse decision criterion is then

$$u(T) \begin{cases} > A/2 , & \text{decide pulse present} \\ < A/2 , & \text{decide pulse not present} \end{cases} \tag{7-32}$$

Detection errors are made whenever the noise sample is instantaneously strong enough to falsify the decision. The frequency of such error occurrences is measured by the *probability of error* P_e. Given that on the average pulses are sent as often as not (i.e., 50% of the time), the probability of error is one-half the probability that $u(T)$ exceeds the threshold when a pulse is not present, plus one-half the probability that $u(T)$ falls below the threshold when a pulse is present. Thus the probability of a decision error is

$$P_e = \frac{1}{2} \text{ prob. } [u(T) > A/2 \,\big|\, u(T) = n(T)]$$

$$+ \frac{1}{2} \text{ prob. } [u(T) < A/2 \,\big|\, u(T) = n(T) + A] \qquad (7\text{-}33)$$

Since all systems are limited ultimately by thermal noise, we assume the noise process $n(t)$ to be zero-mean Gaussian noise with mean power $\overline{n^2} = N$, where N is the total average noise power in the filter output. Then, when a pulse is not present, $u(T)$ is simply a sample of zero-mean Gaussian noise. Its probability density function is

$$u(T) = n(T) : \qquad p(u) = \frac{1}{\sqrt{2\pi N}} e^{-u^2/2N} \qquad (7\text{-}34)$$

On the other hand, when a pulse is present, $u(T)$ is a sample of a *biased* (nonzero-mean) Gaussian process with p.d.f. given by

$$u(T) = n(T) + A : \qquad p(u) = \frac{1}{\sqrt{2\pi N}} e^{-(u-A)^2/2N} \qquad (7\text{-}35)$$

The only difference between these two p.d.f.'s is the bias or mean value of the distributions. Under these symmetrical circumstances (see also Chap. 10), it is easily shown that the two probabilities of (7-33) are identically the area under the tail of the same Gaussian p.d.f. from the same point on the tail. The probability of error reduces to simply

$$P_e = \text{prob. } [u > A/2 \,\big|\, u = n] = \frac{1}{\sqrt{2\pi N}} \int_{A/2}^{\infty} e^{-u^2/2N} \, du$$

$$\qquad (7\text{-}36)$$

$$= \frac{1}{\sqrt{\pi}} \int_{\frac{A}{2\sqrt{2N}}}^{\infty} e^{-\lambda^2} \, d\lambda$$

Apart from a constant factor, this latter expression is recognized as the complementary error function erfc ( ), as defined earlier in Sec. 4-2. Thus the probability of erroneously detecting the binary pulses is

$$P_e = \frac{1}{2} \text{ erfc} \left[\frac{A}{2\sqrt{2N}} \right] = \frac{1}{2} \text{ erfc} \left[\frac{1}{2} \sqrt{\frac{P}{2N}} \right] \qquad (7\text{-}37)$$

where $P = A^2$ is the peak (signal) pulse power and N is the average noise power.

As the signal-to-noise ratio P/N is increased, P_e decreases very rapidly so that eventually only a very small increase in signal power will make the transmission of pulses almost error-free. The curve of Fig. 7-13 indicates how rapidly this improvement accrues with peak pulse SNR. Clearly a threshold effect exists here (not to be confused with the decision threshold) as is evident from examination of this curve. Although it is more appropriate to speak about a threshold *"region"* of improvement rather than a definite point, we may state that there is a threshold in the vicinity of about 20-dB peak SNR below which system performance may involve significant numbers of errors, and above which the effect of transmission noise is negligible.

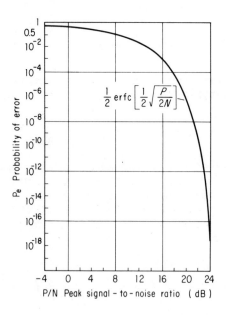

Fig. 7-13 Detection of binary on-off pulses.

This discussion has assumed a system with on-off pulses of peak pulse power P. Since pulses are sent on the average only 50% of the time, the average signal pulse power is $P/2$. In terms of average SNR, the data of Fig. 7-13 should be decreased by 3 dB. If instead bipolar (plus-minus) pulses are used, the peak-to-peak signal swing must remain the same as for the on-off pulses in order to achieve the same margin over the noise. In this case the bipolar pulse amplitudes would be one-half the amplitude of the on-off pulses $(A/2)$ and the average signal power is then only $P/4$, a reduction of 6 dB from the peak power of the on-off system.

Therefore for a bipolar pulse system the threshold of performance occurs at about roughly 14-dB average signal-to-noise ratio.

Output SNR and Quantization Noise

In a PCM system two types of noise are of concern. One of these is the transmission noise we have just been discussing, the other is the quantization noise mentioned earlier. Transmission noise may be introduced anywhere between the transmitter and the detector, whereas quantization noise is introduced only at the transmitter and is carried along to the final output. As pointed out, transmission noise causes detection errors that result in the reconstruction of "clean" but incorrect code groups. The decoder then interprets these incorrect code groups as false signal amplitudes. Aside from these occasional errors, transmission noise does not otherwise appear at the output; that is, there is no continuous output component of transmission noise as in analog modulation systems. As we have seen, the quality of the detection process improves so rapidly as the signal power is increased above the threshold region that the effect of transmission noise can often be made negligible by design. In such a PCM system operating with SNR well above threshold, the final output signal-to-noise ratio is determined by the quantization noise alone. However, this quantization noise can also be reduced to any desired degree by choosing the quantization levels fine enough.

To examine quantization noise, we consider a quantizer with equal spacing between quantization levels. A typical "staircase" input-output transfer characteristic of such a quantizer is shown in Fig. 7-14, where the step size (i.e., the distance between levels) is a volts. The input signal $v(t)$ to the quantizer is assumed to have zero average value and to have a peak-to-peak amplitude swing of V volts,

$$V = v(t)_{\max} - v(t)_{\min} \qquad (7\text{-}38)$$

As mentioned previously, when binary coding is employed with code groups of n pulses each, the quantizer can accommodate 2^n amplitude levels. Therefore, the step size is determined by

$$a = V/2^n \qquad (7\text{-}39)$$

and the discrete output levels are the allowed values $\pm a/2$, $\pm 3a/2$, $\pm 5a/2$, $\ldots$, $\pm(2^n - 1)a/2$. The quantized output signal $v_q(t)$ has the value $ka/2$ whenever the input signal is within plus or minus one-half a step size ($\pm a/2$) of that value as described by

$$v_q(t) = \frac{ka}{2}, \qquad \text{when } \left| v(t) - \frac{ka}{2} \right| < \frac{a}{2} \qquad (7\text{-}40)$$

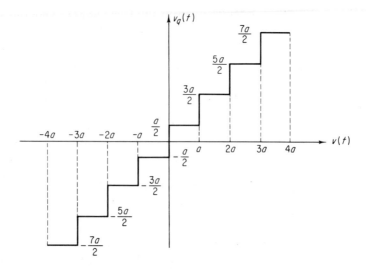

Fig. 7-14 Input-output transfer characteristic of a quantizer.

where k is an odd integer. Note that whereas the input signal covers the amplitude range $V = 2^n a$, the quantized signal amplitudes cover only the range

$$(2^n - 1)a = V - a \qquad (7\text{-}41)$$

Quantizing the signal amplitude introduces an initial error into the system that can never be removed. Once a signal is in a quantized state, the original signal cannot be recovered because of this error. The time-varying error $q_n(t)$, the difference between the input signal and the quantized signal, is referred to as the *quantization noise*

$$q_n(t) = v(t) - v_q(t) \qquad (7\text{-}42)$$

A unique feature of this noise is that its magnitude is always less than one-half a quantizing step height

$$|q_n(t)| < a/2 \qquad (7\text{-}43)$$

as distinctly different from transmission noise which could theoretically take on all possible amplitudes. Bennett (Ref. 5) and others have shown that quantization noise affects a PCM system as though it were an additive random fluctuation component with a zero mean and an r.m.s. value determined by the quantizing step size. When a signal is reconstructed from quantized samples, the original signal is obtained plus a noise having a uniform power spectrum over the bandwidth of the signal. Based on the assumption that over a long period of time all values of error voltage in the range $(- a/2, a/2)$ eventually appear the same number of times, the mean-squared value of the error will be

$$\overline{q_n^2} = \frac{1}{a} \int_{-a/2}^{a/2} q_n^2 dq_n = \frac{a^2}{12} \tag{7-44}$$

With the assumption made that the average value of the error is zero, the r.m.s. fluctuation error is then $1/\sqrt{12} = 1/(2\sqrt{3})$ times the height of a single quantizing step. This r.m.s. error voltage then represents the effect of quantization noise at the output of a PCM system.

A measure of the fidelity of signal reproduction in a PCM system can now be defined as the ratio of signal power to quantization noise power in the reconstructed signal, for signals that fully load the quantizer (i.e., input signals with the maximum peak-to-peak amplitude swing $V = 2^n a$). Four different types of signals are examined here.

1. *Uniformly distributed signal.* For this signal waveform all possible amplitudes are equally likely; that is, on a probabilistic basis the signal amplitudes are uniformly distributed over the full range $2^n a$. Therefore all possible quantization levels are equally likely also. A simple nonrandom signal that fits this description is a waveform with triangular excursions covering the maximum peak-to-peak swing of the quantizer. For this type of signal the average signal power of the reconstructed samples is given by

$$S_\Delta = \frac{2}{2^n} \sum_{i=1}^{2^{n-1}} (2i - 1)^2 \left(\frac{a}{2}\right)^2 = \frac{a^2}{12} (2^{2n} - 1) \tag{7-45}$$

The output signal-to-noise power ratio is then

$$\frac{S_\Delta}{\overline{q_n^2}} = \frac{S_\Delta}{a^2/12} = 2^{2n} - 1 \tag{7-46}$$

2. *Gaussianly distributed signal.* Another possible type of information signal is a noise-like waveform with a band-limited power spectrum and a Gaussian amplitude distribution. Such a noise-like waveform might be a possible model for a description of voice signals in PCM systems. Since peaks of Gaussian noise seldom exceed four times its r.m.s. value, we take the r.m.s. value of this signal before quantizing to be one-fourth of the peak overload voltage of the quantizer; i.e., $\sigma = 2^{n-1}a/4$. It can be shown that the average signal power of the reconstructed samples is also approximately σ^2 for $n > 4$ (the number of quantizing levels greater than 16). Therefore the output signal-to-noise ratio is approximately

$$\frac{S_v}{\overline{q_n^2}} \approx \frac{(2^{n-1})^2 a^2/16}{a^2/12} = \frac{3}{16} 2^{2n} \tag{7-47}$$

3. *Rectangular wave.* For a rectangular input waveform with the maximum peak-to-peak amplitude swing $2^n a$, the quantized samples would have the two values $\pm(2^n - 1)a/2$. The average signal power of these samples is

$$S_r = (2^n - 1)^2 a^2/4 \tag{7-48}$$

and the corresponding output signal-to-noise ratio is

$$\frac{S_r}{\overline{q_n^2}} = \frac{(2^n - 1)^2 a^2/4}{a^2/12} = 3(2^n - 1)^2 \tag{7-49}$$

4. *Sinusoidal signal.* For a full-load sinusoid of peak amplitude $2^n a/2$, it can be shown that the average power of the reconstructed samples is given by

$$S_s = \frac{1}{8}(2^n - 1)^2 a^2 \left[1 + \frac{1.6}{2^n}\right] \tag{7-50}$$

However, as expected for large $n\,(n > 4)$, the average reconstructed signal power approaches the r.m.s. power of a sinusoid of peak value $(2^n - 1)a/2$. Thus the output signal-to-noise ratio in this case is approximately

$$\frac{S_s}{\overline{q_n^2}} \approx \frac{(2^n - 1)^2 a^2/8}{a^2/12} = \frac{3}{2}(2^n - 1)^2 \tag{7-51}$$

which is just 3-dB smaller than for the rectangular waveform. Note that for all four signal types studied here the output SNR is roughly proportional to the square of the number of quantizing levels. Figure 7-15 illustrates the SNR improvement with the number of levels in a PCM system using these signals. Also indicated is the relative bandwidth as discussed previously. Since the bandwidth is proportional to n, the number of pulses per code group, and the SNR is on the order of 2^{2n}, with respect to quantization noise the output SNR in PCM systems increases *exponentially* with bandwidth, or the SNR in dB varies linearly with transmission bandwidth.

7-4 Delta Modulation

A somewhat different example of a coded binary modulation system is *delta modulation* (DM). For a more complete discussion of DM and references, see Ref. 2. DM is perhaps best described as a one-digit code PCM system which involves a form of differential

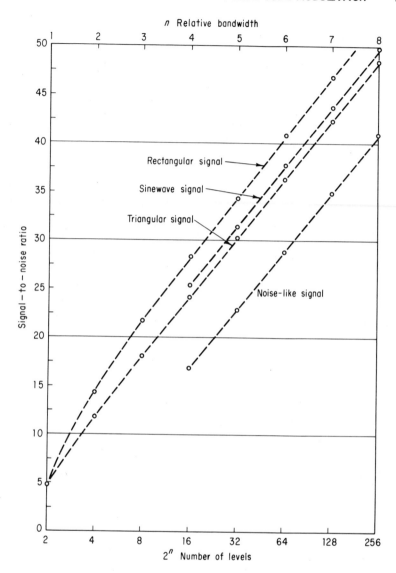

Fig. 7-15 PCM SNR improvement with number of quantization levels.

encoding of analog waveforms. Whereas PCM utilizes n digits to transmit a sampled signal amplitude, simple DM uses only one digit to indicate *changes* in the sampled value of the derivative of the signal amplitude. The outstanding feature of DM is the simplicity of the circuitry needed to implement the system, although DM requires a sampling rate much higher than the Nyquist rate, and generally a total wider bandwidth than a comparably performing

PCM system. Again, performance of a DM system is limited by quantization noise, but this limitation can be made small by using higher sampling rates and/or higher-order DM techniques. As is true of PCM systems, SNR in DM systems is determined solely by the quantization noise whenever the external system noise is not strong enough to interfere with pulse decisions at the detector. Most of the general aspects of transmission and reception are similar to those already discussed for PCM.

REFERENCES

1. H. S. Black, *Modulation Theory* (D. Van Nostrand and Co. Inc., Princeton, New Jersey, 1953).
2. P. F. Panter, *Modulation, Noise, and Spectral Analysis* (McGraw-Hill Book Company, New York, 1965).
3. M. Schwartz, *Information Transmission, Modulation, and Noise* (McGraw-Hill Book Company, New York, 1959).
4. B. M. Oliver, J. R. Pierce, and C. E. Shannon: "The Philosophy of PCM," *Proc. of the IRE*, pp. 1324-1331 (November 1948).
5. W. R. Bennett: "Spectra of Quantized Signals," *The Bell Sys. Tech. Journal*, Vol. 27, pp. 446-472 (July 1948).

8

Multiplexing Techniques

In the preceding chapters we have discussed several of the basic modulation techniques in terms of their ability to convey messages generated by a *single* information source. In practice the need frequently arises for a communication system to simultaneously convey multiple messages from a large number of information sources in one location to a large number of users at another. *Multiplexing* schemes (*multichannel operation*) economically meet this need by combining the messages from several information sources, which are then transmitted as a composite group over a single transmission facility, with provision at the receiver(s) for separation (demultiplexing) back to the individual messages. Since only one (though more complicated) transmitter and receiver is needed instead of many, one advantage of multichannel operation is a lessening of the total quantity of necessary equipment. Each of the individual streams of information that form a multiplexed group are often denoted as a *channel*.

Two generic forms of multiplexing are of interest. These are frequency division multiplexing (FDM) and time division multiplexing (TDM). FDM, which is directly applicable to continuous waveform (analog) sources, in essence involves "stacking" side-by-side in frequency several information channels so as to form a composite signal. This composite frequency-multiplexed signal is then used to modulate a carrier in some conventional manner. Recovery of the individual messages after reception and initial demodulation is accomplished by bandpass filtering and frequency selection of the channels. TDM, a logical extension of pulse modulation, involves interleaving in time the narrow pulses of several ordinary pulse modulation signals, such as PAM or PCM, and thus forming one composite pulse transmission system. Separation of the time multiplexed pulse streams at the receiver is accomplished by gating appropriate pulses into individual channel filters. A third technique, phase multiplexing, is possible also, but it appears to be of less practical interest than either FDM or TDM; however, it has been used to some extent to combine two channels in phase quadrature.

8-1 Frequency Division Multiplexing

A very commonly employed FDM system utilizes SSB modulation techniques to achieve the frequency multiplexing in a minimum transmission bandwidth. A block diagram of such a typical FDM system is shown in Fig. 8-1, and Fig. 8-2 illustrates the spectral relationships for this system. Examination of these figures reveals some pertinent aspects of FDM systems. Note that each of the input information channels is band-limited to some maximum frequency f_m assumed to be the same for all channels. Band-limiting of the information channels is necessary to prevent *crosstalk* through overlapping spectra of adjacent channels when stacked side-by-side in frequency and also to simplify channel separation at the receiver. Each channel waveform is modulated onto a sinusoidal *subcarrier* of the proper frequency to translate the channel to its allotted position in frequency. The subcarrier frequencies must be closely controlled to avoid crosstalk and other spurious effects between channels. Usually all subcarriers are generated from a master oscillator to ensure good regulation. In connection with this problem vacant frequency bands, termed *guard bands*, are placed between

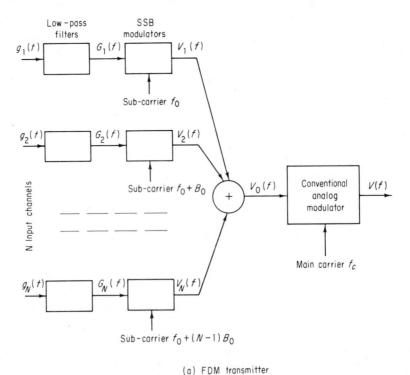

(a) FDM transmitter

Fig. 8-1 A frequency division multiplex system.

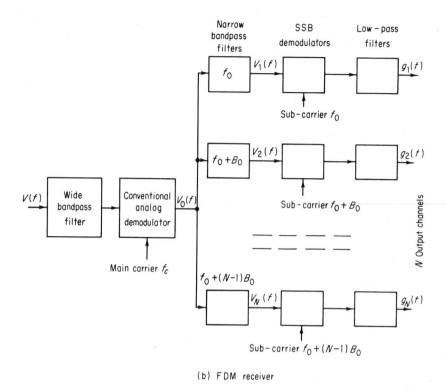

(b) FDM receiver

Fig. 8-1 A frequency division multiplex system.

channels to help minimize crosstalk and to ease the requirements of filtering and frequency selection involved with channel separation. For SSB modulation with information bandwidth f_m and guard bandwidths B_g, each channel has an overall bandwidth

$$B_0 = f_m + B_g \qquad (8\text{-}1)$$

An FDM system utilizing SSB consists then of a group of N such channels and requires a total transmission bandwidth

$$B = NB_0 = Nf_m + NB_g \qquad (8\text{-}2)$$

The FDM signal may then be modulated onto the main radio carrier, typically either by frequency modulation (FDM-FM) or as single-sideband modulation (FDM-SSB). At the receiver, the carrier is demodulated, and each channel of the multiplexed group individually separated out by channel filters of bandwidth f_m located at the sub-carrier frequencies. Typically (when SSB is used to form the multiplex group) the channel filter outputs are individually SSB demodulated with subcarriers of appropriate frequency to recover the original channel waveforms.

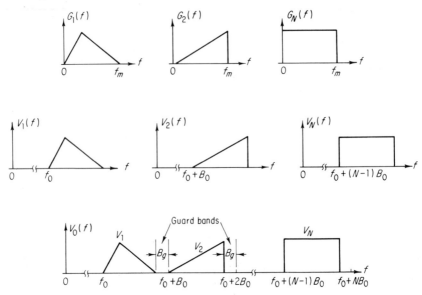

Fig. 8-2 Spectral relationships for the FDM system of Fig. 8-1 (only positive frequencies shown).

An important equipment and power advantage accrues to FDM systems known as the *"nonsimultaneous load advantage."* This refers to the fact that the channel waveforms rarely add to an instantaneous amplitude even approaching N times the peak value for any one channel. This means that the required dynamic range of an FDM system transmitting N channels increases slowly with N. This is particularly true for analog voice signals. Based on empirical data, for conversational speech, current telephone "toll quality" transmission practice provides for relative power capacity roughly as described in the table below (Ref. 1). The values listed for the required relative power capacity permit overload of the system to occur approximately 1% of the time. To emphasize the strikingly large nonsimultaneous load advantage obtainable on the

Nonsimultaneous Multiplex Load Advantage

Number of Channels	Required Relative Power Capacity	Advantage over N Separate Channels
1	0 dB	0
10	6 dB	20 − 6 = 14 dB
100	9 dB	40 − 9 = 31 dB
500	13 dB	54 − 13 = 41 dB
1000	16 dB	60 − 16 = 44 dB

average with conventional speech, note for instance that the 1% overload level of a 1000-channel FDM voice system is equivalent to adding peak instantaneous voltages of only six full-load tones. This property of FDM systems represents an important savings in equipment and power utilization.

8-2 Time Division Multiplexing

A typical TDM system is illustrated by the block diagram of Fig. 8-3, where the indicated pulse transmission system is any one of the conventional pulse modulation processes such as PAM or

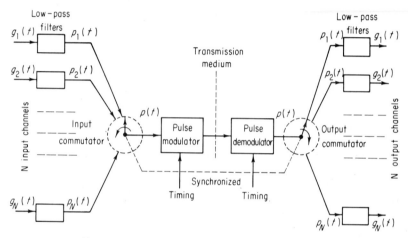

Fig. 8-3 A time division multiplexed pulse system.

PCM. Some pertinent pulse timing plots are shown in Fig. 8-4. As in all pulse modulation systems, the first operation in a TDM system is the sampling or digitizing process. In TDM systems waveform sampling is performed by the input "commutator" (Fig. 8-3), a device that sequentially samples all N input channels once per revolution (i.e., once per each sampling period T or at a rate $f_c = 1/T$ samples per second). Just as for FDM systems, the input channels of a TDM system must also be band-limited to avoid distortion owing to the sampling process. The low-pass filter on each input channel constrains the input spectrum to lie below some frequency f_m. Therefore the sampling rate must be at least as great as twice the highest frequency component in an information waveform or

$$f_c \geq 2f_m \qquad\qquad (8\text{-}3)$$

The function of the input commutator is than twofold, first to take a narrow sample of each of the N input waveforms and second to sequentially interleave these N pulse samples in the space of T seconds. This latter function is the time multiplexing operation.

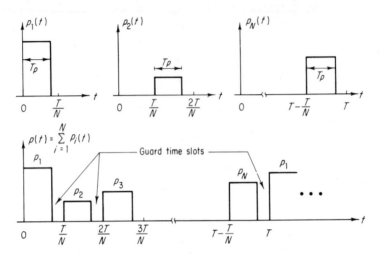

Fig. 8-4 Pulse timing diagram of a TDM system.

Following the commutation process, the multiplexed pulse group is introduced into the pulse modulator where, according to the particular modulation technique employed, each pulse is modulated and transmitted to the receiver. Since this TDM scheme must squeeze N pulses into the space of just one pulse of a single-channel system, this introduces a bandwidth widening factor N. If the chosen pulse modulation technique requires a transmission bandwidth B_0 for single-channel operation, its transmission bandwidth must be increased to

$$B = NB_0 \tag{8-4}$$

to accommodate N multiplexed channels. If, for example, PCM is employed, an additional bandwidth expansion factor is introduced by the coding as described in Chap. 7.

At the TDM receiver the narrow pulse samples are reformed and then distributed by the output commutator (operating synchronously with the input commutator) to appropriate channel filters. A final low-pass filtering operation recovers each of the N channel waveforms.

As indicated, separation or demultiplexing of the pulse streams is accomplished by the output commutator, which must be accurately synchronized with the input commutator process. If a loss of synchronism occurs between the input and output commutators, the pulse samples will be gated into the wrong output channel filters, resulting in confusion of the message waveforms appearing in all channels. Perhaps the most significant problem in TDM systems is the acquisition and tracking of synchronization information. Most TDM systems transmit synchronization signals by occasionally inserting special *sync* pulses into the transmission, which enable the receiver circuitry to lock to the timing of the transmitter. Still other TDM systems use very stable "clocks" or master oscillators at both receiver and transmitter, which after an initial *sync* procedure maintain synchronization for long periods of time. A common device used in TDM systems to help ease the problems associated with channel separation and synchronization is to include *guard time slots* or vacant time intervals between pulses. Guard time slots have the effect of further decreasing pulse widths and causing an additional widening of the transmission bandwidth.

As discussed previously for PCM, the one big advantage of all pulse systems is the possibility of reshaping or reforming the pulses followed by amplification, to improve the signal-to-noise ratio at any point during transmission and at the final receiver. In this *regeneration* process the effects of transmission noise and disturbances can be almost completely eliminated, provided the noise is not overwhelming. Thus several repeater stations can be spaced along the transmission path to restrengthen the TDM signal and to almost completely remove the noise introduced along the previous path. This regeneration advantage does not accrue to continuous waveform systems since amplification of these signals amplifies any noise that is present as well as the signal, and so the signal-to-noise ratio steadily worsens in analog systems such as FDM.

REFERENCE

1. C. B. Feldman and W. R. Bennett: "Bandwidth and Transmission Performance," *The Bell System Tech. Journal,* Vol. 28, pp. 490-595 (July 1949).

9

Introduction to Digital Signaling

In the preceding chapters we have briefly reviewed conventional signal and modulation theory, and some aspects of reception in additive Gaussian noise. Primarily analog signals were discussed in these chapters, and in all cases emphasis was on signal-to-noise ratio as an intuitive figure of merit describing the *fidelity* with which demodulation recovers the original modulating waveforms in the presence of additive noise. The concept of encoding analog information into binary or other digital format, such as PCM, was also introduced. It was indicated that a digitally encoded (quantized) system can tolerate more signal distortion and noise prior to initial demodulation than can an analog modulation system. The important factor in reception of PCM is only that the interfering noise and distortion should not be so great as to produce incorrect *decisions* on the sequence of transmitted digits. *Fidelity* in receiving and processing the pulses in demodulation becomes unimportant. Indeed, as we shall point out later (Chap. 13), the best demodulation techniques in the *decision* sense involve rather extreme distortion of the pulse shapes prior to decision and waveform reconstruction.

In other words, in PCM systems the *quality* of the final reconstituted analog output, measured as a signal-to-noise ratio or in any equivalent sense, is a function only of the *probability of correct reception* of the pulse sequences. Since the latter probability is usually near unity, a more sensitive criterion is its difference from unity, termed the *probability of error*. For example, high-quality voice transmission by PCM may require a probability of error on each pulse of 10^{-5}. That is, on the average, one allows at most about one erroneous decision per 100,000. On the other hand, minimal intelligibility for PCM systems may be possible with error-rates exceeding 0.01.

PCM is only one special example of a digital transmission. A more familiar example is telegraphy, or Teletype. Here the information being transmitted is the *written* language, which in the generic sense is already in *digital* form. By this one means that using, say, only upper-case letters, the information symbols being transmitted are selected from a *finite, discrete* set: 26 letters,

10 numbers, and about 10 punctuation symbols. This set of less than 50 *symbols* comprises the total *alphabet* of both the source information and the receiving terminal output. Each symbol can, for example, be assigned a number (or ordered in a list) for reference purposes; hence the allusion to the set as a *digital alphabet*. Usage of the word digital in this context does not imply that only number messages are being sent but implies only *discreteness* of the set of possible information symbols. This discreteness is in contrast to, say, an analog voice transmission. If one could make up a waveform dictionary of all possible voice utterances, it would also be possible to convey speech in some direct digital form, with an alphabet size equal to the total number of entries in the dictionary. Indeed, one could assign each utterance a number and send it by transmitting only a number or some other equivalent symbol.

By digital communications, then, one implies no more and no less than that the information content can be represented by a discrete sequence, where each entry in the sequence is drawn from some *finite* set of symbols or waveforms. If the information is basically *binary*, the alphabet need contain only two symbols or two waveforms, one used to transmit a "1" in the message sequence, the other to transmit a "0". If the information is language, a higher-order alphabet is required for presentation in the usual printed form. However, note carefully that the symbols in this higher-order alphabet may also be constructed as particular sequences of more elementary units. Braille is one such example. Another familiar example is the Morse Code representation of each alphanumeric by a particular dot-dash sequence. In the latter case, the set of character sequences forms a large alphabet (about 50 in size), but all are made up from the elementary dot-dash symbols and corresponding spaces. Similarly, in PCM, each PCM-*code word* represents a particular quantized amplitude level in the original intelligence, but the code word is commonly transmitted as a sequence of binary symbols.

In the last case mentioned, the actual electrical transmission involves a binary sequence. In discussing system operation in such a case, one often considers separately the operations involved in recovering the binary information (say, for purposes of signal and receiver design) and then only subsequently considers the overall performance achieved with respect to the groupings of these binary symbols as PCM code words or alphanumeric characters. Thus the transmission facility may be basically binary in nature (this is the most common situation in present-day communications) and, despite the *character* nature of the final output, the design or optimization of the overall operation may be premised almost completely on the "*binary channel*" performance.

On the other hand, under certain conditions such as in the presence of intermittent interference or when the signal is fading up and down in level, there may be a tendency for errors to cluster, i.e., occur in localized groups. In this case, character performance may depend not only upon the long-term average probability of error for any individual binary symbol but also upon the statistics of the clustering. For such a *transmission channel* (channel being used to connote the entire transmission environment), meaningful design calculations then involve the overall character performance. Some simple calculations of this type will be described in Chap. 15. As will be seen, the first step in such computations involves calculations of the probability of error for each binary symbol. The remainder of the calculations then involves particular properties of the grouping of the binary symbols into characters or properties of the transmission channel causing the error clustering. Such calculations are overly specific for our purposes in this book, and our attention in the chapters which follow will dwell rather on symbol *error-rate* (probability of error) as the performance criterion, with most of the detail on binary transmission.

Accordingly, the purpose of the following chapters is to provide a general introduction to digital communication techniques and their performance. The emphasis will be on reception of steady (non-fading) signals in additive Gaussian noise. Basic binary signaling techniques are introduced in Chaps. 10 to 12, followed in Chap. 13 by a general discussion of matched-filtering and correlation detection. Higher-order (M-ary) signaling is then described in Chap. 14, followed by a brief discussion in Chap. 15 of the role of error-control coding in radio communications. Finally in Chap. 16 a mathematical model is given for the so-called Rayleigh fading which typifies many long-distance radio channels, and a discussion is given of its effect upon performance, and Chap. 17 outlines the effects of various forms of diversity as antifading measures.

As mentioned earlier, our emphasis in these chapters will be on carrier (bandpass) signaling, in additive Gaussian noise. These are not the only channel models which occur in communications. Low-pass noncarrier channels may be involved in telephone or cable networks. In such networks, the important error-causing mechanisms may be distinctly non-Gaussian in nature, often involving random channel distortions or noises of an impulsive character. Impulsive noise arising from atmospherics (lightning pulses) propagated over long distances may also be dominant or significant for radio communications in the high-frequency (h.f.) band, or at lower radio frequencies. The reader is referred to the literature for discussion of such other channels (e.g., Ref. 1 on data transmission over the telephone network).

REFERENCE

1. W. R. Bennett and J. R. Davey, *Data Transmission* (McGraw-Hill Book Company, New York, 1965).

10

Binary On-off Keying (OOK)

10-1 Some General Principles

In describing binary signaling in this and succeeding chapters, we will often use the descriptive telegraphy terms Mark and Space to refer to the two binary signaling states. These states are often also termed $+1$ and -1, or 1 and 0. In any event, for our purposes, these are all only convenient labels for denoting the binary states.

Also, in Chaps. 10 to 12, we will discuss primarily sinusoidal waveforms, generated by modulation of sinusoidal carriers with simple waveshapes. In addition to simplicity of both the signals and the associated receivers, such waveforms constitute the bulk of the signals used in digital radio communications. However, effective signaling can be carried out with much more arbitrary classes of waveforms; this topic is discussed in Chap. 13.

In this chapter we describe binary on–off keying. Although this mode of signaling is no longer very common in modern digital radio communication design, as compared to the FSK and PSK signaling described in Chaps. 11 and 12, it still serves as a convenient basis for introducing many of the basic concepts.

A binary *on-off keyed* (OOK) radio system is a specialized form of amplitude modulation. It has sometimes been termed *amplitude-shift keying* (ASK), particularly in connection with discussions which extend to multilevel signaling (as in Chap. 14). An idealized OOK system may be described as transmitting pulses of the form

$$s_T(t) = \begin{cases} u_T(t)\cos(2\pi f_c t + \phi_T) \,, & \text{for Mark} \\ \\ 0 \quad\quad\quad\quad , & \text{for Space} \end{cases} \tag{10-1}$$

where $u_T(t)$ is some low-pass waveform often, but not necessarily, a rectangular pulse. We will assume for now that the communication medium introduces no distortions on the signal waveform. As shown in our simplified model of a binary receiver (Fig. 10-1a), the received signal is contaminated at the receiver input with additive Gaussian noise, originating either as pickup by the antenna (antenna noise) or as receiver thermal noise in the r.f. amplifiers or mixer stages. The combined waveform of signal plus noise is then translated to some convenient frequency and filtered. Frequency translations are assumed not to affect the *relative* levels, statistics, or waveforms of signal and noise, and hence these operations are not included in our analytical model. For Chaps. 10 to 12 we will also not comment on the details of the bandpass filtering action beyond stating that these filters limit the spectrum of the signal and noise waveforms presented to the detector to that band needed for appropriate processing of the signaling waveform. After examining and becoming familiar with detection results in a number of cases, we will discuss in Chap. 13 the detailed implications of filter parameters.

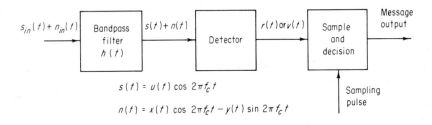

$$s(t) = u(t) \cos 2\pi f_c t$$

$$n(t) = x(t) \cos 2\pi f_c t - y(t) \sin 2\pi f_c t$$

(a) Elements of a simple receiver

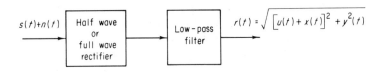

(b) Noncoherent (envelope) detector

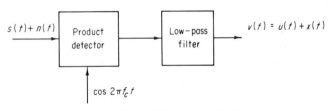

(c) Coherent (synchronous) detector

Fig. 10-1 Elements of a binary digital receiver.

Accordingly we use our representation of bandpass signal and noise (Sec. 4-6) to directly describe the outputs of the band-pass filter. Assuming this output centered on some frequency f_c, the signal term in the filter output arising from the transmitted signal of (10-1) has the form*

$$s(t) = \begin{cases} u(t) \cos 2\pi f_c t , & \text{Mark being received} \\ \\ 0 , & \text{Space being received} \end{cases} \tag{10-2}$$

Two examples of such a signal are shown in Fig. 10-2a, b. The reader will be able to verify that no loss of generality in the results below occurs because of the arbitrary choice of phase reference implied in (10-2). Associated with (10-2), the additive noise term

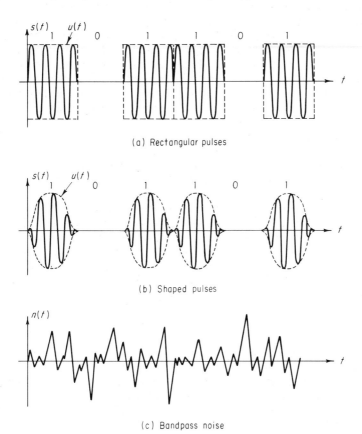

(a) Rectangular pulses

(b) Shaped pulses

(c) Bandpass noise

Fig. 10-2 Examples of OOK signals and bandpass noise.

in the filter output will have the form (Sec. 4-6),

$$n(t) = x(t) \cos 2\pi f_c t - y(t) \sin 2\pi f_c t \tag{10-3}$$

---

*Assuming here that there is no intersymbol interference (discussed further in Sec. 10-2).

where $x(t)$ and $y(t)$ are low-pass Gaussian processes, with statistics governed by the receiver filters, etc. Considering for the moment only the case of a *Mark signaled*, we write the filter output as a sum of the signal and noise terms,

$$s(t) + n(t) = [u(t) + x(t)] \cos 2\pi f_c t - y(t) \sin 2\pi f_c t \qquad (10\text{-}4)$$

This signal is now applied to a detector and decision circuit, to determine whether a Mark or a Space is present. The receiver is assumed to know the timing of the succession of binary waveforms (i.e., it is assumed to maintain *perfect synchronization*). It is also assumed that the binary decisions are made by *sampling the detector output* at some appropriate *instant, once per information pulse.* The sampled voltage will, for example, determine the setting of a telegraph relay or some equivalent operation. As noted in Figs. 10-1b and c, the detector implementation usually involves a nonlinear device whose output includes undesired harmonics at multiples of the frequency f_c, in addition to the desired detected value near zero frequency. The nonlinear device is therefore usually followed by a low-pass filter that rejects these harmonics; however, this filter can have a cutoff frequency well above the signal bandwidth and hence passes the desired detected terms *without distortion or smoothing.* Regarding both the nonlinear device *and* this associated low-pass filter as the detector, we will speak of such detectors as *zero-memory* devices. In the model of Fig. 10-1, accordingly, all *relevant integration, smoothing*, etc., is accomplished in the *predetection filtering*, and there is *no* relevant *postdetection filtering.* This applies to optimum and most near-optimum receivers (Chap. 13). There are some communication receivers which employ filtering (smoothing) following the detector; however, we remark that rigorous or dependable analyses do not generally exist for binary error-rate performance of such systems.

The most common method for detection of on-off keyed signals is noncoherent detection, involving measurement of the amplitude of the *envelope* of the bandpass filter output. Coherent detection methods may also be employed, although we shall see later that once coherent detection techniques are admitted, one may easily achieve higher performance by other than on-off keying. Both forms of detection will be considered below.

10-2 Noncoherent Detection

From (10-4), and as illustrated in Fig. 10-1b, the envelope of the bandpass filter output is a time waveform given by

$$r(t) = \sqrt{[u(t) + x(t)]^2 + y^2(t)} \qquad (10\text{-}5)$$

As already remarked, the forming of the envelope may be regarded as a zero-memory process. We recall that for Gaussian noise $x(t)$ and $y(t)$ are Gaussian and also recall from (4-211) that the probability density function of the envelope at any instant is given by

$$p(r) = \frac{r}{N} I_0 \left(\frac{ur}{N}\right) e^{-(r^2 + u^2)/2N} \tag{10-6}$$

where u is the signal envelope value *at that instant* and $N = \sigma^2 = \overline{x^2} = \overline{y^2}$ is the (ensemble) average power of the total output noise *at that instant*. (We are assuming here that the noise has a zero-mean value.) Thus, in writing this p.d.f., the time-dependence has been suppressed on both $r(t)$ and $u(t)$.

The statement that the envelope will be sampled once per pulse, to determine whether the pulse was Mark or Space, implies a number of assumptions for ideal operation. One already stated is that *synchronous timing* is available at the receiver. That is, we assume an accurate knowledge of the time interval of occurrence of each information pulse in the received waveform and hence of appropriate timings for the successive envelope samplings and binary decisions. Second, the envelope value involved in each sample is assumed to include only the voltages associated with a single information pulse, plus noise. This assumption preempts the possibility of intersymbol interference, in which the binary decisions may be confused by residual voltages in the filter output remaining from previous pulse inputs. In part this in turn implies practically that the information pulses are of finite length. Commonly for a Mark starting at time $t = 0$, the pulse is zero for $t < 0$ and for $t > T$, where T is the spacing between successive pulse starts. If the sampling instant occurs at $T_S(T_S \leq T)$ following the start of each pulse, the further implication is that the filter has, over an interval of length T_S, completely discharged all currents or voltages remaining from the previous pulses.* This problem is discussed in greater length in Sec. 13-7.

One alternative approach for avoiding intersymbol interference is a rapid discharging of the filter, via auxiliary circuitry, at the end of each pulse. The resulting circuit is no longer truly a linear, nontime-varying filter, even though the filter acts in an "ordinary" manner *between* discharge intervals. For such a regularly discharged filter, the filter bandwidth is no longer critical with respect to intersymbol interference and may be as narrow a bandwidth (long ringing time) as desired. Indeed, if one goes to the limit of extremely narrow bandwidths, the result is an ideal integrating

---

*Based on the discussion above, if a continuously operating, nontime-varying filter is in use, its rise time (decay time) ideally must be shorter than T_S. For a simple one-pole (RLC) filter, for example, if rise time is interpreted at the 10-90% interval for the envelope of the filter response to a step input, the 3-dB bandwidth will have to exceed $0.7/T_S$

bandpass filter whose impulse response has an envelope which is a step function. The effect of discharge every T seconds is to convert the effective impulse response to a rectangle of duration T. Such an *integrate-and-dump* filter, as it is often termed, is then (as shown in Chap. 13) a proper filter for optimal reception of constant amplitude pulses, and indeed is the one outstanding instance where so-called matched-filter detection (Sec. 13-1) has been routinely achieved in communication applications.

Returning now to the OOK problem, the first-order p.d.f. (10-6) describes the envelope of the filter output at the sampling instant, this form being applicable whatever the detailed nature of the predetection filters (which, however, do determine how the values of u and N are related to signal and noise in the receiver front-end). We also assume here that the exact r.f. (or i.f.) phase changes randomly over successive Mark pulses and hence is an unknown. Then it is intuitively clear that for this on-off signaling, the Mark/Space decision for each signal pulse can be based only upon comparing $r(t)$ at the sampling instant against some threshold* voltage level.

Specifically let b denote the threshold level. Then when $r(t) \geq b$ at a sampling instant, the decision is Mark, and when $r(t) < b$ the decision is Space. Thus for a Mark transmitted the probability of an error is the probability of a failure to exceed the threshold. With the p.d.f. (10-6), this probability of error is given by

$$P_{eM} = \text{prob}(r < b) = \int_0^b p(r)\,dr = 1 - \int_b^\infty p(r)\,dr$$

$$= 1 - \int_b^\infty \frac{r}{N} I_0\left(\frac{ur}{N}\right) e^{-(r^2 + u^2)/2N}\,dr \qquad (10\text{-}7)$$

This integral can be evaluated in terms of the so-called Marcum Q-function (Refs. 1, 5) defined by

$$Q(\alpha, \beta) = \int_\beta^\infty t\, I_0(\alpha t)\, e^{-(t^2 + \alpha^2)/2}\,dt \qquad (10\text{-}8)$$

which is familiar in radar detection studies. As seen by comparing (10-8) with (10-7), $Q(\alpha, \beta)$ is the probability that the envelope of a sine wave of peak value α plus additive Gaussian noise of unit power will exceed some value β. The Q-function is reasonably well

---

*The fact that a threshold decision on the envelope is the optimum decision criterion when signal phase is not known can be derived from first principles of decision theory (see Chap. 13). Similar remarks apply to the coherent detection discussion in Sec. 10-3.

tabulated (Ref. 3) and excellent machine calculation routines are additionally available (e.g., Refs. 2, 4). The Q-function has the following special properties:

$$Q(\alpha, 0) = \int_0^\infty t\, I_0(\alpha t)\, e^{-(\alpha^2 + t^2)/2}\, dt = 1 \qquad (10\text{-}9a)$$

$$Q(0, \beta) = \int_\beta^\infty t\, e^{-t^2/2}\, dt = e^{-\beta^2/2} \qquad (10\text{-}9b)$$

Its complement

$$R(\alpha, \beta) = 1 - Q(\alpha, \beta) = \int_0^\beta t\, I_0(\alpha t)\, e^{-(\alpha^2 + t^2)/2}\, dt$$

$$= e^{-(\alpha^2 + \beta^2)/2} \sum_{m=1}^\infty \left(\frac{\beta}{\alpha}\right)^m I_m(\alpha\beta) \qquad (10\text{-}10)$$

is well known in other extensive literature (e.g., Ref. 2) as the circular coverage function, e.g., as applied to the two-dimensional target-aiming problem.

Thus in (10-7) the probability of an error when a Mark is signaled is

$$P_{eM} = 1 - Q(\sqrt{2\gamma}, b_0) \qquad (10\text{-}11)$$

where we have introduced the notation

$$\gamma = u^2/2N \qquad (10\text{-}12a)$$

for the *signal-to-noise ratio* (SNR) at the bandpass filter output *at the sampling instant,* and

$$b_0 = b/\sqrt{N} \qquad (10\text{-}12b)$$

for the threshold level normalized to the r.m.s. noise voltage.

Similarly the probability of an error when a Space is signaled is the probability that in the absence of signal the noise voltage alone in the filter output will exceed the threshold. Thus, setting $u = 0$ in (10-6), we have for this case

$$p(r) = \frac{r}{N} e^{-r^2/2N} \qquad (10\text{-}13)$$

and

$$P_{eS} = \text{prob}\,(r > b) = \int_b^\infty p(r)\, dr = e^{-b_0^2/2} \qquad (10\text{-}14)$$

Assuming Marks and Spaces occur with equal probability (each with probability 1/2), the average probability of error* for non-coherent OOK signaling is given by

$$P_e = \frac{1}{2} P_{eM} + \frac{1}{2} P_{eS} = \frac{1}{2} [1 - Q(\sqrt{2\gamma}, b_0)] + \frac{1}{2} e^{-b_0^2/2} \qquad (10\text{-}15)$$

The areas under $p(r)$ involved in this calculation are illustrated graphically in Fig. 10-3. A set of curves for probability of error versus SNR at various fixed threshold levels is shown in Fig. 10-4. Note that curves for *fixed* threshold approach constant values with large SNR. This is due to errors caused by noise alone exceeding the threshold level rather than due to signal-plus-noise failing to exceed threshold. In the terminology of radar detection this is known as a constant false-alarm rate situation. Clearly a fixed threshold is nonoptimum for OOK in the sense of minimizing the error-rate, since the error-rate can never then be made smaller than the false-alarm rate associated with the threshold level.

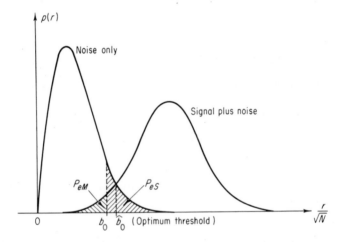

Fig. 10-3 Probability density functions for noncoherent (envelope) detection of OOK signals.

As is clear from Fig. 10-4, there is an optimum value of threshold *for each SNR* which minimizes the error-rate. This optimum threshold is the value $\hat{b}_0$ at which $\partial P_e/\partial b_0 = 0$ in (10-15). It is readily shown that $\hat{b}_0$ is the solution to the transcendental equation

$$I_0(\hat{b}_0 \sqrt{2\gamma}) e^{-\gamma} = 1 \quad \text{or} \quad \gamma = ln\, I_0(\hat{b}_0 \sqrt{2\gamma}) \qquad (10\text{-}16)$$

---

*Error-rate is often used synonymously with probability of error, in the sense that over long sequences, the fraction of total elements in error will closely approach the probability of error for any individual element (large sample interpretation of probability).

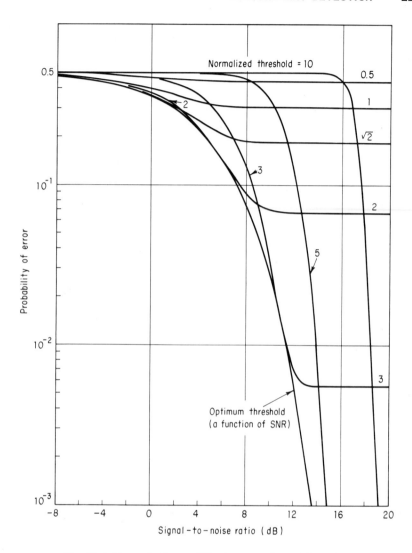

Fig. 10-4 Error-rate for on-off keying, noncoherent detection.

Graphically $\hat{b}_0$ is the normalized envelope value corresponding to the crossover point of the p.d.f.'s of Fig. 10-3. (Note that for this minimum error condition an unbalance exists for the two types of errors in noncoherent OOK.) The solution for $\hat{b}_0$ ranges monotonically from a <u>fixed</u> value of $\sqrt{2}$ for $\gamma \ll 1$ to an asymptotic dependence $\hat{b}_0 = \sqrt{\gamma/2}$ for $\gamma \gg 1$. Recalling (10-12), the latter is equivalent to an unnormalized optimum threshold

$$\hat{b} = u/2 \qquad (10\text{-}17)$$

as might be expected. In other words, for high SNR the optimum unnormalized threshold is one-half the Mark envelope value. The relation

$$\hat{b}_0 = \sqrt{2 + \frac{\gamma}{2}} \qquad (10\text{-}18)$$

is an excellent analytic approximation to the solution of (10-16) for all γ. Using the optimum obtained from (10-16) for each γ, we show the corresponding error-rate (minimum achievable for noncoherent detection of OOK) as the lowest curve of Fig. 10-4. Clearly a reasonable estimate of SNR is needed for proper threshold adjustment. For a channel whose transmission characteristic is slowly changing, an approximation to this desired operation is obtained through use of atuomatic gain control (AGC), followed by a fixed-threshold filter-detector. In effect, as SNR increases, the AGC reduces the receiver gain and consequently reduces the false-alarm rate.

We also note some useful asymptotic forms for high SNR (Refs. 1, 5). For a, b large we have for the Q-function

$$Q(a,b) \approx 1 - \frac{1}{2} \operatorname{erfc}\left[\frac{a - b}{\sqrt{2}}\right] = \operatorname{erfc}\left[\frac{b - a}{\sqrt{2}}\right] \qquad (10\text{-}19)$$

where erfc ( ) is the complementary error function introduced in Chap. 4. Then at high SNR the error-rate in (10-15) achieved with optimum threshold is well approximated by

$$\text{opt. threshold:} \qquad P_e \approx \frac{1}{4} \operatorname{erfc}\left(\frac{\sqrt{\gamma}}{2}\right) + \frac{1}{2} e^{-\gamma/4} \qquad (10\text{-}20)$$

We further have the asymptotic result for the complementary error function*

$$x \to \infty: \qquad \operatorname{erfc} x \approx \frac{e^{-x^2}}{x\sqrt{\pi}}\left[1 + 0\left(\frac{1}{x^2}\right)\right] \qquad (10\text{-}21)$$

so that for $\gamma \gg 1$, (10-20) is well approximated by only its second term (actually a close lower bound on P_e),

$$\text{opt. threshold:} \qquad P_e \approx \frac{1}{2} e^{-\gamma/4} \qquad (10\text{-}22)$$

Note the important implication of this last result. For steady signals in additive Gaussian noise, using on-off keying with noncoherent detection, and *using an optimized threshold,* the error-rate

---

*The notation $0(z)$ indicates terms which approach zero as fast as z approaches zero, i.e., as some constant times z.

decreases *exponentially* with SNR. Note also that under these conditions the errors predominantly occur because of false alarms.

10-3 Coherent Detection

In ideal coherent detection we assume that there is available in the receiver an exact replica of the possible arriving signal, exact even to r.f. phase. This can be achieved, for example, by use of very stable oscillators in both transmitter and receiver. As indicated in Chap. 5 and in Fig. 10-1c, the receiver then in effect multiplies and filters (or crosscorrelates*) this replica against the sum of the received signal and the additive noise. The specific question of deriving such a replica for use in the receiver is deferred to Chap. 12, where it is discussed within the application context of phase-shift keying.

With the signal phase thus defined, we can conveniently use the same phase reference to define the quadrature components of the additive noise. This is just what was done in writing (10-2) and (10-3). In this sense, one-half the noise energy is in phase with the signal and the other half is in phase quadrature to the signal. Coherent detection of a signal may then be viewed as extraction of this signal from a background of noise and interference, along with whatever portion of the background is in phase with the desired signal, while rejecting that part in phase quadrature.** It is the latter rejection operation which tends to diminish the perturbations caused by a given amount of noise energy in the band of the signal and which produces for coherent detection the advantages noted below over noncoherent detection. However, as we shall see later in Chap. 12, the fullest advantage of coherent detection in binary transmission is obtained by using the presumed knowledge of signal phase to encode the binary information as the phase of a single *continuous* waveform (phase-shift keying) rather than the on-off keying case examined below.

At the moment our purposes are well served by considering only the most common signaling—the transmission of a simply modulated sine-wave tone. For now we will assert that the coherent detection operation is equivalent to bandpass filtering of the received signal and noise, followed by a multiplier-filter operation (synchronous detection) as depicted in Fig. 10-1c. That is, the bandpass filter output described in (10-4) is multiplied with a reference signal which (ideally) is perfectly in phase with the signal

---

*Discussed in Sec. 13-2.
**For more general signal waveforms, one can still define the noise to be composed of one component in phase with the signal and one in quadrature with it. Using a replica of the signal for coherent correlation detection (see Chap. 13), one obtains the same rejection of the noise quadrature component as described above.

components, in this case a signal of the form $\cos 2\pi f_c t$. Multiplication is then followed by a not-very-restrictive low-pass filtering which removes the double-frequency components but passes the zero-frequency terms without distortion, as in Fig. 10-1c. The result (ignoring a factor of 1/2 which may be lumped into receiver gain constants) is a detector output*

$$v(t) = u(t) + x(t) \tag{10-23}$$

Again, $x(t)$ is zero-mean Gaussian with average power $\overline{x^2} = N$, where N is the *total* noise power in the filter output. Thus, when the signal is present (Mark signaled), $v(t)$ is simply a *biased* Gaussian variable, with mean value $u(t)$ and variance N. Its p.d.f. is then

$$p(v) = \frac{1}{\sqrt{2\pi N}} e^{-(v-u)^2/2N} \tag{10-24}$$

and its cumulative distribution function (i.e., the probability of exceeding the threshold b) is

$$P(v > b) = \int_b^\infty \frac{1}{\sqrt{2\pi N}} e^{-(v-u)^2/2N} \, dv = \frac{1}{2} \operatorname{erfc}\left[\frac{b_0}{\sqrt{2}} - \sqrt{\gamma} \right] \tag{10-25}$$

where $b_0 = b/\sqrt{N}$ and $\gamma = u^2/2N$ have the same meanings as earlier. In particular γ is again the filter output SNR at the sampling instant for each pulse.

When the signal is *not* present (Space signaled), $u(t) = 0$, and the detector output is simply

$$v(t) = x(t) \tag{10-26}$$

Hence in this event, $v(t)$ is zero-mean Gaussian with variance N. Its p.d.f. and cumulative distribution function are given, respectively, by (10-24) and (10-25) by setting $u = \gamma = 0$. For coherent detection of OOK the only difference between the p.d.f.'s for Mark or Spaced signaled is the bias or mean value u, the Mark signal value in the filter output at the sampling instant. At the sampling

---

*If there is subsequent low-pass filtering which modifies the signal and noise voltages, its modifications to the signal and noise voltage can be accounted for in the usual manner from the filter transfer characteristic, leaving a form exactly like (10-23). However, this lack of change in statistical form applies only in the case of the ideal noiseless-reference coherent detector being discussed here. Within this limitation there is no loss in regarding (10-23) as the basic description of the output after post-detection filtering, at the point where the Mark/Space decision is to be made. In this case bandpass filtering prior to the coherent detection process is completely equivalent mathematically to low-pass filtering following synchronous detection. These remarks apply as well to the ideal coherent phase-shift keying receiver described later in Chap. 12.

instant the decision as to Mark or Space signaled is determined by comparison of $v(t)$ against a threshold b described by the normalized value $b_0 = b/\sqrt{N}$. Thus, proceeding as in (10-15) and assuming Marks and Spaces equally likely, the probability of error for coherent detection of OOK is

$$P_e = \frac{1}{2}\left[1 - \frac{1}{2}\,\text{erfc}\left(\frac{b_0}{\sqrt{2}} - \sqrt{\gamma}\right)\right] + \frac{1}{2}\left[\frac{1}{2}\,\text{erfc}\left(\frac{b_0}{\sqrt{2}}\right)\right] \qquad (10\text{-}27)$$

The areas under $p(r)$ involved in the integration are shown in Fig. 10-5.

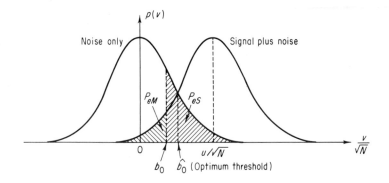

Fig. 10-5 Probability density functions for coherent detection of OOK signals.

Again, for a given SNR γ, setting $\partial P_e/\partial b_0 = 0$ gives an optimum threshold which minimizes P_e. This time it is readily shown to be determined for all signal-to-noise ratios by

$$\hat{b}_0 = \sqrt{\frac{\gamma}{2}} \quad \text{or} \quad \hat{b} = \frac{u}{2} \qquad (10\text{-}28)$$

This is also apparent from examination of Fig. 10-5; it corresponds to the crossover point of the two p.d.f.'s. Using (10-28) and recalling the identity

$$\text{erfc}(-x) = 2 - \text{erfc}(x) \qquad (10\text{-}29)$$

the minimum error-rate when the threshold is optimally adjusted at each SNR is given simply by

$$\text{opt. threshold:} \qquad P_e = \frac{1}{2}\,\text{erfc}\left(\frac{\sqrt{\gamma}}{2}\right) \qquad (10\text{-}30)$$

This is shown plotted versus SNR as the lowest curve in Fig. 10-6, along with plots of (10-27) versus SNR for various fixed thresholds.

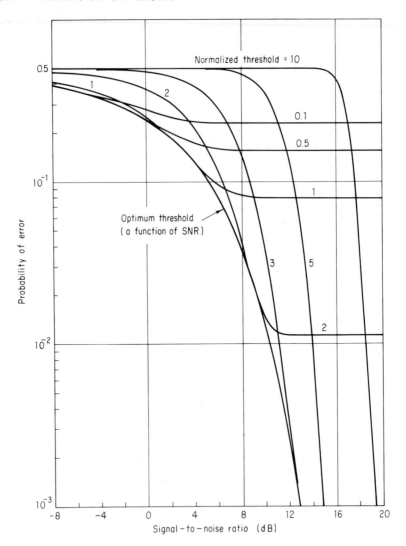

Fig. 10-6 Error-rate for on-off keying, coherent detection.

It may be noted that at the optimum threshold in this coherent detection case the probability of error is identical for Marks and Spaces transmitted. This balance of the two types of errors is apparent in Fig. 10-5. As discussed earlier, this is not generally the case in envelope detection. Note also that with a *fixed* threshold the error-rate for coherent detection of OOK approaches the associated constant false-alarm rate at high SNR.

At high SNR we recall the asymptotic form of (10-21). Then (10-30) becomes

$$\text{opt. threshold:} \qquad P_e \approx \frac{1}{\sqrt{\pi \gamma}}\, e^{-\gamma/4} \qquad\qquad (10\text{-}31)$$

Comparing this result with (10-22) and noting that the exponentials dominate, we see that at high SNR there is only a very slight reduction in the SNR required to achieve a particular error-rate by using coherent rather than noncoherent detection for OOK. That is, the two detection schemes perform almost equally well *at high SNR*. Such blurring of the performance difference between noncoherent and coherent detection is observed quite generally whenever *high* SNR is involved.

REFERENCES

1. J. I. Marcum: "A Statistical Theory of Target Detection by Pulsed Radar," *IRE Trans. PGIT,* IT-6, p. 145, ff (April 1960); earlier *Rand Corp. Report* RM-753 (July 1948).
2. A. R. DiDonato and M. P. Jarnagin: "A Method for Computing the Circular Coverage Function," *Mathematics of Computation, 16,* pp. 347-355 (July 1962).
3. J. I. Marcum: "Tables of the Q-Function," *Rand Corp. Report* RM-339 (January 1950).
4. D. E. Johansen: "New Techniques for Machine Computation of the Q-Functions, Truncated Normal Deviates, and Matrix Eigenvalues," Sylvania Electronic Systems, Applied Research Laboratory, *Sci. Report No. 2* on AF19(604)-7237, AFCRL-556 (July 1961). The routines described here have a relative accuracy of 10^{-5}.
5. M. Schwartz, W. R. Bennett and S. Stein, *Communication Systems and Techniques* (McGraw-Hill Book Company, New York, 1966) (Appendix A).

11

Binary Frequency-shift
Keying (FSK)

11-1 Frequency-shift Signaling

We noted in Chap. 10 that acceptable performance in on–off keying depends critically upon setting the threshold at a reasonably optimum value for each SNR. However, many important radio channels are characterized by continuous fading (Chap. 16), with random fluctuations in received signal amplitude and phase. These amplitude fluctuations often cover a range in excess of 10 dB within one second or less. It is clear that even with AGC an OOK receiver with a fixed threshold may have an excessively high error-rate under such conditions of signal fading. Accordingly it is desirable to find a signaling system less vulnerable to fading effects. To communication engineers an obvious early answer along these lines was the use of frequency modulation which is insensitive to signal amplitudes (at least for signal-to-noise ratios high enough to avoid "noise breakthrough" at the detector). Thus *frequency-shift keying* (FSK) was originally conceived as using a telegraph signal to frequency-modulate a carrier. The frequency deviation or modulation index was chosen by the same criteria as applied to FM with analog modulation (recall Chap. 6), the overall transmission bandwidths so chosen being usually several times the telegraph signal (modulation) bandwidth. The receiving system was the usual FM detector.

However, for binary FSK signals based on rectangular modulating waveforms, the instantaneous frequency actually shifts quite rapidly (the rapidity depending on transmitter bandwidth) between just two frequencies, one representing transmission of Mark and the other of Space. For wide deviations it becomes apparent that two filters, one centered on the Mark frequency and one on the Space frequency, may provide a less noisy discrimination than the conventional wide-band FM detector. Moreover, from the more recent statistical decision theory viewpoint (Sec. 13-5), the optimum detector for an FSK signal involves a pair of crosscorrelators

(Sec. 13-2) which for particular signal classes may be replaced by realizable matched filters. For both reasons the *two-filter receiver* model is the one more commonly encountered in communication applications and is the one we shall emphasize in our discussions.* In some applications demodulation is by the usual FM-related technique of detection of the instantaneous frequency by a standard FM detector. Although some results are available on such receivers (e.g., Refs. 1, 3), this method of FSK detection will not be discussed here in any detail. We can comment, however, that the error-rate variation with SNR is roughly the same as described below for noncoherent detection with dual-filter receivers operating in the same total bandwidth.

As in the on-off keyed case, either noncoherent or coherent detection is possible when one uses a two-filter receiver for FSK. We shall describe results for both cases, although coherent detection of FSK signals is not often encountered in practice. Again the reason is that if one has the ability to maintain a coherent reference it is usually just as easy and more profitable to operate the system with phase-shift keying on a single tone (Chap. 12) rather than to use two tones.

The simplest form of FSK radio system is one with rectangular frequency modulation and constant carrier amplitude. This may be described as ideally transmitting signal pulses of the form

$$s(t) = \begin{cases} A \cos 2\pi f_1 t, & \text{for Mark} \\ A \cos 2\pi f_2 t, & \text{for Space} \end{cases} \quad 0 < t < T \qquad (11\text{-}1)$$

where f_1 and f_2 are constant over a single information pulse (Fig. 11-1). In actual fact, two types of transmitters may be employed to generate the FSK signal. The more common in standard communications is the reactance modulator type of system (Chap. 6). We will primarily discuss rectangular tone pulses as defined by (11-1), but there is also an emphasis in some applications on design of the signal so as to minimize spectral tails. In this case the modulating telegraph waveform is not a rectangular wave with sharp transitions between bipolar levels but rather one in which cosinusoidal or other convenient-shaped transitions are made (e.g., Ref. 2). If such a signal is detected by a dual-filter pair, the detection results below apply, with the analysis of performance limited primarily by the ability to calculate the effects of the bandpass filters upon the FM signal. The alternative method of generating FSK signals is the selective *gating* of one of a pair of *locked* oscillators. This type of system, with the oscillators both

---

*The dual-filter receiver analysis of this section applies equally well to the general problem of reception of binary transmissions employing a pair of distinguishable waveforms to denote the two message states (Sec. 13-3).

frequency and phase stable, would have to be employed for a coherent detection system to be possible. In most cases, with either
method of signal generation, the transmitted carrier amplitude is
held fixed.

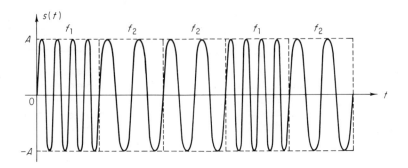

Fig. 11-1 FSK waveform, rectangular pulses.

In this section we will discuss only simple examples involving
use of sine-wave tones as the FSK signals, with two-filter reception and both noncoherent and coherent detection. Even in a two-
filter system, filters designed to be centered on one tone may
partially respond to the other tone. (Remember, we are discussing
a pulsed sinusoid, which is not a simple monochromatic wave but
has a finite spectral width). In addition to such *crosstalk* on the
signaling tones, spectral overlap of the filters *may* produce some
correlation between the portions of front-end noise passed by the
two filters, the degree of correlation depending on the degree of
overlap. However, samples of the noises in the two filter outputs
can be uncorrelated even with overlap (Chap. 13), and we will consider it so. In fact in this chapter we will consider only the important special case in which there is no crosstalk or overlap.

11-2 Noncoherent Detection of FSK

In noncoherent FSK reception using a pair of tone filters, as
illustrated in Fig. 11-2a, the output of each filter is envelope-
detected. The envelopes are sampled once per information pulse.
The Mark-Space decision is made according to whichever is the
larger of these envelope samples. As stated above, our assumption in this section will be that the signals and filtering are ideal
(no crosstalk, etc.). Hence we may again use directly the representations given in Sec. 4-6 for a signal in narrow-band noise, to
represent the output of either filter. In particular let N be the
average noise power level in the filter outputs at the instant of
sampling, assumed the same for both filters, and let u be the

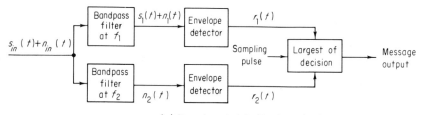

(a) Noncoherent detection tone f_1 signaled

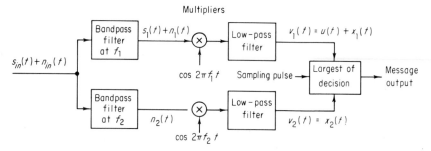

(b) Coherent detection, tone f_1 signaled

Fig. 11-2 Dual-filter detection of binary FSK signals.

signal level at the same instant in the filter momentarily containing the signaled tone (the other filter output containing zero signal component). Then for the filter output containing the signal the p.d.f. for the envelope r_1 is given by

$$ p(r_1) = \frac{r_1}{N} I_0 \left[\frac{ur_1}{N} \right] e^{-(r_1^2 + u^2)/2N} , \quad 0 \le r_1 < \infty \qquad (11\text{-}2) $$

and for the filter containing noise alone, the p.d.f. for the envelope r_2 is given by (the same form with $u = 0$),

$$ p(r_2) = \frac{r_2}{N} e^{-r_2^2/2N} , \quad 0 \le r_2 < \infty \qquad (11\text{-}3) $$

By our assumptions of independent noises in the two filter outputs, r_1 and r_2 are statistically independent.

An error occurs whenever $r_2 > r_1$, so that the probability of error is

$$ P_e = \text{prob}(r_2 > r_1) \int_{r_1=0}^{\infty} p(r_1) \left[\int_{r_2=r_1}^{\infty} p(r_2)\, dr_2 \right] dr_1 \qquad (11\text{-}4) $$

The inner integral is just $e^{-r_1^2/2N}$. Hence

$$P_e = \int_0^\infty \frac{r_1}{N} I_0\left(\frac{r_1 u}{N}\right) e^{-r_1^2/N} e^{-u^2/2N} dr_1 \qquad (11\text{-}5)$$

Setting $x = r_1 \sqrt{2/N}$ and again identifying the SNR as

$$\gamma = u^2/2N \qquad (11\text{-}6)$$

the integral reduces to

$$P_e = \frac{1}{2} e^{-\gamma} \int_0^\infty x I_0(x\sqrt{\gamma}) e^{-x^2/2} dx \qquad (11\text{-}7)$$

In turn this is readily identified from (10-8) and (10-9) as

$$P_e = \frac{1}{2} e^{-\gamma} e^{\gamma/2} Q(\sqrt{\gamma}, 0) = \frac{1}{2} e^{-\gamma/2} \qquad (11\text{-}8)$$

Note that γ is the SNR in only *that filter output which contains the signal.* This simple and well-known exponential error-rate result for noncoherent FSK is shown plotted as the upper curve in Fig. 11-3.

It is interesting to compare this result with that for noncoherent detection of on-off keying at high SNR and with optimized threshold, as given in (10-22). It is apparent that (at high SNR or low error-rates) any particular error-rate is achieved in noncoherent FSK with only one-half the value of SNR required for noncoherent OOK. For equal information rates (pulse lengths), the SNR in both cases is defined with respect to the same filter bandwidths and hence the same level of noise N. However, note that γ is defined for OOK in terms of the power transmitted only during the Marks; zero power is transmitted during the Spaces. The average power used in OOK is then only *one-half* the value used in defining γ. Thus at low error-rates *noncoherent OOK and noncoherent FSK achieve an equivalent error-rate at the same average SNR.* Moreover, because of usage of two keying tones, FSK must use a greater bandwidth allocation, greater by (roughly) at least a factor of 2. Nevertheless, to achieve this performance, there exists for OOK the significant disadvantage of needing to optimize the detection threshold at each SNR. The equivalent operation in FSK is comparing the *envelope difference,* $r_2 - r_1$, against a *zero* threshold; however, the latter threshold is independent of SNR and hence is always the appropriate threshold, independent of SNR. In fading (see also Chap. 16) this fact accounts for the difference in performance of conventional fixed threshold versions of these systems when operated over fading channels, and for the preference for FSK. In OOK, even the use of automatic gain control cannot completely account for signal level variations when a nonzero threshold has to be used.

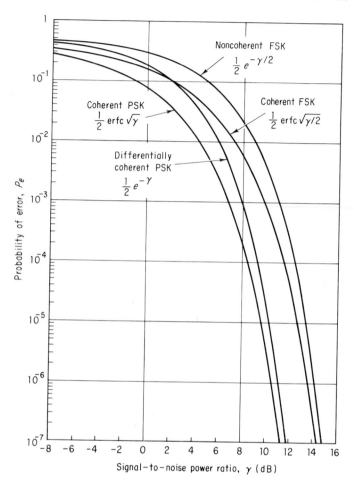

Fig. 11-3 Error-rates for several binary systems.

11-3 Coherent FSK

By coherent (or synchronous) detection of an FSK signal, we mean that there is available in the receiver an exact replica of each of the possible transmissions, exact even to r.f. phase in the received signal. The coherent detection process again has the effect of rejecting a portion of the bandpass noise. As we shall see (Chap. 12), coherent FSK operation involves much the same difficulties as phase-shift keying but achieves lesser performance. We will also observe below that coherent detection of FSK is significantly advantageous over noncoherent detection only at relatively low signal-to-noise ratios, i.e., relatively high error-rates.

Despite all this there are practical applications in which FSK may be utilized because of particular operational problems and in which coherent detection may still be available, for whatever small additional advantage it provides.

Extending the analysis of Sec. 10-3, we now consider coherent detection of the sinusoidal signal plus noise outputs of a *pair* of bandpass filters, as indicated in Fig. 11-2b. The filter at f_1, which momentarily contains the signal, has a sinusoidal output component with envelope u, and hence its output voltage can be written as

$$e_1(t) = [u(t) + x_1(t)] \cos 2\pi f_1 t - y_1(t) \sin 2\pi f_1 t \qquad (11\text{-}9)$$

The other filter, at frequency f_2, has an output (in the absence of crosstalk or interference) containing only noise.

$$e_2(t) = x_2(t) \cos 2\pi f_2 t - y_2(t) \sin 2\pi f_2 t \qquad (11\text{-}10)$$

The coherent detection processes correspond to multiplying $e_1(t)$ by $\cos 2\pi f_1 t$ and $e_2(t)$ by $\cos 2\pi f_2 t$, respectively, followed by low-pass filtering to remove the double-frequency components, as shown in Fig. 11-2b. Ignoring factors in each of 1/2, which again can be lumped with the system gain constants, the respective detector outputs are

$$v_1(t) = u(t) + x_1(t) \quad \text{and} \quad v_2(t) = x_2(t) \qquad (11\text{-}11)$$

Using (11-11), with u, x_1, and x_2 representing voltages at the sampling instant, we now assume that u is positive (it is readily verified that the error probability result below is identical if the opposite is true). Accordingly we expect v_1 to be *algebraically* larger than v_2. If it is not, we make an error. Thus the probability of an error is given by

$$P_e = \text{prob}(v_1 < v_2) = \text{prob}(u + x_1 < x_2) \qquad (11\text{-}12)$$

Since x_1 and x_2 are zero-mean Gaussian with variances $\overline{x_1^2} = \overline{x_2^2} = N$, and u is a constant over the statistical ensemble of noise, P_e can be rewritten as

$$P_e = \text{prob}(w < 0) \qquad (11\text{-}13)$$

where

$$w = u + x_1 - x_2 \qquad (11\text{-}14)$$

is also Gaussian (it is a sum of Gaussian variables plus a constant). The mean and variance of w are just

$$\overline{w} = u \qquad (11\text{-}15)$$

and

$$\sigma_w^2 = \overline{(w - \overline{w})^2} = \overline{(x_1 - x_2)^2} = \overline{x_1^2} + \overline{x_2^2} = 2N \qquad (11\text{-}16)$$

Hence w has a Gaussian p.d.f. given by

$$p(w) = \frac{1}{\sigma_w \sqrt{2\pi}} e^{-(w - \overline{w})^2 / 2\sigma_w^2} \qquad (11\text{-}17)$$

Correspondingly we now obtain straightforwardly

$$P_e = \int_{-\infty}^{0} p(w)\, dw = \frac{1}{2} \operatorname{erfc}\left(\frac{\overline{w}}{\sigma_w \sqrt{2}}\right) = \frac{1}{2} \operatorname{erfc}\left(\frac{u}{2\sqrt{N}}\right) \qquad (11\text{-}18)$$

Or, again defining the SNR $\gamma = u^2/2N$ as in (11-6), we have for the probability of error with coherent detection of FSK

$$P_e = \frac{1}{2} \operatorname{erfc}\left[\sqrt{\frac{\gamma}{2}}\right] \qquad (11\text{-}19)$$

If this result is compared with that in (10-30) for coherent detection of OOK with optimum threshold, it is seen that the same error-rate occurs in the FSK case at a 3 dB lower value of SNR than in the OOK case. Again we recall that this implies that the *same* performance is then obtained at the same *average* power, when the 50% duty cycle of OOK is considered. We will also note in the next chapter (see also Fig. 11-3) that the same form of result is obtained for ideal phase-shift keying, except that identical error-rate performance is then obtained at 3 dB still-lower SNR than for coherent FSK. This simply reflects a doubled noise level associated with the use of orthogonal waveforms in coherent FSK, as opposed to "antiparallel" waveforms in the PSK case (see also Chaps. 12 and 13).*

It is also interesting to compare coherent versus noncoherent FSK at high SNR. Using the asymptotic expansion in (10-21), at higher SNR the probability of error in coherent FSK is well approximated by

$$P_e \approx \frac{1}{\sqrt{2\pi\gamma}} e^{-\gamma/2} \qquad (11\text{-}20)$$

Because the behavior is dominated by the exponential, there is a vanishingly small difference (for increasingly large γ) between the

---

*One can show that with coherent FSK one can do slightly better than the no-crosstalk case analyzed here, by spacing the tones close enough together so that the coherently detected Space filter output is negative when a Mark is signaled (Mark filter detected output positive) and vice versa. Optimally the performance is about 0.85 dB better than the result in (11-19).

SNR required to achieve a certain error-rate in coherent FSK as given by (11-20) and that required in noncoherent FSK, given by (11-8). This is also apparent in the corresponding curves of Fig. 11-3.

An interesting slight variation on coherent FSK is one in which, after coherent detection, the larger *magnitude* signal is chosen rather than the algebraically larger value. This might be used, for example, if for some reason there is 180° uncertainty in the phase references being used for coherent detection. The probability of error in this case can be simply described from (11-11) and (11-12) as

$$P_e = \text{prob}\left(|v_1| < |v_2|\right) = \text{prob}\left(|u + x_1| < |x_2|\right) \quad (11\text{-}21)$$

It can be shown that the result in this case is just

$$P_e = 2P_0(1 - P_0) \quad (11\text{-}22)$$

where P_0 is exactly the probability of error given in (11-13) and (11-19). Thus asymptotically, at high SNR and correspondingly very low P_0, the probability of error in the magnitude comparison operation is only twice that in the algebraic comparison. Since at high SNR, error-rate decreases exponentially with SNR, such a factor of 2 corresponds to negligibly small relative changes in required SNR (i.e., measured in dB). Alternatively viewed, this illustrates that it is the rejection of noise by synchronous detection which is the most important feature of coherent FSK and that the ability to utilize algebraic sign is only of secondary importance.

REFERENCES

1. J. Salz and S. Stein: "Distribution of Instantaneous Frequency for Signal Plus Noise," *IEEE Trans. Information Theory*, vol. IT-10, pp. 272-274 (October 1964).
2. W. Lyons: "Design Considerations for FSK Circuits," *IRE Nat'l. Convention Record*, pt. 8, pp. 70-73 (1954).
3. M. Schwartz, W. R. Bennett and S. Stein, *Communication Systems and Techniques* (McGraw-Hill Book Company, New York, 1966).

12

Binary Phase-shift Keying (PSK)

12-1 Ideal Coherent Phase-shift Keying

Just as FSK can be regarded as a form of frequency modulation, so one can consider the digital equivalent of phase modulation, termed phase-shift keying (PSK). This form of signaling is also of interest from a decision theory viewpoint. As pointed out in Chap. 13, optimum (minimum error-rate) binary signaling/reception requires encoding each information element as the algebraic sign of a single pulsed waveform, with detection by multiplication and integration (crosscorrelation, Sec. 13-2) against a perfect replica of this waveform. Phase-shift keying of a constant-amplitude carrier, with sharp keying transitions between two phase states separated by π radians, fulfills exactly these requirements for optimum signaling. The resulting PSK signal has the form of a sequence of plus-minus rectangular pulses of a continuously generated sinusoid carrier, as shown in Fig. 12-1. Such a signal can be generated by DSB-SC modulation of a carrier by a bipolar rectangular waveform, as well as by direct phase modulation of a carrier.

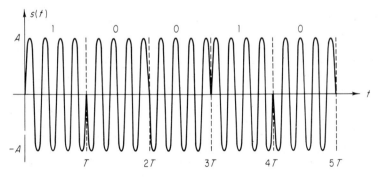

Fig. 12-1 PSK signal, rectangular pulses.

In some PSK applications one may use a waveform more complex than a pulsed sinusoid, with the information still encoded as the algebraic sign.* In that case, commonly the first operation in reception will be to mix (multiply and filter) against a locally generated reference waveform having the same complex modulation as the transmitted waveform but offset in frequency. The difference frequency term in the mixer output is then readily observed to be a sinusoidal waveform with its phase (0 or π radians, say) containing the binary information. Accordingly the remainder of the receiving operation can then be essentially identical with that for simple PSK. Hence while we confine our discussion to the latter case, phase-modulated continuous sinusoidal waveforms, the basic results apply much more generally.

In the case that we analyze, the *coherent detector* or *synchronous detector* requires a reference waveform accurate in frequency and phase. An exactly similar reference waveform would be required to implement a *phase detector* as a means of detecting the binary information. The ideal phase detector, by our definition, is a zero-memory device whose output is independent of the envelopes of the detector inputs and which specifically measures the cosine of their phase difference. Note that the usual balanced phase detector circuit indeed yields the *cosine* of the phase difference between the two input signals. Often, one of the signals is first given an additional 90° phase shift, so that the overall circuit output becomes the *sine* of the phase difference. For differences small relative to 1 radian, this approximates to the phase difference itself, and this is the usual desired output in phase modulation systems. However, we will rather consider throughout here that a "phase detector" is only the balanced detection circuit giving the *cosine* of the phase difference between the input signals. Thus a phase difference of zero degrees results in $+1$, and of 180° in -1, which is directly the kind of detected bipolar output desired in binary systems.

The coherent detector, on the other hand, is also a zero-memory device but has an output proportional to both the input envelopes and to the cosine of the phase difference [see also (12-13) and (12-14)]. In *either* case, however, the binary decision is based upon the *algebraic sign* of the detector output, and hence in this problem both types of detectors will render the identical binary decisions from the same input signals. Both these detection schemes are outlined in Fig. 12-2. Thus, unlike the analogs in FSK, there will be no performance difference in binary PSK between the coherent detector suggested by decision theory and the phase detector suggested by the analogy to demodulation of phase-modulated carriers. Note that there might be some difference

---

*For example, wide-band pseudonoise waveforms have been used to facilitate synchronization in telemetry from deep-space probes. They have also been used in some versions of the Rake technique mentioned in Chap. 17 as a means of resolving multipath in the transmission channel.

between the two types of detectors if one were to consider post-detection smoothing when ideal predetection matched-filtering (Sec. 13-1) is not available. However, error-rate analysis of postdetection smoothing of the output of these detectors represents an unsolved problem.

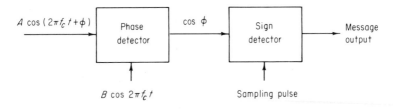

(a) Phase detection

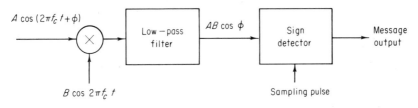

(b) Coherent detection

Fig. 12-2 Two detection schemes for ideal coherent PSK.

The mathematical model for ideal coherent PSK detection is essentially the same as in the coherent detection analyses in the preceding chapters, involving here only a single basic signal waveform. Thus, as in (10-23), the output of the coherent detector has the form

$$v(t) = u(t) + x(t) \qquad (12\text{-}1)$$

where $u(t)$ is either positive (Mark) or negative (Space). Assuming Mark (it is readily shown that the same result is obtained for a Space signal) so that $u > 0$, we note that the probability of error is simply the probability that $v(t)$ is negative at the sampling instant,

$$P_e = \mathrm{prob}(v < 0) = \mathrm{prob}(u + x < 0) \qquad (12\text{-}2)$$

Since $u + x$ is a biased Gaussian variable, we obtain quickly the probability of error for ideal coherent PSK,

$$P_e = \frac{1}{2}\,\mathrm{erfc}\left(\frac{u}{\sqrt{2N}}\right) = \frac{1}{2}\,\mathrm{erfc}(\sqrt{\gamma}) \qquad (12\text{-}3)$$

where again $\gamma = u^2/2N$ is the SNR in the filter output at the sampling instant. This result is shown as the lowest curve on Fig. 11-3, consistent with the earlier remark that ideal coherent PSK can be shown to be the optimum binary communication system in the sense of achieving the minimum possible probability of error for given SNR. At high SNR, as in the earlier asymptotic relations, the error-rate is well approximated by

$$P_e \approx \frac{1}{2\sqrt{\pi\gamma}} e^{-\gamma} \tag{12-4}$$

When we compare (12-3) with (11-9) for ideal coherent FSK, it is clear that a particular probability of error occurs at exactly 3 dB lower SNR in ideal PSK than in coherent FSK. This is also evident in the curves of Fig. 11-3. Thus where one is seeking a system design to operate below some specified error-rate, there is a very real 3 dB design advantage (lesser required SNR) for ideal coherent PSK over ideal coherent FSK. As is also evident, coherent PSK has no greater equipment requirements than coherent FSK (in fact, less, since only one frequency is used), and hence the tendency is for coherent FSK hardly ever to be used.

We have continually identified our model above as *ideal* coherent PSK. There are two important limitations in practical implementation, which in fact apply to coherent detection in general. One would be a possible phase error in the receiver reference with respect to the incoming signal. Coherent detection always selects that component of the additive noise in phase with the *receiver* reference and rejects the component in quadrature with it. A phase change in the reference then merely amounts to a different decomposition of the noise into two quadrature components, one of which is selected, and the nature of the noise term in formulas such as (12-1) does not change. However, if the phase error is $\Delta\phi$, the signal term is diminished by the factor $\cos \Delta\phi$. With the actual SNR prior to coherent detection defined by γ, it is easy to see that the error-rate would then become

$$P_e = \frac{1}{2} \operatorname{erfc}(\sqrt{\gamma}\, \cos \Delta\phi) \tag{12-5}$$

In actual operation such phase errors ($\Delta\phi$) may be due either to relative drifts in the master oscillators at transmitter and receiver or to changes introduced by the propagation medium, which appear as apparent drifts or fluctuations in the relative frequency or phase of the received signal. In either case these changes can be compensated by correcting the receiver reference, but the information required for this correction can usually only be derived by operations on the received signal. In this situation one requires relatively long-term smoothing (filtering) to diminish the additional apparent fluctuations caused by receiver noise. For example, this can be achieved by the use of the technique illustrated in Fig. 12-3. The result (12-5) can be used to estimate the time scale in which such correction must be accomplished. For example, to suffer no more than a 1 dB loss in performance (again meaning a requirement of 1 dB higher SNR to achieve the same error-rate) as compared to ideal coherent PSK, requires

$$(\cos \Delta\phi)^2 > 0.8 \qquad (12\text{-}6a)$$

or

$$|\Delta\phi| < 0.45 \text{ rad (approx. } 25°) \qquad (12\text{-}6b)$$

If one knows the approximate rate of variations of phase and/or frequency and their magnitude, the above result can be used to estimate the time-constants required in the phase correction loops.

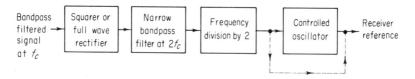

Fig. 12-3 A method of deriving or correcting a receiver reference for coherent detection.

The other important limitation in detection of PSK is the additive noise associated with deriving the reference signal in the receiver. This is discussed below, following the description of differential phase-shift keying.

12-2 Differentially Coherent PSK (DPSK)

An interesting alternative to attempting ideal coherent PSK, with the required long-term stability and/or high-quality phase correction loops, is so-called *differentially coherent phase shift-keying* and detection,* often termed simply differential PSK or DPSK. In this technique it is assumed simply that enough stability is present in the oscillators and the transmission medium that there is negligible change in phase from one information pulse to the next information pulse, aside from changes caused by actual encoding. Information is then encoded, not by absolute identification of, say, 0° phase with Mark and 180° with Space, but rather by

---

*Probably best known in practice at this time as incorporated by Collins Radio Co. in a variety of applications under the trade name *Kineplex* (see Ref. 1). Usually these systems have employed four or eight phases per pulse rather than two; at this point, however, we confine our discussion to the two-phase case.

differentially encoding the information in terms of the *phase change* between successive pulses (Fig. 12-4a). For example, no (0°) phase shift from the previous pulse could designate Mark, and 180° phase shift would then designate a Space. A coherent detector or phase detector is still used, one input being the "current" pulse and the other being the previous pulse appropriately delayed. An example of a possible implementation of differentially coherent phase detection is shown in Fig. 12-4b. A more common implementation, in terms of integrate–and dump filters, will be discussed in Chap. 13.

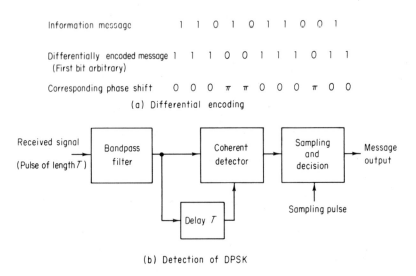

Information message	1 1 0 1 0 1 1 0 0 1
Differentially encoded message (First bit arbitrary)	1 1 1 0 0 1 1 1 0 1 1
Corresponding phase shift	0 0 0 π π 0 0 0 π 0 0

(a) Differential encoding

(b) Detection of DPSK

Fig. 12-4 Differentially coherent phase shift keying.

It should be noted that differential encoding, by itself, can be used in any digital system and is not uniquely associated with DPSK. However, if differential encoding is used in conjunction with signaling and receiving systems such as discussed earlier, additional decoding logic is required at the receiver output to recover the original message. This usually then becomes a disadvantage rather than an asset. An interesting non-DPSK example of a system employing differential encoding is the Duobinary technique (Ref. 2) which does not require decoding logic.

Thus the major difference between the DPSK system as described above and the ideal coherent reference PSK system is not in the differential encoding, which can be employed in any case. Rather it lies in deriving the reference signal for phase detection from the receiver input over a single previous pulse.* The

---

*A generalization of DPSK is to derive the receiver reference from the receiver input over *several* information pulses, as suggested in Fig. 12-3, followed with differential decoding logic. In the limit of a noiseless derived reference this detection technique can

performance difference lies in the fact that the reference is contaminated by additive noise to the *same* extent as the information pulse; that is, both have the same signal-to-noise ratio.

For analysis we can assume that a Mark is transmitted and that in the absence of noise both the signal and the reference portions of the filter outputs have the same phase (and the same frequency, of course). It is easy to show that the subsequent results apply as well if Space were transmitted and hence the two were of opposite phase. Including the noise, the two outputs of the bandpass filter (one being the output delayed by the pulse length) are therefore of the form*

$$e_1(t) = [u(t) + x_1(t)] \cos 2\pi f_c t - y_1(t) \sin 2\pi f_c t$$
$$e_2(t) = [u(t) + x_2(t)] \cos 2\pi f_c t - y_2(t) \sin 2\pi f_c t$$

$$(12\text{-}7)$$

Since the noises arise from different input pulse intervals, they will ideally be uncorrelated (see also Sec. 13-2) but of equal power. Thus the noise quadrature components have the following statistics:

$$\overline{x_1^2} = \overline{x_2^2} = \overline{y_1^2} = \overline{y_2^2} = N$$

$$\overline{x_1} = \overline{y_1} = \overline{x_2} = \overline{y_2} = 0 \qquad (12\text{-}8)$$

$$\overline{x_1 y_1} = \overline{x_2 y_2} = \overline{x_1 y_2} = \overline{x_2 y_1} = 0$$

where N is the noise level associated with *each* pulse at the sampling instant.

It is convenient to rewrite (12-7) and (12-8) in terms of nonzero mean Gaussian processes which have u as their mean value. To this end, we write

$$e_1(t) = X_1(t) \cos 2\pi f_c t - Y_1(t) \sin 2\pi f_c t$$
$$e_2(t) = X_2(t) \cos 2\pi f_c t - Y_2(t) \sin 2\pi f_c t$$

$$(12\text{-}9)$$

where X_1, X_2, Y_1, Y_2 represent the redefined quadrature components of the inputs to the phase detector or coherent detector. These have the following statistics:

---

be shown to result in an error-rate $P_e = 2p(1 - p)$ where p is the error-rate in (12-3) for ideal coherent PSK. If information is not differentially encoded but directly imposed as PSK, the error-rate of course would simply approach p.

*For the implementation of Fig. 12-4, this assumes the pulse length T (the delay in the figure) is an integer multiple of the carrier period. The necessary generalizations when this is not the case are obvious.

$$\overline{X_1} = \overline{X_2} = u, \quad \overline{Y_1} = \overline{Y_2} = 0$$

$$\overline{(X_1 - \overline{X_1})^2} = \overline{(X_2 - \overline{X_2})^2} = \overline{Y_1^2} = \overline{Y_2^2} = N \qquad (12\text{-}10)$$

$$\overline{(X_1 - \overline{X_1})(X_2 - \overline{X_2})} = \overline{Y_1 Y_2} = \overline{(X_1 - \overline{X_1})Y_2} = \overline{(X_2 - \overline{X_2})Y_1} = 0$$

We can also conveniently introduce envelope and phase descriptions of the detector inputs:

$$X_1(t) = R_1(t) \cos\theta_1(t), \quad X_2(t) = R_2(t) \cos\theta_2(t)$$

$$Y_1(t) = R_1(t) \sin\theta_1(t), \quad Y_2(t) = R_2(t) \sin\theta_2(t)$$

$$(12\text{-}11)$$

and

$$e_1(t) = R_1(t) \cos[2\pi f_c t + \theta_1(t)]$$

$$e_2(t) = R_2(t) \cos[2\pi f_c t + \theta_2(t)]$$

$$(12\text{-}12)$$

With these latter quantities as inputs to the coherent detector,* the detector output at the instant of sampling (again ignoring gain or conversion factors) is

$$v_s = R_1 R_2 \cos(\theta_1 - \theta_2) = X_1 X_2 + Y_1 Y_2 \qquad (12\text{-}13)$$

while the output of a phase detector with the same inputs would be simply

$$v_p = \cos(\theta_1 - \theta_2) = \frac{X_1 X_2 + Y_1 Y_2}{R_1 R_2} \qquad (12\text{-}14)$$

Clearly, in either case, the decision is based upon the algebraic sign of $\cos(\theta_1 - \theta_2)$. Thus either the multiplier detector whose output is v_s or the phase detector with output v_p would render identical binary decisions.

As a practical matter, reference has often been made to the phase detector interpretation of implementation. As a result many of the published performance analyses of DPSK system (Refs. 3 to 6) have been based upon studying the distributions of the phase. However, the binary case allows a much simpler analysis based on the coherent detector model, using the "scalar product" representation on the RHS of (12-13). Thus, on the assumption that the same phase has been signaled in both $e_1(t)$ and $e_2(t)$ the probability of error is given by

$$P_e = \text{prob}(X_1 X_2 + Y_1 Y_2 < 0) \qquad (12\text{-}15)$$

---

*Recall that this involves the product of e_1 and e_2 followed by low-pass filtering which removes unwanted harmonics.

There are several simple ways to evaluate this last probability conveniently. One, with an important physical interpretation given subsequently, is to note the algebraic identity

$$X_1 X_2 + Y_1 Y_2 = \frac{1}{4} \left\{ \left[(X_1 + X_2)^2 + (Y_1 + Y_2)^2 \right] - \left[(X_1 - X_2)^2 + (Y_1 - Y_2)^2 \right] \right\}$$
(12-16)

The sign of the quantity on the RHS here can be regarded as determining the larger *envelope* of two conveniently defined Gaussian processes. Thus, we introduce new variables

$$u_1 = X_1 + X_2 \qquad u_2 = X_1 - X_2$$
$$v_1 = Y_1 + Y_2 \qquad v_2 = Y_1 - Y_2$$
(12-17)

Since the original variables are Gaussian, these new variables are obviously also jointly Gaussian. Using (12-10), we see their means and variances to be

$$\bar{u}_1 = \bar{X}_1 + \bar{X}_2 = 2u \quad \bar{u}_2 = \bar{X}_1 - \bar{X}_2 = 0$$
$$\bar{v}_1 = \bar{Y}_1 + \bar{Y}_2 = 0 \quad \bar{v}_2 = \bar{Y}_1 - \bar{Y}_2 = 0$$
(12-18)

$$\overline{(u_1 - \bar{u}_1)^2} = \overline{\left[(X_1 - \bar{X}_1)^2 + (X_2 - \bar{X}_2)^2 \right]} = 2N , \quad \overline{(v_1 - \bar{v}_1)^2} = 2N$$
(12-19a)

$$\overline{(u_2 - \bar{u}_2)^2} = 2N , \quad \overline{(v_2 - \bar{v}_2)^2} = 2N$$
(12-19b)

Similarly, the crosscovariances are

$$\overline{(u_1 - \bar{u}_1)(u_2 - \bar{u}_2)} = \overline{\left[(X_1 - \bar{X}_1)^2 - (X_2 - \bar{X}_2)^2 \right]} = N - N = 0 \quad (12\text{-}20a)$$

and

$$\overline{(u_2 - \bar{u}_2)(v_1 - \bar{v}_1)} = \overline{(u_2 - \bar{u}_2)(v_2 - \bar{v}_2)} = \overline{(v_1 - \bar{v}_1)(v_2 - \bar{v}_2)} = 0$$
(12-20b)

Thus the new variables are all uncorrelated and have fluctuation components whose properties correspond to those of the quadrature components of bandpass Gaussian noise. Furthermore, as already indicated in (12-16), if we define the envelopes

$$R_1 = \sqrt{u_1^2 + v_1^2} , \quad R_2 = \sqrt{u_2^2 + v_2^2}$$
(12-21a)

then

$$P_e = \text{prob}(X_1 X_2 + Y_1 Y_2 < 0) = \text{prob}(R_1^2 < R_2^2) = \text{prob}(R_1 < R_2) \quad (12\text{-}21b)$$

But the statistics in (12–18) to (12–20) and the probability statement in (12–21) are now *identical in form* with those involved in the analysis of noncoherent detection of FSK, in Sec. 11-2, where R_1 is the envelope of a signal-plus-noise and R_2 is the envelope of noise alone. Then we can directly apply (11-8) in particular, to obtain

$$P_e = \frac{1}{2} \exp\left[-\frac{1}{2} \frac{(2u)^2}{2(2N)} \right] = \frac{1}{2} e^{-u^2/2N} \qquad (12\text{-}22)$$

When we define the SNR $\gamma = u^2/2N$ as earlier, the error-rate for differentially coherent phase detection is therefore

$$P_e = \frac{1}{2} e^{-\gamma} \qquad (12\text{-}23)$$

The result (12-23) has also been plotted in Fig. 11-3. It is clear from (12-23) that, at all error-rates, DPSK requires *exactly 3 dB less SNR than noncoherent FSK* for the same error-rate. Recalling the asymptotically exponential behavior of ideal coherent PSK, it is also clear that at high SNR *DPSK performs almost as well as ideal coherent PSK* at the same keying rate and power level.

The mathematical form of the result obtained above indicates a close relationship between DPSK and noncoherent FSK envelope detection. The physical interpretation underlying this relationship is extremely useful for qualitatively understanding the operation of various related systems. Although we have presented the mathematics above, the interpretation is more easily pursued following the discussion of matched-filters and correlation detection and hence reappears as a topic late in the next chapter (Sec. 13-8).

The DPSK result can also be viewed as providing an upper bound on the error-rate for the case of phase-shift keying as described in Sec. 12-1, when a derived and hence noisy reference is used. Thus the DPSK error-rate corresponds precisely to the case where the derived reference is as noisy as the "current" pulse voltages being detected. From a practical point of view this is the noisiest reference which has any meaning. For any less noisy reference, the results will lie between the two lowest curves in Fig. 11-3, which are already quite close at high SNR's (low error-rates) of practical interest. Exact analyses exist for PSK with a general noise reference (e.g., Refs. 7, 8) but are beyond our scope here.

REFERENCES

1. M. L. Doelz, E. T. Heald, and D. L. Martin: "Binary Data Transmission Techniques for Linear Systems," *Proc. IRE, 45,* pp. 656-661 (May 1957).

2. A. Lender: "The Duobinary Technique for High-Speed Data Transmission," *Communications and Electronics*, vol. 82, No. 66, pp. 214-218 (May 1963).
3. J. G. Lawton: "Comparison of Binary Data Transmission Systems," *Proc. Second National Conference on Military Electronics*, pp. 54-61 (1958).
4. J. G. Lawton: "Theoretical Error-Rates of Differentially Coherent Binary and Kineplex Data Transmission Systems," *Proc. IRE, 47*, pp. 333-334 (February 1959).
5. C. R. Cahn: "Comparison of Coherent and Phase-Comparison Detection of a Four Phase Digital Signal," *Proc. IRE, 47*, p. 1667 (September 1959).
6. C. R. Cahn: "Performance of Digital Phase-Modulation Communication Systems," *IRE Trans. Comm. Sys.*, CS-7, pp. 3-5 (May 1959).
7. S. Stein: "Unified Analysis of Certain Coherent and Noncoherent Binary Communication Systems," *IRE Trans. Inf. Theory, IT-10*, pp. 43-51 (January 1964).
8. M. Schwartz, W. R. Bennett, and S. Stein, *Communication Systems and Techniques* (McGraw-Hill Book Company, New York, 1966) (Chap. 8).

13

Matched-filters and Correlation Detection

13-1 Matched-filters to Maximize SNR

We have examined a class of receivers for binary signaling/detection systems which are described in terms of bandpass filtering operations followed by zero-memory detectors (and no significant postdetection filtering). In each case studied the error probability depends *only* upon the *SNR* in the *appropriate filter outputs.* In this chapter we discuss further aspects of these filtering operations.

Previously we have implied several times that SNR has been consistently defined so that different systems are directly comparable. The underlying assumption is that the systems are to be compared for signaling at the same information transmission rate. Then for purposes of comparison all systems may be visualized as using the same individual pulse waveform (e.g., rectangular pulses of length T); hence the *same* bandpass filtering will be appropriate to all systems (in FSK such filtering is applied at *each* tone frequency). The latter statement assumes that, with the "random" nature of the message-bearing pulse sequences, the bandpass filtering in each case will be defined with the common goal of a best processing (in the sense of discrimination against noise) of each individual pulse in the sequence. If one now assumes the same signal power and the same receiver noise level, it is clear that the systems can be directly compared in terms of the defined SNR required to achieve a particular error-rate. If the assumptions on common pulse shape or receiver filtering are weakened, for reasons of engineering implementation or channel characteristics, then the SNR in each case must be related specifically to the basic signal power and noise parameters in order to achieve a realistic comparison.

The SNR used to define error-rate in these preceding chapters was always defined at the *outputs* of bandpass filters, and the error-rates for all the systems studied decrease monotonically with increasing values of this SNR. With only this as the basis, the obvious question is certainly whether general criteria exist for choosing the filters themselves so as to maximize the SNR and thereby minimize the error-rate. We will first treat this problem in general and then illustrate it for the particular important case of rectangular information pulses.

To accomplish this, we return to the representations of band-pass filtering of signal and noise introduced in Chaps. 3 and 4. Let $u_{in}(t)$ be the complex envelope of a signal at carrier frequency f_c at the input to a bandpass filter centered on f_c, and let the equivalent low-pass impulse response and low-pass frequency function of the filter be $h(t)$ and $H(f)$, respectively. Then the filtered bandpass output signal can be represented as a modulated carrier at f_c with a complex envelope

$$u(t) = \int_{-\infty}^{\infty} u_{in}(\tau)\, h(t - \tau)\, d\tau = \int_{-\infty}^{\infty} H(f)\, U_{in}(f)\, e^{j2\pi f t}\, df \quad (13\text{-}1)$$

where $U_{in}(f)$ is the spectrum of $u_{in}(t)$. (Recall that $h(x) = 0$ for $x < 0$, so that the effective upper limit on the first integral is actually t.) Likewise, if the input additive bandpass noise is stationary Gaussian, with equivalent low-pass power density spectrum $N_0(f)$, the filter output noise power is

$$N = \int_{-\infty}^{\infty} N_0(f)\, |H(f)|^2\, df \quad (13\text{-}2)$$

Although the complex envelope $u(t)$ is in general indeed complex, wherever required we have been assuming (without loss of generality) the choice of phase reference at the receiver output to be such that one quadrature component of the noise is always in phase with the signal.

Now we confine our attention to a typical signal pulse over the interval $(0, T)$ and regard $u_{in}(t)$ to be just that signal waveform. Then using (13-1) in our definition of SNR at the filter output, the output signal envelope value at the sampling instant, $t = T_s$ $(T_s \leq T)$, is

$$|u| = |u(T_s)| = \left| \int_{-\infty}^{\infty} u_{in}(\tau)\, h(T_s - \tau)\, d\tau \right| = \left| \int_{-\infty}^{\infty} H(f)\, U_{in}(f)\, e^{j2\pi f T_s}\, df \right|$$

$$(13\text{-}3)$$

and the corresponding output SNR can be written as

$$\gamma = \frac{|u|^2}{2N} = \frac{1}{2} \frac{\left| \int_{-\infty}^{\infty} H(f)\, U_{in}(f)\, e^{j2\pi f T_s}\, df \right|^2}{\int_{-\infty}^{\infty} N_0(f)\, |H(f)|^2\, df} \quad (13\text{-}4)$$

Recall again that this SNR as used in our error-rate results assumes that $u_{in}(t)$ and $U_{in}(f)$ refer to the waveform of a single information bearing pulse, usually regarded as confined to some time interval $(0, T)$, and that there are no intersymbol interference effects. This latter condition will be consistent with a continuous message transmission provided (as is indeed shown below to be true for the optimum filter in the case of spectrally flat noise) that $h(T_s - \tau) = 0$ for $\tau < 0$. Note also that $N_0(f)$ is a power density spectrum and hence is everywhere real and positive.

We seek the equivalent low-pass filter described by $H(f)$ that maximizes the SNR given by (13-4). This is most easily accomplished by applying a mathematical result well-known as the *Schwarz inequality*. This takes the following form: If $A(f)$ and $B(f)$ are any complex functions, then

$$\left| \int_{-\infty}^{\infty} A(f)B(f)\,df \right|^2 \le \left[\int_{-\infty}^{\infty} |A(f)|^2\,df \right]\left[\int_{-\infty}^{\infty} |B(f)|^2\,df \right] \quad (13\text{-}5)$$

This inequality can be regarded as a generalization of the familiar distance relation among vectors, that the magnitude of the scalar product of two vectors is less than or equal to the product of the magnitudes of the two vectors. Furthermore the *equality* in (13-5) is achieved *if, and only if,* the functions are "conjugate parallel," namely when

$$A(f) = KB^*(f) \quad (13\text{-}6)$$

where K is any arbitrary complex constant. To apply these statements to (13-4), we assume $N_0(f)$ is nonvanishing over all regions where $U_{in}(f)$ is nonzero, since otherwise we could make a noiseless (infinite SNR) decision by confining our signaling and filtering to only this portion of this frequency domain. Then we make the identifications,

$$A(f) = \sqrt{N_0(f)}\, H(f) , \quad B(f) = \frac{U_{in}(f)}{\sqrt{N_0(f)}}\, e^{j2\pi f T_s} \quad (13\text{-}7)$$

The inequality (13-5) now yields the result

$$\left| \int_{-\infty}^{\infty} H(f)U_{in}(f)\, e^{j2\pi f T_s}\, df \right|^2 \le \left[\int_{-\infty}^{\infty} N_0(f)|H(f)|^2\, df \right]\left[\int_{-\infty}^{\infty} \frac{|U_{in}(f)|^2}{N_0(f)}\, df \right]$$
$$(13\text{-}8)$$

with *equality if, and only if,* the equivalent low-pass filter's frequency function is given by

$$H(f) = K\frac{U_{in}^*(f)}{N_0(f)}\, e^{-j2\pi f T_s} \quad (13\text{-}9)$$

Thus, for the SNR defined by (13-4), one has the inequality

$$\gamma \leq \frac{1}{2} \int_{-\infty}^{\infty} \frac{|U_{in}(f)|^2}{N_0(f)} \, df \tag{13-10}$$

with equality, giving the maximum possible value of SNR, holding only when (13-9) is satisfied.

Ignoring the complex constant K (which can be regarded as a constant gain and phase factor of the filter, irrelevant in determining SNR), the *optimum* (equivalent low-pass) *filter* is seen now to be one which is "matched" to the complex envelope of the input signal in that:

1. The filter's amplitude variation versus frequency is proportional to that of the signal components.
2. The filter's phase at each frequency negates the signal phase (thus the filter results in phase-aligning all signal components so they add maximally), with an additional phase variation linear in frequency which represents a time delay T_s.
3. If the noise power density spectrum is nonuniform, the weighting of the voltages at each frequency is inverse to the noise power density at that frequency.

The *"matched-filter"* given by (13-9) then maximizes the output SNR *at the sampling instant* T_s for each pulse.

The result above is usually presented for the case when the noise power density spectrum is flat over the band of interest. For white, bandpass noise with (two-sided) spectral density $n_0/2$ over the signal band, the equivalent low-pass noise spectrum (see Sec. 4-6) is

$$N_0(f) = n_0 \text{ watts/hz} \tag{13-11}$$

For such white noise the matched-filter is given from (13-9), to within an arbitrary constant, as

$$H(f) = U_{in}^*(f) \, e^{-j2\pi f T_s} \tag{13-12}$$

and the corresponding maximized output SNR for the bandpass system is

$$\gamma_{max} = \frac{\frac{1}{2} \int_{-\infty}^{\infty} |U_{in}(f)|^2 df}{n_0} \tag{13-13}$$

The numerator in (13-13) is readily recognized (via Parseval's theorem) to be the *total energy E in the received bandpass signal pulse*,

$$E = \frac{1}{2} \int_{-\infty}^{\infty} |U_{in}(f)|^2 df = \frac{1}{2} \int_{-\infty}^{\infty} |u_{in}(t)|^2 dt = \int_{-\infty}^{\infty} S(t) \, dt \tag{13-14}$$

where $S(t)$ is the instantaneous signal power over the pulse. Thus for white noise the *maximum achievable SNR* is the famous result

$$\gamma_{max} = E/n_0 \qquad (13\text{-}15)$$

This maximum SNR is achieved *if, and only if,* one can physically provide a bandpass filter that is matched according to (13-12) to the spectrum of the complex envelope of the signal.* Note that in the event of signal distortion by the transmission medium, it is the *arriving* signal waveform, not the transmitted waveform, to which the optimum receiver must be matched.

Let us consider the matched-filter itself in further detail. Its equivalent low-pass impulse response is given by

$$h(t) = \int_{-\infty}^{\infty} H(f) \, e^{j2\pi ft} \, df = \int_{-\infty}^{\infty} U_{in}^{*}(f) \, e^{j2\pi f(t - T_s)} \, df$$

$$= \left\{ \int_{-\infty}^{\infty} U_{in}(f) \, e^{j2\pi f(T_s - t)} \, df \right\}^{*} = u_{in}^{*}(T_s - t) \qquad (13\text{-}16)$$

That is, the equivalent low-pass impulse response of the matched-filter is a *time-reversed* and *delayed* version of the signal complex envelope waveform, the time-delay being taken with respect to the sampling instant. Since $u_{in}(t) = 0$ for $t < 0$, the matched-filter impulse response $h(t) = 0$ for $t > T_s$. At the same time, if the signal persists for $t > T_s$, the matched-filter impulse response would be noncausal. That is, one would *not* have $h(t) = 0$ for $t < 0$. In order to obtain a causal filter, it is necessary *at the outset* to regard $u_{in}(t)$ as vanishing for $t > T_s$, with the value of E in (13-14) modified accordingly. Usually, therefore, T_s and T are regarded as identical. This does not yet mean that $h(t)$ will be readily realizable physically. As illustrated in Fig. 13-1, $u_{in}(t)$ might typically have a form dominated by a decaying exponential. Then $h(t)$ would have to involve a growing exponential, and this is not a controlled impulse response easily achieved in a filter design.

The one outstanding practical situation in which a matched-filter has been simply realized physically occurs when the signaling pulses (envelopes) are rectangular. In this case

$$u_{in}(t) = \begin{cases} A, & 0 < t < T \\ 0, & \text{elsewhere} \end{cases} \qquad (13\text{-}17)$$

and if $T_s = T$ is taken as the sampling instant, (13-16) requires

---

*In general, we remind the reader, a separate matched–filter may be required for each possible signal waveform, e.g., the pair of filters required for binary FSK.

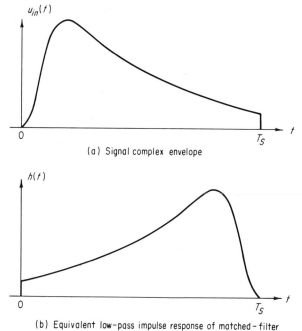

(a) Signal complex envelope

(b) Equivalent low-pass impulse response of matched-filter

Fig. 13-1 Illustration of matched-filter.

merely that to within an arbitrary complex constant

$$h(t) = \begin{cases} A, & 0 < t < T \\ 0, & \text{elsewhere} \end{cases} \tag{13-18}$$

This filter is an ideal *integrating filter* with time constant T. That is, its response to a waveform with complex envelope $v_{in}(t)$ is given by the complex envelope

$$v(t) = A \int_{t-T}^{t} v_{in}(t)\,dt \tag{13-19}$$

It is well known that an ideal bandpass integrating filter is generally realizable as an extremely narrow bandwidth (high Q) filter. For example, a filter with equivalent low-pass impulse response of the form $\exp(-t/T_c)$ closely approaches ideal integration action as its time constant $T_c \to \infty$ (i.e., its bandwidth approaches zero). Specifically it closely approaches an ideal integrating filter for all t such that $t \ll T_c$. As shown in Fig. 13-2, such a filter could conceivably be used here with $T_c \gg T$. Its output is sampled at time T

after the beginning of the signal pulse, and any filter output voltages extending (owing to ringing) after time T are ignored. The difficulty with this implementation from a communications viewpoint is simply that immediately after time T, a new signal pulse begins to enter the filter, and decisions relative to it will be made at the time $2T$. Thus the ideal integrating filter would suffice for a single isolated rectangular pulse, but its ringing would create intolerable

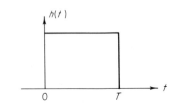

(a) Desired matched–filter impulse response

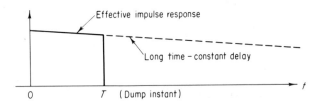

(b) Low–pass equivalent of extremely narrow–band (High – Q) filter

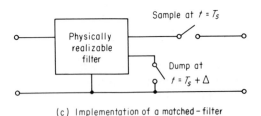

(c) Implementation of a matched–filter

Fig. 13-2 Integrate-and-dump filter.

intersymbol interference in a pulse-sequence situation. One solution has been to artificially discharge (''dump'') all currents and voltages in the filter, in an extremely short interval immediately after the filter output has been sampled for the decision operation and before any signficant portion of the next pulse is received, in effect restarting the filter for each new signal pulse interval. This realization is often called an *integrate-and-dump filter*. Note, however, that such a filter is effective only if its dump times are synchronized with the pulse train, and its *output conforms* to (13-19) *only at the sampling instants.* We will return in Sec. 13-6 to further detailed discussion of the operation of this filter.*

Returning now to (13-15), we call attention to the remarkable result of the matched-filter operation: For spectrally flat noise *the output SNR depends only upon the ratio of the energy in the signal pulse to the noise power spectral density.* It is *independent* of any detail of the *pulse envelope waveform,* or of the *bandwidths* used in the signal or receiver. As is shown later in Sec. 13-7, the E/n_0 ratio is also a parameter quite descriptive of reasonable suboptimum filter results. Thus, the E/n_0 ratio provides an extremely valuable qualitative parameter for understanding the performance to be expected of signals which may possibly have extremely complicated signal structures, as discussed further in Sec. 13-3. It has sometimes been termed the *energy contrast ratio,* or simply the energy contrast.

13-2 Correlation Receivers as Matched-filters

The result in (13-16) has another important interpretation, which leads to alternative and more generally realizable methods of implementing matched-filter operation. Let $w_{in}(t)$ be the complex envelope of signal-plus-noise presented to the matched filter, with the signal component described by $u_{in}(t)$. The complex envelope of the matched-filter output *at the sampling instant* is just

$$w(T_s) = \int_{-\infty}^{\infty} h(T_s - \tau)\, w_{in}(\tau)\, d\tau \qquad (13\text{-}20)$$

But, with (13-16), and the implicit assumption that $u_{in}(t) = 0$ for $t < 0$ or for $t > T_s$,

$$w(T_s) = \int_{0}^{T_s} u_{in}^*(\tau)\, w_{in}(\tau)\, d\tau \qquad (13\text{-}21)$$

The integrand in (13-21) is recognized (recall (3-68)) as a complex envelope generally obtained by a mixing operation. That is, if a waveform with complex envelope $u_{in}(t)$ and carrier frequency $f_c - f_0$ is multiplied with a waveform of complex envelope $w_{in}(t)$ and carrier frequency f_c, then $u_{in}^*(t)\, w_{in}(t)$ is the complex envelope associated with the difference frequency carrier component at f_0. If $f_0 \neq 0$,

---

*In principle, a filter which continuously conforms to (13-19) can be constructed by feeding a perfect integrating filter a difference signal, constructed as the difference between the input and a version delayed precisely by T, with carrier frequency assumed an integer multiple of $1/T$. As is readily seen, the overall response to an impulse modulation is precisely (13-18).

the remainder of the operation indicated in (13-21) is a bandpass integration operation at frequency f_0, over the interval $(0, T_s)$; this integration is of the same type described earlier. In turn, the output characterized by $w(t)$ is detected and sampled in line with the kind of signaling being used, to give $w(T_s)$ as in (13-21).

The multiplication and integration operation described above is closely related to the basic operation of crosscorrelation. We term it *bandpass crosscorrelation* and discuss it in more detail in Sec. 13-4. The receiver which implements (13-21), illustrated in Fig. 13-3b, is for this reason termed a *correlation receiver*. The multiplication and integration operation is, of course, carried out over each pulse interval, and the voltage resulting from it at each sampling instant is identical with that which would be derived via any other form of matched-filter and with the same statistical properties described above in Sec. 13-1.

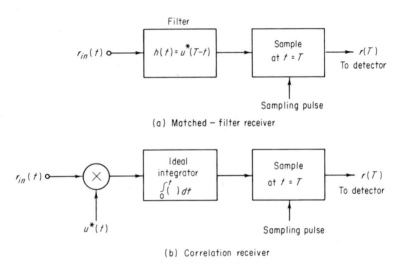

Fig. 13-3 Demonstrating the equivalence of matched-filtering and correlation.

Note again that in the event of signal distortion by the transmission medium, replicas of the *received* pulses must be used as the crosscorrelation reference signals for optimum discrimination against noise.

13-3 Signaling with Arbitrary Waveforms

An important conclusion to be derived from considering matched-filters is that, at least for signals received in additive white noise and not unpredictably distorted by the transmission medium, *signal structure* is *not* per se an important parameter of communications error-rate performance. In actual application the associated bandwidth and equipment complexity (and reliability) may become important as engineering parameters, but *so long as the reception process can closely approximate matched-filtering, error-rate performance is not affected by signal structure.*

For this reason it is relevant to restate our previous discussions of OOK, FSK, and PSK systems in terms of using extremely *arbitrary waveforms* rather than sinusoidal pulses, the condition being only that the receiver know enough about the waveforms so that proper filtering or crosscorrelation can be carried out.

For OOK systems only a single arbitrary pulse waveform is either transmitted or not transmitted for each information element, and the receiver is simply matched to this known waveform. The resulting SNR at the receiver output at the sampling instant is then maximized and the error-rate performance in terms of SNR is identical to that discussed in Chap. 10. For coherent detection it is assumed in addition that the phase of the waveform, as received, is included in the known information, and hence that coherent detection of the waveform is achievable. Moreover the *same* arbitrary waveform need not be transmitted for each pulse, provided only that the receiver *knows the sequence of waveforms* utilized and has available information (either supplied by the transmitter or derivable from the received signal) about the ordering of the pulses in the sequence. The receiver then can supply the proper matched-filter for every successive pulse, and error-rate performance is unaffected.

For binary PSK systems, including DPSK, again only a single arbitrary waveform is used for each information element, with an associated algebraic sign (± sign) to convey the information. In ideal coherent PSK the assumption is that the given waveform, say $u(t)$, is known precisely at the receiver, so that one can detect whether it has been sent in its basic form (0° phase shift), or with 180° phase shift, i.e., $-u(t)$ transmitted as the complex envelope rather than $+u(t)$. In DPSK the requirement is the ability to detect, based on the matched-filter outputs at the end of each T-length pulse interval, whether two successive pulses were sent with the same relative phase or with a 180° change in phase.

In generalizing FSK, either coherent or noncoherent, there must be two different, but otherwise arbitrary, transmitted waveforms (analogous to the two tone frequencies of the conventional system). Let us describe these waveforms as having the complex envelopes $u_M(t)$ and $u_S(t)$ for Mark and Space respectively. There are then two separate matched-filters, respectively having equivalent lowpass impulse responses

$$h_M(t) = u_M^*(T - t) , \quad h_S(t) = u_S^*(T - t) \qquad (13\text{-}22)$$

Our previous analyses are still applicable now provided there is *no crosstalk.* That is, if $u_M(t)$ is signaled, the signal component in the output of the filter characterized by $h_S(t)$ shall be zero (i.e., only a noise output), and vice versa. This assumption is mathematically the statements that

$$\int_0^T u_S(t) h_M(T - t) dt = 0 , \qquad \int_0^T u_M(t) h_S(T - t) dt = 0 \quad (13\text{-}23)$$

Using (13-22), we see the requirement in both cases to be simply that

$$\int_0^T u_M(t) u_S^*(t) dt = 0 \qquad (13\text{-}24)$$

Thus the statement is that the complex functions $u_M(t)$ and $u_S(t)$ are *orthogonal* (hence uncorrelated) over the interval (0, T), in the usual mathematical sense of orthogonality.* Note this is completely general—the two signals may even occupy the same bandwidth, so long as they are orthogonal owing to internal structuring. By Parseval's theorem, (13-24) is equivalent to a statement on the pulse spectra, namely

$$\int_{-\infty}^\infty U_M(f) U_S^*(f) df = 0 \qquad (13\text{-}25)$$

A more general parameter characterizing the distinguishability of two pulse waveforms is their *complex correlation coefficient*

$$\lambda = \frac{\frac{1}{2} \int_0^T u_M(\tau) u_S^*(\tau) d\tau}{\sqrt{E_M E_S}} = \frac{\int_{-\infty}^\infty U_M(f) U_S^*(f) df}{2\sqrt{E_M E_S}} \qquad (13\text{-}26a)$$

where

$$E_M = \frac{1}{2} \int_0^T |u_M(t)|^2 dt , \qquad E_S = \frac{1}{2} \int_0^T |u_S(t)|^2 dt \qquad (13\text{-}26b)$$

are the respective pulse energies. In this context the usual binary FSK corresponds to $\lambda = 0$, and the usual PSK in which one possible signal is merely the negative of the other corresponds to $\lambda = -1$. In the latter situation the signals are often said to be *antiparallel*

---

*Note that coherent FSK still presumes accurate phase knowledge of each.

or *antipodal.* In general, two signals are said to be completely "unalike" or orthogonal, or uncorrelated when $\lambda = 0$. If $\lambda > 0$, the two have some commonness which reduces their distinguishability, and if $\lambda < 0$, they become more distinguishable, *provided* that the receiver has sufficient knowledge of their phase to allow coherent detection procedures.

A further obvious statement, already mentioned above, is that the waveforms representing Mark and Space during one symbol interval $(0, T)$ may be completely different from those in any preceding interval, *so long as the receiver knows what they are* so that the appropriate matched-filtering can be accomplished. One can recognize here some of the rudiments of a *secure* system, in which quite arbitrary ("noise-like") waveforms can be used to represent the information symbols, and there is no particular relation between the waveform alphabet for one message element and that used for any successive elements. Only a receiver having knowledge of the successive waveform alphabets being employed can meaningfully detect the signals.

Finally note that the detection analyses of Chaps. 10 to 12 apply completely to these more general signaling systems so long as they are generically equivalent to one of the types (OOK, FSK, DPSK, PSK) examined. This statement includes further generalizations described later, such as the extension to M-ary signaling in Chap. 14. Without further comment we will therefore continue to describe models in terms of relatively simple forms of modulation of sinusoidal carriers.

13-4 Bandpass Crosscorrelation

In Sec. 13-2 the multiplication and integration process required in a *correlation receiver* was termed *bandpass crosscorrelation.* In this section we consider this process in more detail and indicate its relation to true crosscorrelation.

Let $q_1(t)$ and $q_2(t)$ be bandpass signals at the carrier frequencies f_1 and f_2, with complex envelopes $r_1(t)$ and $r_2(t)$,

$$q_1(t) = \text{Re}\left\{r_1(t)\, e^{j2\pi f_1 t}\right\} \tag{13-27a}$$

$$q_2(t) = \text{Re}\left\{r_2(t)\, e^{j2\pi f_2 t}\right\} \tag{13-27b}$$

Then bandpass crosscorrelation of $q_1(t)$ and $q_2(t)$ involves first a mixing operation, with extraction of the difference frequency component (recall Sec. 3-4),

$$q_{12}(t) = \text{Re}\left\{r_{12}(t)\, e^{j2\pi(f_2 - f_1)t}\right\} \tag{13-28a}$$

where

$$r_{12}(t) = \frac{1}{2} r_1^*(t)\, r_2(t) \tag{13-28b}$$

This is followed (Fig. 13-4a) by smoothing or averaging over a time interval,* to produce again a waveform at the difference frequency,

$$q(t) = \text{Re}\left\{r(t)\, e^{j2\pi(f_2 - f_1)t}\right\} \tag{13-29a}$$

where

$$r(t) = \int_0^t r_{12}(\tau)\, d\tau = \int_0^t \frac{1}{2}\, r_1^*(\tau) r_2(\tau)\, d\tau \tag{13-29b}$$

We have arbitrarily assumed here that the waveforms begin at $t = 0$. If, in addition, they end at (or our instant of interest occurs at) the time $t = T$, then we are only interested in the value of $r(t)$ at that instant, as given by

$$r(T) = \int_0^T \frac{1}{2}\, r_1^*(t) r_2(\tau)\, d\tau \tag{13-30}$$

Finally again (Fig. 13-4b), detection is carried out on $q(t)$, resulting in measurements as follows:

noncoherent detection: Measurement of envelope of $q(t) = |r(t)|$ (13-31a)

coherent detection: Measurement of in-phase component of $q(t) = \text{Re}\{r(t)\}$ (13-31b)

Note that the coherent detection operation assumes use of a local reference, at the difference frequency, which (in some derived manner) is exactly in phase with the carrier form in (13-29a). If instead, the local reference has the form $\exp j[2\pi(f_2 - f_1)t + \Delta]$, the coherent detection measurement would result in $\text{Re}\{r(t) e^{j\Delta}\}$. If $r(t)$ is real, as it will be for example when $r_1(t)$ and $r_2(t)$ in (13-28b) are identical, then

$$\text{Re}\left\{r(t) e^{j\Delta}\right\} = r(t) \cos\Delta$$

If $r(t)$ is not real (say, because one of the correlated waveforms contains noise) and has the form

$$r(t) = r_R(t) + j\, r_I(t) \tag{13-32}$$

---

*Averaging over an interval T usually implies the operation $\frac{1}{T} \int_0^T (\ ) \, dt$. The factor $1/T$ is omitted above since it does not enter naturally into the receiver equations and in any case can be regarded as another irrelevant gain constant insofar as ratios of signal and noise.

then

$$\text{Re}\left\{r(t)\,e^{j\Delta}\right\} = r_R(t)\cos\Delta - r_I(t)\sin\Delta \qquad (13\text{-}33)$$

Note that the detectors, particularly the envelope detectors, can be the usual detectors of a carrier signal provided $q(t)$ in (13-29) is a narrow-band signal at the carrier frequency $f_2 - f_1$, i.e., provided the bandwidth of $r(t)$ is small compared to $|f_2 - f_1|$.

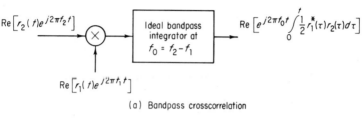

(a) Bandpass crosscorrelation

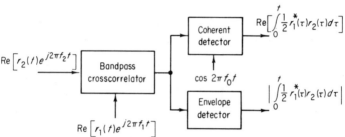

(b) Coherent and noncoherent detection after bandpass crosscorrelation

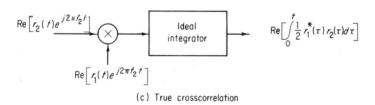

(c) True crosscorrelation

Fig. 13-4 Comparison of some crosscorrelation operations.

Now consider instead the case when $r_1(t)$ and $r_2(t)$ are the complex envelopes of waveforms at the *same* carrier frequency, say $f_1 = f_2$ in (13-27). The waveforms are

$$\hat{q}_1(t) = \text{Re}\left\{r_1(t)\,e^{j2\pi f_1 t}\right\} \qquad (13\text{-}34a)$$

$$\hat{q}_2(t) = \text{Re}\left\{r_2(t)\,e^{j2\pi f_1 t}\right\} \qquad (13\text{-}34b)$$

Now the effect of bandpass correlation is to produce a signal defined from (13-28) as

$$\hat{q}_{12}(t) = \text{Re}\{r_{12}(t)\} \qquad (13\text{-}35\text{a})$$

where

$$r_{12}(t) = \frac{1}{2} r_1^*(t) r_2(t) \qquad (13\text{-}35\text{b})$$

This $\hat{q}_{12}(t)$ is now directly a low-pass quantity, so that the desired integration is now in fact a true integration (rather than a bandpass integration) operation. The result is

$$\hat{q}(t) = \text{Re}\{r(t)\} \qquad (13\text{-}36\text{a})$$

where

$$r(t) = \int_0^t r_{12}(\tau)\,d\tau = \frac{1}{2} \int_0^t r_1^*(\tau) r_2(\tau)\,d\tau \qquad (13\text{-}36\text{b})$$

Now first we remark that a true crosscorrelation of $\hat{q}_1(t)$ and $\hat{q}_2(t)$, including a time lag τ, and integration over the interval $(0,\,T)$ under the assumption that the waveforms vanish outside this interval, would yield (cf. Sec. 3-5) the result

$$R_{\hat{q}_1 \hat{q}_2}(\tau) = \text{Re}\left\{ e^{j2\pi f_1 \tau} \int_0^T \frac{1}{2} r_1^*(t) r_2(t + \tau)\,dt \right\} \qquad (13\text{-}37)$$

Particularly, the functional dependence on the lag time τ is such that at the value $\tau = 0$,

$$R_{\hat{q}_1 \hat{q}_2}(0) = \text{Re}\left\{ \frac{1}{2} \int_0^T r_1^*(t) r_2(t)\,dt \right\} \qquad (13\text{-}38)$$

This is identical to the result in (13-36) when one sets $t = T$ in the latter (Fig. 13-4c). Thus bandpass crosscorrelation is identical with true crosscorrelation when the signals being correlated are in the same band (have the same nominal carrier frequency). The terms bandpass crosscorrelation and correlation receiver derive from this relationship.

Now consider further the result, described in (13-36), of bandpass crosscorrelation when both carriers are the same (true crosscorrelation at zero time lag). Clearly $\hat{q}(t)$ in (13-36) no longer provides a full description of $r(t)$ but only of its real part. Indeed, comparing with (13-31b), what is obtained is strictly that part of $r(t)$ which is desired in a coherent detector receiver implementation. This is not surprising. We have already noted that synchronous detection ("zero-frequency beat") has the effect of singling out only the component in phase with the detector's reference signal, and rejecting any component in phase quadrature with it. Thus, *bandpass crosscorrelation followed by coherent detection is entirely equivalent to true crosscorrelation.*

To obtain the effect of envelope detection from a true cross-correlator, on the other hand, would require some supplementary operation to recover the additional quadrature component. To this end, suppose that coherent detection is performed on the bandpass crosscorrelator output, but with a + 90° phase shift introduced into the local oscillator, i.e., using $-\sin 2\pi f_1 t$ in place of $\cos 2\pi f_1 t$. Instead of (13-31b), the result of this "quadrature coherent detection" is

$$\text{Im}\,\{r(t)\} \;=\; \text{Im}\left[\frac{1}{2}\int_0^t r_1^*(\tau)\,r_2(\tau)\,d\tau\right] \tag{13-39}$$

which is the *imaginary part* of the desired complex envelope. This output is in a sense a quadrature component to the output of a true crosscorrelator. The envelope can now be obtained as the square root of the sum of the squares of the outputs (13-31b) and (13-39). Alternatively it can be obtained directly by envelope detection of the bandpass crosscorrelator output.

The process of *bandpass crosscorrelation is the general basis for design of receiving systems* for signaling with complex signal structure, such as pseudonoise waveforms. The operation is fully equivalent in performance to matched-filtering and is often termed another form of implementing matched-filtering, even though the only significant filtering operation involved is the final integrating filter. Note incidentally that this last operation, integration, is required independently of the detailed signal design. Additionally, in some types of signaling with complex waveforms, the complexity of the signal structure lies in the variation of its instantaneous frequency or phase (i.e., angle modulation). In such cases the multiplication operation in crosscorrelation is a very natural one in which the transmitted carrier is regarded to be a nonpure tone and the receiver *local oscillator* waveform is taken to have exactly matching variations which are cancelled out by mixing and extraction of the difference-frequency component.

13-5 Maximum-likelihood Reception*

Optimum Receivers

While details are beyond our scope here, it is useful to point out the relation of the matched-filter results to the so-called *maximum-likelihood*, statistical decision theory approach to optimum reception. For a general statement, consider that a digital symbol is transmitted during an interval $(0, T)$ by transmitting one of a set

---

*For more details, see for example Refs. 1 to 3.

(alphabet) of waveforms $\{s_k(t)\}$, $k = 1, \ldots, M$. For example, $M = 2$ for binary systems. The transmitted waveform, say some $s_m(t)$, is received in a wide band in the presence of additive noise $n(t)$ so that the observed waveform is some *real* waveform $q(t)$,

$$q(t) = n(t) + s_m(t) \qquad (13\text{-}40)$$

(In writing this last equation, we have conveniently redefined the $\{s_k(t)\}$, so that they include attenuation or other effects of the channel.) Assuming that for one message element, the $\{s_k(t)\}$ are known to be confined to some interval $(0, T)$, the totality of information available at the receiver about the signaled symbol is contained in $q(t)$, $0 < t < T$. The question then is: Knowing the statistics of the noise and the nature of the signals, how should one operate on the observed $q(t)$ so as to render a digital decision with minimum probability of making an error?

The philosophical answer is that one should calculate for each of the $\{s_k(t)\}$ the relative probability or likelihood that the observed $q(t)$ represents transmission of the kth waveform. The minimum probability of error decision is then made by selecting the most likely as indicated by these calculations. Mathematically each likelihood is the so-called *posterior* conditional probability of the corresponding $s_k(t)$, given the observed $q(t)$. We assume all M symbols to be equally likely and of equal energy (if they are not, certain biases appear in the decision processes described below but their essence is unchanged). Then it is easily shown that in the case of coherent signaling where the phases of all the $\{s_k(t)\}$ are assumed precisely known, in fact the maximum likelihood occurs for that symbol for which the quantity

$$\int_0^T q(s)\, s_k(t)\, dt = \mathrm{Re}\left[\int_0^T r(t)\, u_k^*(t)\, dt \right] \qquad (13\text{-}41)$$

is a maximum; and that for noncoherent signaling it occurs for that symbol for which

$$\left| \int_0^T r(t)\, u_k^*(t)\, dt \right| \qquad (13\text{-}42)$$

is a maximum, where $r(t)$ and $u_k(t)$ are the complex envelopes of $q(t)$ and $s_k(t)$, respectively.

Note that *(13-41) is exactly identical to bandpass crosscorrelation followed by coherent detection*; and *(13-42) to bandpass crosscorrelation followed by envelope detection.**

Formulas such as (13-41) and (13-42) describe the calculations which should be performed for nondistorted signals in additive

---

*An interesting discussion along these lines is presented in Ref. 4.

Gaussian noise to enable *optimum* decisions, and in this sense they describe the basic *design* (filtering, detection, and comparison for decision) of the optimum receiver. As just noted, this optimum design is bandpass matched-filtering or bandpass crosscorrelation, followed by the appropriate coherent or noncoherent (envelope) detection, and choice of the "largest" detector output as the decision. As it turns out therefore, the optimum decision theory receiver is identical in form to the linear-filter receivers we have examined earlier, when in the latter the filter is optimized on the basis of optimizing the SNR at the detector. Thus the decision theory results do not here provide improved methods of reception over those derived from more intuitive insights. However, they do provide the additional satisfaction of knowing that the receiver structure derived from intuition is the *best* that can be done, and that, for example, postdetection filtering prior to decision could never add anything in performance to our already SNR-optimized receivers.

None of this is very surprising. It is a basic maxim that whenever one has many samples, each comprising a deterministic quantity plus a random Gaussian perturbation independent from sample to sample, maximum contrast is achieved by adding the samples so that the deterministic parts add coherently while the random parts add noncoherently. If the random noise terms do not have equal variance from sample to sample, each sample should additionally be weighted inversely to the noise variance. This latter weighting is a trivial constant for white noise, as shown in Sec. 13-1, but note the more general result expressed in the frequency domain in (13-9). In the time domain, a nonflat noise spectrum implies correlations in successive noise values, and the corresponding time-domain interpretation of (13-9) would accordingly be more complex than the simple matched-filters for white noise. However, it can be shown that the basic rule described above is fully equivalent in the frequency and time domains. It may be additionally remarked that the result for maximal-ratio diversity combining described in Chap. 17 is precisely again an example of the same basic rule.

The decision theory result likewise provides a guarantee that the matched-filter error-rate performance is an *absolute* bound on the detection performance achievable. In Sec. 13-7 we shall discuss suboptimum receivers. The knowledge of an upper bound, as we shall see, often provides a valuable reference for assessing on an *absolute* scale just how good such suboptimum receivers are.

Optimum Signals

The decision-theory results described above indicate the optimum reception system for a given set of signals. A natural next question is whether one can in turn optimize the waveforms comprising the set of signals. That is, assuming that the appropriate optimum reception is employed for each set of signals considered, performance may still vary with the nature of the set, and one seeks the optimum set. To pursue this question, we return to our bandpass crosscorrelation representation and confine the discussion to the binary case.

Consider the coherent detection case, with perfect phase reference in the receiver. Thus, let $u_1(t)$ and $u_2(t)$ represent the two possible complex envelope waveforms (remember, one may simply be only the negative of the other), with equal energies.

$$E = \frac{1}{2} \int_0^T |u_1(t)|^2 dt = \frac{1}{2} \int_0^T |u_2(t)|^2 dt \qquad (13\text{--}43)$$

and let λ be their normalized complex crosscorrelation or correlation coefficient,

$$\lambda = \frac{1}{2E} \int_0^T u_1(t) u_2^*(t) dt \qquad (13\text{--}44)$$

We assume conceptually that we will perform *both* bandpass crosscorrelation operations (i.e., using both u_1 and u_2) on the received signal-plus-noise whose complex envelope is $r(t)$, coherently detect each, and examine the difference. That is, we will make our decision according to whether the *decision variable*

$$\nu = \mathrm{Re} \left\{ \int_0^T r(t) [u_1^*(t) - u_2^*(t)] dt \right\} \qquad (13\text{--}45)$$

is positive or negative. Since $r(t)$ is a linear combination of the signal and additive complex zero-mean Gaussian noise of power spectral density n_0, it is clear that ν will be Gaussian. Assume, for example, that $u_1(t)$ was transmitted, so that $r(t) = u_1(t) + z(t)$ where $z(t)$ represents the noise. Then the mean of this Gaussian random variable is

$$\bar{\nu} = \mathrm{Re} \left\{ \int_0^T u_1(t) [u_1^*(t) - u_2^*(t)] dt \right\} = 2E(1 - \lambda_r) \qquad (13\text{--}46)$$

where

$$\lambda_r = \mathrm{Re}\,\lambda \qquad (13\text{--}47)$$

The variance of ν is

$$\sigma_\nu^2 = \frac{1}{2} \left| \int_0^T z(t) \left[u_1^*(t) - u_2^*(t) \right] dt \right|^2 = n_0 \int_0^T | u_1^*(t) - u_2^*(t) |^2 dt$$

$$= 4En_0 (1 - \lambda_r) \qquad\qquad (13\text{-}48)$$

The probability of an error, i.e., the probability that ν will be negative when it should be positive, is then

$$P_e = \frac{1}{\sigma_\nu \sqrt{2\pi}} \int_{-\infty}^0 e^{-(\nu - \bar{\nu})^2 / 2\sigma_\nu^2} d\nu = \frac{1}{2} \operatorname{erfc} \left(\frac{\bar{\nu}}{\sigma_\nu \sqrt{2}} \right)$$

$$= \frac{1}{2} \operatorname{erfc} \left[\sqrt{\frac{E(1 - \lambda_r)}{2 n_0}} \right] \qquad\qquad (13\text{-}49)$$

It follows that the best performance possible in coherent detection is obtained when the argument of the complementary error function is as large as possible. That is, λ_r should be as negative as possible, $\lambda_r = -1$. This is exactly the case in ideal coherent PSK, and the result is of course exactly the same as observed earlier (recalling that with matched-filtering, $\sqrt{\gamma} = \sqrt{E/n_0}$). It is also clear now that this is the best performance achievable with *any* binary signal design and the same E/n_0. Likewise our earlier result on coherent FSK corresponds, as noted earlier, to coherent detection of orthogonal waveforms, represented by $\lambda = 0$, hence, $\lambda_r = 0$. From this point of view, the lesser performance of coherent FSK relates to the signals being less separated than in the ideal PSK case.

The argument as to the ideal value of λ in the case of noncoherent detection is somewhat more complicated, since the case $\lambda \neq 0$ involves "crosstalk" in the matched-filter envelope outputs. We will not here analyze this problem. However, it can be shown (e.g., Refs. 4 or 5) that in this case $\lambda = 0$ gives the *best* error-rate performance available among all possible binary signal sets at the same E/n_0, and that there is no other parameter of performance from an error-rate viewpoint. Thus with noncoherent operation, orthogonality of the waveforms is the desired characteristic in the signal set to optimize error-rate performance.

13-6 Integrate-and-Dump Matched-filters

In Sec. 13-1 we have already defined the matched-filter for rectangular pulses. For a rectangular pulse received over the interval $(0, T)$, the equivalent low-pass impulse response of the matched-filter is

$$h(t) = \begin{cases} A - \text{constant}^* , & 0 < t < T \\ 0 & , \quad \text{elsewhere} \end{cases} \qquad (13\text{-}50)$$

This type of filter has been termed previously an integrate-and-dump (I & D) filter. A rectangular pulsed sinusoid itself can be defined as having the complex envelope

$$u(t) = \begin{cases} \sqrt{2S} , & 0 < t < T \\ 0 & , \quad \text{elsewhere} \end{cases} \qquad (13\text{-}51)$$

where S is the average power level over the pulse duration. It is interesting and useful to examine the detailed nature of the time response of this particular matched-filter to this pulsed sinusoid.

To achieve additional insight, we consider the more general problem of a bandpass I & D filter characterized by (13-50), centered on some frequency f_0 and responding to a rectangular pulse at frequency $f_0 + f$. This input signal is characterized with respect to f_0 by the complex envelope

$$u(t) = \begin{cases} \sqrt{2S}\, e^{j2\pi ft} , & 0 < t < T \\ 0 & , \quad \text{elsewhere} \end{cases} \qquad (13\text{-}52)$$

The output response is, of course, a bandpass signal at frequency $f_0 + f$, but can be represented in terms of f_0 as its nominal carrier frequency. Then for time t within the interval $(0, T)$, the complex envelope of the filter output, relative to f_0, is

$$v(t) = A\sqrt{2S} \int_0^t e^{j2\pi f\tau}\, d\tau = A\sqrt{2S}\, e^{j\pi ft}\, \frac{\sin \pi ft}{\pi f} \qquad (13\text{-}53)$$

This is usefully written as

$$v(t) = A\sqrt{2S}\, t\, e^{j\pi ft}\, \frac{\sin \pi ft}{\pi ft} \qquad (13\text{-}54)$$

When the pulsed sinusoid and matched-filter are aligned in frequency, $f = 0$, this response has the special form

$$f = 0: \quad v(t) = A\sqrt{2S}\, t \qquad (13\text{-}55)$$

and the envelope voltage, $|v(t)|$, builds up linearly as shown in Fig. 13-5a. The average output noise *power* level also builds up linearly

---

*The constant A is often written as $1/T$ so that the filter can be thought of as averaging over a duration T.

with time, as

$$N(t) = n_0 \int_0^t |A|^2 dt = n_0 |A|^2 t \qquad (13\text{-}56)$$

Thus for the special case of the pulse centered on the band-center frequency of the filter, the resulting output SNR builds up linearly as

$$\gamma(t) = \frac{|v(t)|^2}{2N(t)} = \frac{S\,t}{n_0} \qquad (13\text{-}57)$$

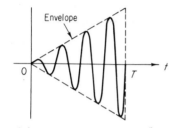

(a) Buildup of filter output on "centered" rectangular pulse

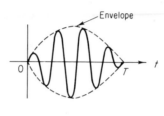

(b) Buildup of filter output on pulse offset in frequency by $1/T$

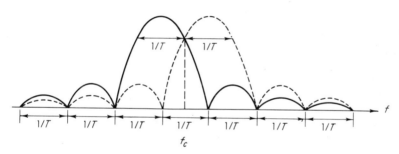

(c) Spectra of tones spaced by $1/T$ cps

Fig. 13-5 Waveforms and spectra in matched-filter detection.

For the more general case, we examine (13-54) at the sampling time T,

$$v(T) = A\sqrt{2S}\,T\,e^{j\pi fT}\,\frac{\sin \pi fT}{\pi fT} \qquad (13\text{-}58)$$

This is shown in Fig. 13-5b. Thus, in responding to a pulse offset in frequency by an amount f, there will be zero response at time T if the amount of frequency offset is such that $f = k/T$, where k is any integer. This has particular application to noncoherent FSK, implying that if the two signaled tones are spaced by $1/T$, or any multiple thereof, then matched-filter detection will result in zero *crosstalk*. Likewise, frequency division multiplexing becomes possible with tones spaced at only $1/T$, provided all other channels are synchronized in pulse timing. Note that this zero-crosstalk holds even though the spectra of rectangular pulses spaced by $1/T$ overlap considerably (Fig. 13-5b). In fact the spectra are easily shown to overlap at the -3 dB points. Note also, by examining the magnitude of (13-54) at times other than $t = T$, as shown in Fig. 13-5b, that zero-crosstalk at multiples of $1/T$ depends critically on all timing factors being perfect and the signals being undistorted from perfect rectangular form. Under conditions of radio multipath and fading, for example, modern frequency division multiplex communications systems designed with this tightness of tone packing may seriously degrade because of crosstalk arising because the received signals do not precisely meet these specifications.

13-7 Suboptimum Filtering

We continue to confine ourselves here to bandpass signals modulated by rectangular pulses described as in (13-51). We consider, however, using a suboptimum, but perhaps more readily realized, passive filter instead of the matched-filter. The suboptimum filter is also centered on the same frequency as the signal pulse. Terming the filter's equivalent low-pass impulse response $h(t)$, and its frequency function $H(f)$, the signal complex envelope at the filter output for $t = T$ is

$$u(t) = \sqrt{2S} \int_0^T h(T - \tau) d\tau \qquad (13\text{-}59)$$

The noise power in the filter output, assuming stationary white noise of equivalent low-pass power spectral density n_0, is

$$N = n_0 \int_{-\infty}^{\infty} |H(f)|^2 df = n_0 \int_{-\infty}^{\infty} |h(t)|^2 dt \qquad (13\text{-}60)$$

The SNR at the output of the suboptimum filter is thus

$$\gamma = \frac{|u(T)|^2}{2N} = \frac{S}{n_0} \frac{\left| \int_0^T h(T - \tau) d\tau \right|^2}{\int_{-\infty}^{\infty} |h(t)|^2 dt} \qquad (13\text{-}61)$$

For comparison purposes this can be written as

$$\gamma = \frac{ST}{n_0} \frac{\left| \int_0^T h(T - \tau)\, d\tau \right|^2}{T \int_{-\infty}^{\infty} |h(t)|^2\, dt} \tag{13-62}$$

Recognize that

$$\frac{E}{n_0} = \frac{ST}{n_0} \tag{13-63}$$

appears here as a conspicuous parameter, even for nonmatched-filtering. It will become evident that the remaining factor in (13-62) is indeed near unity for reasonable suboptimum filtering.

Note that if we are now using a continuously operating, nontime-varying filter, it must represent a compromise between the narrow bandwidth required to minimize the noise level in detection, and the requirement of sufficiently rapid time response (decay) to avoid intersymbol interference. The latter problem, it may be recalled, is implicit in the requirements for matched-filter design, and is avoided for example by the regular discharge action in integrate-and-dump filters. As an example of a useful compromise sub-optimum filter with reasonable selectivity and little after-ringing, consider a single pole (e.g., RLC) bandpass filter. The equivalent low-pass transfer function of such a filter can be conveniently written (ignoring gain constants) as

$$H(f) = \frac{1}{2\pi} \frac{1}{f_c + jf} \tag{13-64}$$

where f_c is the cutoff frequency. The corresponding equivalent low-pass impulse response is

$$h(t) = \begin{cases} e^{-2\pi f_c t}, & t > 0 \\ 0, & t < 0 \end{cases} \tag{13-65}$$

For this filter we readily evaluate (13-59) and (13-60) as

$$u(T) = \sqrt{2S} \left[\frac{1 - e^{-2\pi f_c T}}{2\pi f_c} \right] \tag{13-66}$$

and

$$N = \frac{n_0}{4\pi f_c} \tag{13-67}$$

However, this being a continuously operating, nontime-varying filter, energy residing in the filter at the end of each pulse is not discharged but only decays at a rate characteristic of the filter. Whenever the previous pulse represents the binary state other than the present pulse, this residual energy produces intersymbol (adjacent-symbol) interference. We will here ignore energy from any but the last previous pulse by assuming it to have negligible effect. For the filter of (13-65), the voltage caused by the previous pulse decays from a value such as (13-66) by the additional factor

$$\alpha = e^{-2\pi f_c T} \qquad\qquad (13\text{-}68)$$

We remind the reader that there are available (Refs. 1, 5) general formulas applicable to precisely determining the effect of such intersymbol interference on error-rate. However, here we apply the empirical criterion that the filter bandwidth, as determined by f_c, must be sufficiently large to render negligible the factor α, the ratio of the undesired to the desired voltage component. For example, consider negligibility to be interpreted as -20 dB or $\alpha = 0.1$. Then (13-68) requires

$$e^{-2\pi f_c T} = 0.1 \qquad\qquad (13\text{-}69)$$

or

$$f_c = \frac{1.15}{\pi}\frac{1}{T} \qquad\qquad (13\text{-}70)$$

Using this value in (13-66) and (13-67), the SNR of (13-62) at the instant of sampling becomes

$$\gamma = \frac{|u(T)|^2}{2N} \approx 0.7\,\frac{ST}{n_0} = 0.7\,\frac{E}{n_0} \qquad\qquad (13\text{-}71)$$

Hence there is a loss of approximately 1.5 dB in SNR in using this particular RLC filter as compared to the matched-filter. Relaxation of the intersymbol interference requirement could further reduce this, the limit being still about a 1-dB difference even if intersymbol interference could be completely ignored and the RLC filter bandwidth chosen only to optimize the SNR for an isolated pulse. On the other hand, ideal matched-filter performance may itself not be completely achievable for other reasons, such as waveform distortion or synchronization jitter introduced by the transmission medium. It is perhaps not surprising therefore to find that in many systems applications, the 1-2 dB additional margin available through matched-filtering may be of relatively little consequence in coping with the major system design problems. In h.f. radiotelegraphy, for example, the problem is that of severe signal fading (see Chap. 16).

There is one further point of substantial practical importance. Matched-filtering represents perhaps the ultimate in processing of a digital signal in additive Gaussian noise. For every pulse it gives at some appropriate instant a voltage which can be used to make the minimum probability of error binary decision. However, the matched-filter output waveform generally bears little resemblance to the input waveform. For example, for rectangular pulses the matched-filter output will be triangular in shape during the course of the pulse. In contradistinction there are many applications such as h.f. radiotelegraphy, where there is much emphasis on radio receiving systems which do not of themselves include telegraph terminal (decision-using) equipment. In such systems the reception goal of the radio systems is only to *relay* the signals (e.g., via land lines) to the users who have the telegraph terminals. Indeed, the radio receiving system of itself may have no equipment which is in any sense "aware" of the timing of the telegraph signal pulses. In such operation the desired reconstitution of the telegraph signal may be most easily accomplished by demodulating the radio signal with a maximum *fidelity*, and then "sharpening" the resulting noisy telegraph signal via hard limiting or some equivalent. Such "maximum fidelity" requires a filter which has a sufficiently fast response, or wide bandwidth, that there is very little rounding or other distortion of the telegraph signal transitions, i.e., such as to cause overlap of successive information pulses. This can be accomplished only at a cost in noise reduction. With the random telegraph transitions occurring T seconds apart, or at multiples of T, the radio signal may be regarded as having a sideband structure extending out to well beyond $1/T$ on either side of the radio carrier, and near-faithful reproduction requires that the filter be wide enough to pass a major part of this sideband structure. Typically, total bandpass filter bandwidths of the order of $3/T$ to $5/T$ may be used in such operations. It is also apparent that in such relay systems, the matched-filter per se has no useful role, since its output is a much distorted version of the transmitted signal, aimed only at producing at the end of the integrate cycle a voltage which is an optimum indicator of the binary content. Of course, a telegraph signal could also be reconstituted by making binary decisions and then regenerating the telegraph waveform. This, however, requires explicit attention in the receiver to the timing of every telegraph signal. This can become particularly burdensome in a multiplex situation in which the several channels are unsynchronized in timing. On the other hand, the wide-band filter-demodulator can efficiently demodulate the signal with *no* attention to pulse timing, and timing synchronism is necessary only at the terminal where the final filtering and binary decisions are being made.

13-8 DPSK as Orthogonal Waveform Signaling

We will now pursue further the discussion started in Sec. 12-2 on differentially coherent phase-shift keying. This has become an extremely important signaling mode in modern systems, and the purpose here is to further discuss its implementation and to deepen the qualitative understanding of its behavior.

The most common implementation of DPSK has been with rectangular pulses, with constant signal amplitude. As explained in Secs. 13-4 and 13-6, the bandpass integrate-and-dump filter is then the essence of an optimum receiver.

With the specific use of *I & D* filters, the DPSK reception concept of Fig. 12-4 can be simplified by using the extremely high-Q nature (long ringing time) of the basic filter circuits to effect the required delays. If the *input* to such a circuit is gated off but the circuit is not discharged, it will simply ring at the filter center frequency, with the complex envelope *holding* at its last output value. Thus DPSK reception can be implemented by *commutating* alternate pulses of the sequence of input pulses of duration T between a *pair* of such *I & D* filters. This operation is shown in Fig. 13-6. In alternation, each filter charges up with an input signal pulse over a period T, holds for a second period of length T, and then is discharged and ready for a new input. During the second interval, the other filter is being charged up with the next signal pulse. If the two filter outputs are connected to a coherent detector (or phase detector), it is readily seen that the desired outputs for the binary decision are available just prior to the end of each time interval T.

There are practical restrictions on the use of *I & D* filters in DPSK reception (indeed on *I & D* filters in general). If the filter is

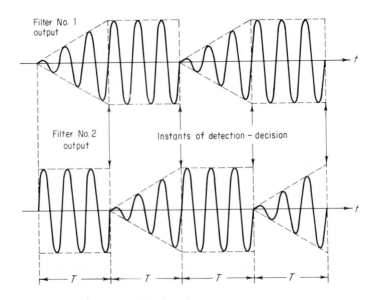

Fig. 13-6 Integrate and dump detection of DPSK.

operated at some center frequency f_0, the time for discharge ("dump") T_D will take at least one and usually several r.f. cycles,

$$T_D = k/f_0, \quad k \text{ a small integer} \tag{13-72}$$

For the loss of energy contrast in processing to be kept small, T_D must be small compared to the pulse length T,

$$T_D = pT, \quad p \approx 0.1 \text{ or less for } 0.5 \text{ dB or smaller loss} \tag{13-73}$$

Finally the actual filter circuit must be sufficiently high Q, or narrow-band, that integrating action is closely approximated over the interval T. Thus the filter bandwidth B must be

$$B \approx q/T, \quad q \approx 0.1 \text{ or less} \tag{13-74}$$

The net result is that the filter Q must be such that

$$Q = \frac{f_0}{B} = \frac{k}{pq} \approx 100 \, k \text{ or more} \tag{13-75}$$

Desirably, then, Q is of the order of 1000. Another restriction from our statements above is

$$\frac{1}{T} = \frac{p}{k} f_0 \approx 0.1 f_0 \text{ or less} \tag{13-76}$$

That is, the keying rate must be an order of magnitude less than the filter center frequency. Thus there are restrictions on the keying rate achievable in view of the limited frequencies at which the desired filters can be built. In actual fact it appears that well-functioning bandpass $I \& D$ filters have not been built for operation at rates above 10–20 kilobits/sec and that circuit design for higher rates would not be a trivial problem.

This does note mean that DPSK is infeasible at higher keying rates, merely that bandpass $I \& D$ filtering may not be the appropriate approach. Certainly RLC filters such as considered in the last section could be employed, along with a delay line as in Fig. 12-4 or some equivalent. Also crosscorrelation reception, with lowpass $I \& D$ operation, is certainly outside these restrictions.

To examine another aspect of DPSK, we return to further interpretation of the mathematics of Sec. 12-2. The derivation of error-rate, particularly (12-17) and (12-21), may be interpreted as follows: For convenience we consider only bandpass $I \& D$ filters, although the results are readily seen to apply to more general filtering action. If the $I \& D$ outputs for two successive pulse intervals are alternately added and subtracted, a comparison of *envelopes* of the *resulting sum and difference* will determine the information conveyed by the phases of the two pulses. However, note now that the sum can also be realized by processing the input through an $I \& D$ filter which operates over the total time $2T$, and the difference by processing through another $I \& D$ filter operating over $2T$ but which includes an additional $180°$ phase inversion switched onto the input at time T. We have thus defined a pair of matched-filters which operate on a *waveform of length* $2T$, with decision based upon envelope comparison of their outputs.* Indeed, if we examine each pair of pulses, we see that, owing to differential encoding, a Mark (say) is represented by either of the phase combinations

$$0° - \quad 0°$$
$$180° - 180°$$

on the successive pulses, and a Space by either of the combinations

$$0° - 180°$$
$$180° - \quad 0°$$

It is in fact clear that, in the earlier sense of (13–26a), either of the Mark combinations is *orthogonal*, over the $2T$ interval, to either of the Space combinations, and that this orthogonality is the significant feature of the signaling. In this light, DPSK is merely *a generalization of noncoherent FSK*, in which *every running pair of pulses represents one of two possible orthogonal waveforms*. Note, however, that each pulse energy is used twice, because of the stratagem effected by the differential encoding. Thus, for power level S, the E/n_0 ratio is $2ST/n_0$ rather than ST/n_0, and this can be viewed completely as the source of the exact 3–dB improvement for DPSK ever noncoherent FSK.

Note that the ratio $2ST/n_0$ is available because of the use of orthogonal waveforms, where by the stratagem employed, the first half of each successive pair of waveforms is identical. Because the first halves are identical, there appears to be no way to extend this stratagem to an ideal coherent PSK system wherein the normalized crosscorrelation of the two waveforms could be negative. Thus, coherent detection of the DPSK waveforms could afford only the equivalent of coherent FSK (coherent detection of orthogonal signals) which, as we have seen, has only slight advantages over noncoherent FSK at reasonably low error-rates.** In a nutshell,

---

*Note that, since each such pair of matched-filters is fully occupied for a period $2T$ and makes one decision every $2T$ seconds, a second pair would be needed for processing the alternate decisions.

**Note that, since phase stability must still apply in DPSK over overlapping intervals of length $2T$, the transmitter must retain a stable carrier. It is as if one had stable gated oscillators for transmitting FSK but chose the slightly poorer noncoherent rather than coherent detection because of the simpler implementation. A major reason for such a choice, as already indicated in Sec. 12–2, may also be that the transmission medium (rather than oscillators) is responsible for sufficient phase variations to negate deriving phase references from the received signal by smoothing over very many pulses.

ideal coherent PSK operation (antiparallel waveforms) appears to be limited to a case where any particular signal energy is only "used once" in a pulse decision, hence with $E/n_0 = ST/n_0$, while the DPSK stratagem allows a noncoherent operation with twice this E/n_0 ratio and hence almost makes up completely for the difference between ideal coherent and ideal noncoherent operation (as was evident in Fig. 11-3).

We may also note that just as the simple RLC filter appears to provide a reasonable suboptimum engineering approximation to the action of an $I \& D$ filter, it appears possible to achieve similar approximations for the desired $2T$-duration reception filters for DPSK regarded as orthogonal waveform signaling.

The interpretation of DPSK as orthogonal waveform signaling is often very useful in understanding the effects of channel instabilities, fading, etc., upon the signals, since interpretations are then often a simple adaptation of similar considerations for FSK. These interpretations are also often readily extendable to systems where pilot tones are being used, say to monitor the channel phase, and the information-bearing waveforms are perhaps even antiparallel. Such systems approximate ideal coherent PSK, with the pilot tone information being used to set up the necessary phase references. If, instead, the pilot tone is now considered to be part of the total information signal, then the *total* alternate waveforms are no longer antiparallel; and one can often gain a useful picture of the overall performance as a function of *total* received power by recognizing a close kinship to the DPSK problem and applying the known results for matched-filter detection of these composite waveforms. Unfortunately more detailed examination of such considerations are beyond our scope here (see, e.g., Ref. 1).

REFERENCES

1. M. Schwartz, W. R. Bennett and S. Stein, *Communication Systems and Techniques* (McGraw-Hill Book Company, New York, 1966).
2. J. M. Wozencraft and I. M. Jacobs, *Principles of Communication Engineering* (John Wiley and Sons, Inc., New York, 1965).
3. W. B. Davenport, Jr. and W. L. Root, *Random Signals and Noise* (McGraw-Hill Book Company, New York, 1965).
4. C. W. Helstrom: "Resolution of Signals in White, Gaussian Noise," *Proc. IRE 43*, pp. 1111-1118 (September 1955).
5. S. Stein: "Unified Analysis of Certain Coherent and Noncoherent Binary Communications Systems," *IRE Trans. Information Theory* (January 1964).

14

M-ary Signaling

14-1 *M*-ary and Coded Signal Alphabets

We have up to now discussed only binary digital signaling, with a two-symbol waveform alphabet utilized to transmit one *binary source* digit (termed a *bit* of information) per transmitted symbol. Each transmitted symbol, however, can convey much more information if a larger signaling alphabet is allowed. Specifically an M-symbol alphabet (M distinct waveforms) will convey $\log_2 M$ information bits per transmitted symbol. M-ary signaling may be accomplished by multiamplitude, multitone, or multiple phase signaling, the obvious generalizations of binary OOK, FSK and PSK, respectively. One may also employ signaling waveforms constructed as sequences of binary waveforms of the previously discussed types. PCM and algebraically coded binary systems (Chap. 15) are examples of sequences of binary waveforms. The distinction commonly drawn is that such a sequence is regarded as a single M-ary waveform and detected as a unit in an M-ary system, whereas detection and decision is carried out on the individual binary waveforms in the usual operation of PCM or algebraic coded binary systems.

A typical data communication system model is shown in Fig. 14-1. The message *source* is assumed to produce statistically independent, equally likely binary digits (bits), at a rate of R per second where R is the *source* or *information rate.* No loss in generality is introduced by this assumption since all data sources may be coded into such binary sequences. The information per source digit is, of course, 1 bit. In a time interval T_M, a total of $M = 2^{RT_M}$ different, equally probable message sequences are then possible, conveying R bits of information per sequence interval.

The *coder* accepts blocks of $k = RT_M$ source digits and instructs the modulator to produce one of an available set of $M = 2^k$ waveforms. For the previously discussed binary signaling case, $k = 1$, the modulator makes its choice between just two waveforms, each of duration $T = T_M$. For the *algebraic binary coding* case to be discussed in Chap. 15, the coder accepts blocks of $k > 1$ source digits and instructs the modulator to produce one of $M = 2^k$ distinct sequences or code words; each such sequence contains n binary waveforms, $n > k$, each binary waveform being of duration $T = T_M/n$. Detection will be on the individual binary waveforms of duration T and not on the composite waveform of duration T_M, and is followed by logic which converts the n decisions to k information decisions. In *M-ary signaling*, the coder again accepts blocks of $k > 1$ source bits and instructs the modulator to produce one of $M = 2^k$ distinct waveforms of duration T_M. In reception, however, the waveform will be considered an indivisible entity, and decision will be performed on the waveform as a whole.

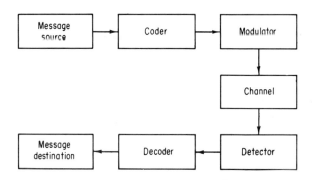

Fig. 14-1 Model of a data communication system.

The *modulator* provides the selected waveform which is transmitted over the channel where it is assumed in our model to be corrupted with additive white Gaussian noise. The *signaling rate* may refer either to the rate of transmission of M-ary symbols $(1/T_M)$, or to the binary source rate $(1/T)$. Its meaning will be clear in context.

At the receiver, for the *uncoded binary* case, the detector examines the binary waveform and produces one of two possible output values. The *decoder* is not necessary in this case since the decision output is directly a binary digit or bit of information. For the *algebraic coded binary* system the *detector* (decision) produces one of two possible output values for each binary waveform, and the *decoder* associates with each block of n such values, a particular sequence of k binary digits or information bits. In the *M-ary signaling* case the detector examines each M-ary waveform and produces one of M possible output values. The decoder, in turn, produces a distinct sequence of k bits for each of the M possible input values.

Comparison of such diverse systems in a meaningful manner is not simple. If bandwidth is not at a premium (a reasonable assumption for many applications involving M-ary or algebraic coding techniques), then a comparison of systems operating at the *same information rate* may be of interest. For purposes of graphically depicting system performance, we make this assumption and plot probability of M-ary symbol or code word error P_e as a function of the energy or signal-to-noise ratio required per bit of information (source digit). The energy per source bit E_b is related to the energy per symbol E by the expression

$$E_b = \frac{1}{k} E \qquad (14-1)$$

where k is the number of information bits per symbol. With a fixed source rate R, this parameter determines the required received power S according to the relation

$$S = E_b R \qquad (14-2)$$

Symbol error probability will be used here in preference to *bit* error probability for comparison purposes because there is no single universal deterministic relationship between the two. However, deterministic relationships can be formulated for particular cases. Perhaps the most meaningful *general* assumption that can be made in relating symbol error probability to bit error probability is the following: Whenever an M-ary symbol is in error, *assume that the decoder randomly selects the k binary digits associated with any of the other (2^k − 1) M-ary symbols.* Now, considering any arbitrary bit position in the M-fold set of k-bit sequences, $M/2$ of the sequences contain a binary 1 in that position and $M/2$ contains a binary 0. Then considering any arbitrary bit in the binary sequence corresponding to the symbol signaled, it is apparent that the same binary state occurs in that identical position for 2^{k-1} − 1 of the remaining 2^k − 1 possible sequences and that the other binary state occurs in that position in the remaining 2^{k-1} sequences. Under these assumptions the average probability of binary error P_{eb} is related to the probability of symbol error P_e by

$$P_{eb} = \frac{2^{k-1}}{2^k - 1} P_e = \frac{1}{2} \frac{P_e}{1 - (1/2^k)} \qquad (14-3)$$

and in any case a reasonable choice of coding will guarantee that on the average

$$P_{eb} \leq \frac{1}{2} \frac{P_e}{1 - (1/2^k)} \qquad (14-4a)$$

---

*This is certainly a reasonable assumption when all M symbols are mutually orthogonal and equally likely. When they are not orthogonal, errors are likely to result in symbols which are "close" to that transmitted, and hence the erroneous symbol choice may contain more than an average number of bits in common with the correct set, in this binary representation; this is reflected in the upper bound statement of (14-4).

For large k, this bound is practically indistinguishable from

$$P_{eb} \leq \frac{1}{2} P_e \qquad (14\text{-}4b)$$

If, on the other hand, a bandwidth constraint is assumed, then a comparison of systems utilizing the same r.f. bandwidth is of interest. Unfortunately, as will be seen, the bandwidth required for any M-ary or coded signal depends upon the system type. For multiamplitude or multilevel signaling, the bandwidth is essentially independent of M; but, as will be shown later, for large M such systems generally do not offer sufficient signal discrimination against noise for radio communications. For multitone or other orthogonal waveform sets as are more generally applicable for radio, the system bandwidth is proportional to M. At the same time, in all these systems, the information rate is proportional to $\log_2 M$. For a given M, the probability of symbol error versus SNR (E_b) at some fixed information rate may be considered a curve for some fixed bandwidth (over the entire range of SNR values). However, a second curve drawn for another value of M will have to be rescaled to the same bandwidth (and now a different information rate) if a comparison based on fixed bandwidth is desired. These remarks will be clearer when actual performance curves are examined. The general system design problem, which usually involves compromises between quality of performance, information flow rate, and required bandwidth is a multiparameter problem which does not always allow a single, generally applicable basis of comparison in the M-ary or coded situations.

14-2 Multiamplitude Signaling*

In this technique M different amplitudes of a single basic waveform are transmitted, with decisions based upon threshold levels following either coherent or noncoherent detection. There are two important limitations of such a system—power requirements and channel gain stability.

If one assumes uniformly spaced levels to be transmitted, the *average* transmitted power varies with M approximately as

$$P_{av} = \frac{1}{M} \sum_{q=1}^{M} q^2 = \frac{(M + 1)(2M + 1)}{6} \approx \frac{M^2}{3} \qquad (14\text{-}5)$$

This varies slightly according to whether the zero level is also being used as in binary OOK, and also according to whether coherent

---

*Sometimes termed amplitude shift keying (ASK).

detection is available and being used to encode algebraic sign as well as level, halving the required number of different amplitudes.* Recognize now that

$$M = 2^k \qquad (14-6)$$

where k is the number of information bits per symbol. Hence

$$P_{av} \approx \frac{2^{2k}}{3} \approx \exp(2k \ln 2) \qquad (14-7)$$

That is, the average power required increases *exponentially* as the increase in information rate in a multilevel system. In low-powered systems this might be feasible; in high-powered radio systems, using multiple levels to increase the information rate over binary operation (assuming a fixed signaling rate) seems unattractive. In addition, use of a multilevel system raises the need for linear power amplifiers in transmission. Another important difficulty in radio operation is the effect of fading upon any detection technique using fixed thresholds, although it has been shown (Ref. 1) that thresholds can be continuously adapted by transmitting and monitoring a pilot tone which utilizes a negligible fraction of the transmitted power.

The significance of multiamplitude or multiphase signaling (see below) as compared to multitone FSK is that they require no greater bandwidth to increase the information rate over the binary case. In effect, however, the choice is added bandwidth versus added power. In radio applications where M-ary signaling has been discussed, the decision has been in favor of the added bandwidth. The only area where multiamplitude signaling has been prominently considered is in digital data transmission on voice channels of the telephone network. Here the problem is the finite bandwidth available for transmission and this leaves only multiamplitude or multiphase possibilities. Fortunately telephone lines can be made to have a high degree of channel stability and low additive noise level and hence to allow multiamplitude signaling.

Error-rate calculations for multiamplitude systems involve simple modifications of the formulas in Chap. 10.

14-3 Multiphase Signaling

The concept of signaling with several phases on a single tone is the natural M-ary generalization of PSK.

---

*In the binary case this would yield a *bipolar* system rather than the on-off system examined in Chap. 10; this bipolar system corresponds actually to the binary PSK of Chap. 12. However, in the extension to M-ary, multiphase rather than multiamplitude is the natural extention of the PSK concept.

First, however, we give special consideration to the four-phase case. Let us visualize that if a binary PSK signal is employing, say, the 0°-180° phase positions of a carrier, then with respect to coherent detection a completely independent binary signal can be transmitted on the 90°-270° phase positions. One signal may be visualized as DSB-SC modulation (multiplication by ±1) of $\cos 2\pi f_0 t$, and the other as DSB-SC modulation of $\sin 2\pi f_0 t$. After receiver filtering, and assuming perfect phase reference, coherent detection by a $\cos 2\pi f_0 t$ reference (compensated for any additional phase produced by the transmission medium and receiver filters) will retrieve the first signal, with the noise component in phase with it, and coherent detection by $\sin 2\pi f_0 t$ will retrieve the other signal and the other quadrature component of noise. Note that the two noises are independent at any single instant of time, such as the sampling instant for the binary decisions. Thus, without changing signaling bandwidth, we have doubled the information rate. The corresponding average probability of error for any bit will be determined by the value ST/n_0 where S now is the power in *one* of the quadrature components. Hence to double the information rate *without changing the bit error probability* will require doubling the transmitted power. The final point to be made here is that it is clear that no other phase positions exist which will allow any additional binary PSK signals to be transmitted without producing crosstalk with both quadrature signals already described. This does not mean that more such binary PSK signals could not be introduced, e.g., at the 45°-225° and 135°-315° phase positions. However, one should then anticipate that, because the crosstalk will reduce the discriminability against noise, a disproportionately large increase in total transmitted power will be required to reduce the effects of the additive noise.

Now let us turn to an M-ary signaling point of view. In the case discussed above, binary PSK on each of two quadrature components, the signal transmitted at any instant has the form

$$s(t) = a \cos 2\pi f_0 t + b \sin 2\pi f_0 t \qquad (14\text{-}8)$$

where for each information pulse $a = +1$ or -1 and independently $b = +1$ or -1. Clearly the total signal transmitted at any instant has the form

$$s(t) = \sqrt{2} \cos(2\pi f_0 t + \theta) \qquad (14\text{-}9)$$

where θ has one of the values 45°, 135°, 225°, 315°. Thus the same signals viewed previously as occupying 0° or 180°, and 90° or 270°, can be alternately regarded as involving just one out of four possible phases (45°, 135°, 225°, 315°), each such selection conveying two information bits. The generalization of (14-9) to M phases is that for each signal pulse of length T,

$$s(t) = \sqrt{2S} \cos(2\pi f_0 t + \theta) , \quad 0 < t < T \qquad (14\text{-}10)$$

where θ is one of a set of uniformly spaced values θ_m given, for example (see Fig. 14-2), by

$$\theta_m = \frac{2\pi}{M}(m-1), \quad m = 1, \ldots, M \qquad (14\text{-}11)$$

Usually, M is taken as some power of 2,

$$M = 2^k, \quad k = \text{integer} \qquad (14\text{-}12)$$

The power S in (14-10) is now the *total* signal power received.

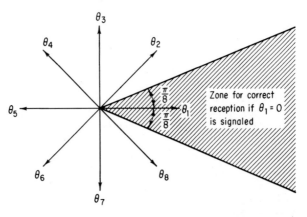

Possible signal phases $\theta_m = (m-1)\dfrac{2\pi}{M}$, $m = 1,2,\cdots M$

Fig. 14-2 M-phase signaling (illustrated for M = 8).

The problem of detecting the value of θ is interesting. It is *not* sufficient to simply use the common form of phase detector with $\cos 2\pi f_0 t$ as a reference. This measures $\cos \theta$, and the latter is ambiguous [$\cos \theta_m = \cos(2\pi - \theta_m)$, and only in the binary case where the choices are $\theta_m = 0$ or π is there no ambiguity]. It would be sufficient to employ two phase detectors, with $\cos 2\pi f_0 t$ and $\sin 2\pi f_0 t$ as respective references, along with a logic circuit to determine the ratio of the two detected components. However, an equally interesting detection process would be to employ a set of M coherent detectors or phase detectors, using $\cos(2\pi f_0 t + \theta_m)$ as the respective reference signals, and to choose the (algebraically) largest output. This is in fact the receiver which would be directly indicated by a maximum-likelihood approach. This is basically also the model we will analyze for error probability.

The situation is pictured in Fig. 14-2 for the case M = 8. Consider, without loss of generality, that $\theta_1 = 0$ is the signaled phase. At the input to the detector (following the bandpass filters), denote the receiver noise components in phase with the signal and in quadrature with it as $x(t)$ and $y(t)$, respectively. Then the voltage at the detector has the form

$$v(t) = [\sqrt{2S} + x(t)] \cos 2\pi f_0 t - y(t) \sin 2\pi f_0 t \qquad (14\text{-}13)$$

where S is the signal power level and $N = \overline{x^2} = \overline{y^2}$ is the noise power level. Since the possible phasors are spaced by $2\pi/M$, it is clear from Fig. 14-2 that reception will be correct provided the phase of the waveform defined by (14-13) is within π/M on either side of the signaled phase. An exact expression for the probability of symbol error (Ref. 2) is

$$P_e = 1 - \frac{1}{2\pi} \int_{-\pi/M}^{\pi/M} e^{-\gamma} \left[1 + \sqrt{4\pi\gamma} \cos\theta \, e^{\gamma \cos^2\theta} \frac{1}{\sqrt{2\pi}} \int_{-\infty}^{\sqrt{2\gamma}\cos\theta} e^{-x^2/2} \, dx \right] d\theta$$

$$(14\text{-}14)$$

where we have again denoted the total SNR at the detector input by

$$\gamma = S/N \qquad (14\text{-}15)$$

If we assume matched-filtering,

$$\gamma = \frac{S}{N} = \frac{E}{n_0} \qquad (14\text{-}16)$$

where E is the received energy associated with each M-ary symbol. The symbol error probability P_e is plotted in Fig. 14-3 as a function of normalized *SNR per information bit*, defined by

$$\gamma_b = \frac{\gamma}{k} = \frac{\gamma}{\log_2 M} \qquad (14\text{-}17a)$$

or, in the matched-filter case,

$$\gamma_b = \frac{E_b}{n_0} = \frac{1}{k} \frac{E}{n_0} = \frac{1}{\log_2 M} \frac{E}{n_0} \qquad (14\text{-}17b)$$

Curves are given for $M = 2, 4, 8, 16$ and 32. Figure 14-3 shows that for fixed symbol error probability, under the assumption that all systems are operating at the same information rate, the normalized SNR γ_b, and hence the transmitter power, must be *increased* with increasing M, while the required signaling bandwidth is decreasing.

A better quantitative feeling for the relationships in Fig. 14-3 can be obtained by deriving a simple bounding result, the derivation being instructive in its own right. We rewrite (14-13) so that

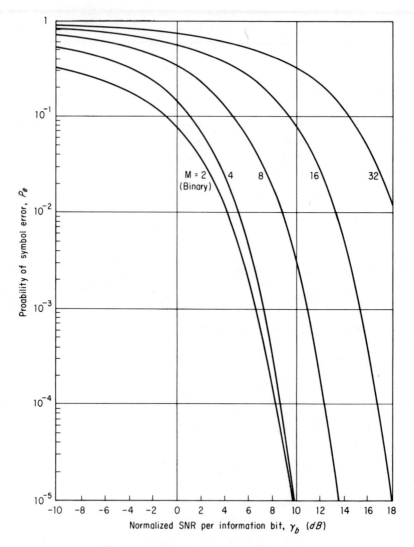

Fig. 14-3 Coherent multiphase signaling.

the probability of error is the probability that the phase θ of

$$v(t) = x \cos 2\pi f_0 t - y \sin 2\pi f_0 t \qquad (14\text{--}18)$$

lies outside the zone

$$-\frac{\pi}{M} < \theta < \frac{\pi}{M} \qquad (14\text{--}19)$$

where now x and y are independent Gaussian variates with means

$$\bar{x} = \sqrt{2S}, \quad \bar{y} = 0 \qquad (14\text{-}20a)$$

and variances

$$\overline{(x - \bar{x})^2} = \overline{y^2} = N \qquad (14\text{-}20b)$$

As opposed to the exact calculation already cited, a simple but very close approximate result is obtained by calculating the sum of the probabilities

$$P_1 = \text{prob}\left[y > x \tan\frac{\pi}{x}\right] \qquad (14\text{-}21)$$

and

$$P_2 = \text{prob}\left[y < -x \tan\frac{\pi}{M}\right] \qquad (14\text{-}22)$$

As shown in Fig. 14-4, these calculate the probability that the phasor lies outside the zone of correct reception, except that the zone of width $2\pi/M$ centered (in this case) on $\theta = \pi$ is included twice. Hence

$$P_1 + P_2 - P_3 = P_e \qquad (14\text{-}23)$$

where P_e is the probability of error and P_3 is the probability of lying in the added zone. However, the joint p.d.f. of x and y is circularly symmetrical about the point $x = \sqrt{2S}$, $y = 0$; hence the probability P_3 is certainly strongly bounded (very strongly for large SNR) by

$$0 \le P_3 \le \frac{1}{M - 1} P_e \qquad (14\text{-}24)$$

Accordingly, in (14-23) we can write

$$P_1 + P_2 \ge P_e \ge P_1 + P_2 - \frac{P_e}{M - 1}$$

or

$$P_1 + P_2 \ge P_e \ge \frac{M - 1}{M}(P_1 + P_2) \qquad (14\text{-}25)$$

Thus, for M large,

$$P_e \approx P_1 + P_2 \qquad (14\text{-}26)$$

to within an extremely small algebraic factor. Because of the exponential dependence of error-rate on SNR, such a factor becomes negligible in any system evaluation.

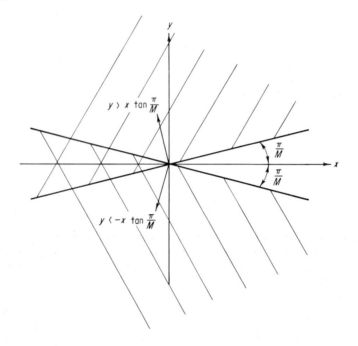

Fig. 14-4 Bounds for errors in multiphase signaling.

To calculate P_1, we set

$$w = y - x \tan \frac{\pi}{M} \qquad (14\text{-}27)$$

Then w is Gaussian, with

$$\overline{w} = -\overline{x} \tan \frac{\pi}{M} = -\sqrt{2S} \tan \frac{\pi}{M} \qquad (14\text{-}28\text{a})$$

$$\sigma_w^2 = \overline{(w - \overline{w})^2} = \overline{y^2} + \overline{(x - \overline{x})^2} \tan^2 \pi/M = N \sec^2(\pi/M) \qquad (14\text{-}28\text{b})$$

It follows that

$$P_1 = \text{prob}(w > 0) = \frac{1}{2} \text{erfc} \left[-\frac{\overline{w}}{\sigma_w \sqrt{2}} \right] = \frac{1}{2} \text{erfc} \left[\sqrt{\frac{S}{N}} \sin \frac{\pi}{M} \right]$$

$$= \frac{1}{2} \text{erfc} \left(\sqrt{\gamma} \sin \frac{\pi}{M} \right) \qquad (14\text{-}29)$$

where γ is used according to its earlier definition. Similarly

$$P_2 = \frac{1}{2} \text{ erfc} \left(\sqrt{\gamma} \sin \frac{\pi}{M} \right) \tag{14-30}$$

Hence

$$P_e \approx \text{erfc} \left(\sqrt{\gamma} \sin \frac{\pi}{M} \right) \tag{14-31}$$

As expected from (14-25), for $M = 2$ (binary PSK) this is too large (by exactly a factor of 2) compared to the earlier exact results in Sec. 12-1.

An exact result for symbol error-rate is also available for $M = 4$. In this case it is convenient to regard the signaled phases as $45°$, $135°$, $-45°$, $-135°$, so that the coordinates are rotated by $45°$ from those in Fig. 14-4. Regarding the $45°$ phasor to be the one transmitted, the received quadrature components x and y of signal plus noise are each independently Gaussian, with variance N, and *each* with mean value

$$\bar{x} = \bar{y} = \sqrt{2S} \cos(\pi/4) = \sqrt{S} \tag{14-32}$$

The probability of *correct* reception is then

$$P_c = \text{prob}(x > 0, y > 0) = \text{prob}(x > 0) \text{ prob}(y > 0)$$

$$= \left[\frac{1}{2} \text{ erfc} \left(-\sqrt{\frac{\gamma}{2}} \right) \right]^2 = \left[1 - \frac{1}{2} \text{ erfc} \sqrt{\frac{\gamma}{2}} \right]^2 \tag{14-33}$$

and the probability of error is

$$P_e = 1 - P_c = \text{erfc} \sqrt{\gamma/2} \left[1 - \frac{1}{4} \text{ erfc} \sqrt{\gamma/2} \right] \tag{14-34}$$

As is evident, (14-31) and (14-25) indeed provide upper and lower bounds on the exact result (14-34) for $M = 4$.

In the approximate result (14-31), for large M,

$$\sin \left(\frac{\pi}{M} \right) \approx \frac{\pi}{M} \tag{14-35}$$

and the symbol probability of error is approximately

$$P_e \approx \text{erfc} \left[\sqrt{\gamma} \frac{\pi}{M} \right] = \text{erfc} \left[\sqrt{k \gamma_b} \frac{\pi}{M} \right] \tag{14-36}$$

If one now assumes fixed information rate operation, it is evident that the SNR per bit γ_b and hence the transmitter power S must increase as $M^2/\log_2 M$ if the symbol error probability is maintained constant with increasing M. At the same time the required signaling bandwidth diminishes as $1/\log_2 M$. If instead one assumes a fixed signaling bandwidth, maintaining the same symbol error probability with increasing M requires that the SNR per bit γ_b be increased as $M^2/\log_2 M$ while the information rate increases as $\log_2 M$. Note, however, that to compensate for the increased information rate the signal power S must be increased as M^2 and not as $M^2/\log_2 M$.

If we assume that whenever an M-ary symbol is in error the decoder has randomly selected the k binary digits associated with any of the other $2^k - 1$ M-ary symbols, then the bit error probability is related to the symbol error probability by (14-3), and the dependences discussed above in terms of symbol error probability also hold for bit error probability. However, in the multiphase case, as Fig. 14-2 shows, an error is much more likely to occur with the adjacent phase selected then with any of the other phases selected at random. If one then selects a binary-to- M-ary coding such that the binary sequences representing adjacent phasors differ in *only one bit position* (one such coding is the so-called Gray code), then each M-ary symbol error is more likely to represent only one binary error in the sequence of k bits.* In the extreme (which would tend to hold in the multiphase case at extremely high values of SNR),

$$P_{eb} = \frac{1}{k} P_e = \frac{1}{\log_2 M} P_e \qquad (14-37)$$

Equations (14-37) and (14-3) represent two extremes in relating bit error probability to M-ary symbol error probability. In either case, the error probabilities are related by an algebraic factor and the dependence of error-rate on signal energy, in additive Gaussian noise, is still dominated by the exponential dependence on γ/M^2 implied in (14-36). Thus multiphase signaling with any value of M larger than M = 4 implies a power increase closely proportional to M^2. Compounded with this problem is the need for excellent channel phase stability implied in our calculations above. (The latter problem can be alleviated by going to a DPSK type of

---

*In the four-phase case, for example, one may choose encoding so that either phase on each side of the correct one represents one of the two bits being in error, and choice of the opposite phase represents both bits in error. Then by simple extension of the earlier analysis of the M = 4 system, it may be shown that the binary error-rate is precisely

$$P_{eb} = \frac{1}{2} \operatorname{erfc} \sqrt{\gamma/2}$$

This is exactly the same result obtained earlier when we considered the four-phase system as two quadrature binary PSK systems, if we additionally take into account the division of the total power S between the two quadrature components.

keying. However, we shall comment upon DPSK by viewing it as an extension of orthogonal waveform signaling, and hence this discussion is deferred to Sec. 14-5. The large requirement on SNR remains in any event.) Again multiphase keying with M exceeding four has found application in phone-line data transmission but not in radio systems.

14-4 Multitone Signaling

Multitone signaling, or *multiple FSK* as it is often termed, implies the use of M spaced frequencies or tones as the M-ary symbols. Reception is via a set of M filters, each centered on one of the possible tones. If phase references were available for *all* the tone frequencies, coherent FSK reception would be possible. (In fact use of multiple phases per tone would be feasible.) However, because of the multiplicity of frequencies, such phase references are at best difficult to maintain in a true multitone system. Accordingly we shall here consider only noncoherent reception, with each tone filter followed by an envelope detector and the decision based on the largest envelope output. For the moment we also consider only the case where the tone spacing and receiver filtering is such that there is no crosstalk among the filter outputs, i.e., the symbols and filters are orthogonal. With matched-filters, with each symbol pulse of length T_M, the required tone spacing is $1/T_M$, and the total bandwidth occupied by the overall system (to the $-$ 3-dB points on the spectra of the outermost tone pulses) is

$$B_M = M/T_M \qquad (14\text{-}38)$$

To obtain error probabilities, note that of the M filter outputs, $M - 1$ contain only noise of intensity N. From (4-198), for example, the probability that the envelope of each of these latter exceeds some level x is

$$f(x) = \int_x^\infty \frac{r}{N} e^{-r^2/2N} \, dr = e^{-x^2/2N} \qquad (14\text{-}39)$$

Since all are independent, the probability that *none* of these envelopes exceeds the level x is

$$[1 - f(x)]^{M-1} \qquad (14\text{-}40)$$

and hence the probability that one or more does exceed the level x is

$$g(x) = 1 - [1 - f(x)]^{M-1} = 1 - \left[1 - e^{-x^2/2N}\right]^{M-1}$$

$$= \sum_{k=1}^{M-1} (-)^{k-1} \binom{M-1}{k} e^{-kx^2/2N} \qquad (14\text{-}41)$$

The last result above is obtained from the ordinary expansion of a binomial. Now for the filter output containing both noise and the signaled tone, the latter with signal envelope $u = \sqrt{2S}$, the envelope p.d.f. is given from (4-211) as

$$p(r) = \frac{r}{N} I_0\left(\frac{r\sqrt{2\gamma}}{\sqrt{N}}\right) e^{-\gamma} e^{-r^2/2N} \tag{14-42}$$

where again we have introduced γ as the SNR at that *filter output containing the signal,*

$$\gamma = \frac{1}{2}\frac{u^2}{N} = \frac{S}{N} \tag{14-43}$$

Then the probability of error is the probability, over all possible values of r in (14-42), of any other filter having a larger envelope,

$$P_e = \int_0^\infty p(r)\, g(r)\, dr$$

$$= e^{-\gamma} \sum_{k=1}^{M-1} (-)^{k-1} \binom{M-1}{k} \int_0^\infty \frac{r}{N} I_0\left(\frac{r}{\sqrt{N}}\sqrt{2\gamma}\right) e^{-(1+k)r^2/2N}\, dr \tag{14-44}$$

Setting $x = (r/\sqrt{N})\sqrt{1+k}$, the integrals are readily evaluated [recall (10-9), for example], giving

$$P_e = e^{-\gamma} \sum_{k=1}^{M-1} (-)^{k-1} \binom{M-1}{k} \frac{1}{1+k} e^{\gamma/(1+k)}$$

$$= \sum_{k=1}^{M-1} (-)^{k-1} \binom{M-1}{k} \frac{1}{k+1} e^{-\gamma k/(k+1)} \tag{14-45}$$

The leading term above provides an upper bound on the probability of error

$$P_e \leq \frac{M-1}{2} e^{-\gamma/2} \tag{14-46}$$

However, because of the alternating nature of the series in (14-45), and the fact that $\binom{M-1}{k}$ increases with k at small k, it is not simple to establish this bound from (14-45). Instead, the bound may be shown mathematically by starting with the observation that

$$1 - y^n = (1 - y)(1 + y + y^2 + \cdots y^{n-1}) \tag{14-47}$$

Thus instead of (14-41) one can write

$$g(x) = 1 - \left(1 - e^{-x^2/2N}\right)^{M-1} = e^{-x^2/2N} \sum_{k=0}^{M-2} \left(1 - e^{-x^2/2N}\right)^k \tag{14-48}$$

Furthermore

$$\left(1 - e^{-x^2/2N}\right) < 1 \qquad (14\text{-}49)$$

and hence all factors in the sum are below unity. Thus one can immediately write

$$g(x) < (M - 1) e^{-x^2/2N} \qquad (14\text{-}50)$$

and the result (14-46) immediately follows upon inserting this into the defining integral in (14-44).

The exact result for error probability in (14-45) is plotted in Fig. 14-5 as a function of normalized SNR per information bit γ_b defined again by

$$\gamma_b = \gamma/k \qquad (14\text{-}51)$$

Curves are drawn for the values $M = 2, 4, 8, 16$, and 32. If we assume that all systems are operating at the same information rate, Fig. 14-5 shows that, for fixed symbol error probability, the normalized signal energy γ_b and hence the required transmitter power *decreases* with increasing M, while by (14-38) and (14-12) the required signaling bandwidth increases, as discussed further below. One may also note that in the multitone case, a symbol error results strictly in any other symbol, randomly, as the output; and hence with $M = 2^k$, binary error-rate is exactly related to symbol error-rate by (14-3).

The bound in (14-46), which highlights existing dependences, may be more intuitively derived as follows: Let γ be the SNR in the tone filter output containing the signal. Then the probability that noise in any *single* one of the other filter outputs will produce a larger envelope is given from our earlier binary FSK result (Chap. 11) as

$$P_1 = \frac{1}{2} e^{-\gamma/2} \qquad (14\text{-}52)$$

The probability of error is the probability of a larger envelope in *any* of the other $M - 1$ outputs than the correct one. Since all filter outputs have independent noises, the latter probability is certainly bounded by

$$P_e \leq (M - 1) P_1 \qquad (14\text{-}53)$$

That is, $(M - 1)P_1$ ascribes as statistically separate errors any occurrence when two or more envelopes are simultaneously larger than the correct one, whereas only one symbol error actually occurs—hence the inequality. This is the same bound stated earlier

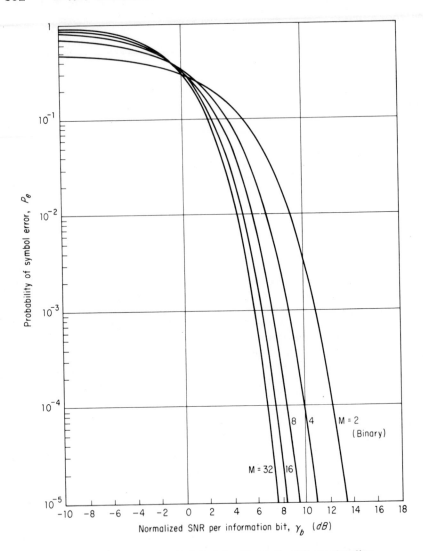

Fig. 14-5 Noncoherently detected orthogonal multitone signaling.

in (14-46). At high SNR, or low error-rates, where one can expect most errors to occur owing to only one false larger output, this bound should be very close to the actual value of error-rate. It should be considered reasonable only when $MP_1 \ll 1$, which is, however, the low error-rate case of usual interest.

Consider (14-46), and for illustration recall that for matched-filtering

$$\gamma = ST_M/n_0$$

Then if we consider keeping the symbol lengths T_M constant, using an increasing number of tones to increase information rate, the bound indicates that S need only increase as $\ln M$ to keep the symbol error-rate constant. Thus, if $M = 2^k$, the signal power S need increase only linearly with k, while the required energy per bit γ_b does not depend upon k or M. The price paid is that, from (14-38), the bandwidth increases exponentially with k,

$$B_M = 2^k/T_M \qquad (14\text{-}54)$$

As we have commented earlier, it is exactly such increases in bandwidth which are often more readily available in radio systems than signal power increases or receiver noise level reductions. Hence multitone FSK (or appropriate variants) have been of major interest when M-ary signaling is considered in radio applications.

Now consider instead the use of bandwidth expansion via higher values of M, while maintaining the binary source information rate fixed. With $M = 2^k$, and binary source symbols occurring at rate $1/T$, the M-ary symbol lengths then increase with k (or M) as

$$T_M = kT \qquad (14\text{-}55)$$

Alternately stated, the symbol SNR changes with respect to the SNR per information bit, by just (14-51):

$$\gamma = k\gamma_b \qquad (14\text{-}56)$$

The bound in (14-46) can then be written

$$P_e \leq \frac{M-1}{2} e^{-k\gamma_b/2} \qquad (14\text{-}57)$$

A weaker bound, with $M = 2^k$, is

$$P_e \leq M e^{-k\gamma_b/2} = \exp\left[-k\left(\frac{\gamma_b}{2} - \ln 2\right)\right] \qquad (14\text{-}58)$$

This leads to the interesting result that, as $k \to \infty$ ($M \to \infty$) with binary source rate fixed, the *error-rate can be made to approach zero exponentially*, provided the SNR per information bit γ_b is such that

$$\gamma_b > 2 \ln 2 \qquad (14\text{-}59)$$

That is, if the ratio of energy per *binary* symbol exceeds 1.39 (about 1.4 dB), then one can obtain arbitrarily small error-rate by using a sufficiently large value of k. Of course, this is a bandwidth tradeoff—the error-rate decreases exponentially with k, while the bandwidth increases exponentially as $2^k/k$, only slightly less rapidly then in (14-54). Since the receiver complexity (number of tone filters) also increases exponentially, the value of k would always be limited in practical applications, although the limiting value considered practicable may tend to increase as appropriate variants of multitone keying (such as discussed in the next section) are considered.

It is apparent from (14-46), (14-58), and (14-59) that for fixed information rate operation at values of γ_b well above the limiting value, the error probability may be maintained essentially constant with increasing M if the symbol SNR γ is increased as ln M or the energy per bit decreased as $1/\log_2 M$. The bandwidth of course increases as M/k. These characteristics are in sharp contrast to the coherent multiphase case discussed in Sec. 14-3 where the required SNR per bit γ_b increased or $M^2/\log_2 M$ and the required bandwidth decreased as $1/\log_2 M$.

We have considered only the case of *orthogonal* multitone symbols. As was indicated, for rectangular pulses with matched-filtering orthogonal tones can be separated by spacings of just $1/T_M$. For closer tone spacings or other receiver filters the symbol waveforms will be *nonorthogonal*. Likewise, extending our earlier discussion in Sec. 13-8 on binary DPSK, multiphase DPSK signaling with each phase symbol of length T_M can be regarded as nonorthogonal M-ary signaling with symbol lengths $2T_M$, noncoherently detected. In the nonorthogonal case we can again bound the error-rate as being less than M times the probability of any single symbol exceeding the correct one. However, the latter probability should now be taken with respect to the nearest "adjacent" symbol; i.e., that which is most correlated or least orthogonal with respect to the correct one. In Ref. 3, for example, it is shown how to calculate such a result in the binary case. For the M-ary case the approximation to the probability of symbol error is given (Ref. 4) by

$$P_e = \text{erfc}\left(\sqrt{2\gamma} \, \sin\frac{\pi}{2M}\right) \qquad (14\text{-}60)$$

where γ is again the symbol SNR. The approximate symbol error probability P_e is plotted in Fig. 14-6 as a function of normalized SNR per information bit, $\gamma_b = \gamma/k$ for M = 4, 8, 16, 32. For M = 2, the previously derived expression for binary DPSK,

$$P_e = \frac{1}{2} e^{-\gamma} \qquad (14\text{-}61)$$

is plotted. Equation (14-60) provides an upper bound for the symbol error probability. Notice that the multiphase DPSK case in (14-60) and Fig. 14-6 involves signal power-information rate tradeoffs similar to those of the ideal PSK case, in (14-36) and

Fig. 14-3. This suggests that *crosstalk* in the *nonorthogonal multi-tone* system will have much the same effects. Indeed the same *levels* of crosscorrelation among the symbols should produce roughly the same results in the two cases.

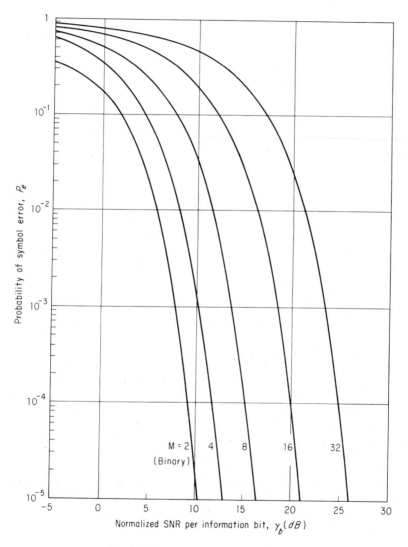

Fig. 14-6 Differentially coherent PSK.

14-5 Binary Orthogonal Sequences

The use of M orthogonally spaced symbols, each of length T_M and totally occupying a bandwidth B proportional to M, involves a time-bandwidth product BT_M which can be very generally viewed as involving BT_M "degrees of freedom." These degrees of freedom are closely analogous to concepts in Fourier series theory or in interpretation of the sampling principle, which state, respectively, that a function of bandwidth B and duration T can be described by $M = BT$ independent Fourier coefficients on tones spaced by $1/T$, or by $M = BT$ time samples at intervals $1/B$. (Actually the number $2BT$ is usually involved; this corresponds to taking, for example, both sine and cosine terms at each frequency. In our case, assuming lack of knowledge of phase, we are restricted to the factor $M = BT$.)

Now M independent numbers are much like M dimensions of a vector, and M mutually orthogonal vectors can be constructed from a basic set by appropriate choices of M coefficients. In multitone FSK as we have described it, with the set of spaced tones as the basis, each of the set of vectors corresponds to choosing $M - 1$ coefficients zero and one of value unity—a different one for each of the M vectors. In general, however, the *communications properties of any set of orthogonal waveforms is independent of the basis* upon which the waveforms are formed. Thus our statements above for M-ary multitone FSK apply more generally to orthogonal waveform sets of M waveforms as digital symbols. In addition such a set of waveforms will require at the least a minimum *time-bandwidth product* $BT = M$, no matter how constructed.

A particularly useful orthogonal set of this type are the so-called binary orthogonal sequences. A *sequence* of M binary pulses of individual length T occupy a bandwidth $B = 1/T$ (the bandwidth of the individual pulses), and a total time duration $T_M = MT$. Hence the time-bandwidth product is $BT_M = M$, and exactly M orthogonal sequences can be constructed by proper choices of the binary sequences. If we regard the binary sequences as, say, imposed with $0°-180°$ phase shift onto a carrier, the resulting bandpass signals are orthogonal. Note, however, that the M-*pulse sequence*, being used to create an alphabet of M symbols, can convey just $k = \log_2 M$ information bits.

For all cases where the M-ary symbol is transmitted as a sequence of binary PSK waveforms, a real possibility exists for practical implementation of the phase reference required for phase coherent reception. Since each symbol is a sequence of M pulses, all at the same frequency, and involving only a $0°-180°$ phase shift, a phase reference for coherent detection can be established in a manner similar to that suggested in Sec. 12-1 for binary PSK. Notice that we are still discussing the use of M different filters for reception, although these are possibly more appropriately realized as bandpass crosscorrelators. At any rate we have here the possibility of coherent detection of an M-ary orthogonal set.

For the case of orthogonal signals with coherent detection, an exact expression (Ref. 5) for the probability of symbol error is given by

$$P_e = 1 - \frac{1}{\sqrt{2\pi}} \int_{-\infty}^{\infty} e^{-u^2/2} \, du \left[\frac{1}{\sqrt{2\pi}} \int_{-\infty}^{u+\sqrt{2\gamma}} e^{-z^2/2} \, dz \right]^{M-1} \tag{14-62}$$

A plot of symbol error probability P_e is given in Fig. 14-7 as a function of normalized SNR per information bit γ_b for M = 2, 4, 8, 16 and 32. It is apparent from this figure that if fixed information rate operation is assumed, constant symbol error probability may

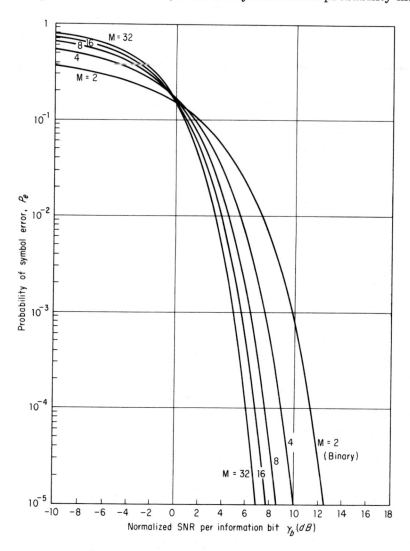

Fig. 14-7 Coherent detection of orthogonal signals.

be obtained with increasing M by decreasing the SNR per bit γ_b. The bandwidth is, of course, increasing as M.

If for every one of the orthogonal sequences we consider also its complement (replacing all 1's with 0's and all 0's with 1's, or in the carrier case, reversing the 0°–180° phase shifts and hence in effect adding 180° phase shifts to the entire waveform), then the total set of 2M signals forms a *"biorthogonal"* symbol alphabet. Here M/2 pulse sequences or M/2 degrees of freedom are used to create an alphabet of M symbols, each symbol conveying $k = \log_2 M$ information bits. Use of the biorthogonal alphabet requires a phase reference and is equivalent to multitone *coherent PSK*. The difficulty of achieving an adequate phase reference in the multitone case has been cited and may be contrasted with the possibility of practical implementation which exists for biorthogonal binary sequences. An exact expression (Ref. 6) for the probability of symbol error is given by

$$P_e = 1 - \frac{1}{\sqrt{2\pi}} \int_{-\sqrt{2\gamma}}^{\infty} e^{-v^2/2} \, dv \left[\frac{1}{\sqrt{2\pi}} \int_{-(v+\sqrt{2\gamma})}^{v+\sqrt{2\gamma}} e^{-z^2/2} \, dz \right]^{\frac{M}{2}-1} \quad (14\text{-}63)$$

The symbol error performance as a function of normalized SNR γ_b is better than that exhibited by orthogonal sequences but worse than that of simplex codes (see below) for small M. However, the performance of all three rapidly becomes indistinguishable as M is increased. Utilization of biorthogonal signals requires only M/2 correlators as contrasted to M correlators for orthogonal signals, for equal-sized alphabets of M symbols each. It is also true that a biorthogonal signal set requires one-half the bandwidth of an orthogonal signal set, if the source rate is considered fixed.

Another interesting set of codes is the set of *simplex* or maximal length sequence codes. Although the crosscorrelation between any two orthogonal code words is zero, and that existing between any two biorthogonal code words is either 0 or − 1, the simplex codes are characterized by a crosscorrelation of − 1/(M − 1) between any two code words.* Here M − 1 degrees of freedom or pulses are used to create an alphabet of M symbols. For coherent detection an exact expression (Ref. 6) for the probability of symbol error for codes with equal crosscorrelation between any two code

---

*A simplex code is a waveform alphabet in which all members have identical mutual crosscorrelation. For an M-member set it can be shown that the most negative value possible (maximum discrimination between waveforms) for this mutual crosscorrelation, normalized, is − 1/(M − 1). An example of construction of such a set is the following: Consider a biorthogonal sequence set of 2M waveforms where each waveform contains M pulses. Of each pair in the set which differ only by a minus sign, choose that member whose first pulse is +1. A set of M *orthogonal* waveforms is so chosen. Delete the first pulse from all. Then all the M waveforms, each consisting of M − 1 pulses, have normalized crosscorrelation − 1/(M − 1).

words is given by

$$P_e = 1 - \frac{1}{\sqrt{2\pi}} \int_{-\infty}^{\infty} e^{-u^2/2} \, du \left[\frac{1}{\sqrt{2\pi}} \int_{-\infty}^{u+\sqrt{2\gamma(1-\lambda)}} e^{-z^2/2} \, dz \right]^{M-1} \qquad (14\text{--}64)$$

where λ is the value of the correlation coefficient. For the previously discussed orthogonal case, substitution of $\lambda = 0$ in (14-64) yields (14-62). For the simplex case $\lambda = -1/(M-1)$, and it is apparent that for the same symbol error probability a simplex code requires only $1 - (1/M)$ as much energy per symbol as the corresponding orthogonal code. Hence plots of probability of symbol error P_e as a function of normalized SNR per information bit γ_b may be obtained from Fig. 14-7 by shifting the curves to the left by an amount equal to $|10 \log [(M-1)/M]|$ dB. For large M the error performance (as a function of γ_b) of orthogonal, biorthogonal, and simplex codes is equivalent.

REFERENCES

1. D. A. Chesler, "Multi-Amplitude Transmission Through a Fading Channel," Sylvania Electronic Systems, Waltham, Mass., Applied Research Laboratory, *Research Note 558* (August 1963).
2. C. R. Cahn, "Performance of Digital Phase-Modulation Communication Systems," *IRE Trans. Commun. Systems, CS-7*, pp. 3-6 (May 1959).
3. S. Stein, "Unified Analysis of Certain Coherent and Noncoherent Binary Communication Systems," *IRE Trans. Infor. Theory* (January 1964).
4. S. Stein, "Noncoherent Detection for Differential Phase Shift Keying," Sylvania Electronic Systems, Waltham, Mass., Applied Research Laboratory, *Research Report 473* (June 1965).
5. A. J. Viterbi, "On Coded Phase Coherent Communication," Jet *Propulsion Lab. Technical Report No. 32-35*, J. P. L., Pasadena, California (August 15, 1960).
6. A. H. Nuttall, "Error Probabilities for Equicorrelated M-ary Signals Under Phase Coherent and Phase Incoherent Reception," *IRE Trans. Information Theory, IT-8*, pp. 305-314 (July 1962).

15

Channel Capacity and
Error-control Coding

15-1 Channel Capacity

A very basic result in information theory is Shannon's formula for the capacity of the Gaussian noise channel (Ref. 1). This is usually stated for a low-pass band-limited channel, extending from 0 to B hertz on a one-sided spectral basis, or from $-B$ to B hertz on a two-sided basis. For a spectrally flat (white) additive Gaussian noise of one-sided power density spectrum n_0 and total noise power

$$N = n_0 B \tag{15-1}$$

and for a total signal power S, *the maximum binary rate at which information can be transmitted without error* over this channel is termed the *channel capacity C,*

$$C = B \log_2 \left(1 + \frac{S}{N}\right) \quad \text{bits/sec} \tag{15-2}$$

Shannon's result includes proof that message sequences exist in principle such that this maximum rate could actually be achieved, with zero error-rate, although infinite length symbols would be required (i.e., encoding on a message basis). We shall not attempt here either to prove these important results or to discuss detailed ramifications, for which excellent references are available (e.g., Ref. 2). Rather we confine ourselves to some remarks of engineering interest.

A more general statement than (15-2) is that if the one-sided noise power density spectrum is $n(f)$ and the signal power density spectrum is $S(f)$, the channel capacity is

$$C = \int_0^\infty \log_2 \left[1 + \frac{S(f)}{n(f)}\right] df \quad \text{bits/sec} \tag{15-3}$$

The further statement is that if $n(f) = n_0$ and if $S(f)$ is confined to any finite spectral range, then for a given total signal power the maximum value for C is obtained when $S(f)$ is uniformly distributed over this band. In this case the result obtained is again (15-2), with B the total bandwidth occupied (with the spectrum regarded as one-sided), whether low-pass or bandpass.

The capacity C in (15-2) was cited as the maximum information rate for errorless transmission. In practice one is always willing to allow a certain error-rate, and the actual rate of transmission of information bits should be higher if an average error-rate p per decoded bit is allowed. This higher rate C' exceeds the error-free-rate C by a so-called *equivocation* or *rate of information loss* owing to perturbing noise. However, at normally useful error-rates, C' is negligibly different from C, and it is usually reasonable and meaningful to compare information rates of practical systems at some nonvanishing error-rate to the channel capacity for error-free transmission.

Several useful interpretations follow from the channel capacity formulas. One qualitative statement is that practical systems tend to operate at some *"information-rate efficiency"* relative to channel capacity, the efficiency being somewhat characteristic of the system type; and in many instances the change in channel capacity resulting from a change in the channel parameters is very similar to the change in performance of an actual system operating over the same channel. For example, in Chap. 14 we examined multiphase and multiamplitude transmission. In these systems, with bandwidth maintained constant, one can increase information rate by appropriately increasing the signal power. As seen from (15-2), however, for $S/N \gg 1$ (or $E/n_0 \gg 1$) the channel capacity increases only logarithmically with increases in SNR. Thus, with fixed bandwidth, the SNR will have to increase exponentially with increased channel capacity. This is, of course, similar to the conclusion reached in detailed examination of information rates of these systems in Chap. 14. On the other hand, for multitone FSK, we found the required bandwidth increases exponentially with increasing information rate, whereas (15-2) suggests that a more efficient use of spectrum should be possible.

An interesting result follows by examining (15-2) with (15-1) in the limit as $B \to \infty$, with S and n_0 fixed. Recalling that, for $x \ll 1$, $\ln(1 + x) = x - (x^2/2) + \ldots \approx x$, the capacity C_∞ obtained in this limit is

$$C_\infty = \lim_{B \to \infty} \left[B \log_2 \left(1 + \frac{S}{n_0 B} \right) \right] = \lim_{B \to \infty} \left[B (\log_2 e) \ln \left(1 + \frac{S}{n_0 B} \right) \right]$$

$$= \lim_{B \to \infty} \left\{ B (\log_2 e) \left[\frac{S}{n_0 B} + 0 \left(\frac{1}{B^2} \right) \right] \right\} = \frac{S}{n_0} \log_2 e = \frac{S}{n_0} \frac{1}{\ln 2} \quad (15\text{-}4)$$

It is in fact easily shown from (15-2) that the maximum value of C versus B occurs as $B \rightarrow \infty$, and hence that, for a *given S and n_0*, the greatest transmission rate is available by letting the *bandwidth* become as *large as possible.* Thus for any single signal on the additive Gaussian noise channel the limits on information rate are established by S/n_0 and not at all by bandwidth. In fact in a time T the maximum total information transfer rate possible is

$$I_{max} = C_{\infty} T = \frac{ST}{n_0} \log_2 e = \frac{E}{n_0} \log_2 e \quad \text{bits} \qquad (15\text{-}5)$$

Thus, going to a *wider bandwidth does not in itself degrade performance*, and band spreading may actually be helpful. In this context it is instructive to recall the earlier statements in (14-58) and (14-59) for M-ary orthogonal signaling. Recall that it was shown that the error-rate would approach zero exponentially with increasing symbol length (constraint length, in our present terms) provided the SNR per information bit exceeds the value $\gamma_b = 2 \ln 2$. For an information rate R (bits/sec), power S, and noise power density n_0, this implies the requirement

$$\frac{1}{R} \frac{S}{n_0} \geq 2 \ln 2$$

or

$$R \leq \frac{1}{2} \frac{S}{n_0} \frac{1}{\ln 2} \qquad (15\text{-}6)$$

Note that this is just half of the value in (15-4), implying that the degrees of freedom in the channel are not being used as efficiently as they might be. Aside from this, the result in (14-58) also implied use of exponentially increasing symbol length and hence is quite consistent with the infinite-bandwidth channel capacity in (15-4).*

Further, whenever S/N or $S/n_0 B$ is very much below unity, for whatever the value of B, then the channel capacity is already given by (15-4), and changing the bandwidth does not change (in either direction) the capacity for information rate transmission in additive Gaussian noise if S/N remains small. For example, the *weak-signal communication* problem is in fact defined by $S/N \ll 1$, (e.g., communication from a deep-space probe), and hence, insofar as such a communications signal is concerned, there is *nothing wasteful* in extending to a bandwidth much wider than the information bandwidth without increasing the information rate (except, that is, that the band is thereby foreclosed from being used for other communication purposes). In such a channel, the rate of transmission

---

*As a general comment (Ref. 2) it appears that signaling models for which one can show the error-rate to decrease *exponentially* with increasing degrees of freedom never quite indicate the channel capacity of (15-3).

relative to channel capacity does not change by changing the band-width utilized. In fact the use of wider bandwidths actually enables one to approach the theoretical capacity *more* closely. Actually, wide bandwidths are often used for reasons other than combating noise in communication performance. Examples are the noise-like transmissions of the Rake technique (Chap. 17), or the use of wide-band signaling to provide range resolution by crosscorrelation in radar astronomy, or in ranging on communication signals from space probes.

It is also interesting to note that the result of matched-filter detection in additive Gaussian noise can be expressed in terms of the ratio E/n_0 which is also bandwidth-independent. In any actual operating system (particular mode of signaling and detection), the tolerable error-rate fixes a particular value y for the required SNR. With matched filters this required y relates to the received signal power S and noise power density spectrum n_0 through

$$\gamma = \frac{E}{n_0} = \frac{ST}{n_0} \qquad (15\text{-}7)$$

The rate of transmission R is then

$$R = \frac{1}{T} = \frac{S}{n_0 \gamma} \qquad (15\text{-}8)$$

Hence in the weak signal environment when $S/n_0 B \ll 1$ so that (15-4) is satisfied, the ratio of actual information rate to information theory channel capacity (the information-rate efficiency suggested earlier) becomes simply

$$\eta = \frac{R}{C_\infty} = \frac{1}{\gamma \log_2 e} = \frac{0.693}{\gamma} \qquad (15\text{-}9)$$

Thus, for example, if $\gamma = 6.93$ (8.4 dB) is being used in binary DPSK to achieve an error-rate (from Fig. 11-3) of $5(10)^{-4}$, the system is operating at an information rate efficiency of 10%. Recognizing the law of diminishing returns in trying to approach theoretical channel capacity, with the maximum improvement possible limited to 10 dB, one may regard such an information rate efficiency to be quite high and anticipate that practical systems which pose further significant gains in information rate efficiency in additive Gaussian noise may prove very difficult and expensive to achieve. Similar conclusions will be noted in the next section in examining coding for the Gaussian channel.

15-2 Algebraic Coding for Error Control

The usual digital message transmission contains very little redundancy; that is, there is no simple way to predict from knowledge of all but one of the bits what that one should be. As a counterexample, if the message represents teleprinter information, language context which is highly redundant would enable one to do such prediction. For this reason one can easily read language telegrams with occasional garbles but one cannot usually correct garbles in purely numerical data. We are considering the latter as exemplifying the more general case of digital operation when we ascribe an absence of redundancy.

In many applications it is desirable to consider artificially adding a small degree of redundancy, at the very least to enable one to spot inconsistencies in the output stream which would indicate the presence of errors. A typical example is the use of parity checks. In simplest form an extra *parity check bit* is added to a block of bits so that, say, the total number of 1's is even. That is, if the block already contained an even number of 1's, the added bit would be a 0; if the block contained an odd number of 1's, the added bit would be a 1. A single error in the *coded block* (including the parity check bit) would be detected because it would cause a parity error. Normally such detection would be followed operationally by a repeat of the operation.

If one adds many check bits to an information block, each comprising a parity check over some different subset of the information and parity digits, it becomes possible to structure these so that the pattern of parity failures in the code block can be used to determine which bits are in error and hence to *correct* them. As a general rule the ability to *correct* a given number of errors in a code block of given length requires that a much greater fraction of the bits in the block be parity check bits than is required to *detect* a like number of errors. That is, error correction requires a greater degree of redundancy than error detection. This is equivalent to a lower fraction of each total code block being available for the information carrying bits. Often, in coding discussions, one refers to the information rate not in terms of actual rate of flow (bits/sec), but as the fraction (bits/bit) of total transmitted bits which are carrying information. Thus, for some maximum number of errors per code block to be perfectly detectable or correctable, detection will generally have a higher rate associated with it than correction. At the same time, as the fraction of bits in error to be controlled grows larger, more check bits are needed. In general it turns out that, in fact, efficient rates (rates of the order of 0.5 bit/bit), coupled with ability to cope with errors occurring with probability 0.01 or thereabouts require code blocks ("constraint lengths") several hundred bits long. However, information rate is critical here. We cite later a code with blocks only 15 bits long, rate one-third (five information bits/block), and able to correct up to three errors per code block.

We have implied above the association of redundancy with information bits in well-defined code blocks. The need for long constraint lengths and the associated equipment complexity in fixed-block coding has led to development of various other concepts, termed *sequential* or *convolutional coding*, in which parity checks are introduced on a "running" basis and where equipment complexity grows significantly less fast with constraint length than in fixed block length coding. However, explanation of the latter systems lies beyond our purposes here and we shall confine our remarks to fixed block length codes.

In addition to practical interests and obvious applications which motivated some of the early work in coding, much of the spur to coding research has been results (e.g., Ref. 2) which indicate that coding on binary channels can be used to approach channel capacity without the need for detection operations based on large signaling alphabets. Accordingly, extensive literature on coding exists at both elementary and advanced levels (e.g., Refs. 2 and 3), and we shall present here only some of the simpler aspects, and concentrate largely on remarks concerning the communications utility of such codes.

To this end recall the model of a typical binary data communication system previously described in Fig. 14-1. (Coding has been applied almost exclusively to binary data formats, although in principle algebraic coding can also be applied to M-ary systems.) The message *source* produces one of $M = 2^{RT_M}$ distinct, equally likely message sequences in each time interval of duration T_M, where R is the source information rate in bits per second. For algebraic coding in fixed blocks the *coder* accepts a block of $k = RT_M$ bits and produces a block of $n > k$ binary digits (code words), the $n - k$ redundant digits being formed in accordance with a specified encoding rule. The structure imposed is such that certain error patterns may be detected and/or corrected by the decoder. The information per binary digit is reduced from 1 bit per binary digit before encoding to k/n bits per digit after encoding. The *modulator* then generates one of two waveforms in each interval of length $T = T_M/n$, for each of the n digits of the code word. At the receiver the *detector* examines the waveform received during each pulse time T and produces one of two output values. The *decoder* accepts a sequence of n values, performs a specified error detection and/or correction routine. Correction implies a decision (a best guess) on the sequence of k *information digits* transmitted.

A significant statement is that adding structure in the form of check digits to sequences of information digits and subsequently utilizing that structure to detect and/or correct digit errors has been shown to be an efficient form of redundant transmission. Information theorists have produced an array of performance bounds which clearly indicate the gains achievable through the use of sophisticated coding techniques, and a number of classes of codes, *some* with reasonable decoding equipment implementations, have been found. Nevertheless except for simple parity check schemes there is not yet extensive use of such coding in data communication systems.

One important theoretical result in coding (e.g., Ref. 2) is that for fixed transmitter power S and information rate R, such that R is less than some channel capacity which closely approaches that of (15-2), it can be shown that parity-check codes exist for which the code words, regarded as M-ary sequences and detected accordingly, form alphabets for which the probability of code word error P_e *decreases exponentially with code length* n, *while signaling bandwidth B is maintained fixed.** From the system model

$$B \approx n/T_M \qquad\qquad (15\text{-}10)$$

where n is the number of binary waveforms per code word and T_M is the duration of the code word. Accordingly, n may be increased without affecting the signaling bandwidth if T_M is increased proportionately. This increase in T_M need not affect the information rate R if k, the number of information bits per code word, is also increased as T_M, since

$$R = k/T_M \qquad\qquad (15\text{-}11)$$

Notice that the energy per symbol (code block) E increases linearly with T_M, since

$$E = ST_M \qquad\qquad (15\text{-}12)$$

but the energy per information bit E_b is independent of T_M. Thus the above states that it is in principle possible, with binary signaling employing strategically added redundancy, to construct sequences with which it is possible to approach channel capacity in the limit of long constraint lengths. The final statement is that the use of bit-by-bit detection, followed by decoding logic, can be shown in the large-alphabet limit (e.g., Ref. 2) to represent only a small loss in performance while providing much simplified receiver design compared to detection of the sequences as a whole.

It is worth comparing these statements with those given earlier in (14-58) and (14-59) and discussed further in (15-6). With M-ary orthogonal signaling one can reach zero error-rate in the limit, but only by using exponentially increasing bandwidth. With algebraic coding, on the other hand, one can reach channel capacity for a fixed bandwidth. The difference between the finite-bandwidth and infinite-bandwidth capacities is relatively small, moreover, so that the important distinction lies in avoiding the necessity for bandwidth expansion. What is further clear is that if one regards the set of 2^k code words as an M-ary alphabet, this alphabet is

---

*However, in fact, it does not appear that any of the known practical block coding schemes have this limiting property.

nonorthogonal, so that the real distinction from the results in Chap. 14 lies in the statement that it is not necessary to have orthogonal waveforms to achieve zero error-rate in the limit, and in fact the set of waveforms can be so closely packed that they can remain within a finite bandwidth, as k increases without limit.

15-3 Properties and Examples of Use of Algebraic Codes

As stated earlier algebraic codes involve generalizations of the familiar concept of parity-checking, adding an additional code bit to a sequence such that the total number of 1's, say, in the enlarged sequence is always even. The extensions involve adding many check-bits, each of which constitutes a parity check over a different selected subset of the sequence. One often-discussed general class of such codes (Ref. 3) are the *Bose-Chaudhuri-Hocquenghem* (BCH) codes, which include many earlier discovered algebraic codes as special cases. In reception, comparisons among the parity checks are used either to detect errors or to correct them.

The algebraic codes are described as (n, k) codes, the parameter k representing the number of information bits per code sequence (or code block, or code word), and n representing the total number of digits in the code sequence. Thus, $n - k$ is the number of parity check digits in each sequence. The degree of redundancy is described by the ratio of the signaling rate to information bit rate n/k, which is also the ratio by which the bandwidth is expanded. *E*ncoders for codes such as the Bose-Chaudhuri-Hocquenghem codes are easily implemented via shift register circuits. The problem lies in achieving inexpensive *de*coders. The communication designer contemplating the possibility of a system improvement via coding must ordinarily refer to the coding experts for recommendations as to codes and code properties of the proper type. We shall emphasize here only the issue of how, given such codes and their properties, one evaluates their communication performance.

We implied above that the redundancy can be used either for detection of errors in the code sequence or for the correction of errors. The basic parameter indicating the degree of error control is the *minimum Hamming distance d* among the set of allowed code words. The *Hamming distance* between two code words is the number of bit positions in which they differ. As stated earlier, since there are only k bits of information per sequence (which determine the other $n - k$ digits), there are only 2^k "legitimate" code words among all possible 2^n digit sequences. Thus, as n becomes large, it may be visualized that the minimum Hamming distance d between all code words may also become large. It is also readily seen that if the number of errors is $d - 1$ or less, so that there are transpositions (errors) in $d - 1$ or fewer of the binary digits of the transmitted sequence, then the word received cannot appear to be a legitimate code word (i.e., some of the parity checks fail to be satisfied), and hence the decoder is always capable of detecting $d - 1$ or fewer errors per code sequence. There are, of course, many patterns of d or more errors which also do not result in transposing the transmitted code word into another legitimate code word and hence can be detected; however, some patterns of d or more errors will result in undetected errors, and the error-detecting capability is rather commonly described in terms of the maximum number of errors per sequence which are *guaranteed* to be detected.

With the decoding of code sequences on an error detection basis, while errors can be detected at the receiver, the only way the intended user can learn the correct message is to request a retransmission. This involves use of a two-way or *feedback communications* circuit. Some properties of such circuits have been studied in communications applications. In the conventional communications application, over fading radio circuits for example, error detection with feedback is a desirable mode for "riding through" a deep fade of the signal. The system merely "waits" until the fade condition disappears. The intricacies of error-detection feedback communications (or *repeat-request*) systems lie in the strategies by which message repetition is requested and carried out, particularly when errors may occur in both directions of communication. We will, however, limit our discussion only to the error-correcting codes, which can correct errors upon reception in a one-way transmission. The calculations exemplified below are similar to those needed for determining the basic probabilities of detecting or missing errors in error-detection systems. Our limitation is really in not discussing the many variants associated with feedback communication schemes.

Referring again to the minimum Hamming distance d, it is easily shown that any number of errors smaller than $(d - 1)/2$ can in principle be corrected. The decoder is made to choose as its output the legitimate code word "nearest," in the Hamming distance sense, to that detected in reception. Again some error patterns with larger numbers of errors can be corrected but not with any guarantee. Furthermore in error correction, as the number of errors becomes significantly larger than those guaranteed to be corrected, there is a rapidly diminishing likelihood of a correct decoding. As opposed to error detection capability, whose strength depends on the "density" of legitimate code words in the n-dimensional code space, error correction capability depends strongly on the mutual separations of the code words. Hence a given degree of redundancy conveys a much greater error detection than error correction capability. This often leads designers in two-way communication applications to a preference for error detection because of the more favorable spectral occupancy and power tradeoffs.

There is another important difference in practical implementation. Error detection for any parity-checking code can be accomplished via a shift register decoder. Error correction, involving logical decisions among sets of parity checks, is much more complex, and one of the major problems in practical realization is that of determining codes with reasonably inexpensive decoders. One well-known short code, the (15,5), is known to allow a shift register decoding and is reasonably efficient, and it has been used for that reason. Decoders for certain codes, including the (73,45), (21,11), and (15,7), may be implemented with n-state shift registers, modulo-2 adders, and majority decision elements. Only a relatively few codes are known which possess such relatively equipment-simple decoding algorithms (although the number keeps growing), and a better feeling for the equipment complexity of existing error-correcting decoders is obtained by citing (Ref. 4) a decoder implementation (ca. 1962) for the (127,92) Bose-Chaudhuri code. It consists of a 127-stage shift register and a special purpose digital computer approximately the size of a desk drawer. This decoder corrects all patterns of five or fewer errors or detects all patterns of 10 or fewer errors, per 127-element code block.

Now let us consider the performance of an (n, k) error-correcting code in stationary Gaussian noise. For each code there is some value r such that all patterns of $r - 1$ or fewer errors per code word are completely corrected. Some patterns involving r or larger numbers of errors are also properly corrected. The total possible number of patterns of exactly j errors in the n elements of the code word is the combinatorial,

$$\binom{n}{j} = \frac{n!}{(n - j)! \, j!} \tag{15-13}$$

For each j we denote by α_j the number of patterns of j errors which will not be properly corrected. Note that for $j \gg r$,

$$\alpha_j \to \binom{n}{j} \tag{15-14}$$

In fact for most short or moderate length codes α_j differs significantly from $\binom{n}{j}$ only for $j \leq r$ and possibly $j = r + 1$, and it is not unreasonable to ignore *any* of the capability for correcting more than $r - 1$ errors in estimating performance. With the latter, one sets

$$\alpha_j = \binom{n}{j}, \quad j \geq r \tag{15-15}$$

In stationary Gaussian noise the occurrence of errors is independent from bit to bit. If p is the probability of any one bit being detected in error and $1 - p$ is the probability that it will be correct, the probability of a decoded word error (the probability that r or more detection errors occur) is given with (15-15) by

$$P_e \approx \sum_{j=r}^{n} \alpha_j p^j (1 - p)^{n-j} \approx \sum_{j=r}^{n} \binom{n}{j} p^j (1 - p)^{n-j} \qquad (15\text{-}16)$$

For low probabilities of error, $p \ll 1$, this is usually well approximated by its leading term

$$P_e \approx \binom{n}{r} p^r \qquad (15\text{-}17)$$

Furthermore let us assume as an example that the signaling of bits uses noncoherent FSK. Then, with γ_b the *SNR per information bit*, the SNR per transmitted bit is

$$\gamma = \frac{k}{n} \gamma_b \qquad (15\text{-}18)$$

and

$$p = \frac{1}{2} e^{-\gamma/2} = \frac{1}{2} e^{-(k/n)\gamma_b/2} \qquad (15\text{-}19)$$

In addition a useful approximation truly valid only for $n \gg r$, but not introducing significant error here because $\binom{n}{r}$ appears only as an algebraic factor, is

$$\binom{n}{r} = \frac{n(n-1)\cdots(n-r+1)}{1 \cdot 2 \cdots r} \approx n^r \qquad (15\text{-}20)$$

Then to excellent approximation, (15-17) becomes

$$P_e \approx \exp\left[-r\left(\frac{k}{n} \frac{\gamma_b}{2} - \ln \frac{n}{2}\right)\right] \qquad (15\text{-}21)$$

In contrast each information bit could alternately be transmitted as an individual *uncoded* binary symbol, with SNR γ_b, and hence with a *binary* probability of error

$$P_{eb} = \frac{1}{2} e^{-\gamma_b/2} \qquad (15\text{-}22)$$

Ignoring the algebraic factor which distinguishes bit-error probability from the probability of a code-sequence error (recall the discussion in Sec. 14-1) and the similar term $\ln (n/2)$, we see that coding will be an improvement provided roughly that

$$r \frac{k}{n} > 1 \qquad (15\text{-}23)$$

Furthermore, in fact, the transmitted power per information bit required with coding relative to that for the uncoded case, for equivalent error-rate at the same information rate, is then roughly the factor

$$\eta = \frac{1}{r} \frac{n}{k} \qquad (15\text{-}24)$$

The (15,5) code, for example, corrects all patterns of three or fewer errors. Hence $r = 4$ and (15-23) is satisfied. Furthermore, however, the value of η is just

$$\eta = 3/4 = 0.75 \qquad (15\text{-}25)$$

Thus, there is only about a 25% saving in SNR, less than 1.3 dB, which must be measured against the expense of the additional equipment in such a case.

In general one can always satisfy (15-23) and improve the benefits described by (15-24) by going to longer and longer codes. Roughly (recall the geometric arguments), one should be able to increase n with both k and r increasing proportionally to n, say

$$k = a n$$
$$r = b n \qquad (15\text{-}26)$$

Then

$$\eta = 1/abn \qquad (15\text{-}27)$$

where for the (15,5), for example, $1/ab = 11.25$ and extrapolation of the same properties to longer codes indicates

$$\eta \approx 11/n \qquad (15\text{-}28)$$

The saving in transmitter power may thus be estimated at 3 dB for every doubling of the code length. This would be true at extremely low error-rates but would fail as soon as our approximations failed. For example, in (15-21) we would require in our example $(\gamma_b/6) \gg \ln (n/2)$, and as soon as n were too large or γ_b too small, the code would fail. In fact this illustrates two well-known phenomena in using error correction coding in problems involving additive stationary Gaussian noise: In general more improvement is available by coding as the error-rate requirements become more stringent (lower), and second, for any given code there is an error-rate threshold such that the code works well when *lower* error-rates are required but is of dubious or negative value when higher error-rates can be tolerated.

The performance of a few representative codes in additive Gaussian noise is presented in Figs. 15-1 to 15-4. Probability of symbol error P_e is plotted as a function of SNR per information bit γ_b. The curves of Figs. 15-1 and 15-2 assume PSK transmission

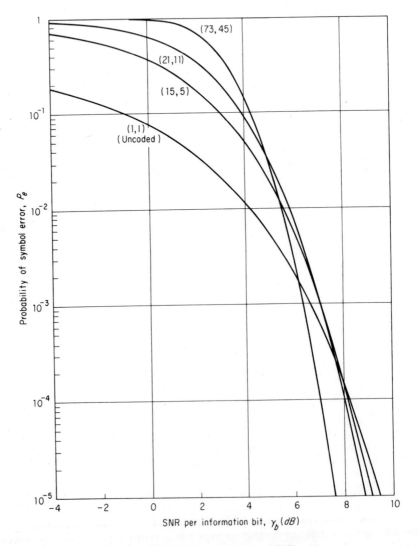

Fig. 15-1 Coherent reception of PSK.

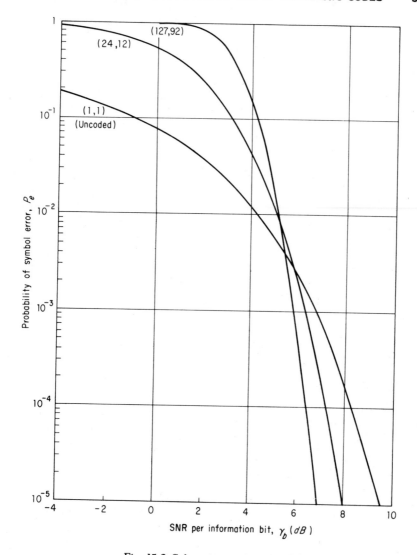

Fig. 15-2 Coherent reception of PSK.

with ideal coherent reception and result from applying (15-16) with

$$p = \frac{1}{2} \operatorname{erfc} \left(\sqrt{\frac{k}{n} \gamma_b} \right)$$ (15-29)

while the curves of Figs. 15-3 and 15-4 assume FSK transmission with noncoherent envelope detection and result from applying

(15-16) with

$$p = \frac{1}{2} e^{-(k/n)\gamma_b/2} \tag{15-30}$$

The uncoded or (1,1) code is presented for reference in each figure. Notice that each curve has an error-rate threshold of the type mentioned above. Note only is no single code better than the uncoded case for all energy levels but no single code out-performs

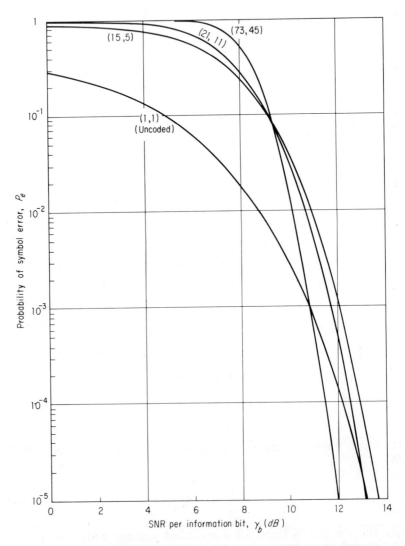

Fig. 15-3 Noncoherent reception of FSK.

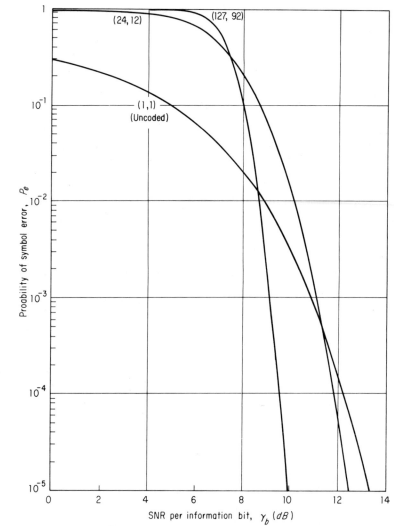

Fig. 15-4 Noncoherent reception of FSK.

all others over the range of energy levels. Longer codes tend to perform better at high signal levels whereas the shorter codes perform better at low signal levels. Note also that for the range of symbol error probabilities under consideration, the gains attributable to coding over the additive Gaussian channel are not especially impressive. However, the Gaussian channel, because of the rapid decrease in bit error probability with increasing signal power, represents in any event a relatively unfavorable environment for achieving major SNR improvements by any coding means at all.

More significant coding gains are obtained over real-life channels which are additionally characterized by fading or impulsive noise. By fading we specifically mean here that the channel has the characteristic of tending to remain in any particular condition for periods of time, long compared to an information bit length, then shifting to another condition in which it again remains for some interval before changing again. There is a certain probability of bit error associated with each each condition, and there is a *high correlation* (more accurately, a high conditionality) between the probabilities of error for adjacent bits, rather than independence as in the steady signal-stationary additive Gaussian noise channel. That is, when errors occur, they tend to occur in clusters during intervals of poor channel condition rather than randomly in time. Such a "burst-noise" channel might be created by relatively slow (but at times deep) fading of the signal level or by impulsive disturbances which are long compared to one bit duration.

Block codes of the type discussed earlier can be found which have significant *burst-error* correction capabilities (Ref. 3). An error burst in this connection usually means the total number of bits between the first and last bits in the block which are in error, inclusive, regardless of whether the intermediate ones are in error or not. Thus it is possible to implement error correcting codes and decoders which are guaranteed to correct for a burst of length up to some value b (note the remaining $n - b$ bits are being assumed to be received correctly); for a given (n, k), b can be significantly larger than the number of *random* errors which might be guaranteed correctible with the same (n, k) and a different implementation. Multiple burst-error correcting codes are also known. The apparent difficulty in employing these codes in radio applications is that most burst-error channels are not simply describable as having error bursts not exceeding a certain length and error-free bursts exceeding a certain other minimum length. Usually both these numbers are random variables so that it appears difficult to choose an efficient code design.

A useful alternative which has been discussed, especially for signal fading applications, is the concept of *interleaving* (or interlacing). The principle is most readily explained with reference to Fig. 15-5. Imagine successive n-bit code words A, B, C, D, etc., read into the rows of a rectangular storage array as shown in Fig. 15-5a, each word already having been encoded for error correction of randomly occurring errors. Then imagine that the sequence to be transmitted is obtained by reading out along the columns of the array, as shown in Fig. 15-5b. The bits belonging, say, to code word A appear interleaved at relatively wide spacings in the transmitted sequence, the spacings being determined by the overall size of the array. If this spacing is large enough, then the successive occurrences of these bits will relate to *statistically independent* channel conditions, and each bit associated with the word A will have associated with it an independent probability of being in error $\bar{p}$, where $\bar{p}$ is the probability that any bit at random is in error on the channel (hence is an average channel property). If one now reconstitutes the code words at the receiver (through another storage matrix) and then decodes each code word, one has generally reduced the burst-error problem to a random error problem, with errors occurring at the average error-rate of the channel (note, however, not generally with the kind of exponential dependence on SNR which characterizes the additive Gaussian channel).

$$A_1 \quad A_2 \quad A_3 \quad A_4 \quad A_5 \quad A_6 \quad A_7 \ldots$$

$$B_1 \quad B_2 \quad B_3 \quad B_4 \quad B_5 \ldots$$

$$C_1 \quad C_2 \quad C_3 \ldots$$

$$D_1 \quad D_2 \quad D_3 \ldots$$

$$E_1 \quad E_2 \ldots$$

$$F_1 \quad F_2 \ldots$$

(a) ARRAY INPUT

$$A_1 B_1 C_1 D_1 E_1 \ldots A_2 B_2 C_2 D_2 \ldots$$

$$A_3 B_3 C_3 \ldots A_4 B_4 C_4 D_4 \ldots$$

(b) OUTPUT SEQUENCE FOR TRANSMISSION

Fig. 15-5 Example of interleaving.

To indicate the strength of this process, consider the (15,5) code used with each code word and a channel which intermittently completely destroys clusters of, say, 10 bits, with these clusters occurring on a random basis with an average duty cycle of 0.01. Since the code corrects three errors, each error cluster can be assumed to fairly well completely destroy one or two code words, depending upon how it falls. Hence the average rate of error of decoded sequences will lie between 0.01 and 0.02. On the other hand, with interleaving over a sufficiently long time scale, the average probability of error in each bit of a received (reconstituted) code sequence will be 0.01, and using our previous results the estimate of the probability of error (or error-rate) for the decoded sequences is

$$P_e \approx \binom{15}{4}(0.01)^4 \approx 1.5(10)^{-5} \tag{15-31}$$

The improvement is obvious. The interleaving technique plays an extremely important role in newer concepts for employing coding over fading radio channels, as well as in designs for channels characterized by intermittent interference.

REFERENCES

1. C. G. Shannon and W. Weaver, *The Mathematical Theory of Communication* (University of Illinois Press, Urbana, 1959).
2. J. M. Wozencraft and I. M. Jacobs, *Principles of Communication Engineering* (John Wiley and Sons, Inc., New York, 1965).
3. W. W. Peterson, *Error Correcting Codes* (M. I. T. Press, 1964).
4. T. C. Bartee and D. I. Schneider: "An Electronic Decoder for Bose-Chaudhuri-Hocqueghem Error-Correcting Codes," *IRE Trans. Information Theory, IT-8,* pp. S17–S24 (September 1962).

16

Fading Radio Channels

16-1 Importance of Fading Channels

We have confined our attention in the preceding chapters to the case of steady signal levels on a channel characterized by additive, stationary Gaussian noise. There are many radio channels of this type, mainly of the line-of-sight (l.o.s.) variety. Short-range u.h.f., v.h.f., or h.f. groundwave transmissions are examples. Others are ground-to-air or air-to-ground l.o.s. links, air-to-air links, and ground-to-satellite or space probe and vice versa. Satellites involve both the case where the satellite is actually a communication terminal (e.g., command or telemetry signals) and where it is merely a radio repeater or relay (i.e., active or passive relay). In all these basically l.o.s. channels there may be changes in the SNR owing to relative motion of one or both terminals. However, such changes occur relatively slowly compared to the fractional second or shorter time scale on which digital data is transmitted, and the basic operation is still deduced from the results presented earlier.

On the other hand, as we have also remarked from time to time, some of the most important channels for communications are only partially described by this characterization of steady signal and additive stationary Gaussian noise. The two most familiar deviations are signal fading on long-distance beyond-the-horizon terrestrial radio links, and impulsive noise on wire or cable links, or on radio links at frequencies below the m.f. band (i.e., below about 500 kc). With our emphasis on radio applications we shall discuss just the first of these at length. This chapter will be devoted to discussion of the fundamental aspects of fading channels; associated aspects of reception will be discussed in Chap. 17.

Most radio channels vary in their characteristics because of natural changes. For this reason propagation through the troposphere will vary with general variations in refractive index, which in turn may vary meteorologically, seasonally, and climotologically. Likewise propagation via the ionosphere may change as a function of geomagnetic activity, solar activity (e.g., the 11-year solar cycle), solar storms, and nuclear detonations. All such changes take place on a time scale that is long compared to, say, one second. On the other hand, signal and receiver design are primarily affected by fluctuation phenomena which occur in fractions of a second, usually in the order of milliseconds or even microseconds. Neither signal design, filter design, nor detection design can alter the effects of the slower fluctuations, and one must simply design enough power, antenna size, etc. (so-called *system margin*) into the system to achieve satisfactory operation under whatever conditions of *long-term* degradation of signal are anticipated in the operational requirement. Thus the resulting system may often appear greatly overdesigned for the performance routinely achieved, but the reason for the overdesign is to still provide adequate performance under the relatively rare conditions upon which the design is predicated.

One may also cope with a degraded environment by an alteration in the signaling. Such a system is what is usually meant by an *adaptive* system. Usually, when the SNR drops, such adaptation takes the form of a reduction in the information transmission rate (i.e., per Chap. 15 the channel capacity decreases). Other common forms of adaptation for coping with long-term variations on fading channels include such simple expedients as changing the frequency in use on a long-distance h.f. circuit.

Our more detailed concern will be with fading fluctuations of a shorter-term variety, typically evidenced in fractions of a second, which arise because of *multipath conditions* on these radio channels rather than from the longer-term variations in the gross nature of the medium. By multipath is meant, in simplest terms, that there are many *rays* (paths) along which electromagnetic energy can travel from the transmitting point to the receiving point, all within the respective antenna beams, and such that the total propagation time from transmitter to receiver differs among these rays. For now we assert that this occurs in long-distance propagation, leaving details of the media aside, and we proceed in the next section to the characterization of the parameters of such channels that affect communications.

16-2 The Rayleigh Fading Multipath Channel

If one could transmit an extremely sharp impulse over a multipath medium, the received signal would appear as a train of impulses. The overall spread in time of arrival of these impulses T_M is termed the *multipath spread* (measured in time units). The multipath spread is a gross characteristic of the medium, defined in the same nominal way as is bandwidth for describing a filter. As a result of variations in the detailed structure of the medium, the nature of the multipath observed will vary in time. That is, if one could repeat the impulse-sounding experiment over and over, he would observe changes in the nature of the received impulse trains. In general these changes will include changes in the sizes of the individual impulses, in the relative delays among the impulses, and, quite often, changes in the number of impulses observed in the received impulse train.

Physically the multipath arises because long-distance propagation involves reflection or scattering processes in the medium, and the "reflectors" or "scatterers" or "irregularities of the medium" are in constant change owing to the dynamic nature of the medium. A given gross characterization of the medium such as the overall multipath spread or the average attenuation over the channel may remain fixed over time intervals ranging from many minutes up to hours or more, but within such an interval we have a *stationary* fluctuation process owing to the dynamic state of flux of the medium. As we have described it up to this point, this fluctuation process consists of random changes in the detailed structure of the multipath, within the overall multipath spread. Returning once more to the impulse-sounding experiment, repeated many times, if all delays within the overall multipath spread are observed to occur more or less uniformly, it is said that one is observing a *continuous multipath* or a *multipath continuum*. If the delays observed are confined to certain nonoverlapping ranges, it is said that one is observing a discrete multipath. Note, however, that the discrete multipath still may include a continuum within each nominal discrete delay interval. As will be observed later, the signal bandwidth strongly controls whether there is any observable distinction, *in effects upon the signal*, between discrete and continuous multipath, or indeed whether even the size of the multipath spread enters as a factor.

Let us now examine quantitatively the effects on a general modulated signal. Returning to the notation of Chap. 3, let this signal be a modulated carrier of center frequency f_c,

$$s_0(t) = \text{Re}\left\{u(t)\, e^{j2\pi f_c t}\right\} \tag{16-1}$$

where the complex envelope function $u(t)$ denotes the amplitude and phase variations owing to modulation. Then, corresponding to the multiplicity of propagation times, the received signal will have the form

$$s(t) = \sum_k \alpha_k(t - t_0)\, s_0[t - t_0 - \tau_k(t)] \tag{16-2}$$

where $\alpha_k(t)$ is the amplitude of the signal being received via the kth path at time t, with delay $\tau_k(t)$ relative to some *nominal average path propagation time* t_0. In the event of a multipath continuum this would be written

$$s(t) = \int_{-\infty}^{\infty} \alpha(\tau; t - t_0) s_0(t - t_0 - \tau) d\tau \qquad (16\text{-}3)$$

where $\alpha(\tau; t - t_0) d\tau$ represents the amplitude at time t of all rays arriving with relative delay times in the range $(\tau, \tau + d\tau)$. We can include discrete paths in the formalism of (16-3) by allowing $\alpha(\tau; t)$ to include δ-functions, and will tend to use this latter formalism because of its notational convenience. Note that the *second* argument in $\alpha(\tau; t - t_0)$ denotes how the *functional dependence* of α upon τ *changes with time* owing to the dynamic multipath structure. We have referenced the state of the medium to the *nominal* time $t - t_0$ at which a signal arriving at time t was transmitted.

Using (16-1) in (16-3) results in

$$s(t) = \text{Re} \left\{ \int_{-\infty}^{\infty} \alpha(\tau; t - t_0) u(t - t_0 - \tau) e^{j2\pi f_c(t - t_0 - \tau)} d\tau \right\}$$

$$(16\text{-}4)$$

$$= \text{Re} \left\{ v(t - t_0) e^{j2\pi f_c(t - t_0)} \right\}$$

where

$$v(t) = \int_{-\infty}^{\infty} \alpha(\tau; t) u(t - \tau) e^{-j2\pi f_c \tau} d\tau \qquad (16\text{-}5)$$

Now defining

$$h(\tau; t) = \alpha(\tau; t) e^{-j2\pi f_c \tau} \qquad (16\text{-}6)$$

we can write

$$v(t) = \int_{-\infty}^{\infty} h(\tau; t) u(t - \tau) d\tau = \int_{-\infty}^{\infty} h(t - \tau; t) u(\tau) d\tau \qquad (16\text{-}7)$$

Therefore to within the nominal propagation time t_0 the complex modulation component of the received signal is seen to be related to that which was transmitted as through a linear filter, with $h(x; t)$ in its dependence on x (i.e., on the first argument) playing the role of a complex-valued equivalent low-pass filter impulse response. Through its dependence on its second argument, t, $h(x; t)$ is said to be a linear *time-varying* filter. As we shall see momentarily, the nature of the time-varying functionality is such that $h(x; t)$ can be regarded as a *random variable* in its t-dependence.

To complete the description in (16-7), we can define the complex-valued equivalent low-pass, time-varying transfer function for the medium, $H(f;t)$, as the Fourier transform of $h(\tau;t)$ with respect to its *first* argument,

$$H(f;t) = \int_{-\infty}^{\infty} h(\tau;t) \, e^{-j2\pi f\tau} \, d\tau \tag{16-8a}$$

$$h(\tau;t) = \int_{-\infty}^{\infty} H(f;t) \, e^{j2\pi f\tau} \, df \tag{16-8b}$$

Then we can rewrite (16-7) as

$$v(t) = \int_{-\infty}^{\infty} H(f;t) \, U(f) \, e^{j2\pi ft} \, df \tag{16-9}$$

where we have identified the spectrum of the transmitted modulation component $u(t)$ as

$$U(f) = \int_{-\infty}^{\infty} u(\tau) \, e^{-j2\pi f\tau} \, d\tau \tag{16-10}$$

To understand the interpretation of the time-varying filter response and transfer function defined in (16-6) and (16-8), consider the transmission of an unmodulated carrier at frequency f' relative to f_c, that is, at the actual frequency $f = f_c + f'$. In (16-1) this corresponds to

$$u(t) = A \, e^{j2\pi f't} \, , \qquad A = \text{constant} \tag{16-11}$$

and in (16-10) to the single-line spectrum

$$U(f) = A \int_{-\infty}^{\infty} e^{-j2\pi(f - f')\tau} \, d\tau = A \, \delta(f - f') \tag{16-12}$$

Thus, in (16-9) and (16-4),

$$v(t) = A \, H(f';t) \, e^{j2\pi f't} \tag{16-13a}$$

$$s(t) = \text{Re} \left\{ A \, H(f';t - t_0) \, e^{j2\pi(f_c + f')(t - t_0)} \right\} \tag{16-13b}$$

That is, with a monochromatic transmission at frequency $f_c + f'$, the received signal contains amplitude and phase changes described in their *time-variation* by the t dependence of $H(f';t)$. In particular the received signal *is not monochromatic*. It has a nonvanishing spectral width determined by the t-variations in $H(f;t)$. Thus in (16-9), if we were to take the spectrum of $v(t)$, we would have in general

$$V(f) = \int_{-\infty}^{\infty} v(t) e^{-j2\pi ft} dt = \iint_{-\infty}^{\infty} H(\lambda;t) U(\lambda) e^{j2\pi(\lambda - f)t} d\lambda \, dt \qquad (16\text{-}14)$$

and this is not in general simply relatable to $U(f)$, as would be the case in the more familiar nontime-varying filter situation. The important useful statement is that the complex-valued function $H(f';t)$ represents additional multiplicative modulation in the signal received when a monochromatic signal of frequency f' (relative to f_c) is transmitted.

We still have not detailed the actual character of $h(\tau;t)$ or of $H(f;t)$. To do this, we consider further the transmission of an unmodulated carrier, this time regarding it in the time domain. Using (16-11) in (16-7) with $f' = 0$ for convenience so that the unmodulated carrier is at f_c, we have (for unit carrier amplitude)

$$v(t) = \int_{-\infty}^{\infty} h(\tau;t) d\tau = \int_{-\infty}^{\infty} \alpha(\tau;t) e^{-j2\pi f_c \tau} d\tau \qquad (16\text{-}15)$$

In (16-4) then, the received signal is

$$s(t) = \operatorname{Re}\left\{ e^{j2\pi f_c(t-t_0)} \int_{-\infty}^{\infty} h(\tau;t-t_0) d\tau \right\}$$

$$= \operatorname{Re}\left\{ e^{j2\pi f_c(t-t_0)} \int_{-\infty}^{\infty} \alpha(\tau, t-t_0) e^{-j2\pi f_c \tau} d\tau \right\} \qquad (16\text{-}16)$$

Momentarily let us assume the multipath is discrete so as to return to the sum representation of (16-2),

$$\alpha(\tau;t-t_0) = \sum_k \alpha_k(t-t_0) \, \delta[\tau - \tau_k(t-t_0)] \qquad (16\text{-}17a)$$

Then

$$s(t) = \operatorname{Re}\left\{ e^{j2\pi f_c(t-t_0)} \sum_k \alpha_k(t-t_0) e^{j2\pi f_c \tau_k(t-t_0)} \right\} \qquad (16\text{-}17b)$$

At any given instant t the sum is that of a set of phasors, of form $\sum \alpha_k e^{j\phi_k}$. As time proceeds the phasors change because of changes in both α_k and τ_k. It may readily be visualized, however, that α_k has the nature of a scattering cross section or of a reflection coefficient. Hence rather gross dynamic changes in the medium are required for α_k to change enough for significant observable changes to occur on the received signal in (16-17b). On the other hand, the phase ϕ_k associated with each one of these phasors will change by 2π radians whenever τ_k changes by $1/f_c$, i.e., whenever the physical path length associated with a scatterer changes by one wavelength of the *carrier* frequency. This can occur with relatively small motions in the medium. Furthermore, because of the irregularity of the typical radio medium it may be expected that different of the τ_k will change at different rates. Accordingly one can expect the more rapidly changing effects on signals from the dynamic nature of the medium to be primarily evidenced by random changes among the relative path delays or phases of the phasors in the sum of (16-17b).

Furthermore, if there are a sufficiently large number of "scatterers" (phasors) of roughly equivalent size, and their phases are changing randomly and independently of each other, it is well known that the resultant phasor will tend toward the following behavior: Via essentially the central limit theorem (Chap. 4), the two quadrature components of the resultant will each tend to be distributed as a zero-mean *Gaussian* variable, with equal variances, and *independent* fluctuations. These properties are identical with those of the quadrature components of bandpass Gaussian noise. The amplitude of the resultant phasor will then (Sec. 4-6) have a Rayleigh distribution, and its phase will be uniformly distributed. Exactly such Rayleigh-distributed envelope fading is observed quite often with c.w. transmissions on many long-distance radio circuits and is what is commonly termed Rayleigh fading. Because our physical knowledge of the media leads us to expect multipath structure of the type described above, and because this leads to an expectation of Rayleigh fading, and finally because this expectation is *consistent with the experimentally observed envelope fading, it is generally accepted that the observed fading is indeed due to multipath structure.* The fading is also often termed *wave-interference fading*, and sometimes (loosely) *short-term* fading. The latter differentiates that this fading is typically evident in seconds or fractions thereof, as contrasted to longer-term gross changes in the medium over periods of many minutes or, often, hours.

It should be noted that experimentally observed Rayleigh Law distributions for the stationary short-term signal envelope fading statistics are limited in significance on the "tails" of the distribution because of the necessarily finite duration of observation times (owing to the longer-term variations). On the other hand, the central limit property of the two quadrature components implies that the strongest tendency toward Gaussianness for each should be around its zero mean value. For the envelope statistics this will mean that the strongest tendency for the Rayleigh distribution to be a valid description will be at *low* envelope levels (i.e., when both quadrature components are near zero). As will be seen later, it is exactly this end of the envelope distribution which is of most concern in studying the degradation of performance owing to signal fading. Thus, when the Rayleigh Law is found to hold over the bulk of the distribution, we infer that it must also strongly hold near zero envelope level. That the Rayleigh Law may not be a good description at extremely high envelope levels may be expected since the asymptotic central limit argument is weakest there; on the other hand, the exact nature of the signal level distribution at very high levels is irrelevant for communications performance.*

We may further note that it has been shown that as few as six independently varying phasors of roughly equal magnitude will closely approximate a Rayleigh distribution in the sense described above (i.e., except for the upper few-percentile tail). It is also clear that if any one phasor (path) has a level equal to or above the sum of the rest, the distribution will not tend to the central limit in the same way. Such a strong component is often termed a *specular* or *steady* component, it being assumed to arise from a relatively stable ray path such as a well-formed layer reflection. Then the remaining paths contribute a Rayleigh fading component, and the total is termed *specular-plus-Rayleigh* fading. The resultant envelope fading statistics in the latter case are exactly those for the envelope of a sine wave plus additive Gaussian noise and hence have a Rice distribution. Hence the specular-plus-Rayleigh fading is also often termed *Rice* or *Rician* fading.

We have described how a multipath structure with enough discrete paths will lead to Rayleigh or Rice fading on a single transmitted tone and that this is consistent with experimental data. For a continuous multipath we have in effect an infinity of such paths, and the same consequences are apparent. Recall now the interpretation of $H(f;t)$ as the complex modulation received for a tone transmitted at relative frequency f. Thus the statement is that $H(f;t)$ is a *complex Gaussian time process* with respect to its dependence on t. That is, its two quadrature components are random, *independent Gaussian*, with equal variances, and with zero-mean for pure Rayleigh fading, or nonzero mean if a specular component is present. This is an *extremely* important interpretation, since it allows reliable analysis of expected behavior by use of the well-developed mathematics surrounding Gaussian processes.

---

*The exact high-level distribution might be significant in assessing the detectability of a fading signal at a site where only the high-level portions exceed the noise level. However, even here, for levels giving any significant percentages, the Rayleigh Law appears experimentally to hold well. By significant we refer to values in at least, say, the 1%-10% (or 90-99%) range, as opposed to, say, the 0.01%-1% range.

For transmission of intelligence, however, one must send more than a single tone, and hence must be concerned with the relations among the $H(f;t)$ over a spectrum of values of f. Since all the $H(f;t)$ basically arise from the same multipath process, we can extrapolate our previous arguments to the statement that the set of variates $H(f_i;t_i)$, $i = 1, 2, \ldots$, form a *jointly* complex Gaussian process. The only parameter required then to characterize the joint distribution is the *normalized complex frequency cross-covariance* (or correlation coefficient), which we define for a zero-mean (pure Rayleigh fading) process by

$$\rho_F(\Delta f; \Delta t) = \frac{\frac{1}{2}\overline{H(f;t)H^*(f + \Delta f; t + \Delta t)}}{\sqrt{\frac{1}{2}\overline{|H(f;t)|^2}}\sqrt{\frac{1}{2}\overline{|H(f + \Delta f; t + \Delta t)|^2}}} \qquad (16\text{-}18)$$

(If there is a specular component, it should be subtracted from $H(f;t)$ to define the covariance.) This is the complex crosscovariance for the signals received when two tones, spaced by Δf, are transmitted. In writing the covariance in the form (16-18), we are making two assumptions. One, that the dependence on the second argument depends only on the time-differential, is essentially the statement that $H(f;t)$ can be regarded as a stationary process.* The other, that the covariance depends only on the differential in frequency and not on the frequency itself, seems also physically reasonable (at least over the fractional bandwidths characteristic of radio systems); as shown below, this "stationarity" in frequency has an interesting implication for the multipath structure.

The nature of the crosscovariance in (16-18) can be understood with respect to the set-of-phasors picture used earlier. Consider the case $\Delta t = 0$ involving simultaneous received tones. At each of two transmitted tone frequencies, the multipath causes a set of phasors to be produced whose resultant is the corresponding received signal. If the two tones are very close in frequency, the set of phasors corresponding to one will always be closely similar in alignment to those at the other, and fading on the two tone frequencies will be highly correlated. As the frequencies are more widely spaced, the correspondence in alignment becomes much weaker, and the fluctuations will tend to be less correlated (just as earlier we described the unfolding of the fading process in time). Since the phase factors involved have the form $e^{j2\pi f \tau_k}$, it is clear that the correspondence in phasor alignment will tend to break down when $(\Delta f)(\tau_k)_{max}$ is of the order of 2π radians. We

---

*That is, it can be regarded as a locally stationary process. As the long-term variations occur on the medium, the statistics of the parameters of the short-term fading, such as $H(f;t)$, will also change. The distinction is a useful one for signal and receiver design, since the latter impacts only on the rapid fluctuations.

physically expect then that the "width" $(\Delta f)_c$ of the crosscovariance function in (16-18) with $\Delta t = 0$ is of the order of the reciprocal of the overall multipath spread

$$(\Delta f)_c \approx \frac{1}{T_M} \qquad (16\text{-}19)$$

We will obtain a more precise criterion later.

When a signal is transmitted whose bandwidth is of the order of, or exceeds, the frequency crosscovariance width, spectral components of the received signal will be subjected to different gain levels and nonlinear phase shifts across the band. Both of these effects can cause severe and random distortion of the waveform. The phenomenon is known as *selective fading*. This is often so destructive of communications performance that signaling systems for fading channels are usually limited to bandwidths over which the normalized frequency crosscovariance $\rho_F(\Delta f; 0)$ is near unity. This bandwidth is sometimes termed the *coherence bandwidth*, or *coherent propagation bandwidth* of the medium. It is usually only loosely defined as an order of magnitude, since the detailed value of tolerable distortion will depend upon the signal and receiver design and the performance required. Within such a bandwidth all signal components are supposedly fading in the same instant-to-instant manner. This is also sometimes termed *flat fading*, meaning simply *nonselective fading*, and the coherence bandwidth is hence sometimes also termed the *flat-fading bandwidth* (looked at from the contrary view, it is also sometimes termed the *selective-fading bandwidth*).

If we assume that $\rho_F(\Delta f; 0)$ is strictly unity over all Δf relevant to the signal (the ideal flat-fading channel), then it is apparent in (16-18) that

$$H(f + \Delta f; t) = H(f; t) = H(0; t) \quad \text{for all } f, \Delta f \text{ of interest} \quad (16\text{-}20)$$

In this case, returning to the representation of the received signal waveform in (16-9), we can write

$$v(t) = H(0; t) \int_{-\infty}^{\infty} U(f) e^{j2\pi ft} df \qquad (16\text{-}21\text{a})$$

and hence

$$v(t) = H(0; t) u(t) \qquad (16\text{-}21\text{b})$$

That is, for the ideal flat-fading channel (flat over the signal spectrum), and aside from the overall path delay, the received signal complex modulation component is equal to that transmitted, *multiplied by a complex Gaussian process*. Thus the ideal *nonselective fading* case is often described mathematically as being equivalent to introducing *multiplicative Gaussian noise* upon the signal, or as a *multiplicative noise channel*, or simply as *multiplicative Rayleigh fading*. Most analyses of fading, excepting only some recent work, have dealt with the assumption of multiplicative noise as a model for the channel (e.g., see Sec. 16-3). Unfortunately multiplicative noise is at best a first-order approximation to any actual channel, and when one is interested in rare events (seeking low error-rates), it has become clear that one should always properly ask whether the small discrepancies from this idealizing assumption may not account for significant errors in predicting system performance.

Returning now to the relation of the crosscovariance defined in (16-18) to the multipath structure, we substitute (16-8a), and thereby obtain

$$\frac{1}{2} \overline{H(f;t) H^*(f + \Delta f; t + \Delta t)}$$

$$= \frac{1}{2} \iint_{-\infty}^{\infty} \overline{h(\tau_1;t) h^*(\tau_2; t + \Delta t)} \, e^{-j2\pi f\tau_1 + j2\pi(f + \Delta f)\tau_2} \, d\tau_1 \, d\tau_2 \qquad (16\text{-}22)$$

$$= \iint_{-\infty}^{\infty} R(\tau_1, \tau_2; \Delta t) \, e^{j2\pi\tau_2 \Delta f} \, e^{j2\pi f(\tau_2 - \tau_1)} \, d\tau_1 \, d\tau_2 \qquad (16\text{-}23)$$

where we have defined a nonnormalized crosscovariance for the time-varying impulse response of the medium,

$$R(\tau_1, \tau_2; \Delta t) = \frac{1}{2} \overline{h(\tau_1;t) h^*(\tau_2; t + \Delta t)} \qquad (16\text{-}24)$$

We have assumed the latter to be time stationary, as it must be if the left-hand side of (16-22) is to be time-stationary, as we required earlier in (16-18). However, we also required in writing (16-18) that the left-hand side be independent of f (i.e., dependent only on Δf), and we now see in (16-23) that this can only be true for arbitrary f if the double integral has nonvanishing values only when $\tau_2 = \tau_1$. That is, $R(\tau_1, \tau_2, \Delta t)$ *must* have the form

$$R(\tau_1, \tau_2; \Delta t) = \rho_T(\tau_1; \Delta t) \delta(\tau_1 - \tau_2) \qquad (16\text{-}25)$$

In this case

$$\frac{1}{2} \overline{H(f;t) H^*(f + \Delta f; t + \Delta t)} = \int_{-\infty}^{\infty} \rho_T(\tau; \Delta t) \, e^{j2\pi\tau\Delta f} \, d\tau \qquad (16\text{-}26)$$

The strict interpretation of (16-25) is that each delay interval in the multipath structure is causing *independent fluctuations* of the signal components. Actually, closer examination of (16-23) indicates that all that is required is that the integrand vanish for all values of $\tau_1 - \tau_2$ for which $e^{j2\pi f(\tau_2 - \tau_1)}$ is not very near unity. Since the values of f of interest are only those occupied by the signal spectrum, the requirement is really that the multipath structure is fading independently over delay intervals which are any sizable fraction of the signal bandwidth.* If this is true, then pretending that independence is more finely structured will have no effect on calculations. (This is analogous to assuming thermal noise at a receiver input to be infinitely wide-band rather than physically band-limited; the resolution of the filter then discards the pretended additional components, so there is no actual difference in calculations except for the mathematical convenience of dealing with the pretended infinite bandwidth noise.) In any case, we see that the stationarity in the frequency domain expressed in (16-18) will break down if one employs a sufficiently wide-band signal. For practical purposes, however, it has always been assumed to hold in any calculations involving fading media.

The other interpretation in (16-24) to (16-26) is that $\rho_T(\tau;0)\,d\tau$ represents the relative average intensity of the contributions from that part of the multipath in range $(\tau, \tau + d\tau)$. Hence $\rho_T(\tau;0)$ may be termed the *multipath intensity profile*. Correspondingly, $\rho_T(\tau;\Delta\tau)$ is the autocovariance describing the rate of fluctuation of this contribution and may be termed the *multipath time-covariance*. Returning now to (16-18), we can write

$$\rho_F(\Delta f;\Delta t) = \frac{\int_{-\infty}^{\infty} \rho_T(\tau;\Delta t)\, e^{j2\pi\tau\Delta f}\, d\tau}{\int_{-\infty}^{\infty} \rho_T(\tau;0)\, d\tau} \tag{16-27}$$

and in particular

$$\rho_F(\Delta f;0) = \frac{\int_{-\infty}^{\infty} \rho_T(\tau;0)\, e^{j2\pi\tau\Delta f}\, d\tau}{\int_{-\infty}^{\infty} \rho_T(\tau;0)\, d\tau} \tag{16-28}$$

*More particularly, with the signal bandwidth $B \ll f_c$ as a definition of the bandpass signal, we can visualize the multipath structure broken into segments of width $\Delta\tau$ such that $B \ll (1/\Delta\tau) \ll f_c$ with the inequality symbol indicating one order of magnitude. All multipath within such a narrow delay shell will combine as a multiplicative noise on the modulation component, whereas the shell-thickness is wide enough to guarantee (assuming a sufficient density of scatterers) that the multiplicative noise is a complex Gaussian process. In a sense a discrete multipath model based on delay shells of such a thickness is the true physical-mathematical model, and our continuum representations are merely mathematically convenient equivalent forms.

That is, there is a Fourier transform relationship between the complex frequency crosscovariance and the multipath time-covariance, or (at $\Delta t = 0$) the multipath intensity profile. Particularly, as suggested earlier in (16-19) on physical grounds, it now follows from standard Fourier transform relations that the width of $\rho_F(\Delta f; 0)$ will be roughly the reciprocal of the width of $\rho_T(\tau; 0)$, the latter being just the multipath spread.

It is worth commenting that measurements made on the cross-covariance of spaced tones on fading channels have commonly been based upon the crosscovariance of the observed envelopes. When the latter is expressed as a normalized envelope cross-covariance (with mean envelope values subtracted), it very closely gives the value $|\rho_F(\Delta f; 0)|^2$. While this measures $|\rho_F(\Delta f; 0)|$, it unfortunately may yield only sparse information concerning the multipath structure itself, since unless the latter has even symmetry about its mid-value, $\rho_F(\Delta f; 0)$ will be complex. The measured information is then insufficient for detailed information about the skewed multipath intensity profile. Unfortunately, also, there is good reason to expect the profile to be highly skewed in most long-distance fading radio channels.

A final comment on characterization of the channel lies in the nature of the time-variations. In (16-27) we have defined how selectivity in frequency is related to multipath structure but have not defined how either varies with time. For example, the complex autocovariance for the signal received with a single tone transmitted is $\rho_F(0; \Delta t)$. Such an autocovariance describes the rapidity with which the medium changes, i.e., the rapidity of changes in the functional forms $h(\tau; t)$ and $H(f; t)$. The question of fading rapidity is obviously important for any systems (e.g., diversity operation as discussed later) which depend on obtaining a relatively noiseless monitoring of the "instantaneous" state of the channel. Such noiseless monitoring requires relatively long smoothing times, which will be limited in useful duration by the rapidity of fading. Fading rapidity will also represent a limitation in the performance of DPSK systems, or indeed in any digital system when the fading becomes sufficiently rapid to affect coherence within a single pulse.

Recalling our model, rapidity of fading is obviously also related to motions in the medium. Since motion of a reflector or scatterer will be evidenced by a *Doppler shift*, one may expect some relation between rapidity of fading and so-called Doppler broadening of a transmitted spectral line. Indeed, if one thinks of the discrete multipath model as in (16-17b), it is clear that any linear changes in $\tau_k(t)$ as a function of time, say,

$$\tau_k(t) = \tau_{k0} + \frac{v_k t}{c} + \cdots \qquad (16\text{-}29)$$

will be evidence as a Doppler frequency shift, by the amount $f_c v_k/c$

where $c = 3 \times 10^8$ m/s is the velocity of light. Since many different scatterers, all on rays having the same overall path delay τ_k, may have different velocities, the return from any one component of the multipath (assuming a high density of scatterers) will comprise lines with *many different Doppler shifts*. Alternatively if we focus on $H(f;t)$ as the return caused by a continuous transmitted tone at relative frequency f, we see that $H(f;t)$ will in general represent a number of lines, with randomly varying amplitudes, all closely packed around the transmitted tone frequency. The *average spectrum* associated with the *time* variations of $H(f;t)$ is the same on either a time or ensemble-average basis and hence is just the power density spectrum whose transform is the time autocovariance function $\rho_F(0;\Delta t)$. Thus $\rho_F(0;\Delta t)$ is closely characterized in its spectrum (transform on the Δt variable) by the Doppler broadening expected of the channel. Exactly this line of reasoning in fact was applied in arriving at the pre-experimental predictions of the fading rapidity of the orbital dipole belt (Project Westford). Particularly the width in Δt of $\rho_F(0;\Delta t)$ is roughly the reciprocal of the Doppler spread.

Defining the multipath spread for a channel as T_M and the Doppler spread as B_D, another important characteristic of a fading channel is the *spread factor*,

$$L = T_M B_D \qquad (16\text{-}30)$$

If one, for example, attempts to determine the state of the medium by sending a sounding pulse periodically, the period between successive pulses must be at least T_M to avoid ambiguities. On the other hand, the medium *changes* state in a time of the order $1/B_D$. Hence the "instantaneous" state of the medium is measurable using periodic pulses only if

$$T_M \ll \frac{1}{B_D} \qquad (16\text{-}31)$$

i.e., the spread factor must be well below unity. Another important interpretation of the spread factor is as follows. If signal pulses are of length T, one must have $T \gg T_M$ to avoid significant intersymbol interference, since only then will the energy arriving at any instant all primarily relate to one signal pulse. On the other hand, to avoid severe time-fading distortion of the pulse (or equivalently, destruction of coherence over the pulse owing to channel phase fluctuations within the pulse duration), one must also have $T \ll 1/B_D$. Both conditions can be satisfied only if

$$T_M \ll T \ll \frac{1}{B_D} \qquad (16\text{-}32)$$

which again requires a spread factor well below unity. For all terrestrial radio channels the spread factor is indeed well below unity, and only in the case of the orbital dipole belt has the problem arisen of a spread factor of the order of unity.

Operationally, fading rapidity is usually measured by referring to the rate at which the received *envelope* crosses its median level with a c.w. tone transmitted. If $G(f)$ is the power density spectrum of $\rho_F(0, \Delta t)$,

$$G(f) = \int_{-\infty}^{\infty} \rho_F(0, \Delta t) e^{j2\pi f \Delta t} d(\Delta t) \qquad (16\text{-}33)$$

then the basic parameter of all such "zero-crossing" statistics is the so-called r.m.s. frequency contained in $G(f)$, more accurately the "radius of gyration" of the spectrum shape,

$$f_{\text{r.m.s.}} = \sqrt{\int_{-\infty}^{\infty} f^2 G(f)\, df} \qquad (16\text{-}34a)$$

Then it can be shown that the so-called *fade rate at median level*, the rate at which the envelope crosses its median level in, say, a positive-going direction, is given for Rayleigh fading by

$$f_m = 1.475\, f_{\text{r.m.s.}} \qquad (16\text{-}34b)$$

With the general characteristics of fading channels now set down, we can describe the particular parameters of some of the media of practical importance to which these characterizations apply:

1. In conventional long-distance h.f. skywave propagation, at frequencies below the MUF, the fade rate at median level is usually cited as lying between the extremes 0.01-1 fade per second, with 0.1 fade per second (6 fades per minute) being a typical number. The multipath consists of two portions. Each so-called layer reflection, owing to irregularities and depth of the layer, typically corresponds to a multipath continuum no more than a few hundred microseconds long, with 50-200 μs perhaps typical. However, the dominant multipath restricting signaling bandwidths at h.f. arises because of the multihop nature of long-distance propagation, so that some of the energy arrives at a distant receiving point via, say, one, two, or perhaps by as much as five, seven, or ten hops. The differences in path delay time between such modes are anywhere from a few hundred microseconds for relatively short (few hundred mile) paths to many milliseconds on extremely long paths. Typical multipath delays on circuits 1000-3000 miles long are in the range 1-3 ms. Because of this, signaling bandwidths at h.f. are generally

below 500 Hz for any individual signal (many may be sent on parallel channels in a multiplex arrangement).

2. Ionospheric scatter propagation is a one-hop transmission via the ionosphere, using the 30-80 Mhz band above the MUF, over distances of 600-2000 mi. The fading rapidity is again apparently of the order 0.1 fade per second, and the multipath spread is typical of single layer scattering, hence in the range around 100 μsec.

3. Tropospheric scatter propagation uses the frequency range 100 to 10,000 Mhz, over distances ranging from just beyond the radio horizon up to 400-600 mi. Observed fade rates are roughly proportional to operating frequency (as expected from the Doppler interpretation), and are about 0.1-1 fade per second at median level in the 400-1000 Mhz band.* Multipath spread appears to vary from about 0.1-0.5 μs at ranges below about 200 mi to perhaps 5 μs at 600 mi. The exact multipath spread is a function both of range and of antenna beamwidths (the latter dependent on antenna size and electrical wavelength). Usable conventional bandwidths are thus in the few Mhz or hundreds of kilohertz range.

4. Lunar reflections exhibit multipath owing to echoes arising from the entire moon surface, and hence the multipath spread is several milliseconds. Fading rapidity is due to relative motion and libration, and appears again to be in the 0.1/s range at, say, 400 Mhz.

5. The orbital dipole belt tested experimentally in 1963 had a multipath spread (when formed) of several hundred microseconds and a Doppler spread of several hundred hertz. As stated earlier this is the only medium of those listed for which the spread factor approaches close to unity, affecting antimultipath techniques and also affecting the basic nature of the signaling techniques. The experimental systems in fact used a kind of radiometric (energy-sensing) receiver rather than a linear receiver as the signal detection system.

16-3 Error-rates in Rayleigh Fading

Having discussed above the character of fading channels, we turn to their effects upon communications performance. Most of our discussion in this section will be based upon the model of slow, nonselective, purely Rayleigh fading, which can be readily analyzed and is the only model discussed in the bulk of the literature. This model is useful in that it covers (to first-order) a practically meaningful regime for terrestrial communications.

---

*Aircraft echoes can cause fading to fluctuate a factor of 10-100 times faster.

To review, nonselective fading implies that the transmitted signals are received with the fading appearing completely as a multiplicative Gaussian noise. Particularly this assumes that the medium does not introduce any pulse lengthening and hence that there is no intersymbol interference owing to the *medium*. There could still be some introduced by the receiver filters, but for our purposes here we will also assume that there are no such effects whatsoever. Again by this we include the assumption that adequate synchronization is available in the receiver so that, at the sampling instant for a pulse, the signal components of voltages at the detector are due only to that pulse being received.

In assuming purely Rayleigh fading, we are also specifically in this section excluding models involving an additional specular component. Hence the multiplicative noise is a zero-mean complex Gaussian process.

We have not earlier placed a quantitative specification on the term *slow fading*. Specifically the assumption is that the multiplicative noise varies so slowly with respect to the signal pulse lengths that it may be regarded effectively *constant* during the course of each signal pulse, although varying over a long succession of such pulses. Combining this with the other assumptions leads to a mathematical model in which each pulse has associated with it 1) a *simple multiplier on its magnitude*, chosen from a Rayleigh ensemble of the fading envelope, and 2) an *additive carrier phase shift* chosen from the associated uniform distribution of phase. The same multiplier on magnitude and the additive phase shift then also appear on the *output* of the receiver filters as applied to the detector at the sampling instant for making the binary decision for that pulse.

On this basis we can calculate the probability of error for any individual pulse by adapting the results given earlier in Chaps. 10 to 14 for the probability of error with steady signal in Gaussian noise. In the fading case these formulas will be taken to describe the probability of error for an individual pulse *conditional* on the value of the multiplicative noise over that pulse (an envelope and a phase factor), and hence they describe the conditional probability of a detection error caused by the *additive* stationary Gaussian receiver noise. Alternately stated, results such as in Chaps. 10 to 14 give this conditional probability of error, for each kind of binary communication channel, as some appropriate function of the signal-to-noise ratio for each pulse, where the signal part of the SNR involves the multiplicative envelope factor for that pulse. To determine the average performance over fading then requires averaging such a conditional probability of error over the ensemble of possible values of the multiplicative factor, i.e., over the Rayleigh distribution for the envelope factor and (if it enters) the uniform distribution for the phase. This technique, which is illustrated below, is often employed in analysis of systems under the slow-fading assumption. It is especially convenient when the probability of error has already been calculated for steady signal in Gaussian receiver noise, and the resulting probability of error expression can be conveniently averaged over the ensemble of values of the multiplicative noise.

On the other hand, the conditional probability of error is itself based simply upon assuming a certain binary state (Mark or Space) transmitted and then determining in view of the additive receiver noise the ensemble p.d.f. for the voltages at the detector at the sampling instant. When, in slow fading, we further average such a result over the *multiplicative* noise ensemble, we recognize then that the *total* probability calculation involves two integrals, *whose order can be reversed*. Namely, for a given binary state transmitted, we can first determine the ensemble p.d.f. for the sampling-instant detector voltages, with respect to *both* the additive Gaussian noise ensemble and the multiplicative Gaussian noise ensemble (the two ensembles being independent). The resulting voltage p.d.f. can then be integrated over the voltage range which produces decision errors to calculate the net overall probability of error. The latter technique has the following mathematical advantage: For a linear receiving system and Rayleigh fading signal the voltages at the filter outputs at the sampling instant are simply sample values from the *sum* of two independent zero-mean Gaussian processes (one the filtered receiver noise, the other resulting from the multiplicative noise factor on the ''signal'' term for pure Rayleigh fading). Thus the filter output ensemble is simply a zero-mean Gaussian process rather than the sum of a Gaussian process and a steady component such as involved in most of the steady-signal calculations in Chaps. 10 to 14. The remaining integral to determine the probability that the detector voltages lie in the error-producing region is usually correspondingly simpler. Although we shall not illustrate this technique here, it has been extremely valuable in solving many intricate reception problems associated with fading channels (e.g., Ref. 1).

It is important to note that both calculation techniques apply equally well to the particular calculation of the probability that *any single* information pulse, chosen completely at random, will be in error. In many calculations, however, one is interested in the behavior of a sequence of pulses, e.g., to determine the probability of character error in radioteletype or to determine the probability of correct decoding for code blocks when redundant coding is being employed. Many calculations which have been described along these lines are based upon extending the *slow-fading* model to the *assumption* that the multiplicative noise remains constant over the entire character or sequence. (Clearly, however, this becomes less and less realistic, or more and more restrictive, as the sequence length increases.) Within this assumption one necessarily falls back on the first calculation technique: All pulses in the sequence are assumed to have the same multiplicative noise factor and the same probability of bit error, and one can now calculate a probability of *sequence* error *conditional* on the value of the multiplicative process. The net probability of sequence error is then obtained by averaging this conditional probability of sequence error over the statistics of the multiplicative noise. Since a number of binary decisions are involved, which are nonindependent (the multiplicative noise is "completely correlated" over all pulses in the sequence), there appears in this case to be no useful alternate mode of calculation. Furthermore the relation of the conditional probability of sequence error to the error probability for the individual bits in the sequence will generally involve a combinatorial expression (particularly with algebraically coded sequences, where errors can occur only when the number of bit errors in the sequence exceeds some minimum value). It is then often still difficult or impossible to carry out the final averages analytically, although numerical quadratures are usually quite feasible. Moreover the combinatorial relation involved is very particularly related to the nature of the character or sequence coding. Such computations are straightforward as outlined, and we shall omit here any detailed examples of such computations. We will remark, however, that very little improvement is offered by coding in a communication system in which the information must be transferred at a fixed rate* with fixed transmitted power over a slowly fading channel. Lower bounds have been derived (Ref. 2) for the probability of symbol error for a given transmitter power, order of diversity (see Chap. 17), and size of symbol alphabet. These bounds lie only a few dB (4 to 7 dB), in terms of transmitted power, below the performance attainable without coding. The implication of the result is that one must remove the requirement of fixed information transfer rate (e.g., by allowing error detection with repeats) or the requirement of fixed transmitter power if improved communication is to be obtained (with or without coding).

Furthermore the really important problem in dealing with sequence errors, particularly if one wants to investigate the utility of "long codes" or "burst-error codes" for increasing transmission rate on a fading channel, is to remove the nonselective, slow-fading assumption and calculate with respect to more rapid or selective fading or both. In general this is a problem which remains almost unexplored analytically. At the other extreme is the assumption that every pulse error in sequence occurs independently of every other pulse error. One might regard this as another kind of assumption on fading rapidity, but it is not realistic to couple it with an assumption of slow-fading over each individual pulse *except* in one very important case. This is the case when one uses interleaving or "interlacing" (as described in Chap. 15),

*By fixed rate, we also here mean without interleaving.

which does produce this effect of error independence within a sequence without regard to fading rate.

Accordingly for the remainder of this section we will examine the effects of slow, nonselective Rayleigh fading on individual bit error-rates, for the basic systems introduced in Chaps. 10 to 12. Since we have already emphasized the predominant importance of FSK and PSK systems in applications, we will omit discussion of on-off keying here and confine our attention to FSK and PSK.

Within the slow, nonselective, Rayleigh fading assumption we can deal simultaneously with FSK and PSK. Thus, as seen from Chaps. 11 and 12, there are only two forms of conditional probability of error on individual pulses:

$$P_\gamma^{(1)} = \frac{1}{2} e^{-\alpha\gamma} \begin{cases} \alpha = \dfrac{1}{2}, & \text{noncoherent FSK} \\[2mm] \alpha = 1, & \text{differentially coherent PSK} \end{cases} \qquad (16\text{-}35)$$

$$P_\gamma^{(2)} = \frac{1}{2} \operatorname{erfc}(\sqrt{\alpha\gamma}) \begin{cases} \alpha = \dfrac{1}{2}, & \text{coherent FSK} \\[2mm] \alpha = 1, & \text{ideal coherent PSK} \end{cases} \qquad (16\text{-}36)$$

Below we will average (16-35) and (16-36) over fading to describe the average probability of single-pulse error for the various signaling techniques. However, for either ideal PSK or coherent FSK we run immediately into the question of the meaning in such a computation of the requirement for a phase reference, in view of the random fluctuations of carrier phase implied by the fading. A superficial answer is that, if the fading is assumed to be *slow enough*, it should be possible to derive a suitable and essentially noiseless phase reference for either coherent FSK or ideal PSK. Correspondingly for DPSK the requirement is just that the received signal phase remain *sensibly* the same over time periods of two pulse lengths. More generally, if a phase reference is derived by a running average over a long stream of pulses, the duration of such an averaging will have to be a compromise between the desire for a high SNR in the derived reference and the limitations imposed by the rate of fading. In the extreme case of frequent loss of coherence within a single pulse, coherent signaling in this sense will no longer be possible at all. Indeed in such a case linear filtering over each pulse becomes inappropriate even in noncoherent FSK. For this chapter, however, we will only explore the simple calculations of fading effects on the assumption of "sufficiently slow fading," so that it is assumed meaningful to average (16-35) or (16-36) over the fading fluctuations.

Under the assumptions then of slow, multiplicative fading and a linear-filter receiver of the types discussed earlier, recalling (16-21) and the implication that the multiplicative noise remains constant over each pulse, the multiplicative noise will appear directly as a multiplicative factor on the signal component of the filter output. Then at a sampling instant for pulse decision the *envelope* value u of the signal at the filter output will be a value drawn from a Rayleigh law p.d.f.,

$$p(u) = \frac{2u}{u_0^2} e^{-u^2/u_0^2}, \quad 0 < u < \infty \tag{16-37}$$

where

$$u_0^2 = \overline{u^2} \tag{16-38}$$

is the statistical average of u^2 over the fading. The filter output noise *intensity* at every sampling instant is still the factor N, unchanged from pulse to pulse, and hence we may also regard the SNR at the sampling instant

$$\gamma = u^2/2N \tag{16-39}$$

as statistically varying from pulse to pulse only because of signal fading. With (16-37) and N regarded as a constant, the p.d.f. for γ is then the exponential distribution

$$p(\gamma) = \frac{1}{\gamma_0} e^{-\gamma/\gamma_0}, \quad 0 < \gamma < \infty \tag{16-40}$$

where

$$\gamma_0 = \overline{\gamma} = u_0^2/2N \tag{16-41}$$

is the mean SNR (averaged over fading) at the sampling instants at the filter output. Thus the averages of (16-35) and (16-36) over the Rayleigh fading p.d.f. are easily determined to be

$$P^{(1)} = \int_{-\infty}^{\infty} \frac{1}{2} e^{-\alpha\gamma} \frac{1}{\gamma_0} e^{-\gamma/\gamma_0} \, d\gamma = \frac{1}{2 + 2\alpha\gamma_0} \tag{16-42}$$

and

$$P^{(2)} = \int_{-\infty}^{\infty} \frac{1}{2} \operatorname{erfc}\sqrt{\alpha\gamma} \frac{1}{\gamma_0} e^{-\gamma/\gamma_0} \, d\gamma = \frac{1}{2} \left[1 - \frac{1}{\sqrt{1 + \dfrac{1}{\alpha\gamma_0}}} \right] \tag{16-43}$$

(The latter result is obtained by an integration by parts.) Accordingly we have the following average probabilities of error in slow, nonselective Rayleigh fading:

$$\text{noncoherent FSK}: \quad P = \frac{1}{2 + \gamma_0} \tag{16-44}$$

$$\text{coherent FSK:} \quad P = \frac{1}{2}\left[1 - \frac{1}{\sqrt{1 + \dfrac{2}{\gamma_0}}}\right] \qquad (16\text{-}45)$$

$$\text{ideal PSK:} \quad P = \frac{1}{2}\left[1 - \frac{1}{\sqrt{1 + \dfrac{1}{\gamma_0}}}\right] \qquad (16\text{-}46)$$

$$\text{differentially-coherent PSK:} \quad P = \frac{1}{2 + 2\gamma_C} \qquad (16\text{-}47)$$

These results are shown in the curves of Fig. 16-1. Again there is an exact 3 dB difference in performance between coherent FSK and ideal PSK, as well as between noncoherent FSK and DPSK. These are simply a reflection of the exactly 3 dB difference in the relative performance of these systems (represented exactly by the differences in the constant α) at *all* levels of SNR. The kind of results presented in Fig. 16-1 are observed as well experimentally (e.g., Refs. 3,4).

For comparison the noncoherent FSK and ideal PSK curves of Fig. 11-3 for error-rate with steady signal are reproduced as the dotted curves in Fig. 16-1, using the same abscissa to now denote the steady SNR. The severe degradation owing to fading fluctuations about the mean received signal level is obvious. For a single binary channel subject to slow, nonselective Rayleigh-fading, additional system margins of the order of 10 dB (mean level received in fading as compared to required mean SNR in the absence of fading) must be provided for error-rates around 0.01, with approximately an additional 10 dB required for every order of magnitude (factor of 10) further decrease in allowed system error-rate. Indeed, from (16-44)–(16-47) the asymptotic performance for large average SNR is given by

$$P^{(1)} \to \frac{1}{2\alpha\gamma_0} \begin{cases} \text{noncoherent FSK,} & P \to \dfrac{1}{\gamma_0} \qquad (16\text{-}48) \\[2em] \text{DPSK,} & P \to \dfrac{1}{2\gamma_0} \qquad (16\text{-}49) \end{cases}$$

$$\Biggr\} \; \gamma_0 \gg 1$$

$$P^{(2)} \to \frac{1}{4\alpha\gamma_0} \begin{cases} \text{coherent FSK,} & P \to \dfrac{1}{2\gamma_0} \qquad (16\text{-}50) \\[2em] \text{ideal PSK,} & P \to \dfrac{1}{4\gamma_0} \qquad (16\text{-}51) \end{cases}$$

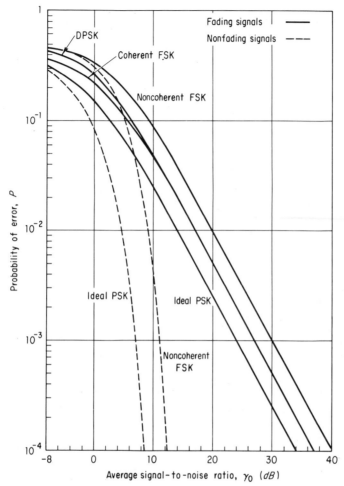

Fig. 16-1 Probability of error for several binary systems in Rayleigh fading.

Thus, at large SNR, error-rate for all these systems is exactly inversely proportional to the mean SNR (the 3 dB performance differences are also recognizable then as factors-of-2 differences in error-rate at any fixed γ_0). By way of comparison, changes in SNR produce *exponential* changes in error-rate with steady signals, whereas with Rayleigh fading changes are only on a 1:1 basis. This is perhaps the dominant qualitative difference. It also indicates the nature of the additional design burden imposed upon systems required to operate in fading and the resulting importance of techniques (such as the diversity techniques discussed in Chap. 17) for overcoming the effects of fading.

Qualitatively the severe degradation introduced by fading is, of course, due to the finite percentage of very low signal levels occurring in Rayleigh Law fading, during which the conditional probability of error is correspondingly very close to 0.5. In this sense one may view the importance of diversity techniques described in Chap. 17 to lie in modifying the p.d.f. for γ, so that it tends to be very small for small γ, rather than the exponential behavior implied in (16-40) for which the p.d.f actually peaks at $\gamma = 0$. To more quantitatively illustrate this interpretation of fading effects, one can examine the ranges of γ responsible for the errors, still under the assumption of the Rayleigh distribution (see also Refs. 5, 6). To this end, we can examine two integrals whose relation to (16-42)-(16-43) is rather obvious,

$$N^{(1)}(\gamma_1) = \int_0^\gamma \frac{1}{2} e^{-\alpha\gamma} \frac{1}{\gamma_0} e^{-\gamma/\gamma_0} \, d\gamma = \frac{1}{2} \frac{1 - e^{-\alpha\gamma_1(1 + 1/\alpha\gamma_0)}}{1 + \alpha\gamma_0} \tag{16-52}$$

$$N^{(2)}(\gamma_1) = \int_0^{\gamma_1} \frac{1}{2} \operatorname{erfc}(\sqrt{\alpha\gamma}) \frac{1}{\gamma_0} e^{-\gamma/\gamma_0} \, d\gamma$$

$$= \frac{1}{2} \left\{ \left[1 - e^{-\gamma_1/\gamma_2} \operatorname{erfc}\sqrt{\alpha\gamma_1} \right] - \frac{1}{\sqrt{1 + \frac{1}{\alpha\gamma_0}}} \left[1 - \operatorname{erfc}\sqrt{\alpha\gamma_1 \left(1 + \frac{1}{\alpha\gamma_0}\right)} \right] \right\} \tag{16-53}$$

For given values of α and γ_0, $N^{(1)}$ and $N^{(2)}$ obviously represent the probabilities or error *conditional* on γ lying in the range $0 < \gamma < \gamma_1$. If we interpret probabilities of error in the large-sample sense as the average fraction of bits in error (over infinitely large populations of bits), then dividing $N^{(1)}$ and $N^{(2)}$, respectively, by $P^{(1)}$, $P^{(2)}$ from (16-42) and (16-43) will give in each case the fraction of all the errors which occur owing to fading signal levels (for fixed γ_0) which are in the range $0 \leq \gamma \leq \gamma_1$. These fractions are

$$\Pr^{(1)}(\gamma_1) = 1 - e^{-\alpha\gamma_0(1 + 1/\alpha\gamma_0)} \tag{16-54}$$

$$\Pr^{(2)}(\gamma_1) = 1 - \frac{e^{-\gamma_1/\gamma_0} \operatorname{erfc}(\sqrt{\alpha\gamma_1}) - \dfrac{1}{\sqrt{1 + 1/\alpha\gamma_0}} \operatorname{erfc}\sqrt{\alpha\gamma_1}(1 + 1/\alpha\gamma_0)}{1 - \dfrac{1}{\sqrt{1 + 1/\alpha\gamma_0}}} \tag{16-55}$$

These are shown plotted in Fig. 16-2, with $\Pr^{(1)}(\gamma_1)$ and $\Pr^{(2)}(\gamma_1)$ as functions of $\alpha\gamma_1$, for various values of $\alpha\gamma_0$ as a parameter. In

(16-54) it is particularly apparent that for $\alpha\gamma_0 \gg 1$ (as is necessary for any reasonably low error-rate, the fraction $\mathrm{Pr}^{(1)}(\gamma_1)$ is *independent* of γ_0. That is, regardless of the overall average rate of errors (i.e., how small or large the total is), a certain *fraction* always occur in a range of SNR determined only by the particular fraction being considered. This is particularly related to the exponential conditional probability of error involved in $\mathrm{Pr}^{(1)}(\gamma_1)$. However, as shown by Fig. 16-2, the general behavior is characteristic also of ideal coherent detection processes.

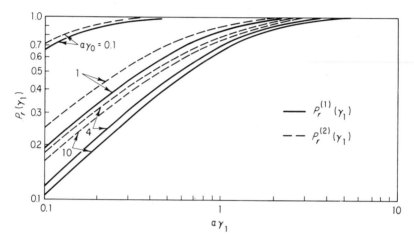

Fig. 16-2 Location of SNR levels at which errors occur in Rayleigh fading.

Again the significance of these last results is the observation that any operation which can alter the fading p.d.f. so as to reduce the relative concentration near $\gamma = 0$ can be expected to greatly reduce the error-rates at a given mean level γ_0. As will be seen in Chap. 17, this is precisely one useful interpretation of the manner in which diversity and other adaptive receiving techniques effect system improvements.

Finally we should remind the reader that all the results presented above are premised upon the assumption of slow and nonselective fading. As stated in the beginning of this section, this model is applicable over a wide range of practical applications but is only a first-order model. For example, for every Rayleigh fading channel there are instants of time during which the signal level fades through or near zero value. At such instants the signal level may be rapidly changing, even though on the average (averaged over all fading levels) it is slowly fading. A pulse at that instant may be badly distorted, so badly that the wrong waveform might be chosen even if there were *no* additive noise. If, for example, this occurs on the average to one pulse out of every 10^4 pulses, there would be an *irreducible* error-rate of 10^{-4}. That is, an analysis with a more accurate model of the channel would show an error-rate dependence on SNR as derived in the equations above, down to an error-rate of about 10^{-4}, and then a "bottoming" of the curve to an asymptotic error-rate of 10^{-4}, no matter how high the ratio of mean signal power to mean noise power. Selective fading will produce similar implications. That is, there are significant changes in the channel response at frequency spacings of the order of the reciprocal of the multipath spread. These must often take the form of near nulls (since at any single frequency, Rayleigh fading implies occasional near-nulls). Furthermore no matter how narrow the signal bandwidth such nulls or near-nulls will occasionally fall within the signal band, with concomitant selective distortion of the signal spectrum. Again the result is an irreducible error rate, or a bottoming in the curve of error rate versus mean SNR. More detailed discussion of these effects and references to associated literature can be found in Ref. 1.

REFERENCES

1. M. Schwartz, W. R. Bennett, and S. Stein, *Communication Systems and Techniques* (McGraw-Hill Book Company, New York, 1966).
2. D. Chesler: "Optimum Performance of Codes Transmitted at Fixed Information Rate Over Slowly Fading Channels," *Applied Research Laboratory*, Sylvania Electronic Systems, *Research Report 367* (October 1963).
3. J. W. Allnatt, E. D. J. Jones, and H. B. Law: "Frequency Diversity in the Reception of Selectively Fading Binary Frequency-Modulated Signals," *Proc. IEE, 104*, Pt. B, pp. 98-110 (March 1957).
4. E. F. Florman and R. W. Plush: "Measured Statistical Characteristics and Narrow-Band Teletype Message Errors on a Single-Sideband 600-Mile-Long Ultrahigh-Frequency Tropospheric Radio Link," *Jour. Res. NBS, 64D,* pp. 125-133 (March-April 1960).
5. B. B. Barrow: "Error Probabilities for Data Transmission Over Fading Radio Paths," Doctoral Dissertation, Delft, 1962; *NATO Tech. Memo* TM-26, SHAPE Air Defense Technical Centre (1962).
6. H. F. Law: "The Detectability of Fading Radiotelegraph Signals in Noise," *Proc. IEE, 104*, Pt. B, p. 130-140 (March 1957).

17

Diversity Techniques*

17-1 Methods of Diversity

The results in Chap. 16 indicate the performance degradation introduced by Rayleigh fading for digital data transmission on a single binary channel, relative to performance with nonfading signal at the same mean SNR. The differences are measured in tens of decibels and imply major additional costs if such differences are to be supplied by increased transmitter power, antenna size, etc. In many systems (notably scatter transmission), the maximum reasonable transmitter power and antenna sizes are already being used in any case. Even where this is not true, the increased costs of an order-of-magnitude increase in transmitted power or antenna sizes make any alternate possibilities very attractive economically. Note also that while our specific performance calculations referred only to digital data transmission, it is obvious that the basic problem is the exponential p.d.f. for the power level of the fading signal and that this will likewise drastically degrade the performance of any analog transmission systems. That is, an extremely high mean signal level will be needed to avoid having the signal "drop into" the noise over too large a percentage of the time.

Alternative to such use of increased power, etc., is the utilization of more sophisticated modulation and reception techniques which are less sensitive to or reduce the fading effects. Of these techniques the best known and most widely used are the multiple-receiver combining techniques categorized as *diversity*. The diversity principle is applicable to both analog and digital transmission in the sense that it is predicated simply on reducing the fading range (especially the probability of near-zero fades, or "deep fades" as they are often termed) for the signal-to-noise ratio. There is an extensive literature on diversity. We will confine ourselves here to outlining the general concepts.

Diversity possibilities for counteracting short-term fading effects were first discovered in experiments with spaced receiving

---

*For a more detailed discussion of diversity techniques see Ref. 1.

antennas at h.f. With sufficient spacing between antennas it was observed that the (short-term) fading fluctuations on the signal received at one antenna are essentially independent of the fluctuations on the signal from the second antenna. It then was suggested and shown that a "switch" operating so as to derive the system output from the stronger of the two signals at each instant* will greatly reduce the depth of fading effects that would be observed with either signal alone.

Obviously there are mechanisms other than spaced receiving antennas for achieving independently fading signals. Depending on the propagation mechanism, diversity techniques may include the following:

1. *Spaced antenna* diversity.
2. *Frequency* diversity.
3. *Angle (-of-arrival)* diversity.
4. *Polarization* diversity.
5. *Time (signal-repetition)* diversity.
6. *Multipath diversity (Rake).*

Of these, the last two are presently primarily applicable only to digital data transmission.

In theory (except for polarization diversity) there is no limit to the number of diversity branches or the number of more-or-less independently fluctuating signals which can be made available to be combined, by duplication of equipment. One is also not limited to selecting only the instantaneously stronger signal. Other combining methods are possible. Linear combining techniques have been commonly identified in the recent literature as follows:

1. *Selector* (or selection) combining.
2. *Maximal-ratio* combining.
3. *Equal-gain* combining.

All these methods involve linear combining networks. Such combiners are the only type applicable in principle for *distortionless* reception of *analog transmissions.* For reception of a serial digital data stream, however, other types of processing can be usefully employed (more or less by extending the matched-filter concept to determining optimum diversity combining techniques), the most familiar of which is *square-law combining.*

We will first briefly describe how "independently" fading diversity branches are achieved in practice. Later we will indicate that signficant diversity effectiveness can still be achieved even when fairly high correlations exist among the complex Gaussian processes which characterize the individual diversity branches.

---

*Or using one output until it becomes too weak relative to some desired threshold, and then automatically switching to the other if it is at that time above the threshold.

Therefore there is a degree of imprecision associated with any specification of the "separation" (in antenna spacing, frequency, angles, time, etc.) required to achieve satisfactory diversity operations, and we will merely note the numbers usually quoted for engineering purposes.

The use of spaced transmitting or receiving antennas is by far the most common diversity technique encountered in present practice. In simplest form a single transmitter (single transmitting antenna beam) is employed. This "illuminates" a certain portion of the "scattering" (or "reflecting" or "refracting") medium. As viewed from a *receiving* site, the angular extent of this "illuminated volume" depends on the transmitting beamwidth and on directional aspect factors of the "scattering" or "reflection." The rays (paths) from any point in this volume will have different electrical lengths to different receiving points. Hence for the same illumination condition different sets of phasors will be seen at separated receiving sites. Recalling our discussion in Sec. 16-2 on the phenomenological origin of Rayleigh fading as caused by addition of randomly varying phasors, we see that we can expect *uncorrelated fading at the two spaced antennas* if the set of phasors being received at one is substantially different than the other (analogous to the interpretation of selective fading in Sec. 16-2). For antennas spaced perpendicular to the arriving radiation, it can be shown that an estimate of the required spacing D for uncorrelated fading is

$$D \gg \lambda/\theta \quad \text{(i.e., at least a few times } \lambda/\theta\text{)}$$

where λ is the carrier wavelength and θ is the lateral angular extent of the illuminated volume (i.e., the solid angle over which rays appear to arrive) as viewed from the receiving site. This is only an order-of-magnitude statement, and then only as an estimate of the spacing required for obtaining complete decorrelation between spaced antennas.

At h.f. where angle-of-arrival fluctuations appear usually to be limited to the order of 1° to 5° (Refs. 2, 3), this would imply a "correlation distance" between spaced antennas of the order of 10 to 100 λ. At 10 Mhz, for example, the required spacing would be of the order of several hundred meters. This is substantially larger (by a factor of 2 to 5) than that found necessary in practice (Refs. 4-7) which is more of the order of a couple of hundred meters at 10 Mhz (probably, as pointed out earlier, because diversity can be effective even with relatively high correlations). Dual spaced-antenna diversity *is* quite common in high-quality h.f. circuits, although more than dual-diversity is quite uncommon.

In tropospheric scatter at relatively short ranges (say, 100 to 300 mi), θ is governed by the antenna beamwidths, typically of the order of 1° to 3°. Again a separation of the order of 10 to 100 λ is usually estimated to be required for complete decorrelation and roughly confirmed experimentally (Ref. 8). At longer ranges, θ may become more controlled by geometry and aspect (i.e., giving smaller angular extents than the beamwidths), and relatively larger antenna spacings may then be required for decorrelation. In tropospheric scatter dual spaced-antenna receiving diversity is *extremely common*, often coupled with a use of dual transmitting antennas to achieve a form of quadruple diversity (see later discussion on polarization diversity).

Although the description above has emphasized antennas spaced perpendicular to the direction of propagation, one can also achieve diversity by spacing on the ground along the direction of propagation. The angle θ in this case would measure the apparent vertical extent of the "scattering volume" rather than the lateral extent. At h.f. with moderately high elevation angles of arrival the effect on the required spacing appears to be less significant than for troposcatter. The result is to multiply by perhaps an order-of-magnitude in troposcatter the estimated correlation distances required for longitudinal antenna spacing as compared with lateral spacing. Almost all space-diversity systems in operation appear to employ essentially lateral spacing (although both might be employed, for example, in an L-shaped layout for triple diversity).

In a similar vein, receiving antennas may be spaced in height; except for the change in aspect relationships governing the angular extent of the "scattering volume," one would expect the required spacings here to be much the same as for lateral spacing on the ground.

In discussing a model for space diversity, we drew an analogy to selective fading. It should already be obvious therefore that transmission of the same signal at sufficiently spaced carrier frequencies will also provide independently fading versions of the signal, hence "frequency diversity." To obtain relatively complete decorrelation, one would want a spacing an order-of-magnitude larger than the nominal width of the frequency crosscorrelation function defined in Sec. 16-2. The bandwidths separately occupied at each carrier frequency can be, of course, narrow enough so that fading is nonselective on the individual branches. Frequency diversity has been employed both at h.f. (Refs. 6, 9) and in tropospheric scatter (Ref. 10), in both cases apparently primarily for experimental purposes (although, as discussed later, a hybrid form of space-frequency diversity is in fact quite common on troposcatter systems). The disadvantages of frequency diversity appear primarily to lie in the need for a doubled frequency allocation, for use of two transmitters, and for combining of receivers operating at two different frequencies.

In discussing space diversity, we noted that the diversity is available basically because the "scattering volume" has nonzero angular extent. In the subsequent discussion we assumed that both spaced receiving antennas (having identical beam patterns) are oriented toward the same bearing. Hence even when the receiving beamwidths are narrower than the inherent angular extent of the "scattering volume" (as determined by transmitter bandwidth and scattering or reflection aspect relationships), the two beams in space diversity are viewing the same portion of the "scattering volume." Diversity is obtained by the relative phasings between rays from this one portion of the volume. Equally well, however, with sufficiently narrow receiving beams, the two beam axes could be oriented toward different or at least partially nonoverlapping portions of the "scattering volume." The signals received via the two beams would then be decorrelated, to the extent that different (nonoverlapping) portions of the "scattering volume" are being viewed. There have been two different suggestions as to how the associated transmitting beam should be designed. One is that a single broad beam should be used; the other is that as many individual transmitting beams should be employed as there are receiving beams, each transmitting beam illuminating specifically that section of the "scattering volume" corresponding to an associated receiving beam. It has not been conclusively shown that the additional costs of this latter implementation are warranted (Ref. 11) except insofar as the total transmitted power may be increased if the maximum available rating of power amplifier is involved with each transmitter, and it would be inefficient to parallel a group of these together in a single transmitter. (It may also be simplest when the same antennas are to be used for communication in both directions.)

Because angle diversity requires antenna beamwidths (1° or so) very narrow compared with the angular extent limitations of the scattering volume owing to both geometric and aspect relationships, it has apparently never been seriously suggested for h.f., where unusually large and therefore expensive antenna sizes would be required. On the other hand, it has very seriously been suggested and studied for tropospheric scatter use (Refs. 11, 12) as a means of using more effectively the already large reflectors required to provide sufficient antenna gain as part of the system "margin." These suggestions arose when very detailed interferometer-scanning measurements in tropospheric scatter indicated significant fluctuations in the apparent angle-of-arrival at the receiving point, implying that squinted antennas, each individually detecting only a narrow cone in these apparent angles-of-arrival, could achieve significant diversity effect. The engineering advantage accrues in realizing the multiple beams via multiple feeds with a single large reflector. An alternative suggestion which has received some study is that of using a tracking feed on the receiving antenna, to track on the instantaneous apparent angle-of-arrival (Refs. 13, 14). It has been shown that this should be closely equivalent in performance to a high order of angle diversity utilizing the same size of reflector.

There are other engineering problems associated with multiple-beam angle diversity, notably problems associated with realizing a set of squinted beams via multiple feeds on a single reflector. For reasonably narrow beams the physical occupancy problem precludes beam overlaps at closer than roughly their 3 dB points. On the other hand, unless the beams can be tightly clustered, it will not be possible to fit a large number of beams within a sufficiently narrow cone, beyond which the aspect sensitivity of the "scattering" will too greatly reduce the power received by the individual beams. There are two other effectiveness problems associated with such clustered beams. One is the possibility that, owing to interactions, the plane-wave receiving cross section of any individual beam will fall below that associated with reflector size (Ref. 15). The other is that, owing to beam overlaps, there will be crosscorrelation in the fading observed on different beams, again reducing the diversity effectiveness (Refs. 11, 12, 16). There have also been disagreements as to the actual effectiveness vis-a-vis space diversity (Refs. 11, 17). At the present time there has not appeared any significant intent to apply angle diversity in operational systems.

Next on the list of diversity techniques is polarization diversity. This implies use of a single polarization at the transmitter, with the action of the propagation medium such that two separate orthogonal receiving polarizations will result in signals not fading in a correlated manner. This has been shown to occur for long-distance reception in the h.f. band, where magneto-ionic effects in the medium cause a varying elliptic polarization to be received when a linear polarization is transmitted. In fact with crossed linearly polarized feeds there is a tendency for the pair of received signals to fade in an anticorrelated manner (Refs. 4, 5) indicative of such rotating ellipticity.* For practical applications there is a limitation to only essentially dual diversity by this technique (there are only two orthogonal polarization modes; any third polarization would yield a linear combination of the other two and hence cannot contribute significantly to any diversity effectiveness). Even dual polarization diversity might be quite useful; for example, as mentioned, more than dual-diversity of any type is rarely used at h.f. However, for high-quality long-distance h.f. circuits, it has been common to use highly directive antennas (e.g., rhombics); for these it appears to be awkward to construct two high-directive, orthogonally polarized antennas in one unit, whereas if they are to be constructed separately, spaced, the spacing itself will tend to produce diversity without the additional effort of two

---

*Note that anticorrelated envelope fading (about the mean) must necessarily refer to specular components changing in polarization. For jointly Rayleigh fading processes, if they are Rayleigh, the envelope correlations are necessarily positive, as pointed out in Sec. 16-2.

different receiving polarizations. More recently, orthogonal log-periodic antennas have been suggested for polarization diversity.

In tropospheric scatter, on the other hand, the inhomogeneities producing the propagation effect are dielectric in nature so that there is little change in the polarization as the wave propagates. This has been observed experimentally (Ref. 18) in tests with nominally linear transmitted polarization in which the orthogonal polarization component received was of the order of 12-20 dB below that received in the nominal transmitted polarization. More-over the dielectric nature of the "scattering" implies that the "scattering" will not be polarization dependent and hence that there will be a near-unity correlation on the fading observed in the two polarizations (Refs. 18, 19). Thus polarization diversity per se is not usefully available in tropospheric scatter.

It is relevant to describe here a hybrid frequency-space diversity, dual-polarization system which is in very common use on tropospheric scatter networks (Refs. 19-22). This is a quadruple diversity system shown schematically in Fig. 17-1. Two large antenna reflectors are used at each end of the link, each with a multiple feed for simultaneous transmission at one frequency and reception at two other frequencies. For one direction of communication, one antenna at the transmitting end transmits in a horizontal polarization and the other at a conveniently spaced

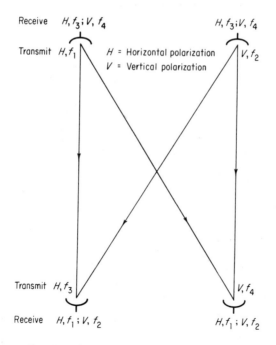

Fig. 17-1 Quadruple-diversity configuration.

different frequency *and* in a vertical polarization. Thus at the receiving terminal two signals are received at *each* antenna, distinguishable *both* in frequency and polarization, and hence readily separable into separate receivers. If the *transmitting* antennas are spaced by the diversity distance, then (by the law of electromagnetic reciprocity) the two signals received at each single receiving antenna are themselves in *space* diversity (and would be even if they were at the same frequency), with the difference in polarization and frequency serving primarily to conveniently "tag" the signals so that they can be separated for use in a diversity combiner. Note, however, that the convenient frequency spacing will itself often be sufficient for frequency diversity action. Thus in such operation a "twofold" mechanism may be involved in producing the diversity action. Likewise the pair of signals at the second receiving antenna are also in diversity with each other. Finally the *receiving* antenna *spacing* is sufficient for diversity between signals received at the same frequency on the two antennas. However, significant diversity action may not be obtained between the two "crossing" paths without use of different frequencies. In fact experiments with a single frequency and only polarization discrimination (Ref. 19) indicated a fairly high degree of correlation for the crossing paths. Here the frequency diversity effect will be important in producing totally a quadruple diversity with relativity large mutual independence between the fading fluctuations on the four receiving channels.

The last two diversity techniques listed earlier, time diversity and multipath diversity, are closely related and have been particularly applied only to digital data transmissions. Briefly, the time diversity concept assumes that if the same bit of information is repetitively transmitted over widely separated intervals of time, the separations being reasonably long compared to the reciprocal of the average fading rate, then the fade levels associated with the various repetitions will be essentially independent samples of the fade distribution. Then any reasonable combination of the repetitions will give a diversity performance insofar as the fading is concerned. Unlike most of the other techniques mentioned, time diversity is attained without any concomitant increase in average received power, since it involves a modulation technique rather than added equipment. In space diversity, for example, there is an increase in average received power because of the added antenna aperture, and in frequency diversity or in multiple-transmitting beam angle diversity there is increased received power because of the increased transmitter power implied by the multiple transmitters (assuming there is no limitation on total primary power at each terminal).

In addition, unlike any of the other diversity techniques, time diversity requires information storage both at the transmitter and receiver. Such storage and particularly the diversity combination of the repeated signals (or of their processed forms) is much simpler for digital than for analog transmissions. Most discussions of time diversity have therefore been in terms of digital transmissions. In this case the concept of using interleaving to extend the capabilities of error-control codes (Chap. 15) may be considered still another version of the use of time diversity.

Finally a kind of time diversity can be achieved in multipath situations when sufficiently wide-band signals are transmitted that the multipath may be viewed as creating a series of echoes. If, in addition, the wide-band signal can be properly "tagged" so as to carry an inherent time base indicator, then the contributions arriving via the different (independently fading) parts of the multipath structure can be separated in the course of reception and combined in diversity. Such a multipath diversity is one interpretation of the Rake technique, where the time base "tagging" is accomplished by use of wide-band pseudonoise waveforms (for a fuller discussion see, e.g., Ref. 1).

17-2 Diversity Performance

It should be apparent from our discussion of the techniques for achieving diversity, and is to be emphasized, that long-term fading effects which represent gross changes in the medium affect all diversity branches identically, and diversity operation cannot therefore compensate for such long-term variations. Diversity performs in reducing fading effects only over the statistically stationary short-term fading.

Second, diversity operation presumes the availability of M distinguishable, dissimilarly fading, signal receiving channels (the *"diversity branches"*). The diversity receiver chooses at each "instant" the best of the M signals or some desirable additive combination of all. Since the system has not infinite bandwidth, however, it cannot truly function on an instant-to-instant basis. The word "instant" therefore refers to a brief time span consistent with the time constants of such estimating and control circuits as are involved in the combiner. It is apparent that to function successfully when estimation is involved, that is, to then be capable of mitigating the effects of short-term fading, the combiner time constants just mentioned must be substantially shorter than the reciprocal of the fading rate mentioned earlier.

At the same time some of the combiners we shall describe (the *linear combiners*) are based upon deriving an estimate of the signal level on each diversity branch. In such cases the estimate ideally is noiseless, free of noise introduced by the receiver on that branch. In most of the theoretical literature on linear diversity combiners (Refs. 1 and 23-26) the assumption is in fact made that *completely noisefree estimates* of the signal levels on the individual diversity branches are available. We will also use this assumption throughout the relevant discussions below. The assumption is justifiable for most terrestrial fading radio channels but must always be employed with care. In effect, in these cases we assume that one can discuss *subintervals* of time *short enough so that the fading signal in each radio channel remains approximately constant* during each interval (many signal pulse durations in length), but which are at the same time *long enough so that they can be expected to include full statistical samples of the receiver noise*, to allow averaging out of the latter for purposes of obtaining noise-free estimates of the "instantaneous" signal levels.

At the same time, while the assumption above may be justified for many combinations of system parameters, it may not be appropriate to all. An example is a narrow-band signal on a channel which is not fading too fast for linear-filter processing of any individual signal pulse but which is fading too fast to allow the longer integration interval needed for deriving noiseless diversity indicators. One could not then expect to be able to apply to such a system the kind of linear combining technique discussed immediately below. However, it is pointed our subsequently that a satisfactory combining technique, termed *square-law combining*, or appropriate variations thereof can be optimum or nearly optimum in such cases, with diversity performance almost as good as the linear combiners.

We shall define the linear diversity combiners on the basis of how they operate within a typical short interval during which some arbitrary but unchanging signal level is assumed to exist on each diversity branch (different on each). Then we describe their error-rate performance over a longer interval, during which the signal levels on the several branches each change within a Rayleigh fading law (averaging over a period during which the signal fading can be regarded as statistically stationary and characterized by some mean SNR).

Throughout we will be considering slow, nonselective fading (multiplicative fading) on each diversity branch. We will also assume that the additive noises on the various diversity branches are stationary Gaussian and mutually independent. This is consistent with the important case in conventional communications in which the major noise arises owing to thermal noise in the receivers in each diversity branch. However, it may specifically not be true, for example, when the major noises arise as external interference. If such interference is of nearby origin, the "noise" will be highly correlated in all the branches. If it arrives over long radio paths, its intensity may fade independently (slow multiplicative noise) in the various diversity branches, but the detailed "noise" waveforms may still be highly correlated in the several branches. Such considerations are beyond our scope here, save to point out that, under such circumstances, by proper instrumentation one should be able to always achieve at least the performance of the selection combiner described below.

In describing the effectiveness of various diversity configurations, the term "diversity improvement" or "diversity gain" is often employed. This is sometimes defined in terms of so-called outage rate. This recognizes that while the median or average value of the signal-to-noise ratio at the diversity combiner *output* represents a greater value than that available on any single diversity branch, the most significant aspect of diversity lies in reducing significantly the *fraction of the time* in which the signal drops down to unusable levels. The latter fraction is termed the *outage rate* at some particular specified level, the level usually being specified relative to the mean output noise level of the combiner. Since similar reductions in outage rates can be obtained in principle by increased transmitter powers, antenna sizes, etc., a criterion on *diversity improvement* then is the saving in median carrier-to-noise ratio required per radio channel (per diversity branch) when using diversity, in order to stay within some specified outage rate, as compared to the median carrier-to-noise ratio required on a single channel for the same outage rate. For very low outage rates (e.g., 0.1 or 1%), calculations of the outage rate involve the near-zero "tails" of the probability density functions, and since the relation between outage rate and median signal-to-noise ratio is not linear, diversity improvement as defined by outage rates is only *distantly* related to improvement in average signal-to-noise ratio.

However, the definition of diversity improvement or diversity gain given above will have a direct engineering meaning only if signal legibility is directly determined by outage rate at some particular "threshold" value specified with respect to the mean receiver noise. For our purposes, with an emphasis on digital data transmission, a more directly meaningful definition can be given in terms of the requirements for meeting a certain error-rate specification. With diversity a significantly lower median (or average) signal level will be required on each diversity channel than for the single nondiversity channel, to achieve a specified error-rate performance. Any such decrease is immediately equatable to a saving in required nondiversity system margin and hence represents a more specific definition of diversity gain.

Before plunging into the mathematics, we can also draw some useful intuitive conclusions about the relative effectiveness of various forms of diversity combining. First, it is apparent that any more general combining, properly done, should permit better results than just selection of the instantaneously strongest branch. This follows since the combiner can at the very least be made capable of using the instantaneously best signal; anything usefully added then must, by definition, represent an improvement. Let us define an "acceptable" signal as corresponding to an SNR for which the error probability is very much less than the design specification. Then selection will itself furnish an acceptable signal whenever any one of the M signals is acceptable, and all that a more general combiner can provide in such cases is "greater acceptability" through, for example, an even higher instantaneous signal-to-noise ratio. For all such events the basic lack of error is the same for both arrangements. The greater improvement possible by more general combiner operation can come only from those other intervals when there is no acceptable signal in any one individual channel, but where at least some of the signals are still high enough so that an effective combination can still produce an acceptable combiner output signal-to-noise ratio. Of the two classes of events just described, it is readily visualized that, for small values of M such as used operationally and for reasonably low error-rates, the first class is *very much* the larger. Therefore for relatively small orders of diversity M, the amount of *added* diversity improvement obtained by using a more general combiner rather than a selector must be significantly *smaller* than the diversity improvement which would be inherent in the use of just the selector. This effect will be strongly evident in the quantitative results below.

We will not here enter into elaborate details on analysis of diversity systems. The literature on analysis of linear diversity combiners is reasonably straightforward (Refs. 23 to 28, or see Ref. 1) and our discussion will emphasize the results and interpretations. We have already indicated how instantaneous and mean SNR are defined for a multiplicative Rayleigh fading channel. Let Γ_i, $i = 1, \ldots, M$ represent the mean SNR (averaged over the assumed stationary short-term fading) in each of the M diversity branches, and let γ_i be the instantaneous SNR, with the variations in the γ_i assumed mutually independent. Then for *selection combining*, which instantaneously selects that channel with the largest γ_i, the combiner *output* SNR γ can be shown to have the probability distribution

$$\text{prob}(\gamma < x) = \prod_{i=1}^{M} \left[1 - e^{-x/\Gamma_i} \right] \tag{17-1}$$

and the corresponding p.d.f.

$$p(\gamma) = \frac{d}{d\gamma} \prod_{i=1}^{M} \left[1 - e^{-\gamma/\Gamma_i} \right] \tag{17-2}$$

When all the Γ_i are equal

$$\Gamma_i = \Gamma \tag{17-3}$$

$$p(\gamma) = \frac{M}{\Gamma} e^{-\gamma/\Gamma} \left[1 - e^{-\gamma/\Gamma} \right]^{M-1} \tag{17-4}$$

Next, it can be shown that with an accurate estimate of eacn channel state presumed available, there is an *optimum (best) combiner* which produces the maximum possible SNR at every instant. This has been called the *maximal-ratio combiner.* Here a weighted sum is formed, each channel output being weighted by a factor proportional to the instantaneous channel envelope level, *with a phase adjusted to cancel out the channel phase,* and an additional factor inversely proportional to the mean noise power in that branch. The effect is to add all signals coherently, with relatively greater weighting to the instantaneously stronger channels. It is readily shown that the *instantaneous* SNR at the combiner output is then just the *sum* of the instantaneous SNR's in the various branches

$$\gamma = \sum_{i=1}^{M} \gamma_i \qquad (17\text{-}5)$$

Over the short-term fading it can then be shown that, when all the $\Gamma_i = \Gamma$, the p.d.f. of γ is

$$p(\gamma) = \frac{1}{(M-1)!} \frac{\gamma^{M-1}}{\Gamma^M} e^{-\gamma/\Gamma} \qquad (17\text{-}6)$$

There is no simple expression for the case when the several Γ_i are unequal.

The third combiner is the so-called equal-gain combiner (Ref. 23), in which no attempt is made to weight the amplitude of the various branch contributions but only to align them in phase via phase-lock circuitry so as to achieve coherent signal additions. This has significant practical advantages in simplicity of implementation. It works well provided that the noise levels in all branches are equal (as they usually are), almost as well as the maximal-ratio combiner. Although there is no simple closed-form result for the p.d.f. of the resulting SNR, extensive numerical evaluations are available.

The effective SNR distribution achieved by the various combiners is shown in the curves of Fig. 17-2 for several values of M, in the case where all channels are of equal strength Γ. These are the probability distributions on arithmetic probability paper, with the no-diversity curve for the same Γ plotted for reference (0 dB being chosen as the median for the latter curve). It is clear that increasing orders of diversity increasingly narrow the range of fading. Also, as remarked earlier, the differences between the results for any particular combiner types are much less significant than the difference between any one of them and the no-diversity curve. Equal-gain combining for all orders of diversity shown is within 1 dB of the optimum, maximal-ratio combining.

The near parallelism and *nature* of the various combiner curves is most significantly demonstrated by examining the p.d.f.'s of the

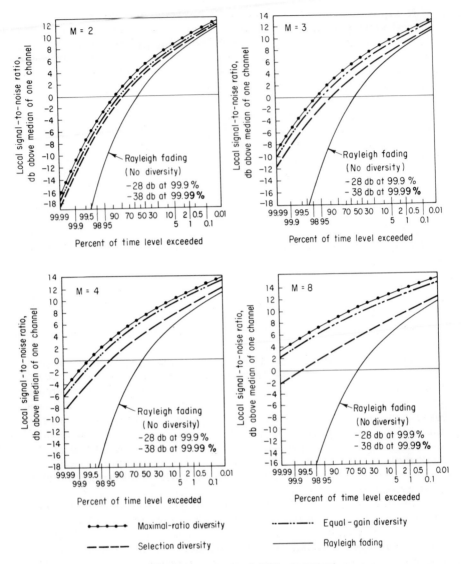

Fig. 17-2 Combiner output probability distributions.

combiner outputs at values of y well below the average. For generally unequal strengths Γ_i in the several branches, these p.d.f.'s can be shown to be approximated as follows:

$$\text{selection:} \quad p(y) = \frac{My^{M-1}}{\displaystyle\prod_{i=1}^{M}\Gamma_i} \tag{17-7}$$

$$\text{maximal-ratio}: \quad p(\gamma) = \frac{1}{(M-1)!} \frac{\gamma^{M-1}}{\prod\limits_{i=1}^{M} \Gamma_i} \qquad (17\text{-}8)$$

$$\text{equal-gain}: \quad p(\gamma) = \frac{(2M)^M}{(2M)!} \frac{\gamma^{M-1}}{\prod\limits_{i=1}^{M} \Gamma_i} \qquad (17\text{-}9)$$

That is, the functional variation of the p.d.f. for M-fold diversity is always of the form γ^{M-1} for small γ. For increasing M, there is an increasing flattening of the p.d.f. at small γ; $p(\gamma)$ and its first $M-2$ derivatives are zero at $\gamma = 0$, as opposed to the no-diversity ($M = 1$) case in which $p(\gamma)$ actually peaks at $\gamma = 0$. Furthermore the dependence on the various channel strengths (mean SNR's) is the same for all the combiner types, and in fact one can define an effective mean SNR (i.e., an equivalent situation in which all the Γ_i are equal) as just the geometric mean of the Γ_i,

$$(\Gamma_{\text{eff}})^M = \prod_{i=1}^{M} \Gamma_i \qquad (17\text{-}10)$$

The differences among the curves in Fig. 17-2 at low γ are therefore only the algebraic factors involving M. As seen in the figure, while the near parallelism was derived above for the p.d.f. at low γ, it holds over almost all the range. The further importance of the formulas (17-7) to (17-10) is that they accurately describe the p.d.f. of γ in the low region of the combiner output fading that accounts for most of the digital errors. Hence (see below) at any given order of diversity, the differences among combiners in the mean diversity-branch SNR required for given error-rate performance are accurately measured by the SNR *differences* depicted in Fig. 17-2. This is important for *theoretical analysis* in complicated situations in that sometimes mathematical analysis can be conveniently carried out assuming one form of combining but not any of the others. The comments here imply that one can sharply infer from any one such analysis the performance to be expected from the other combiner types.

The results above were based on *independently* fading diversity channels. It has also been shown that fairly high levels of correlation can appear in the fading before any significant degradation occurs in diversity performance. The most general analysis of this effect has been carried out assuming maximal-ratio combining (Refs. 1 or 26). If R is the $M \times M$ covariance matrix describing the mutual correlations among the (complex) multiplicative noises which represent the fading on the several branches, then it has been shown that the M eigenvalues of R (which are positive real because R is Hermitian positive definite) define the *effective* intensities of the M-fold diversity operation. (If any of these are very near zero, there is effectively less than M-fold diversity operation; we assume below that this is not the case.) Then for the p.d.f. of γ at low values of γ, the effective mean single-channel intensity is given by

$$\Gamma^M_{\text{eff}} = \prod_{i=1}^{M} \lambda_i = \det R \qquad (17\text{--}11)$$

where λ_i are the eigenvalues of R, and we have used the well-known fact that the product of the eigenvalues is just the determinant of the matrix.

As an example, in dual-diversity with two branches of equal strength Γ and a normalized covariance in their fadings denoted by ρ, one would have

$$R = \Gamma \begin{pmatrix} 1 & \rho \\ \rho & 1 \end{pmatrix} \qquad (17\text{--}12)$$

$$\det R = \Gamma^2 (1 - |\rho|^2) \qquad (17\text{--}13)$$

Thus the effective mean SNR may be regarded as

$$\Gamma_{\text{eff}} = \Gamma \sqrt{1 - |\rho|^2} \qquad (17\text{--}14)$$

and even for $|\rho|$ as large as 0.6, the effective mean SNR is $\Gamma_{\text{eff}} = 0.8\Gamma$ or a decrease of slightly less than 1 dB. In Fig. 17-3 are shown curves (from Ref. 1) for dual-diversity selection combining for many values of $|\rho|$.

Finally we return to the evaluation of performance of digital data streams over a diversity-reception fading radio link. Again we consider the slow-nonselective fading situation, with binary signaling, and again (recall Sec. 16-3) average the conditional probability of error, as a function of γ, over the p.d.f. for γ given by the diversity statistics. The conditional probabilities of error are the forms $P_\gamma^{(1)}$ and $P_\gamma^{(2)}$ given in (16-35) and (16-36).

One simple case which can be readily analyzed is for non-coherent signaling with maximal-ratio combining and independently fading channels. In this case we can write the probability of error as

$$P^{(1)} = \frac{1}{2} \int_0^\infty p(\gamma) e^{-\alpha\gamma} \, d\gamma \qquad (17\text{--}15)$$

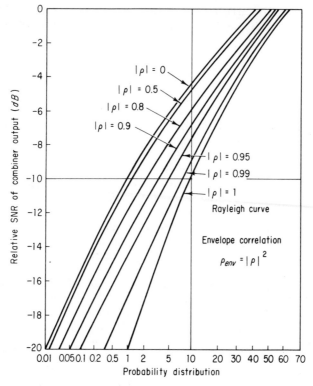

Fig. 17-3 Effect of correlation on the probability distribution of the combiner output, for dual-diversity selection combining.

where for all channels having equal strength, $p(\gamma)$ is the form given in (17-6). But instead of averaging over γ, we can recall the basic operation of this combiner, giving

$$\gamma = \sum_{i=1}^{M} \gamma_i \qquad (17\text{-}16)$$

and instead write (17-15) as the average over the γ_i. Since these are independently fading, we derive

$$P^{(1)} = \frac{1}{2} \int_0^\infty \cdots \int_0^\infty \cdots \int_0^\infty \exp\left[-\alpha \sum_{i=1}^{M} \gamma_i\right] p(\gamma_i) \cdots p(\gamma_M)\, d\gamma_1 \cdots d\gamma_M$$

$$= \frac{1}{2} \prod_{i=1}^{M} \int_0^\infty e^{-\alpha\gamma_i}\, p(\gamma_i)\, d\gamma_i = \frac{1}{2} \prod_{i=1}^{M} \int_0^\infty e^{-\alpha\gamma_i} \frac{1}{\Gamma_i} e^{-\gamma_i/\Gamma_i}\, d\gamma_i$$

$$= \frac{1}{2} \prod_{i=1}^{M} \frac{1}{1 + \alpha\Gamma_i} \qquad (17\text{-}17)$$

When the several Γ_i are much greater than unity, and $\alpha = 1/2$ or 1, this reduces within excellent approximation at low error-rates of interest to

$$P^{(1)} = \frac{1}{2(\alpha)^M} \frac{1}{\displaystyle\prod_{i=1}^{M} \Gamma_i} \qquad (17\text{–}18)$$

It is readily verified that this is *exactly* the result which would have been obtained had we instead approximated $p\,(\gamma)$ in (17–15) by its approximate form in (17–8). The obvious statement is that the error-rate depends (in this slow-fading case) only on the probability distribution of output SNR *at low* γ. From this observation one can immediately now expect the *difference in performance* between the several combiners to be exactly the same as noted earlier in comparing outage rate performance. Furthermore one can expect that the *comparative* results should also not be importantly changed when one goes over to the error-function form of error-probability which characterizes coherent detection systems. Both these statements can indeed be shown (e.g., Ref. 1).

The result (17–17) is shown in the dashed curves of Fig. 17–4 for various M, in the case when all the $\Gamma_i = \Gamma$. In line with our earlier remarks, the curves apply also to the case of unequal Γ_i, when Γ is regarded as their geometric mean.

For coherent signaling with maximal-ratio combining one obtains at low error-rates the result (either by using the approximate pd.f. or by approximating from the exact result),

$$P^{(2)} = \frac{1}{2\sqrt{\pi}} \frac{\left(M - \dfrac{1}{2}\right)!}{M!} \frac{1}{(\alpha\Gamma)^M} \qquad (17\text{–}19)$$

when all the Γ_i are equal. Again it is apparent that use of the p.d.f. for low SNR is sufficient to describe the probability of error for all reasonably low error-rates, and performance of any other combining form (say, equal-gain) can be estimated from the earlier comparisons of diversity gain. One is also led to expect that, if the branch mean SNR's are unequal, it will as earlier again be the geometric mean of their SNR's which will describe performance.

An interesting and useful observation (Ref. 28) from (17–7) is that, for the ith branch operating *by itself*, the error-rate would be

$$P_i^{(1)} = \frac{1}{2} \frac{1}{1 + \alpha\Gamma_i} \qquad (17\text{–}20)$$

and hence with maximal-ratio combining the resultant *error-rate* is

$$P_{\text{m.r.}}^{(1)} = \frac{1}{2} \prod_{i=1}^{M} \left(2 P_i^{(1)}\right) \qquad (17\text{–}21)$$

Thus, with maximal-ratio combining each diversity branch has the effect of reducing the overall error-rate by a factor just exactly equal to twice its own error-rate when operating alone. Since no matter how low the branch SNR, always

$$P_i \leq \frac{1}{2} \tag{17-22}$$

note that for *ideal* maximal-ratio combining there is always some advantage in adding additional branches, no matter how weak they are. (The latter need not, however, be true for less optimal combiners.) Owing to their simplicity the formulas in (17-21) can be especially useful during preliminary design calculations in rapidly estimating the effects of added diversity on error-rate.

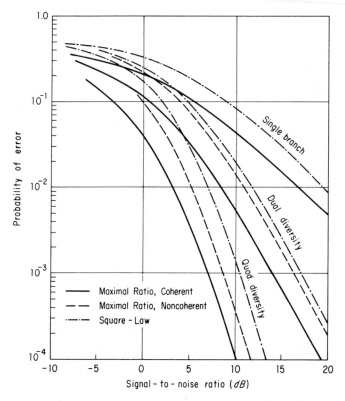

Fig. 17-4 Comparison of diversity combining techniques for binary FSK with Rayleigh fading.

Our discussion up to now has been based on diversity systems which can monitor signal level and use this to effect useful combining. Oftentimes circumstances are such that monitoring of this kind cannot be accomplished. In such a case one cannot use coherent signaling and detection, since channel phase fluctuations are completely unknown. With noncoherent signaling, such as two-tone FSK, it has been shown (Ref. 27) that under the assumptions of slow multiplicative fading one can define the best possible combining, termed "square-law combining." In each diversity branch, noncoherent matched-filter detection (or any reasonable suboptimal filtering) is carried out separately for each binary state (e.g., Mark and Space tones). Assuming that all branches fade independently and have the same mean SNR, the squares of all the Mark filter output envelopes from the several branches are then added, and separately the squares of the Space envelopes, and the decision is made on the basis of the larger sum.

If the mean SNR differs on some of the branches, then an additional weighting factor should be added on each term. If there is correlated fading, then again the eigenstates of the covariance matrix effectively describe the independently fading components, with effective mean SNR's given by the corresponding eigenvalues, and the optimum combiner involves a quadratic form in the filter outputs which is equivalent to weighted square-law combining on the eigenstates. However, it has been shown that simple square-law combining is still quite effective even in these more general situations. We shall confine our detailed remarks below to the specific case of mutually independent fading on all diversity branches, with equal mean SNR's.

In this case with Γ the mean SNR in the filter output of any branch (for the signaled tone), the probability of error (Ref. 27) is

$$P_e = \sum_{m=0}^{M-1} \frac{(2M-1)!(-)^m}{(M-1)!(M-1-m)!m!(M+m)} \frac{1}{(2+\Gamma)^{M+m}} \qquad (17\text{-}23)$$

with the approximation at low error-rates ($\Gamma \gg 1$)

$$P_e = \frac{(2M-1)!}{(M-1)!M!} \frac{1}{\Gamma^M} \qquad (17\text{-}24)$$

These results are also shown in Fig. 17-4 as the broken-line curves.

The most intriguing result from the comparisons in Fig. 17-4 is the following: At high signal-to-noise ratios (low error-rates of practical interest), there is only 6 dB performance difference between square-law combining with noncoherent signaling (and no monitoring of the channel) and maximal ratio combining with ideal coherent PSK (perfect monitoring of the channel).* Furthermore, of this 6 dB, 3 dB may be "picked up," provided the channel is slowly fading, by replacing noncoherent FSK by DPSK signaling with *envelope* detection (recall Sec. 12-2) and square-law combining (or the equivalent sum of scalar products) as the combining technique.

---

*Coherent PSK being 3 dB better than the coherent FSK portrayed in Fig. 17-4.

Square-law combining has another interesting implication. Consider a channel known to be fading so rapidly that there is frequent loss of coherence (i.e., fluctuations in channel phase) even over the duration T of a single information pulse. For such a channel a linear receiver which smooths over intervals of duration T is no longer appropriate since it will tend to average over each of the quadrature components of the received signal, each of which tends to average to zero. On the other hand, there will be subintervals of duration, say, T/k (k = integer), over which coherence may be regarded to hold, and over which linear-filter smoothing is appropriate. Over the duration T one can then obtain k smoothed samples of the received waveform, for which the signal contents do not further add coherently but which we wish to combine for decision purposes. The optimum combining is immediately obvious: One should take the envelope of each of the k samples, square it, and add the total for the Mark filter outputs, and compare it to a similar total for the Space waveform. In the limit, then, one continuously forms the *squared envelope* of the received signal plus noise (e.g., in a square-law detector) and integrates this over the signal pulse duration. It is easily shown that even when k is finite this square-law detection-integration is equivalent to choosing the k envelope samples for the processing described above.

This type of detection is known as *energy detection* or *radiometric detection* and is a common concept in radio or radar astronomy. Its performance can be regarded as a form of time-diversity operation. If E is the average received energy per pulse, and k is the effective number of independent samples of the fading during the pulse duration T, the result is that of k-fold diversity with each diversity branch having mean SNR $\gamma_k = E/kn_0$, where n_0 is the additive receiver noise power density spectrum. For k small (i.e., in the range where increasing orders of diversity provide large improvements), the availability of the diversity effect owing to fading rapidity will in fact give better operation for a single channel than if the fading were constant over each pulse. For quite large k, the required SNR may be of the same order as if the fading were slow, and only for extremely large k is there significant degradation below the slow fading case (there is optimum performance when the order of diversity is such that each "branch" has a mean SNR of about 5 dB).

One word of warning here is that in radiometric detection the binary waveforms must be *orthogonal over the subintervals* if distinguishability is to be preserved, since the result from each of these subintervals is noncoherently detected. This is readily achieved with sufficiently wide tone spacing in FSK. However, the usual DPSK signal would no longer satisfy this criterion over subintervals.

References

1. M. Schwartz, W. R. Bennett, and S. Stein, *Communication Systems and Techniques* (McGraw-Hill Book Company, New York, 1966).
2. M. Balser and W. B. Smith: "Some Statistical Properties of Pulsed Oblique HF Ionospheric Transmissions," *NBS Journal Research*, D, 66, pp. 721-730 (Nov.-Dec. 1962).
3. E. N. Bramley: "Some Aspects of the Rapid Directional Fluctuations of Short Radio Waves Reflected at the Ionosphere," *Proc. IEE*, Pt. B, *102*, pp. 533-540 (July 1955).
4. S. H. Van Wambeck and A. H. Ross: "Performance of Diversity Receiving Systems," *Proc. IRE, 39*, pp. 256-264 (March 1951).
5. G. L. Grisdale, J. G. Morris, and D. S. Palmer: "Fading of Long-Distance Radio Signals and a Comparison of Space- and Polarization-Diversity Reception in the 6-18 Mc/s Range," *Proc. IEE*, Pt. B, *104*, pp. 39-51 (January 1957).
6. R. E. Lacy, M. Acker, and J. L. Glaser: "Performance of Space and Frequency Diversity Receiving Systems," *IRE National Convention Record*, Pt. II, pp. 148-152 (1953).
7. J. Grosskopf, M. Scholz, and K. Vogt: "Korrelations messungen in Kurzwellenbereich," *NTZ, 11*, pp. 91-95 (February 1958).
8. J. H. Chisholm, W. E. Morrow, Jr., B. E. Nichols, J. F. Roche, and A. E. Teachman: "Properties of 400 Mcps Long-Distance Tropospheric Circuits," *Proc. IRE, 50*, pp. 2464-2482 (December 1962).
9. C. D. May, Jr.: "Doubling Traffic Capacity of Single-Sideband Systems," *IRE National Convention Record*, Part II, pp. 145-147 (1953).
10. N. H. Knudzton and P. E. Gudmandsen: "Results from a Three-Hop Tropospheric Scatter Link in Norway with Parallel Operations on 900 Mc and 2200 Mc," *IRE Trans. Comm. Systems*, *CS-8*, pp. 20-26 (March 1960).
11. R. Bolgiano, Jr., N. H. Bryant, and W. E. Gordon: "Diversity Reception in Scatter System Using Angle Diversity," Cornell University, Dept. of E.E., Res. Rept. 359, Jan., 1958.
12. J. H. Vogelman, J. L. Reyerson, and M. H. Bickelhaupt: "Tropospheric Scatter System Using Angle Diversity," *Proc. IRE, 47*, pp. 688-696 (May 1959).
13. S. Stein and D. E. Johansen: "A Theory of Antenna Performance in Scatter-Type Reception," *IRE Trans. Antennas and Propagation, AP-9*, pp. 304-311 (May 1959).
14. D. E. Johansen: "The Tracking Antenna—A Promising Concept for Scatter Communications," *Proc. 7th Nat'l. Comm. Symposium*, Utica, N. Y., pp. 134-149 (October 1961); also, Final Report on Investigation of Antenna Systems for Scatter-Type Reception," *Applied Research Lab.*, Sylvania Electronic

Systems, *AFCRL-742* (August 1961).

15. S. Stein: "Cross-Coupling in Multiple-Beam Antennas," *Trans. IRE PGAP, AP-10*, pp. 548-557 (September 1962).

16. J. H. Chisholm, L. P. Rainville, J. F. Rocye, and H. G. Root: "Angular Diversity Reception at 2290 Mc/s Over a 188 Mile Path," *IRE Trans. PGCS, CS-7*, pp. 195-201 (September 1959).

17. H. Staras and J. H. Vogelman: "Observations on Angle Diversity," *Proc. IRE, 48*, pp. 1173-1174 (June 1960).

18. J. H. Chisholm, P. A. Protmann, J. T. deBettencourt, and J. F. Roche: "Investigations of Angular Scattering and Multipath Properties of Tropospheric Propagation of Short Radio Waves Beyond the Horizon," *Proc. IRE, 43*, pp. 1317-1335 (October 1955).

19. E. F. Florman and R. W. Plush: "Measured Statistical Characteristics and Narrow-Band Teletype Message Errors on a Single-Sideband 600-Mile-Long Ultrahigh-Frequency Tropospheric Radio Lonk," *NBS Journal Research*, Pt. D, *64D*, pp. 125-133 (March-April 1960).

20. G. L. Mellen, W. E. Morrow, Jr., A. J. Pote, W. H. Radford, and J. B. Weisner: "UHF Long-Range Communications Systems," *Proc. IRE, 43*, pp. 1269-1287 (October 1955).

21. R. A. Felsenheld, H. Havstad, J. L. Jatlow, D. J. LeVine, and L. Pollack: "Wide-Band Ultrahigh-Frequency Over-the-Horizon Equipment," *AIEE Trans. 77*, Pt. 1 (*Communications and Electronics*, No. 35), pp. 86-93 (March 1958).

22. K. P. Stiles, F. G. Hollins, E. T. Fruhner, and W. D. Siddall: *AIEE Trans., 77, Pt. I (Communications and Electronics, No. 35)*, pp. 94-96 (March 1958).

23. F. J. Altman and W. Sichak: "A Simplified Diversity Communication System for Beyond-the-Horizon Links," *IRE Trans. PGCS, CS-4*, pp. 50-55 (March 1956).

24. D. G. Brennan: "Linear Diversity Combining Techniques," *Proc. IRE, 47*, pp. 1075-1102 (June 1959).

25. S. Stein: "Clarification of Diversity Statistics in Scatter Propagation," *Proc. UCLA Symposium on Statistical Methods in Radiowave Propagation*, UCLA (June 1958); (published by Pergamon Press, New York, 1960).

26. J. N. Pierce and S. Stein: "Multiple Diversity with Nonindependent Fading," *Proc. IRE, 48*, pp. 89-104 (January 1960).

27. J. N. Pierce: "Theoretical Diversity Improvement in Frequency Shift-Keying," *Proc. IRE, 46*, 903-910 (May 1958).

28. B. B. Barrow: "Error Probabilities for Data Transmission over Fading Radio Paths," *Shape Air Defense Technical Center, TM-26* (February 1962).

QUEEN MARY
COLLEGE
LIBRARY

Index